Mysteries
of the
Unknown

Mysteries
of the
Unknown

By the Editors of
Time-Life Books

QUALITY PAPERBACK BOOK CLUB
NEW YORK

Copyright © 1987, 1988, 1989, 1990, 1992, 1997 by Time-Life Books, Inc.

Library of Congress Cataloging-in-Publication Data

Mysteries of the unknown / by the editors of Time-Life Books.
     p.   cm.
  ISBN 0-7835-4912-1
   1. Parapsychology. 2. Occultism. 3. Curiosities and wonders.
I. Time-Life Books.
BF1031.M95 1997   96-36499
133—dc20   CIP

Compiled by Lizzie Skurnick

Book design by Barbara Sturman

Special thanks to Art Resource, The Bettmann Archive, René Dahinden, Carol Durham, Fortean Picture Library, Monica Elias, Raymond E. Fowler, Deirdre Kennedy, Mary Evans Picture Library, Raymond McNally, and Grey Thornberry.

Printed in the United States of America

CONTENTS

Mysteries
of the
Unknown

1
GHOSTS

Crisis Ghosts and Hateful Hauntings

Corbis-Bettmann

AT DUSK one day in the middle of the nineteenth century, a woman and her son sat peacefully in the garden at the back of their house in Clapham, England. Nothing in their surroundings carried any suggestion of the unusual. The hour was pleasant and serene, the fading light throwing long shadows across a rolling lawn that stretched from the house to a wall and gate. Yet in a moment the lives of their family would be transformed by what they believed to be a phantom encounter.

As the two of them sat talking, the son, whose name was John, shifted suddenly in his chair and pointed at something across the lawn. "Mother," he exclaimed, "there's Ellen!"

His surprise was understandable. Ellen, the older of the family's two daughters, had been sent away to Brighton in the south of England by her parents, in hopes of dampening the ardor of an unacceptable romance. Although the girl had been desperately unhappy away from home and suitor, Ellen's mother realized that her husband would be angry over their daughter's early return against his wishes.

"John," she said to her son, "go quickly and tell Ellen to come into the house. Don't say anything to your father."

The young man started to rise from his chair, but sank down again after trying to put his weight on an ankle sprained earlier that day. "I can't run after her," he said. "You'll have to send Mary."

The mother summoned her other daughter from the house and told her to go fetch her sister. "Father shall not know anything about her coming back," the mother instructed. "We'll send her away again in the morning." Mary, a young and energetic girl, ran across the lawn and through the garden gate. She hailed Ellen and was puzzled when her sister failed to respond. She called out again. Wordlessly, Ellen turned down a path that led away from the house, her dark cloak billowing behind her.

Mary ran in pursuit, following the path across the softly rolling countryside. At last she caught up and reached out to grasp her sister's arm. "Ellen," she said, "where are you going? Why are you—"

Richard Lee

The words caught in her throat. She found that she was unable to take hold of her sister's arm. Her hand seemed to pass directly through the flesh and bone; she felt nothing. A terrible chill ran through her as she watched Ellen turn silently away again and recede.

Numb, the girl walked back to the garden where her mother and brother sat waiting. She told them what had happened. The mother, by now ashen, ran to her husband and repeated the story to him. He shared her conviction that some calamity had befallen their eldest daughter.

The next day, their worst fears were confirmed. The previous evening, at the very hour her image had appeared at the house in Clapham, their distraught daughter had thrown herself into the sea and drowned.

Throughout history, from one end of the earth to the other, people have reported seeing apparitions, ghosts, and phantoms. Many accounts of such sightings eventually took the form of folktales. And those tales, often broadly embellished, fostered a popular impression of terrifying specters wafting like smoke through countryside and town, infecting the very atmosphere. The question of truth, however, was rarely probed deeply.

Yet that question has always hovered close to the edge of the tales. Do these apparitions have some basis in reality? Does their undubitable power as entertainment conceal more fundamental powers—forces that still lie beyond human understanding, mechanisms still to be defined? In the late nineteenth century, students of the paranormal began to collect and analyze reports of thousands of sightings and visitations. It was their conviction that apparitional appearances deserved serious investigation. One of these researchers, Frederic W. H. Myers, wrote: "Whatever else a 'ghost' may be, it is probably one of the most complex phenomena in nature." That sentiment is still widely shared, and the process of gathering a body of evidence continues to this day.

The documentation is highly provocative. A large number of phantom encounters involve some sort of life crisis, most frequently the ultimate crisis of death. Quite often, the apparition seemingly makes itself known at the very moment or within a few hours of death, as claimed by the family residing in Clapham. And as with that family, the viewers, or percipients, often knew and loved the departed. In many other cases, apparitions have reportedly returned—sometimes years after death—to deliver messages to the living, to honor death compacts made in life, to seek justice, or merely to reassure loved ones that all is well in the world beyond the grave.

Yet phantom appearances seem not to be the province only of the dead. Frequently, apparitions of the living have been said to manifest themselves for no particular reason and with no particular intent; people have seen their doubles, or doppelgängers, separated from the body and performing mundane tasks, entirely oblivious to the observer—or observers, for such spontaneous phantoms have on occasion been witnessed by groups of people.

And then there are the rarest of all phantom encounters, the hauntings, so des-

Frederic Myers was a well-known poet, essayist, and classical lecturer at Cambridge when he proposed he and his colleagues form the SPR

Mary Evans Picture Library, London

ignated because a specter seems to inhabit a building or locale, revealing itself over time to percipients who did not have any connection with the apparition during life. Hospitals, museums, mansions, and houses of all sorts, dilapidated or not, have been the supposed abodes of ghosts, which may take the form of humans or animals—or indeed may appear in any physical form at all, including that of long-sunken submarines or spectral armies fighting ancient battles.

Whatever the explanations may be, the investigators believe that they are gaining ground. As the well-known parapsychologist Louisa Rhine put it in 1981: "Parapsychology is the Cinderella of the sciences. The stepmother, Science, has never favored her. She got a late start and the big sisters like physics, chemistry and biology almost cold-shouldered her out of recognition. It remains to be seen if any fairy prince will rescue her."

Frederic Myers and a handful of English colleagues organized the Society for Psychical Research in 1882 in order to investigate apparitional experiences. The founding members, however, boasted impressive credentials. Myers was a well-known poet, essayist, and classical lecturer at Trinity College, Cambridge. Joining him were Edmund Gurney, also a classical scholar at Cambridge; Henry Sidgwick, professor of moral philosophy at Cambridge; the tireless researcher Frank Podmore; and a number of other prominent academics, including Sir Oliver Lodge, an eminent physicist at Liverpool University, and Sir William Barrett, who was professor of physics at the University College of Dublin.

In 1886, Gurney, Myers, and Podmore published what was the most ambitious piece of psychical research to date, a two-volume, 1,400-page survey entitled *Phantasms of the Living*. The purpose of the report, wrote Myers, was "to open an inquiry which was manifestly impending, and to lay the foundation-stone of a study which will loom large in the approaching age." The sheer size of the work indicated the massive volume of evidence and firsthand accounts available to the psychical researchers, and the authors believed that the book banished any remaining doubts about the reality of phantom encounters. The goal, then, was to attempt to classify and understand these experiences. In so doing, the three investigators opened a debate that continues to this day.

In attempting to explain apparitions, *Phantasms of the Living* advanced a theory based on telepathy—a term actually coined by Myers to replace the unwieldy "thought-transference." In the cases collected in *Phantasms,* the authors said, they examined "the ability of one mind to impress or be impressed by another mind other than through the recognized channels of sense." In other words, the percipient might actually be receiving a telepathic signal from the apparent—the person represented by the apparition. In fact, according to this theory of telepathy, the apparent need not be present in any sense in order to be represented as a phantom. As Myers later summed it up: "Instead of describing a 'ghost' as a dead person permitted to communicate with the living, let us define it as a *manifestation of persistent personal energy.*"

SPR founding member Edmund Gurney, a classical scholar at Cambridge

Although this theory proved instantly controversial, there appeared to be much in favor of it. Of the 701 cases discussed in *Phantasms of the Living,* more than half concerned reports of phantom appearances or other impressions in which the manifestation coincided with either the death of the apparent or some other critical moment in that person's life. "On reviewing the evidence thus obtained," wrote Edmund Gurney, "we were struck with the great predominance of alleged apparitions at or near the moment of death. And a new light seemed to be thrown on these phenomena by the unexpected frequency of accounts of apparitions of living persons, coincident with moments of danger or crisis." To these cases, the SPR applied the term "crisis apparitions," suggesting that in such moments of crisis, telepathic communications seem more likely to take place.

Phantasms of the Living proved to be only the first step in a master plan of the society—the "foundation-stone," as Myers had termed it. The next phase, which was pursued over a period of five years, was an exhaustive *Census of Hallucinations,* undertaken with characteristic thoroughness by Professor Sidgwick.

Sidgwick hoped to discover what percentage of the general population had experienced hallucinations that might be considered apparitional. Toward that end, he carefully developed a census question that would encompass three types of hallucinations—those of sight, hearing, and touch—while excluding dream experiences. The question read: "Have you ever, when believing yourself to be completely awake,

Cambridge philosophy professor Henry Sidgwick helped found England's Society for Psychical Research in 1882

had a vivid impression of seeing or being touched by a living being or inanimate object, or of hearing a voice; which impression, so far as you could discover, was not due to any external physical cause?"

The question was printed on a form that required the person being canvassed to state only yes or no and to give name, address, and occupation. Those answering yes were provided with another form on which they were asked to put down the details. Forms were circulated by 410 volunteer census collectors and drew an astounding 17,000 responses. The survey was an international one, with replies coming from Austria, Brazil, France, Germany, Italy, and Russia, along with those from Great Britain.

The results defied all expectations. Nearly ten percent of those polled—1,684 persons—admitted to having experienced sensory hallucinations of the kind described in the census question. The group was made up of 1,029 women and 655 men. Of the total cases reported, 1,087 were visual and 493 auditory, whereas two had involved the sense of touch; 129 of the phantom encounters had been experienced by more than one person.

For purposes of his investigation, Sidgwick defined crisis apparitions according to an arbitrary "margin of coincidence." In effect, he contended, a phantom sighted within a period of twelve hours either before or after a crisis in the apparent's life could reasonably be called a crisis apparition. Given this definition, Sidgwick's data indicated that such apparitions occurred with far greater regularity than any other type of apparitional experience. As a matter of fact, the likelihood of an apparition appearing coincident with a crisis in the apparent's life proved 440 times greater than the chances of one appearing for any other discernible reason.

The accounts of apparitional experiences collected in both *Phantasms of the Living* and the *Census of Hallucinations* shared a number of features. A typical case was that of Mrs. Sabine Baring-Gould of Exeter, England. On January 3, 1840, Mrs. Baring-Gold sat at her dining room table reading the Bible by the light of a candle. Looking up, she reported afterward, she saw her brother, Henry, sitting at the other side of the table. The scene appeared entirely natural—except for the fact that Henry was at that time serving aboard a Royal Navy ship in the South Atlantic.

Although agitated, Mrs. Baring-Gould refused to panic, perhaps calmed by the kindly expression she saw on her brother's face. Neither one spoke, but the woman stared steadily at her brother for several moments, until his form grew dim and faded away before her eyes. Realizing what this might mean, Mrs. Baring-Gould jotted the words "Saw Henry" and the date in the flyleaf of her Bible. A month later, word came that her brother had died at sea—his death had occurred at the very moment his sister saw his figure sitting across from her.

Unfortunately, there were no witnesses to the appearance of Mrs. Baring-Gould's brother. Moreover, the woman did not tell anyone of the experience until after his death became widely known.

The case of Mrs. Anne Collyer of Camden, New Jersey, although similar in many respects to Mrs. Baring-Gould's, provided a crucial element of third-party confirmation. On the night of January 3, 1856, Mrs. Collyer awoke to find her son Joseph standing in the doorway of her bedroom, staring intently at her. As in the case of Mrs. Baring-Gould, the appearance of Mrs. Collyer's son was decidedly impossible, since he was at that time in command of a steamboat on the Mississippi River, more than 1,000 miles to the west. Shocked enough to see her son so unexpectedly, Mrs. Collyer was even more disturbed to note that his face and head were terribly disfigured and wrapped in a crude bandage. He wore a dirty white nightshirt, which she did not recognize, although she later described it as looking something like a surplice.

The next morning, Mrs. Collyer related to her husband and four daughters what she had seen. Her family gave the story little credit, believing that she had simply experienced a very bad dream.

Mrs. Collyer knew better, but it was almost two weeks before the news that she dreaded finally arrived: Captain Collyer had been killed in a steamboat collision. Part of the ship's mast had fallen on him, splitting his skull. His death had occurred at almost the precise moment that his mother had seen his apparition.

The case proved of particular interest to the Society for Psychical Research because of the independent testimony provided by Mrs. Collyer's husband and daughters. All attested to the truth of her story, which she had told in detail well before her son's death became known through more conventional channels. Another of Mrs. Collyer's sons added a further detail after viewing the body: Captain Collyer, roused from his cabin in the middle of the night, had been wearing a white nightshirt, which became soiled in the collision. At the time of his death, he had been attired exactly as his mother saw him.

Most phantom encounters involve apparents whose habits and appearance are extremely familiar to the percipient. Consequently, some skeptics contend that many so-called apparitional experiences are really just the products of overheated imaginations—and no doubt that is sometimes the truth of the matter. In most instances, there is no way of obtaining foolproof evidence of the validity of an apparitional experience, and this inability remains a key stumbling block for psychical research.

Yet a number of cases resist much of the criticism leveled at such studies. Percipients seem to know certain exact details—the soiled nightshirt worn by riverboat captain Collyer—that many researchers maintain could not possibly be acquired except through the agency of a genuine apparition. One such case was the famed "Full Court Dress" incident, which occurred sometime in the 1830s or 1840s and was reported years afterward to the SPR.

The percipient was an Englishwoman who awoke to the sound of loud knocking at two o'clock one morning. Going over to the window, she discovered her mother, from whom she had been estranged for a number of years, standing at the doorstep. At once the woman roused her husband, but when he went to the window he saw nothing. The woman was not only convinced that it had been her mother on the doorstep, but she described in detail her mother's "full Court dress," a gown appropriate for wearing at a royal function.

Later the next day, the woman heard news of her mother, the first she had received in many years. Her mother had indeed been at a royal ball at Kensington Palace the previous evening, but had become ill suddenly and been rushed home—where she died at 2:00 A.M., still wearing her full Court dress.

These cases as well as the numerous others that have been collected and analyzed by the Society for Psychical Research sparked a lively and prolonged debate about the nature and substance of apparitions. One of the central points of contention—and one that is still discussed to this day—is the question of whether apparitions are physical or nonphysical. In other words, do phantoms occupy actual space or are they purely subjective hallucinations that exist only in the mind of the percipient?

Like his colleague Frederic Myers, Edmund Gurney believed in apparitions as subjective phenomena, unique to the percipient, that could be explained only in relation to telepathy. In his opinion, the apparent is not actually present in any sense at the scene of the phantom encounter. Rather, he proposed that the percipient receives a telepathic cue from the apparent, a cue often caused by a crisis or near-death experience, which the percipient then utilizes to project an apparition.

A flaw in Gurney's theory was that it did not adequately account for the occasional occurrence of "collective phenomena," or apparitions seen by more than one person at the same time. Gurney attempted to explain these rare events by introducing the idea of "contagious telepathy," in which an apparition projected by one person might infect the minds of others so that they too see the same figure. The theory, however, was not a very convincing one, and even Gurney himself did not seem to be entirely comfortable with it.

Myers put forward a revised theory that attempted to overcome the limitations of Gurney's hypothesis. Although Myers agreed that phantoms were not physical manifestations in the strictest sense, he did contend that they occupied a physical space that he called "metetherial," a sort of fourth-dimensional field that intertwines with our own physical space. In Myers's view, this explained why some apparitions might appear to have a combination of both physical and nonphysical qualities. The beliefs of Edmund Gurney and Frederic Myers exerted a considerable influence on the psychical researchers who followed them, including G. N. M. Tyrrell, who became president of the Society for Psychical Research in 1945. Tyrrell devoted forty years of his life to the study of apparitions, although, like his predecessors, he had a strong grounding in the physical sciences, holding a degree in physics and mathematics from London University. Throughout his long tenure with the society, Tyrrell attempted to revise and reconsider the existing apparitional theories.

In his book *Apparitions,* which drew on the early cases collected by the SPR, Tyrrell broke down all apparitional incidents into the four broad categories that are still generally recognized: apparitions of the living, crisis apparitions, postmortem apparitions, and continual, or recurring, apparitions. He then went on to postulate the existence of layers of unconscious creative potential in the minds of apparition percipients, to which he gave the rather whimsically theatrical names of "producer" and "stage carpenter." These creative elements, Tyrrell theorized, teamed up with those of the apparent to produce a joint "apparitional drama," which Tyrrell described as "not a physical

Mary Evans Picture Library, London

Ghost hunter Ada Goodrich Freer—shown here in a photograph taken in 1894—worked closely with the SPR during the late 1800s to investigate hauntings

phenomenon but a sensory hallucination." Any flaws in the production, such as the wrong clothing or a mixed-up setting, Tyrrell airily dismissed as nothing more than faulty stagecraft.

Nevertheless, Tyrrell's hypotheses did address many of the difficulties of the earlier theories. Some of the hard-to-explain aspects of certain apparitional experiences could be understood as the "stagecraft" of the apparitional drama. If, for example, an apparition appeared to open a door, the door did not physically open. The idea of the door opening seemed dramatically appropriate, so movement took place in a hallucination—which he interpreted as evidence of an efficient "stage carpenter."

But no single theory, however detailed, has managed to adequately explain each of the hundreds of apparitional cases examined by the society. Tyrrell's views of a subtle creative apparatus at work in both the percipient and the apparent, for example, does not seem to account for several instances of apparitional appearances by dogs, cats, and horses. Sir Henry Rider Haggard, the English novelist, reported in July

1904 a vivid crisis apparition of his daughter's prized retriever. The writer saw the dog lying motionless in a bed of reeds; it turned out that the animal had, in fact, fallen from a bridge to its death in a marshy stream.

On an even more creative level, a phantom animal was not seen but only heard. In this case, a Mr. and Mrs. Beauchamp owned a little mongrel dog humorously named Megatherium, after a species of large sloth. One night the Beauchamps were awakened to hear the sound of their pet's footsteps in the bedroom. But they could not find the animal and assumed that they had been mistaken about the sounds when they saw that the door to their bedroom was closed. A bit later, the couple was awakened again—now by their daughter pounding on the door and shouting that the dog was dying. The Beauchamps rushed downstairs to find Megatherium entangled and strangling in his collar, from which they swiftly rescued him.

Another perplexing variation in the phenomenon of crisis apparitions involves "death compacts," or agreements made between two living people that the first to die will attempt to contact the survivor. Two remarkable instances of death-compact apparitions are recorded in *Phantasms of the Living*. The first involves Lord Henry Brougham, a prominent figure in English civic life in the early half of the nineteenth century and a Lord High Chancellor of England from 1830 to 1834.

As a young, man Lord Brougham attended Edinburgh University with his closest friend, dubbed G in the SPR account. There, the two friends fell into frequent conversation about survival of death and the immortality of the soul. The possibility that the dead would appear to the living intrigued both men, with the result that the two made a solemn vow that the first to die would make every attempt to appear to the survivor in some form.

The two men went their separate ways after leaving the school, and over the years they lost track of each other. Eventually, Lord Brougham later admitted, he had nearly forgotten the existence of his former friend from the university. Many years later, while traveling through Sweden, he had occasion to recall his friend G. One night, as he lay soaking in a hot bath after a long day of travel, Lord Brougham glanced over at the chair where he had left his clothing and saw the figure of G. The next thing Lord Brougham knew, he lay sprawled on the bathroom floor; the apparition had disappeared. Only upon returning to Edinburgh did Lord Brougham discover that his friend had died on the same date and at the same time as the strange appearance.

Despite having made the death compact in his youth, Lord Brougham was far from an ideal percipient. Even when confronted with the sight of his old friend, and upon learning about the coincidence of the time of his death, he continued to harbor strong reservations concerning the validity of the experience. Writing in his journal some years later, he referred to the whole thing as a "singular coincidence" and speculated at length on the nature of dreams and coincidences.

Sometimes, however, the percipient of a ghostly visitor seems to be left with physical evidence of the otherworldly encounter. In 1884, for example, a Professor

Romanes recorded a curious incident involving a handsome young Englishman named Griffiths, who was about to marry a lovely French girl. Chaperoned by their mothers, the betrothed pair had just spent a pleasant holiday in Italy and the south of France and were on their way home, the Griffiths to London and the French girl with her mother to Paris. On the night before crossing the channel to England, young Griffiths was awakened from a heavy sleep to hear the voice of his fiancée pleading with him in French to come instantly to her in Paris.

Griffiths then saw his betrothed coming toward him and felt her reach out to grasp his arm in her hand. An awful fright took hold of him, and the Englishman rushed to his mother's room. As might be expected, she calmly reassured him that everything was all right, and he returned to his bed. He fell briefly asleep but was soon conscious of an intense pain on his arm. Rolling up his nightshirt sleeve, he found an ugly red spot and a rising blister where his love had touched him. Next morning, Griffiths visited a doctor, who told him that he had suffered a severe burn. But that seemed impossible—and doubly so because the doctor could not find the slightest indication of fire or corrosive chemical on the sleeve of the nightshirt.

Later that day, a telegram arrived from Paris bringing news of his fiancée's sudden death, following an illness of only a few hours. Some time after, Griffiths learned that as she lay dying she had called out for him in the very words he had heard in his bedroom.

Deathbed apparitions have been recorded in literature and history for centuries, but they were not studied in any scientific detail until the early 1960s, when Dr. Karliss Osis, using the *Census of Hallucinations* as a pattern, surveyed 10,000 nurses and doctors throughout the United States in an attempt to gather information about near-death experiences. Although one psychic likened the process to "catching a butterfly with a bear trap," Dr. Osis's study led him to conclude that the majority of deathbed hallucinations are truly apparitional, rather than the result of a brain disturbed by the processes of dying.

Despite the continuing researchers of Dr. Osis and others, actual sightings of apparitions seem to be on the decline. In contrast to the Society of Psychical Research in its heyday, today's research into psychic phenomena receives little attention from the world at large.

Dr. Ian Stevenson, head of the Division of Personality Studies at the University of Virginia Medical School, offers two possible avenues of explanation. First, Stevenson contends that it is necessary to determine if there are, in fact, as many apparitional experiences occurring in the world now as formerly. If there are as many cases, why are fewer of them reported? Social conditions, Stevenson suggests, provide at least part of the explanation. When we think of phantoms we almost automatically think of an earlier age; our modern world seems to prohibit such things. Perhaps this climate of disbelief renders people less likely to admit to having had apparitional encounters.

Suppose, on the other hand, that there actually are fewer encounters taking place in the present. If this is the case, Stevenson reasons, perhaps it is also a function of the differences in the eras. First, communications are far more sophisticated now than formerly. In many of the cases collected in the past by the researchers, the percipient had not seen the apparent in many months and often had a desperate need to do so. This urgency may have been a factor in producing apparitions. The more modern communications of today make such a situation less likely, however. Second, the incidence of sudden death is far lower now than it was in the Victorian era, a circumstance that might also contribute to the seeming paucity of phantom encounters. Finally, the same social conditions that might prohibit people from reporting apparitional experiences may inhibit phantoms from appearing.

Even so, some recent experiences, such as the crisis apparition reported by Hilde Saxer in a small village in the South Tyrol, could have happened only during the modern age. On May 4, 1980, Hilde left her job at a local restaurant at her usual time of 11:30 P.M. As the woman began her walk home, she happened to see the distinctive gray Audi belonging to her sister's fiancé, Johann Hofer. The sight surprised her somewhat, because Johann had left the restaurant half an hour earlier, stressing that he needed to go directly home. There was no question that the car was his, however, and when Hilde waved, she saw Johann through the windshield. The young man slowed his car, smiled, and waved back as he passed.

An hour later, Johann's father heard him arrive home at his normal time. The father clearly heard the sound of his son's engine, and he recognized the noise of the distinctive turning maneuver the young man used to get his car into the family yard.

Neither Hilde or Mr. Hofer realized that anything was amiss until the next day, when it was discovered that Johann was nowhere to be found. Although news came over the radio of a major tunnel collapse on the route Johann usually traveled to get home, no one thought anything of it; after all, he had been seen by Hilde and heard by his father shortly after the cave-in.

But as the day wore on and Johann failed to appear, his father began to fear the worst. It was many days before Johann's gray Audi, crushed flat beneath tons of falling rock, could be recovered, and even then his family and friends could scarcely believe the truth. Throughout the ordeal they had comforted themselves with one thought: The tunnel had collapsed at 11:30 P.M., and Johann had been spotted alive afterward.

Both Miss Saxer and Mr. Hofer seemed to have experienced crisis apparitions, made all the more interesting by the importance of Johann's car in helping to document the psychic encounter.

For all its modern trappings, this case seems thoroughly congruent with the body of evidence accumulated in the hundred-plus years since the SPR was formed. Like so many other reports, it is both elusive and tantalizing. Thus, investigators can only press on. Long ago, Frederic Myers offered a rueful summary of the situation: It is the lot of such researchers, he wrote, "to be working (however imperfectly) in the main track of discovery, and assailing a problem which, though strange and hard, does yet stand next in order among the new adventures on which Science must needs set forth."

Since the founding of the SPR in 1882, and its American counterpart, the

ASPR, in 1885, scores of suspected hauntings and poltergeist activities of a terrifying nature have been thoroughly investigated. Occasionally, the investigators have come to suspect that fraud rather than supernatural evil lies at the root of a particularly horrific haunting. One such deceit, which took place in Amityville, New York, in 1975, received widespread attention and became the subject of several books and films. Ronald DeFeo, Jr., the eldest son of an Amityville, New York, auto dealer, claimed the devil made him do it. On a November night in 1974, DeFeo murdered his parents and four brothers and sisters. Despite an insanity plea, he was charged and convicted on six counts of second-degree murder.

Amityville Horror *couple George and Kathy Lutz*

With DeFeo behind bars, the family home was put up for sale. Kathy and George Lutz, a young couple from nearby Syosset, fell in love with the three-story Dutch colonial. Even when they learned the house had been the scene of a grisly crime, they were not dissuaded. On December 18, 1975, the Lutzes and their children moved into 112 Ocean Avenue.

Almost immediately, the Lutzes would later claim, the family felt "unseen forces" in the house. An eerie rapping seemed to come from nowhere. Locked windows and doors mysteriously opened. A priest who agreed to bless the house was met by a disembodied voice that yelled "get out!"

The bizarre events intensified. Kathy Lutz claimed to have levitated above her bed and been beaten by an invisible intruder. A horrific green slime dripped from a ceiling. Finally, just twenty-eight days after moving in, the Lutzes fled in terror from their home.

Soon afterward, the couple teamed up with writer Jay Anson to produce a bestseller about their supposed nightmare, *The Amityville Horror.* A successful movie followed. Although the book was labeled "A True Story," most experts scoffed. Psychical researchers doubted the story, citing inconsistencies and distortions. Most damaging was a claim from DeFeo's lawyer, William Weber. He and the Lutzes, he said, had discussed the murder case and the Lutz family's alleged supernatural experiences in connection with a book Weber was to write. Weber labeled the horror story a hoax created "over many bottles of wine."

Often, though, as in a notable case reported by an English widow in 1943, these terrifying encounters with strange, destructive powers remain unexplained even after the most careful and skeptical examinations. "There is some evil here, which manifests itself in illnesses, our visitors, recent maids, all seem to get ill and my husband died early in July last. . . . Other manifestations . . . are rappings, alarming noises, . . . unpleasant and inexplicable odours. My sister has twice awakened suddenly with a feeling of hands around her throat trying to strangle her, and a sensation of an evil presence." Thus read the letter sent to the SPR by the distraught widow, identified only as Mrs. Knight. She was describing life in her home in a village called Wareham, located about sixty miles southwest of London. Mrs. Knight, her husband, and her sister had moved to the village three years earlier. Mr. Knight's death was just one of many strange and often tragic happenings his wife attributed to an unseen evil in their home.

The house that had brought so much fear and grief into its occupants' lives was described by G. N. M. Tyrrell, a respected SPR investigator and author of the 1953 book *Apparitions,* as "particularly light and cheerful, . . . the last house one would suspect of being haunted." Built in about 1820, it was a two-story brick structure with a slate roof, located on a pleasant country road. A sturdy iron railing anchored by brick pillars separated the front yard from the sidewalk. But according to Mrs. Knight, these charming looks were deceiving.

Among the incidents reported to Tyrrell were two occasions on which Mrs. Knight's sister Miss Irwin claimed to have been jolted awake by the sensation of being strangled by unseen hands. She also reported feeling an evil presence in the room. The second time this happened, the choking feeling and sense of evil were accompanied by the perception of something invisible scrabbling at the bedclothes. Miss Irwin was certain the incidents were not dreams.

At other times, vile smells permeated various areas of the house, including the pantry, the hallway, and the bathroom. There, in fact, Mrs. Knight said she was confronted one morning by the odor of decaying flesh. The stench lingered for more than five minutes, she recalled, filling her mind with thoughts of "death and the grave." Mrs. Knight also reported a bathroom light that turned itself on when nobody was near the switch and a portable radio that suddenly gave off an explosive noise "like a pistol shot" and emitted a quantity of smoke, playing normally all the while. It required no repairs.

In 1943, haunting activity in the house was particularly intense and varied. In January of that year, inexplicable noises sounded in different parts of the house on three consecutive days. The first sounds occurred one afternoon as Mrs. Knight rested in bed, nursing a cold. She heard five loud raps in the room, as if someone were knocking on her door or the head of her bed. The raps were loud enough for her husband to hear them downstairs, although her sister, who was in the kitchen at the time, heard nothing. The following night, both Mrs. Knight and her sister heard a loud thump in one of the upstairs rooms, as if someone had fallen out of bed or a number of books had tumbled off a table and crashed to the floor. They searched but were unable to find any physical cause for this noise. The next day, in the kitchen, Mrs. Knight heard what sounded like a heavy basket of laundry being dumped outside the back door. She opened the door and found nothing.

Three months later, Mrs. Knight awoke in the middle of the night to hear a loud thumping noise directly under her bed. It sounded, she said, like "an animal worrying a big bone on bare boards." She turned on the light and peered under the bed. She saw nothing, but the phenomenon continued. She fetched her sister, and they listened as the noise moved to a different part of the room, then stopped. Mrs. Knight and her husband also twice heard mysterious noises downstairs in the drawing room—slashing sounds like a whip striking the outside of the house's front window.

The house was worse than noisy: It seemed to be unhealthy. Mrs. Knight reported that thirteen visitors and servants fell strangely ill under her roof during the three years she lived there. And when her husband died a week after surgery in July 1943, she attributed his death to the evil presence at work. A month later, a visiting sister, Mrs. Fox, fell ill the morning after her arrival. She was racked with pain. Doctors recorded abdominal swelling and inflammations of the mouth and throat, but the cause of her illness was never determined.

Mysterious accidents also occurred. On the very day that the SPR's Tyrrell arrived to investigate the haunting, Miss Irwin fell in the hall and broke her wrist. She said she had slipped on her way to the door, but Tyrrell found only a foot of the floor space uncarpeted, and those floorboards appeared not to be slick at all.

Mrs. Knight and her sister continued to report strange presences and inexplicable events. On one occasion, Mrs. Knight observed a small oval of light—apparently unconnected with any normal light source—moving along a wall. A few nights later, around midnight, she and her sister saw first a fan of white light near a bedroom door, then a golden pillar next to the wardrobe. The lower half of the pillar was divided by a blue-gray vertical line, as if the light were resolving itself into a two-legged figure. As the two women gazed at this glowing apparition, it suddenly vanished.

About a month later, the two sisters left the house during the day and came home a short while later to find that some unknown force had disturbed one of the brick posts that supported the railing stretching across their front yard. Several bricks were jutting out of the pillar on the side facing the house, and chunks of mortar were strewn about the lawn. A friend who pounded the bricks back into place for the women suggested that a car or truck must have crashed into the railing to cause such damage. However, a careful inspection by Tyrrell revealed that none of the bricks facing the street had been touched and that the paint on both the railings and the pillar was unscratched.

When she first moved in, Mrs. Knight knew nothing about the history of her house. But eventually, when she told her neighbors about the haunting, she learned that previous residents had had similar misfortunes. A woman who had lived in the house had left after her husband's sudden death and her own serious injury in a bicycling accident. Local rumor told of a child who had died in the house with no symptoms of any known disease and of someone else who had fled to a nearby town and drowned himself.

Investigator Tyrrell found Mrs. Knight "a good and accurate witness," who knew nothing of psychic research or of the house's history. Presumably, then, she had formed no bias and had no reason to expect that such menacing happenings would occur. Tyrrell concluded that some of the illnesses, accidents, and deaths that occurred in the house could be put down to chance. The sounds, smells, and visions Mrs. Knight and her sister experienced, however, were "supernormal, hallucinatory or non-physical in character" and provided what Tyrrell felt was good evidence of collective percipience, a phenomenon in which two or more people share the same perception, real or hallucinatory. For their part, Mrs. Knight and Miss Irwin left, to begin anew away from their house's mysterious horrors.

Fetches, Wafts, and Fyes

Marilyn Krauss

IT WAS A festive time in 1845 at the Neuwelcke School, an academy for
daughters of the nobility located in Livonia (later Latvia), on the shores of the
Baltic Sea. Some of the girls were preparing to attend a party, and Mademoi-
selle Emilie Sagée, a popular French teacher who had recently come to the
school, was helping one excited young student to dress for the event.

When Mlle Sagée's charge, Antonie von Wrangel, turned to gaze at her image
in the mirror hanging behind them on the wall, she was astonished to see in the reflection not only Mlle Sagée, but also the teacher's perfect double—both of them
carefully fastening the girl's dress. Antonie, it is said, fell into an immediate faint.

Yet the vision should not have been quite so startling. For weeks there had been
talk about Mlle Sagée among the students. The teacher was attractive, well liked, and
respected, but the girls felt there was something odd about her: Mlle Sagée sometimes seemed to be in two places at once. A student would see her in, say, a hallway,
only to be told by another student that she had been elsewhere on the grounds at the
same moment.

One day, thirteen girls were in a classroom with Mlle Sagée when her double—
or doppelgänger, as such things are called in German—appeared beside the teacher,
mimicking her hand as she wrote on the blackboard. Not long before Antonie von
Wrangel spotted the doppelgänger in the mirror, students and servants alike saw it
standing behind Mlle Sagée at dinner. Naturally, these occasions, witnessed by such
large groups, caused a sensation. But the most remarkable report was yet to come.

On a warm summer day in 1846, all of the school's forty-two pupils were gathered around a table in a large room overlooking the garden, practicing embroidery

under a teacher's watchful eye. Through four open French doors, the group had a clear view of Mlle Sagée, who was picking flowers. At one point the supervising teacher left the room for a few moments; suddenly her empty chair was occupied by Emilie Sagée. The surprised girls could still see the woman moving about in the garden, although her gestures appeared to have become languid. Seizing the opportunity to investigate, two of the bolder girls tried to touch the figure in the chair; they reported a slight resistance. One girl dared to walk in front of the teacher's chair and stepped right through part of the apparition, which remained silent and motionless. Shortly thereafter it began to fade away, and in the garden, Mlle Sagée once again became animated.

A few of the girls later asked Mlle Sagée what she remembered of the incident. She responded only that, from the garden, she had noticed the other teacher leaving the room and had wished that she herself could be in the chair, lest the unsupervised girls get into mischief.

In the months that followed, students continued to report sightings of the teacher's double, an uncanny spirit that seemed to drain her of energy whenever it appeared. Most of the students were less upset by this apparition than they were fascinated, but the girls' parents sought to shield their offspring from so disturbing a phenomenon. A year and a half after Mlle Sagée's arrival, there were only twelve students remaining at Neuwelcke, and the headmaster reluctantly concluded that the teacher, however qualified she might be, would have to leave the school. On being given notice, Mlle Sagée lamented that this was the nineteenth position she had lost in her sixteen-year teaching career.

The Sagée story, one of the most celebrated of such accounts, is not unique. The apparition of the living—the double, doppelgänger, or fetch, as it was called in Victorian England—has a long history and is reported regularly to this day.

Most people—whether believers or not—associate phantoms with the dead. It is thought that ghosts of those who have died materialize to communicate with the living, or to comfort loved ones at the moment of, or just preceding, death. They are also believed to become somehow trapped in a place and haunt it indefinitely. But a number of reported phantom encounters involve apparitions of people still living and of these, an estimated two-thirds are not associated with a crisis in the lives of either the percipient (the witness to the apparition) or the apparent (the person whose apparition is seen). Instead, they are said to occur quite often during life's most ordinary moments (as with Mlle Sagée), frequently without the apparent's awareness and usually without any shattering psychological consequences for the percipient.

Such was the case with Henry J. Purdy of Middlesex, England. By his account, he awoke one night during the summer of 1982 to see his wife standing at their bedroom window, looking out at the garden. This was not unusual, he explained—if Mrs. Purdy had cause to be up during the night, she would often peer out "just to see what the weather outside was like." But a few minutes passed, and Purdy wondered why his wife did not return to bed. "After a time I moved my arm across the

Marilyn Krauss

Modern doppelgängers?

bed and was surprised to find my wife there sleeping peacefully. I looked from her to the figure at the window which gradually faded."

Encounters such as Henry Purdy's might be even more common that supposed, but some people may be reluctant to admit to having had an experience so closely resembling hallucination, usually associated with the mentally ill. However, apparitions of this type have been reported by more than a few whose faculties were not in question, including some distinguished members of the British Parliament. In 1905, for example, Parliament member Sir Frederick Carne Rasch was stricken with influenza, preventing his attendance at the House of Commons during a debate that particularly interested him. During the debate, however, another member and close friend of his, Sir Gilbert Parker, saw Carne Rasch seated near his accustomed place on one of the benches. Knowing Carne Rasch was seriously ill, Parker was surprised to find him present and, as he later told a newspaper, gestured to the man, saying, "I hope you are feeling better."

Carne Rasch made no acknowledgment but merely sat there impassively. A moment later, when Parker looked again, the man was gone. Parker hurried to the lobby to search for his friend, but no one had seen him pass by. Another colleague, Sir Arthur Hayter, reported later that he too had noticed Carne Rasch sitting on the bench and had called this to the attention of a third member.

Told afterward of the apparition, Carne Rasch expressed no doubt at all that his spirit had gone to the debate, since he had been very eager to attend. His family, however, perhaps out of fear that the phantom signaled an ill fate for Carne Rasch, was appalled to hear that his fetch had reportedly visited the Commons. (On returning to his normal parliamentary duties, Carne Rasch himself was a bit annoyed to find that colleagues sometimes poked and prodded him to make sure that he was appearing in the flesh.)

The idea of the fetch (also called waft or fye in England) goes back to pagan times and is found in most cultures. The human double has long been thought to be a manifestation of the soul and, therefore, a precious entity. The ancient Greeks believed it was dangerous to see one's reflection—or double—in a pool of water lest the soul be captured there. The Zulus of Africa still cling to this belief, and they also hold that one's shadow represents the soul as well and that it might be lost or injured by carelessness. And many societies have long-standing superstitions about the breaking of mirrors—which, it is feared, will trap the soul and lead to death.

Although early Christians turned the double into the attractive notion of a kindly guardian angel, the more primitive aspects of the double persisted in folklore, where its appearance was viewed by many as ominous. Tradition held that the double's materialization usually meant the soul had escaped the body and death was imminent. The seventeenth-century English folklorist John Aubrey wrote that Lady Diana Rich, daughter of the Earl of Holland, saw "her own apparition, habit and everything" while strolling about her father's garden in Kensington. A month later she died of smallpox. Lady Diana's sister was also said to have seen her double just before her death. Queen Elizabeth I saw her fetch not long before her death in 1603: According to one chronicler, it was lying in bed looking "pallid, shrivelled and wan." And about a month before he drowned in a boating accident, the poet Shelley saw his fetch.

Psychoanalyst Sigmund Freud was privately fascinated by the uncanny but loath to link himself to what he called "the black tide of mud of occultism"

But the appearance of a double was not always considered to be an omen of impending death. A double could supposedly wander off on its own mysterious business, particularly when one was asleep—leading to the notion that it was not a good idea to wake anyone up too suddenly, lest the double, or soul, be locked out. And the double could, in some cases, be deliberately sent forth. Cotton Mather chronicled some of the grimmer versions of such sallies in his 1692 account of the heyday of witchcraft in the New England colonies. Witches would send their fetches out in the night to "ride" people in their beds—hence the term "hagridden"—paralyzing them and rendering them speechless.

For the pioneering psychoanalyst Sigmund Freud, who explored the human double in a 1919 paper titled "The 'Uncanny,'" the double represented not only the soul, but in some cases the conscience as well. Freud reasoned that the idea of the human double began in the far reaches of human prehistory as a hedge against confronting the death of the ego, or self—a denial of mortality. This notion of an immortal counterpart arises, he wrote, from childish or primitive self-love. When this stage—in a life or in a civilization—is left behind, idea of the double persists, but as "the ghastly harbinger of death." Freud believed that psychic research is a legitimate scientific pursuit but was wary of linking himself with what he had once called the "black tide of mud of occultism." Privately, the founder of psychoanalysis was fascinated by the uncanny and sometimes prone to mystical thinking. In 1905, he saw a man who looked like himself and took the incident as an omen of his own death. He went on to live until 1939.

Freud was not the first to try to unravel the mystery of the human double. Systematic efforts to investigate and explain apparitions had begun with the founding in 1882 of the Society for Psychical Research. In particular, the publication in 1886 of the landmark book *Phantasms of the Living* launched modern inquiry into the phenomenon. Many of the 701 apparitions of the living chronicled in this work were "crisis accounts," in which spirits would appear to loved ones at or near the time of their deaths or during a particularly stressful moment in their lives. But many other encounters occurred during times of calm. A typical case of this sort was reported in 1860 by the Reverend W. Mountford of Boston.

Mountford had been in England, visiting the home of friends. One afternoon, at about four o'clock, he saw through a window his host's brother and sister-in-law approaching along the road in a horse-drawn open carriage. Reverend Mountford informed the host, who, with his wife, came to the window and made small talk about the impending arrival. But the couple in the carriage drove straight past the house and out of sight. The host was amazed by this event: His brother and sister-in-law had passed by without stopping in, "a thing they never did in their lives before."

A few minutes later, the host's niece arrived, looking flustered. Just before four o'clock, the young woman explained, she had left her parents at home by the fire to walk over to her uncle's house. But on the way, her parents had driven past her on the road without looking at her or saying a word. About ten minutes later, Reverend Mountford, looking through the window again, saw the pair coming down the road once more, still in the open carriage. The host was even more perplexed since there was no way, given the configuration of the roads, that the couple could have driven by the house the first time and then have returned to approach again from the original direction. He ran outside and asked them about it, but they assured him that this was the only time they had been on the road that day. Furthermore, they said, they had come directly from home.

"Then you mean to say," the host asked, "that really you did not pass by here ten or fifteen minutes ago?" "No," came the reply, "at that time, probably, we were just coming out of the yard."

In 1923, Eleanor Sidgwick, the wife of one of the SPR's chief founders, published an updated supplement to *Phantasms of the Living,* in which she included many more recent accounts. One aspect of the phenomenon to which all investigators remained alert was the so-called veridical apparition—encounters during which the percipient learns something from the apparition that he or she could not otherwise have known. (This is especially common in crisis accounts, where one person may claim to learn of another's death and even the details of their demise.)

One such instance reported by Eleanor Sidgwick was the case of a boarding school student named J. P. Challacombe. It occurred on a March night in 1898. The boy had gone to bed at about 10:00 but was restless and could not sleep. He began thinking of home and his mother, and before long he heard someone coming up the stairs. His first thought was that it was his mother, and then suddenly she appeared to him. She was wearing "a black dress that I had never seen before, and had on her pink shawl and gold chain, and as she came into the room her shoes creaked." The student was not frightened, but felt that something held him back from getting up to greet her. But the mother soon approached her son's bed and kissed him. "I tried to kiss her but could not," the boy said, "then she disappeared and seemed to vanish in a mist."

Corbis-Bettmann

The boy had no way of knowing it, but at the time of his vision, his mother had just returned from a walk. "My dress Jack had never seen," she testified, "and I am not in the habit of wearing my chain outside my dress. As for the boots, they were a pair I had not worn for years, because they were in the habit of creaking."

Mrs. Sidgwick felt obliged to list this account as "ambiguous," since the mother and son had, after all, had time to discuss the matter before reporting it. But, Sidgwick wrote, not only did the apparition convey information as to the apparent's "actual condition at the moment," it was also a rare instance of a realistic apparition affecting three senses—sight, hearing, and touch. Jack's utterly vivid and three-dimensional impression raised still more questions about the human mind and its powers. Yet the SPR researchers stuck fast to their theory of telepathic hallucination, characterizing as "remembered or represented sensation" the realistic sensory data reported in hallucinations such as young Challacombe's.

At the time of the SPR study, researchers made no attempts to reproduce apparitional encounters in a controlled environment, so the SPR's theories could not be explored fully. But there was a category of alleged apparitions of the living that drew special attention from the early researchers. These cases—in which the apparent consciously tried to appear as an apparition to a particular percipient—were designated "experimental," although they could more precisely be called deliberate.

For example, one December evening in 1882, at about 9:30, a Mr. S. H. B. reportedly went into a room alone at home and, thinking of a lady of his acquaintance, determined "so strongly to fix my mind upon the interior of a house at Kew

. . . in which resided Miss V and her two sisters, that I seemed to be actually in the house." S. H. B. went into something akin to a hypnotic trance for about thirty minutes, and then wrote down his intention on a piece of paper. Later, when he went to bed that night, he once again determined to produce a spiritual presence in Miss V.'s home—this time willing himself to appear in her bedroom at the hour of midnight.

The following day, S. H. B. visited the house at Kew without mentioning his attempts the previous evening at what can be presumed to be a bit of innocent Victorian voyeurism. There he encountered one of Miss V's sisters, who told him, without prompting, that she had seen him twice the night before—once at about 9:30, walking through a corridor in the house, and again at midnight, in the bedroom she was sharing with Miss V. The sister, claiming to have been wide awake, described seeing S. H. B.'s apparition enter the room and take her long hair into his hand. The phantom next took the woman's hand in his, stared at it intently, and then disappeared—whereupon the sister woke Miss V to tell her about the encounter.

After hearing the sister's account, which was confirmed by Miss V, S. H. B. took from his pocket his jottings from the previous evening. He showed the paper to the two ladies—who were, it was said, "much astonished although incredulous."

Rarely, it seems, do percipients take offense at deliberate invasions by apparitions, however astonished they may be. One case of serene acceptance of an apparitional visit involved a colleague of Harvard University psychology professor William James. The gentleman, James reported, was "an able and respected professor" and felt comfortable confiding in the open-minded philosopher and psychologist, but wished to remain otherwise anonymous lest his "experiment" seem frivolous and disgraceful to other, more conservative colleagues.

The professor had been seeing a lady friend, "A," quite often, and the two shared an interest in the theory of the existence of astral (or spirit) bodies. One evening in late 1883 or early 1884, the professor sought to project his astral body into A's presence. He sat in the dark by an open window that faced in the direction of her house, about half a mile away. "I . . . tried as hard as I could to wish myself into the presence of A," the professor recalled, and he remained in "that state of wishing for about ten minutes. Nothing abnormal in the way of feelings happened."

The next day, A. reported that during the previous evening, while having dinner with someone, she had seen the professor peering through the door. She told her companion, whose back was toward the door; the friend reasoned that if the professor were really there, he would come into the room. The apparition retreated, unseen by the friend; nevertheless, both apparent and percipient were convinced of the reality of the event.

As such talents began to be investigated in the laboratory, reports from the field diminished. Indeed, the paucity in the twentieth century of such phenomena gave rise to considerable doubts that there was anything to them at all. But then an incident known as the Landau case occurred, raising several old and unresolved questions.

There are some cases where the presumed agent and the percipient were the same person—a matter of seeing one's own double. Psychical researchers Celia Green and Charles McCreery have called such encounters "autophany." This is distinct from "autoscopy," which refers to allegedly seeing one's own body from outside, as in out-of-body experiences. Autophany is often associated with illness or exhaustion, which may account for the notion of seeing one's double as an omen of impending death. In their 1975 book, titled *Apparitions,* Green and McCreery cite the example of a woman in Brisbane, Australia, who ran a boardinghouse for fifteen young men. One night, utterly exhausted from a day of grueling housework, she sat down with some of the boarders to watch television. Before long, the woman reported, she saw her body floating above her for a few moments, "all white and transparent and lying in the same pose as I did myself. I stared wonderingly and then suddenly it wasn't there. I looked around at my companions but they didn't seem to have noticed anything."

The percipient's state of mind, as well as his or her physical health, may also play a role in autophany, as illustrated by the story of a woman who reportedly saw her double one evening in March 1978, after she had put her children to bed. She had been working at her sewing machine, she recalled, when she heard one of the children tossing restlessly. Upon entering the child's room, she saw "the image of myself stooping over the end of the bed, in a dress which I had not been wearing for some time." The figure appeared to be grieving, although the woman herself was "neither specially sad nor specially excited" that night. Three months before, however, one of her children had died, and it occurred to the woman "that after death my child was laid across the foot of my bed, and I may have stood in that attitude then. The dress, too, was the one I was wearing at the time."

While ill health or psychological suffering, such as this woman may have been feeling, might explain some autophany experiences, Green and McCreery report that the majority of such sightings occur when people are feeling perfectly well. The two researchers cite the story of a man who claimed he was "in excellent fettle" at the time of his alleged encounter. A widower who had lived alone for more than ten years, he awoke one night in late March 1960 "with a convulsive jerk all over, conscious of a nearby presence." In the moonlight, he saw a figure dressed in pajama-like clothing, standing near his bed. He naturally assumed that it was an intruder—probably a burglar—and sat up suddenly with his right fist drawn back. Then, the man reported, "I let fly as hard as I could, but just before contacting I glanced up to the face and saw it was myself! Too late to stop, the fist went through the body." At that, the phantom figure instantly vanished.

One might well be suspicious of a story about an apparition in which both the percipient and the apparent are the same and there are no witnesses. But there is a category of account—a type of veridical apparition—in which people have reported receiving useful information from their own double. The most celebrated such case may be that of the French author Guy de Maupassant. In 1885, he was at work on a short story and was experiencing that familiar hazard of the trade, writer's block.

According to Maupassant, a figure appeared at the door to the writer's study,

Short story author Guy de Maupassant

walked across the room, and sat down opposite him. Maupassant was amazed that anyone had gotten into his study and was even more amazed when the intruder proceeded to dictate the words of the author's story. At that moment, he discovered that the intruder was no stranger, but his own double. Before long the apparition disappeared, leaving Maupassant to continue the tale as it had been dictated—the story of an invisible evil spirit that lives within a man, yet independently of him. The being cannot be escaped, and it tortures its host to madness. The story, titled "The Horla," was, some feel, a harbinger of Maupassant's subsequent madness and death.

A more mundane but equally notable case reportedly took place in Holland in 1944. A repairman was asked by a manufacturing company to fix an adding machine. He visited the plant and began work on the machine, a brand unfamiliar to him. In due course he got the apparatus in working order—except that the machine could not accurately add in the hundreds. The repairman was baffled.

One night, however, he was awakened in his bedroom and saw the machine on a table, next to a lamp that was giving off a bright light. He saw himself, fully dressed, lean over the machine and, with his left hand, remove a little triangular part; the figure pinched one end of the part with pliers and put it back in the machine. The next morning the man returned to the plant, mimicked the action of his double the night before, and repaired the adding machine.

Another type of apparition of the living is said to serve a specific function—that of alerting the percipient to the apparent's imminent arrival. Such a case was reported to the SPR by Dr. George Wyld in 1882; the incident concerned a close friend of his, Miss Jackson. The woman was accustomed to visiting the poor. Once, while making a round of visits, she had an overwhelming desire to be home, warming herself at the kitchen stove. Precisely at that moment, two housemaids in her kitchen saw the doorknob turn and the door open. Miss Jackson then came in and went directly to the stove to warm her hands. The maids took note that on her hands she was wearing handsome green kid gloves. Then suddenly, the woman disappeared.

The astonished maids went to Miss Jackson's mother and told her every detail of the event, down to the gloves the woman had worn. The mother reasoned that since Miss Jackson did not have any green gloves, the appearance was surely imagined. Thirty minutes later, when Miss Jackson herself came home and went to the stove to warm her hands, she was in fact wearing green gloves.

Arrival cases, as they are called, occur with some frequency. In one reported instance, a man was startled to see his twin brother's figure appear in the room; it struck him "like a mild shock of electricity." The vision gradually disappeared, but only moments later the man's twin was actually tapping at the window; he had unexpectedly arrived for a visit. In another case, a major in the British army saw a superior officer enter a mess hall carrying some fishing tackle. The major went to look for the officer, but he was not there, and in fact, no one could recall having seen him for several hours. Shortly thereafter, the officer arrived at the barracks with his fishing gear in hand, dressed in precisely the same clothes that the major had seen him wearing. When asked if he had been in the mess hall about ten minutes before, the officer said no, he had just that moment returned from fishing.

Nowhere, it seems, are arrival cases more common than in Norway. There, the double is referred to as the *vardøgr* and has taken on the special role of forerunner. Thorstein Wereide, a professor at the University of Oslo and an early member of Norway's Society for Psychical Research, wrote in the 1950s that the *vardøgr* appears at one's destination when one is about to leave for that place regardless of the distance or the time involved in the journey. And its appearance in Norway is usually auditory rather than visual. The percipient will hear the rattling of a key in the lock, overshoes being kicked off, the sounds of familiar footsteps. The *vardøgr*'s appearances can become so regular that the percipient addresses the person, saying "Is it you or your *vardøgr*?"

In such situations, it is claimed, the percipient can sometimes put the phenomenon to practical use. This was reportedly done with a student at the University of Oslo, Wiers Jensen, who lived at a boardinghouse early in this century. His evening hours were irregular, making it difficult for the hostess to know when to prepare Jensen's evening meal; however, his *vardøgr* reportedly made regular appearances, and the hostess would know that it was time to start cooking. When Jensen arrived at the boardinghouse, his dinner was ready.

Professor Wereide himself claimed to have a *vardøgr* like Jensen's. His wife would often hear it—and occasionally see it—when Wereide was about to leave the university for the trip home. He believed his wife was particularly receptive, since he had not had such experiences before his marriage. In his opinion, projections of this kind were probably common throughout the world, but Norway had more people who were sensitive to them. The reason, he decided, was that for centuries the Norwegians had lived in remote areas of the countryside and in mountains where communications are especially difficult. "Nature," he wrote, "seems to have made use of 'supernatural' means to compensate for this isolation."

One might argue that such apparitions are what Frederic Myers called "expectation images"—projections of what the observer was hoping to see. But some researchers maintain that the supposed accuracy with which people have noted these forerunners, even when there is no particular schedule involved, suggests that there may be more to many arrival cases than mere wishful thinking.

The Uncanny and Literature

Corbis-Bettmann

"Be thou a spirit of health or goblin damn'd,
Bring with thee airs from heaven or blasts from hell,
Be thy intents wicked or charitable,
Thou comest in such a questionable shape
That I will speak to thee."

THUS DID Shakespeare's Hamlet address his father's ghost, voicing many of the concerns Elizabethans had about the spirit world: Where did ghosts come from? How did they fit with the new Protestant doctrine that denied the existence of Purgatory? Could they be demons in disguise or merely, as Lady Macbeth tells her lord when he recoils from Banquo's ghost, "the very painting of your fear"?

Few in the Elizabethan era doubted the existence of ghosts. A learned treatise on the subject by Ludwig Lavater—his name anglicized to Lewes—was published in 1572. French author Pierre Le Loyer noted in 1586 that "of all the common and familiar subjects of conversation that are entered upon in company, of things remote from nature and cut off from the senses, there is none so ready to hand, none so usual, as that of Spirits, and whether what is said of them is true."

Shakespeare, however, was the first playwright to take ghosts at all seriously. Many of the Shakespearean spirits who stalked the stage of the Globe Theater seemed as real as any of the living characters. In *Hamlet,* for example, the late king of Denmark appears fully armed, his countenance "more in sorrow than in anger," and even gains a certain amount of audience sympathy when he admits that he is "Doom'd for a certain term to walk the night, / And for the day confined to fast in fires."

Shakespeare probably read Lavater's book, but it is not known if he believed in ghosts. It is probably safest to say that the great dramatist had an open mind, believing along with Hamlet that "There are more things in heaven and earth, Horatio, / Than are dreamt of in your philosophy."

Corbis-Bettmann

Charles Dickens

Although Charles Dickens had little patience with the Victorian passion for spiritualism, he loved to write about the supernatural. One such narrative, published with three others under the title "Four Ghost Stories" in the periodical *All the Year Round,* developed into a real-life ghost story so eerie that it evidently convinced even its skeptical author that he had had a brush with the paranormal.

Dickens's 1861 tale concerns a society portrait painter, Mr. H, who, while traveling to a country estate on September 13, meets a delicate-looking young lady on the train. After some conversation, she asks him if he can paint a person from memory. The artist replies that he is not certain but it may be possible.

"Well," says the woman, "look at me again. You may have to take a likeness of me." Mr. H studies her face carefully, and then the travelers go their separate ways.

Two years later, a Mr. Wylde comes to call on the painter and asks if it is possible for him to paint a portrait based only on a description. The visitor goes on to describe his daughter, two years dead, and requests a picture of her. The artist tries several unsuccessful sketches. Then, in a moment of inspiration, he draws the young woman he met on the train. "Instantly," wrote Dickens, "a bright look of recognition and pleasure lighted up the father's face, and he exclaimed, 'That is she!'"

The artist asks when it was that Mr. Wylde's daughter died, and the man replies: "'Two years ago; on the 13th of September.'"

Within a few days of the story's publication, Dickens received a remarkable letter from a portrait painter who informed him that the tale printed in *All the Year Round* matched in astonishing detail a real experience of his own, one that he had written up for publication. The meeting with the young lady on the train and the later request from the bereaved father were all laid out in the real painter's account. The portraitist, naturally enough, believed that Dickens had somehow heard his story and beaten him to publication.

"In particular," wrote the aggrieved artist in his letter to Dickens, "how else was it possible that the date, the 13th of September, could have been got at? For I never told the date until I wrote it."

"Now *my* story," recounted Dickens in apparent wonder, "had NO DATE; but seeing, when I looked over the proofs, the great importance of having *a* date, I wrote in, unconsciously, the exact date on the margin of the proof!"

The Versailles Mystery

Eleanor Jourdain (left) and Anne Moberly

PARANORMAL RESEARCHERS have long been fascinated by a rare type of haunting called retrocognition. In cases of retrocognition—a term based on the Latin for "backward knowing"—percipients say they experience past events and environments as if transported back in time.

One of the most celebrated and sensational of all retrocognitive hauntings first came to public attention in 1911. That year, English schoolmistresses Anne Moberly and Eleanor Jourdain published a book entitled *An Adventure*. It was their account of an uncanny experience a decade earlier at Versailles, the grand palace near Paris that once was the seat of French kings. What these women said they saw there was still being debated more than half a century later.

In the summer of 1901, Eleanor Jourdain invited her new acquaintance Anne Moberly to join her for two weeks of sightseeing in and around Paris. Miss Moberly was the head of a women's residential hall at Oxford University, and Miss Jourdain was considering a job as her assistant. The trip, which was Miss Moberly's first visit to France and Miss Jourdain's second, would allow them to get to know each other.

Despite differences in age and personality, the two women discovered they had much in common. Both were conventional ladies. The fifty-five-year-old Anne Moberly was a shy woman with fierce dark eyes behind a pince-nez straddling a strong nose. She owed her position at Oxford not to her education, which was spotty, nor to her administrative skill, which was deficient, but to her social standing as an Anglican bishop's daughter. Miss Jourdain was capable, outgoing, and charming, twenty years Miss Moberly's junior. She, too, had grown up in a clerical household.

On August 10, the women went by train to Versailles. Neither knew much

VERSAILLES — Palais du Petit Trianon, Façade Nord *and Chapel*

North side of the Petit Trianon from English garden

He saw it in 1901 with no long wall & no bush.
Steps went directly to the west terrace from the English garden.
lady sitting here

The postcard of the Petit Trianon on which Anne Moberly drew an arrow to where she said she saw a seated lady sketching

about French history: Miss Moberly admitted that what she did know came less from scholarly works than from novels, and Miss Jourdain's history courses at Oxford had been classical, stopping short of the era in which Versailles had flourished.

They dutifully completed their tour of the palace. The day was unusually fresh and breezy for August, and they decided to walk to the Petit Trianon, one of two smaller palaces on the grounds. The fact that the Petit Trianon's last royal occupant had been the ill-fated queen Marie Antoinette gave it a romantic appeal. She had been deeply attached to the place, which was her retreat from the stifling etiquette and intrigues of the court. With their Baedeker guidebook in hand and, perhaps, a thought of the queen's death by guillotine in mind, the ladies set out.

Chatting amiably, the Englishwomen strolled through an enormous formal garden and then struck off through a glade. But their directions had been unclear, and they emerged from the woods to find themselves at the wrong building—they had reached the palace called the Grand Trianon. After another look at the guidebook, they started up a lane that appeared to lead toward the Petit Trianon. Miss Moberly noticed a woman shaking a cloth from the window of a building they passed, but to her surprise, Miss Jourdain—who, unlike her guest, was fluent in French and acted as spokeswoman on their outings—did not ask for directions.

The grounds were curiously devoid of other tourists. At a point where three paths branched off from the lane, the women came upon two grave-looking men in green coats and three-cornered hats. They appeared to be gardeners: A wheelbarrow and a spade were at hand. When Miss Jourdain asked which path led to the Petit Trianon, the men answered, but in such a coldly mechanical manner that Miss Jourdain repeated the question, only to receive the same response. Looking about her, she was struck by the old-fashioned clothes of a woman and a girl standing in the doorway of a nearby cottage. Without remarking on them to her companion, she walked on

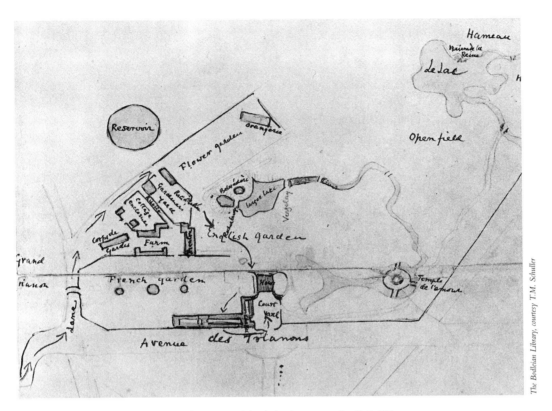

Anne Moberly's map of the ladies' route to the Petit Trianon

with Miss Moberly, taking the path the men had indicated.

For no apparent reason, Miss Moberly suddenly found herself overtaken by an extraordinary depression. Perhaps too shy to reveal her feelings to so recent an acquaintance, she did not mention her gloom, but it grew more oppressive by the minute. At the same time, Miss Jourdain was assailed by an almost overwhelming sense of loneliness and began to feel like a sleepwalker. She, too, kept silent about the feelings that had descended on her as they pressed on toward the Petit Trianon.

In their private, deepening depressions the schoolmistresses followed the path the men in the green coats had indicated until it intersected another path stretching to the left and right. Directly ahead of them, set on rough grass in the shadows of a dense wood, was a small round kiosk, where a cloaked man was seated. The day, which had been so uncharacteristically fresh and breezy, now turned ominous and almost claustrophobic.

Miss Moberly later wrote that everything about her "suddenly looked unnatural, therefore unpleasant; even the trees behind the building seemed to have become flat and lifeless, like a wood worked in tapestry. There were no effects of light and shade, and no wind stirred the trees. It was all intensely still."

The man then turned his head and looked toward the women. Miss Jourdain's uneasy feelings sharpened into fear when she saw a look of evil on his swarthy, pock-marked face. At the same time, she was not certain he was really looking at them. For

33

her part, Miss Moberly was thoroughly alarmed by the face, which struck her as repulsive and odious. But she and Miss Jourdain did not express their fears, talking only of whether to take the path to the right or the left.

As if out of nowhere, a handsome gentleman with long dark curls under a wide-brimmed hat, wearing buckle shoes and a cloak, rushed up to the two women, calling out that they should take the path to the right to reach the palace. Then this unexpected guide dashed off and in a moment was out of view.

Surprised at how quickly he had materialized and then disappeared, but thankful for his help, Miss Moberly and Miss Jourdain resumed their walk, which took them through a somber wood. At its edge, the Englishwomen finally caught their first glimpse of the Petit Trianon.

The two women stepped from the wood and crossed an English-style garden toward the north facade of the Petit Trianon, which, in Miss Moberly's opinion, looked more like an elegant country house than a royal establishment. Near a terrace that wrapped around the north and west sides of the palace, Miss Moberly observed a woman who appeared to be sketching. Fair-haired and rather pretty, she wore a broad-brimmed white hat and a low-cut dress with a full skirt. A light-colored scarf was draped around her shoulders. A distinctly old-fashioned outfit, Miss Moberly concluded, for a tourist to wear. She felt somehow annoyed by the woman, whom she and Miss Jourdain passed in silence.

Miss Moberly was oppressed by an unnatural stillness and a dreamlike feeling as she and Miss Jourdain reached the terrace and made their way around the palace to a courtyard on the south facade. There they entered and fell in with a merry French wedding party—its members all in proper twentieth-century attire—for a tour of the rooms. The dark mood began to dissipate, and their normal good spirits returned.

Perhaps wishing to repress a troubling experience, the ladies did not talk about their excursion until a week later, when Miss Moberly began a letter to her sister in which she mentioned their search for the Petit Trianon. As she wrote, she found herself once again overtaken by depression. She turned to Miss Jourdain and burst out, "Do you think that the Petit Trianon is haunted?" Miss Jourdain promptly replied, "Yes, I do." They then revealed to each other the emotions they had felt that day and tried to account for the odd behavior and dress of the gentleman they had encountered near the kiosk. After this conversation, they did not return to the subject for the rest of their holiday, and several months were to pass before it surfaced once again.

Back in Oxford that autumn, Miss Jourdain was shocked when Miss Moberly mentioned a seated woman they had passed in the garden of the Petit Trianon. Miss Jourdain had seen no seated woman. Later, Miss Jordain learned that August 10, the date of their visit to Versailles, was pivotal in French history, for on that day in 1792 revolutionary forces had arrested the royal family. It had marked the beginning of the end for Marie Antoinette. Ahead lay imprisonment and the guillotine. The women now speculated that they might somehow have tapped into a telepathic trace of the queen's memory lingering near her beloved palace on that black anniversary. It was a fancy that demanded another visit.

Miss Jourdain returned to Paris for the Christmas holidays. On a cold, wet January day, she set off through the Petit Trianon's park for the Hameau, a tiny reproduction of a peasant hamlet, built for Marie Antoinette, who had visited it almost daily. Dreamlike sensations and uncanny perceptions assailed Miss Jourdain as she neared the Hameau. She passed two men in tunics and hooded capes loading sticks into a cart. When she glanced back a moment later, the men had disappeared.

At the Hameau, Miss Jourdain walked from building to building, oppressed by a dreariness that deepened when she paused before the queen's cottage. Reentering the wooded park, she wandered a tangle of paths screened by dense undergrowth. Although she heard the rustling of silk dresses (attire quite

Statens Konstmuseer, Stockholm

When Anne Moberly saw this painting of Marie Antoinette, she became convinced that the lady she had seen sketching in the garden of the Petit Trianon was the queen

foolish for a wet day, she thought) and women talking in French, she saw no one except a grizzled old gardener. Intermittently, faint strains of violin music reached her ears.

Back at the main palace, Miss Jourdain asked if there had been a concert at the Petit Trianon that day. No, she was told, no concert. She began to wonder if she had heard phantom music from the past.

Eleanor Jourdain's second experience at Versailles strengthened the women's conviction that they had experienced something far from ordinary. In comparing their independently written accounts of the August visit, they were struck by several strange discrepancies. In addition to not seeing the woman sketching in the garden, Miss Jourdain had missed the woman shaking a cloth out a window. On the other hand, Miss Moberly had not noticed the cottage with a woman and girl in the doorway. It was as if they both saw across time, but each imperfectly and differently. Somehow, the women decided, they had passively viewed Marie Antoinette's thoughts. According to their hypothesis, the visions that had enveloped them were scenes from a vivid, melancholy daydream that once had filled the queen's mind. Seeking to link their experience to Marie Antoinette's, they tracked down and studied scores of documents. A map drawn by the queen's architect suggested to them that a cottage had indeed stood where Miss Jourdain had seen one, although the site was now empty. In another instance, an architectural record from 1780 noted a small columned structure that they thought must be the kiosk they had seen.

They were also satisfied that their research had uncovered the identities of the figures they had met. The green-coated men with the wheelbarrow, they decided, were not gardeners but members of the Swiss Guard assigned to protect the king and queen. The man seated at the kiosk was identified as the Comte de Vaudreuil, who had proved himself a false friend to the queen by persuading her to allow the performance of a subtly antiroyalist play. The ladies believed they felt the queen's own displeasure at the sight of Vaudreuil.

Converging bits of information led them to October 5, 1789, as a date relevant to some of the events they observed. According to historical tradition, a messenger had rushed to the Petit Trianon on that day to warn the queen of a revolutionary mob approaching from Paris. The researchers matched the messenger with the man running near the kiosk. And, in a paymaster's logbook, they found that a horse cart had been hired to carry away sticks and branches from the park on that date—the very task Miss Jourdain had seen performed near the Hameau.

All the puzzle pieces appeared to fit. The cloaked men, for instance, seemed to have been dressed for fall rather than a warm August day. Whatever the accuracy of their inferences, Marie Antoinette would have remembered that day with a mixture of nostalgia and sorrow, for according to tradition the royal family left Versailles then to take up residence in Paris. The queen never saw her beloved Petit Trianon again.

Psychical researcher G. W. Lambert later proposed that Miss Jourdain and Miss Moberly had a genuine retrocognitive experience but got the year wrong. His research indicated that the kiosk and several other key features of their visions were removed around 1774. He suggests that they saw events from around 1770 rather than 1789.

Then again, Miss Moberly and Miss Jourdain may also have seen nothing more than actors in period costumes. Biographer Phillipe Jullian discovered in researching the life of the flamboyant turn-of-the-century poet Robert de Montesquiou that he and his friends often rehearsed historical plays near the Petit Trianon. And Marie Antoinette was one of their favorite characters. In a 1965 book, Jullian suggested that the Englishwomen might have happened upon these amateur theatricals.

Jullian's theory proved influential. Dame Joan Evans, an art historian and long-time friend to whom Miss Moberly and Miss Jourdain willed the copyright of their book, was convinced that Jullian had hit upon the truth, turning a tantalizing tale of retrocognition into nothing but an honest misperception. Acting on her conviction, Dame Joan refused to authorize any further English editions of *An Adventure*. But many who have read the account still fervently believe that the women did, indeed, somehow briefly view a long-dead world.

The Tower of London

The Tower of London and its surrounding area

ONCEIVED IN conquest and emblematic of violent death, the Tower of London is one of the world's bloodiest historic sites—and also, some say, one of the most ghost ridden. Over the centuries, the Tower has variously been a fortress, a castle, a storehouse, an armory, even a zoo. But it is woven most tightly into British history as a prison and a killing ground, the site of innumerable hangings, burnings, drawings and quarterings, and beheadings. There, nobles met their deaths at royal whim, and even crowned heads were claimed by the executioner's ax.

The Tower site is old beyond reckoning. When William the Conqueror overcame the Saxons in the eleventh century, he found, still standing along the Thames, stretches of ancient Roman walls. Their location was attractive strategically, so William chose to build a fortress within their shelter. A rude military camp served well enough for a while, but in 1078 the king began erecting a vast stone edifice to serve as both fortress and palace. This was the White Tower, which still stands, little changed over the past 900 years, as a monument to Norman architecture. It formed the nucleus of the Tower of London, which is not a single building but an eighteen-acre compound of towers, yards, battlements, houses, and other structures.

Many of William's successors made changes in the Tower, improving its fortifications or expanding its functions. In the thirteenth century, for instance, both Henry III and Edward I spent huge sums on building programs for the complex, some of which were designed to make the royal quarters more comfortable. But by the end of the sixteenth century, the Tower was no longer used as a royal residence, having become mainly a state prison and home to government offices. Eventually, its penal

A 1616 illustation of the Thames and the Tower of London

and bureaucratic functions defunct, the complex became what it is today: an imposing tourist attraction that houses, among other national treasures, the crown jewels.

The Tower of London bears testament to the grandeur of English history, and
also to its periodic cruel perversity. Centuries of monarchical tinkering may have
altered its structural details and lineaments, but the finest architectural revisions could
not begin to expunge the Tower's notorious legacy of death or exorcise its bloody
earth. Legend has it that the complex is haunted by the spirits of many of those
inmates who suffered or died within its grim confines. Evidence that such restless
phantoms actually exist is nothing more than anecdotal, but the ghost stores persist,
clinging tenaciously as London fog to the Tower's cold gray stones.

Not all of the Tower's victims died within its precincts. Many were taken from
imprisonment to Tower Hill, just outside the walled perimeter, to be hanged, beheaded, or otherwise dispatched. Usually their bodies were returned to the Tower
grounds for burial. During World War II, a sentry on night patrol outside the Tower's
main entrance was startled by an odd cortege approaching his post. Several men in
old-fashioned uniforms bore a stretcher. Atop it lay a decapitated body, its head
tucked between one of its arms and its torso. The group vanished only a few yards
from the sentry. No identity was ascribed to the beheaded victim, but there were
indications the sentry had somehow peered into history. In relating his vision, he
accurately described uniforms worn by sheriff's men who, during the Middle Ages,
returned corpses to the Tower for burial.

On the death in 1483 of Edward IV, his twelve-year-old son ascended the throne
as King Edward V, and the new king's younger brother, Richard, became Duke of
York. Their guardian was their uncle, Richard, Duke of Gloucester, who coveted the

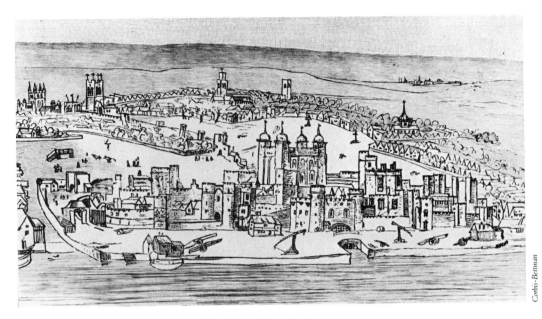

Corbis-Bettman

The Tower of London in 1543

throne himself. Gloucester contrived to have the children declared illegitimate; thereupon he took the crown as Richard III. The boys were confined to the Tower and there disappeared from history. No evidence ever came to light linking Richard to his nephews' departure. Indeed, he had no clear motive for harming them, since they were not a threat to his throne. Nevertheless, legend has it the boys were murdered on Richard's orders in the Bloody Tower, which probably derives its name from that presumed event. Ghosts of the boys, nightgown clad and hand in hand, have reportedly appeared near the Bloody Tower and elsewhere on Tower grounds.

Thomas à Becket was both chancellor and best friend to Henry II, but after Henry named him Archbishop of Canterbury, a rift developed. Henry had expected his long-time crony to side with him in his incessant bickering with the Roman Catholic Church. But Becket put his church before his king, and in 1170 Henry retaliated by having three assassins stab the archbishop to death in his own cathedral. The martyred Becket was canonized three years later, and Henry, bowing to Church demands, was forced to do penance for his old friend's murder. Although Becket did not die at the Tower, he apparently chose the site for vengeance. A new tower and watergate ordered built there by Henry's grandson, Henry III, neared completion twice, only to be destroyed—once by a storm and the second time for no apparent cause. A priest claimed that he had seen Becket's ghost battering the stonework with his cross.

A pious but weak-willed monarch, Henry VI spent most of his reign buffeted by contending forces in the English civil strife known as the War of the Roses. The Lancastrian king eventually found himself imprisoned in the Tower as an opposing Yorkist took the throne to become Edward IV. On the night of May 21, 1471, Henry was stabbed to death, probably at Edward's behest, while praying in a small oratory in the Wakefield Tower. His ghost is said to have been seen sitting outside the oratory, his hands folded in prayer.

One night in the late 1960s, a sentry who was patrolling the walls between the Wakefield and Lanthorn towers rushed into his guardroom, prickling with fear. "Man in cloak! Man in cloak!" was all he could gasp. But when he was calmer, he told how a cloaked figure had appeared from the shadows during his patrol. The sentry was about to challenge the anonymous intruder when he saw that it was headless.

James Crofts was the illegitimate son of Charles II. His father, who had no lawful heir, acknowledged and adored young Jamie, and made him Duke of Monmouth. Charles was to be succeeded by his brother James, a Catholic and therefore unpopular in Protestant England. A movement arose to have Monmouth declared legitimate and a rightful heir, but Charles would not trifle with the succession, and his brother

Edward V and Richard, the doomed princes in the Tower

became King James II in 1685. After Monmouth made a futile try at asserting his own royal claim by force, James sent him to the Tower for treason. The young duke was beheaded the same year as James's ascension. A phantom in cavalier's garb, possibly Monmouth's ghost, supposedly has been seen moving along the battlements connecting the Bell and Beauchamp towers.

The founding of the Tudor dynasty posed a mortal hazard to the Plantagenets, the previous royal family. The last female Plantagenet was Margaret Pole, Countess of Salisbury; although she was seventy years old and politically harmless Henry VIII ordered her beheaded in 1541 on a spurious charge of treason. But proud Margaret refused to bow over the chopping block, telling her executioner that if he wanted her head, he could get it as best he might. She fled the axman, who chased her around Tower Green, gradually hacking her to death. Some claim that there is a ghostly reenactment of the grisly scene each May 27, its anniversary.

Sickly and underage when he became king, Edward VI was a pawn for ambitious nobles. One of them was John Dudley, Duke of Northumberland, who married his son, Guilford Dudley, to Lady Jane Grey in hopes of winning the crown for his family. Lady Jane, grandniece of Henry VIII, had a tenuous claim to the throne. As King Edward was dying, Northumberland persuaded him to name Jane his successor, but soon after Edward's death, the populace recognized Henry's daughter Mary as the rightful heir. Queen for less than a fortnight, Jane was imprisoned in the Tower along with her husband, and soon thereafter both were beheaded. It is said that Dudley's ghost sometimes sits by a window in Beauchamp Tower, weeping, as Dudley himself did while waiting there for his execution.

Jane died under the Tower ax at the age of only fifteen. Prior to her own death, Jane had to watch from her prison window while her young husband was taken to his execution on Tower Hill. Later that same day, February 12, 1554, she was beheaded on Tower Green. Jane's ghost has been reported as recently as 1957, when, on the 403d anniversary of her death, a Tower guard spotted a white shape high on the battlemented roof of the Salt Tower. As he watched, the nebulous mass seemed to form itself into a likeness of Lady Jane. The guard called a second sentry, who also saw the queenly apparition.

The second of Henry VIII's six wives, Anne Boleyn lost the king's favor when she failed to bear him a male heir—and when his wandering eye fell on Jane Seymour. Henry had Anne sentenced to death on dubious charges of adultery and treason. At Anne's request, a swordsman was imported from France for her execution: She feared mutilation under the clumsy ax, which often failed to sever a head with a single blow. The young queen died by the blade on Tower Green in 1536 and was buried in the Tower Chapel of Saint Peter ad Vincula. Her ghost, with head and without, has been reported in many parts of the Tower, including the chapel. There, a spectral Anne is said to lead a procession of ghostly lords and ladies who pace back and forth, then vanish.

Soldier, adventurer, scholar, and scientist, Sir Walter Raleigh was a favorite of Elizabeth I. Incurring her temporary displeasure, he earned himself a brief stay in the Tower in 1592, but his real problems began in 1603, when Elizabeth died and James I took the throne. The new king suspected Raleigh of plotting against him and had him convicted of treason, but Raleigh's public popularity led James to stay the execution. On the whole, the second imprisonment was not unpleasant. Raleigh's family was with him, and he was free to receive visitors, exercise, write, and pursue scientific experiments. He was released in 1616 to voyage to the New World in search of gold. But the expedition failed, and in its course Raleigh violated royal orders against molesting Spanish possessions. Spain demanded vengeance, and in 1618 James had Raleigh beheaded on the old treason charge. A battlement adjoining his apartments in the Bloody Tower came to be called Raleigh's Walk because he often strolled there. It is said that on moonlit nights his ghost walks the battlement still.

In the winter of 1815, a sentry was patrolling the entrance to the Martin Tower when, on the stroke of midnight, he saw a huge bear rear from beneath the door. The guard lunged with his bayonet, but the weapon passed through nothingness and lodged in the oak door. The terrified sentry fainted. The next day he was able to tell his story, but the day after that, he died—some said from fear. Though certainly a departure from ghostly lords and ladies, an apparitional bear in the Tower is not as misplaced as it seems. Henry I was the first king known to have kept a menagerie there, and the custom persisted through the centuries. Lions, tigers, zebras, monkeys, hyenas, and even elephants, as well as bears, were housed from time to time. The zoo

The Norman Chapel of the Tower of London

was not eliminated until 1835, when a Tower lion mauled a soldier.

In the year 1605, the wealthy and erudite Henry Percy, ninth earl of Northumberland, was sentenced to the Tower for complicity in the Gunpowder Plot, whose aim was to blow up Parliament—and along with it, King James I. He stayed there sixteen years before buying his freedom with a £30,000 fine. Like Sir Walter Raleigh, Northumberland had a relatively easy life in the Tower. His children were with him much of the time, and he was able to gather about him other learned inmates— Raleigh among them—for seminars on scientific and literary matters. The fact that the earl was treated well and allowed to leave the Tower with his head still affixed to his shoulders apparently did not, however, deter him from haunting the premises. His ghost is believed to walk the battlements abutting the Martin Tower, where, in life, the earl customarily took the air.

2
SECOND SIGHT

Visions

*Samuel Clemens—who later gained
fame as an author under the pen name
Mark Twain—foresaw his brother
Henry's death in a dream in 1858*

IF SAMUEL CLEMENS of Hannibal, Missouri, had been content to spend his life as a riverboatman, a remarkable episode in psychic lore would have been lost to history. But his often-autobiographical writings in later years as the author Mark Twain made some of his most personal thoughts public. Among them is the story of a dream he had about his younger brother Henry in 1858.

At that time, Sam Clemens was an apprentice pilot on the steamboat *Pennsylvania*, which plied the Mississippi River between New Orleans and St. Louis. Henry, a likable and handsome lad of about twenty, was a clerk on the same vessel. One night, when the *Pennsylvania* was berthed in St. Louis, Henry stayed on the ship while his older brother lodged at a boardinghouse on shore. Sam dreamed that he saw a metal coffin resting on two chairs in the sitting room, and in the coffin the laid-out body of Henry. On Henry's chest was a bouquet of white flowers with a single crimson flower in the center.

Clemens told a sister what he had dreamed, but he mentioned nothing of it to

Henry on their trip downriver together. In New Orleans, Sam was transferred to the steamboat *Lacey,* which was to head back upriver two days after the *Pennsylvania*. On the night before Henry sailed, Sam got to talking about disasters on the river and what to do in case of accident. "Don't lose your head," he advised his brother. "The passengers will do that!" What Henry should do, he said, was to help the women and children into the lifeboat and then swim to shore himself. On that note the brothers parted, and hours later the *Pennsylvania* sailed.

Two or three days later, when Sam and the *Lacey* reached Greenville, Mississippi, they were greeted at the landing with grim news: "The *Pennsylvania* is blown up just below Memphis, at Ship Island! One hundred and fifty lives lost!" According to that first report, Henry was not among the casualties. But the news got worse as the *Lacey* moved from port to port upriver. By the time Sam reached Memphis he knew that four of the *Pennsylvania*'s eight boilers had exploded, that many of the passengers and crew had been killed outright, and that others had been scalded almost to the point of death. Henry was one of the latter.

Sam found his brother in Memphis and stayed with him until he died. A kind citizen of the city then took Sam in and gave him a bed. Exhausted with grief and strain, he fell into a profound sleep. When he woke, he went to the place where Henry's body lay. It was in a room with several other victims of the explosion, all awaiting burial services.

The coffins provided by the city were of plain white pine—except for Henry's. His youth and beauty had appealed to several ladies of Memphis, who had collected sixty dollars to buy him a special metal coffin. Sam Clemens saw his brother lying exactly as he had seen him in his dream: in an open metal coffin, resting on two chairs. About the only item from his dream that was missing was the bouquet of flowers. As he stood there looking on, an elderly woman entered the room with a large bouquet of white flowers—in the center of which was tucked a single red rose—and placed the bouquet on the dead man's chest. In the most awful sense, Sam's dream had come true.

Most people never have an experience as searing as Sam Clemens's. But almost everyone has had experiences that are cause for some slight wonder. Someone thinks of a long-lost friend, and moments later that person calls on the telephone. A young man suddenly senses that his favorite uncle is dead, and a telegram arrives with the bad news. A mother writing to her daughter feels a sharp pain in her writing hand, while at the same time her daughter burns her right hand on the stove. A woman dreams of a disaster at sea, and two days later a great liner sinks with hundreds of passengers.

It is of course possible to attribute any of these and thousands of similar events to coincidence. And yet, so many instances of apparent knowledge have accumulated throughout history that millions of people have come to believe humans possess more than five senses. Some additional faculty, they maintain, enables a person to sense an occurrence before it has happened, apprehend what is in someone else's mind, or be aware of an event taking place far away. This faculty permits a glimpse into another plane of time or space, unreachable by the ordinary senses of hearing, seeing, touching, tasting, or smelling.

IN ANCIENT times, people spoke of prophecies and auguries and miracles. In our more rational age, such things fall under the prosaic-sounding heading of extrasensory perception, defined as the apparent reception of information through means other than the known sensory channels. The experiencing individual is said to be psychic.

Three types of alleged extrasensory perception (ESP) are most commonly studied. The most familiar is telepathy, or mind reading, which is the transference of thoughts from one person to another without the use of words. Telepathy is said to occur most often with people—such as identical twins—who are very close to each other emotionally. Clairvoyance, or second sight, is an awareness of distant objects and events. In its most vivid manifestation it may involve a prolonged vision of a fire or murder taking place a great distance away; more often, it is a quick mental picture of a train wreck or the contents of a sealed envelope or some danger that is creeping up on an unsuspecting loved one. The third type of ESP is precognition, knowing something in advance of its happening—such as in a dream like Mark Twain's.

All ESP phenomena, because they seem beyond the limits of our present understanding, are said to be paranormal; serious investigators describe their research field as the science of parapsychology. But many scientists and other skeptics scoff at ESP research as an extension of old-fashioned spiritualism—the alleged communication, through mediums, with the spirits of the dead. Debate continues to rage over whether parapsychology is a true science, a so-called spiritual science, or no science at all. At the same time, the human belief in psychic powers has been with us always, and it remains strong. Gallup polls, academic questionnaires, and random national samplings by magazines have consistently shown an acceptance of the reality of some psychic phenomena. Often that acceptance is based on personal experience. According to a recent national survey, sixty-seven percent of adult Americans believe they have experienced ESP. The same survey indicated that close to twenty million Americans have undergone profound psychic experiences.

Many well-known figures—the Italian revolutionary patriot Giuseppe Garibaldi, the musicians Charles Camille Saint-Saëns and Robert Schumann, and the inventor Thomas Edison, to name just a few—have experienced psychic episodes. Abraham Lincoln, too, reported paranormal experiences. He believed in omens. According to his close friend and biographer Ward H. Lamon, certain signs assured him that he would rise to power and greatness yet "would be suddenly cut off at the height of his career and the fullness of his fame." Soon after his election as president in 1860, he looked into a mirror and saw a double image of himself. He took it as an image of the future and understood it to mean that he would be elected to a second term but would die before the end of it. After the Cleveland *Plain Dealer* published a story about the president's interest in psychic matters, someone asked Lincoln if the account was true. "The only falsehood in the statement," he replied, "is that the half of it has

Corbis-Bettmann

General Ulysses S. Grant avoided certain death on the night Abraham Lincoln (above) was assassinated because of his wife Julia's premonition

not been told. This article does not begin to tell the wonderful things I have witnessed."

One he had yet to witness was a precognitive dream, which he later related to Lamon "in a melancholy, meditative mood." In the dream, said Lincoln, he had heard the sound of numbers of people weeping and sobbing as if their hearts would break. He could not see the mourners, so he followed the sound through the White House until he arrived at the East Room. "There," according to his account to Lamon, "was a sickening surprise. Before me was a catafalque on which rested a corpse wrapped in funeral vestments. Around it were stationed soldiers who were acting as guards." Mourners wept and gazed upon the corpse, whose face was covered.

"'Who is dead in the White House?' I demanded of the soldiers. 'The president,' was the answer; 'he was killed by an assassin.'"

As every American knows, Lincoln was shot early in his second term by the actor John Wilkes Booth at Ford's Theatre in Washington. Less widely known is the fact that the theater party that night was smaller than had been anticipated because someone else had a premonition, too.

April 13, 1865, was a day of great joy and celebration in Washington. General Ulysses S. Grant had accepted the surrender of Confederate General Robert E. Lee at Appomattox a few days before, ending the Civil War, and was enjoying a brilliant reception given in his honor in the capital. His wife, Julia, took much pleasure in the festivities.

The next day, however, Mrs. Grant awoke with the sense that she and her husband and child must leave Washington immediately and return to their home in Burlington, New Jersey. She begged Grant to take them away at once. The general had appointments that he could not break, but he promised to leave as soon as possible.

As the day wore on, Julia Grant's sense of urgency increased. At noon a messenger came to the door of her hotel room and said: "Mrs. Lincoln sends me, Madam, with her compliments, to say she will call for you at exactly eight o'clock to go to the theater."

Mrs. Grant found the man's appearance strange, disliked his manner, and thought his message peremptory. "You may return with my compliments to Mrs. Lincoln," she replied, "and say I regret that as General Grant and I intend leaving the city this afternoon, we will not, therefore, be here to accompany the President and Mrs. Lincoln to the theater." The man persisted: "Madam, the papers announce that General

Grant will be with the President tonight at the theater." But Mrs. Grant did not care what the papers said. She felt a growing sense that something sinister was about to befall her husband, and she ordered the messenger to deliver her regrets. When he had left, she sent one imploring note after another to General Grant, saying that they must not go to the theater and entreating him to leave for Burlington that evening. At length the general sent word back to her that he would make every effort to be on time for the evening train.

"I am glad I am going away tonight," Mrs. Grant said cryptically to a friend. "Do you know, I believe there will be an outbreak tonight or soon. I just feel it."

The Grants had reached Philadelphia when they heard the news of the

The prescient former prime minister of England, Winston Churchill

assassination. They learned later that not only had the general been expected to sit in Lincoln's theater box but that he was on the assassin's list of intended victims.

It is not unusual for statesmen to be guided by their own intuition or the intuitive powers of others. Throughout his life, and particularly in wartime, Winston Churchill operated on premonitions that went far beyond hunches. One evening during the Luftwaffe assault on London, the prime minister was hosting a dinner at No. 10 Downing Street when the nightly air raid began. So commonplace was the occurrence that no one thought to interrupt the party—except Churchill, who suddenly rose from the table and went into the kitchen. "Put dinner on a hotplate in the dining room," he instructed the staff and then ordered them all down to the bomb shelter. He rejoined the guests and proceeded with the meal. A few minutes later, a bomb fell on the back of the house, obliterating the kitchen but missing staff and diners altogether.

On another occasion, Churchill visisted an antiaircraft battery during a raid. When he returned to his waiting staff car, he walked past the near-side door, which had been opened so that he might occupy his usual seat. He opened the far-side door himself, climbed in, and gave instructions to depart. When the car had driven several blocks, a bomb exploded close to the car and lifted it so precariously onto two wheels that it almost rolled over. Then it righted itself, apparently because of the strategically placed weight of the substantial prime minister. Later, asked by his wife why he had chosen to sit on the other side of the car, Churchill said at first that he did not know. Then he added: "Of course I know. Something said 'Stop!' before I reached the car door held open for me. It then appeared to me that I was told I was meant to open the door on the other side and get in and sit there—and that's what I did." In other words, he just "knew."

ON OCCASION, headline-making disasters have been prophesied by not just one person but by many—psychics and everday citizens, adults and children, the victims themselves, and those who cared about them. Two notable episodes of alleged mass ESP, each involving a major catastrophe, are particularly compelling. Oddly enough, two fiction writers were among those predicting—with remarkable accuracy—a monumental shipwreck. The first was an English journalist by the name of W. T. Stead, who wrote a fanciful account of the sinking of a great ocean liner in the mid-Atlantic for the *Pall Mall Gazette* in the 1880s. His tale, he said, was intended to prod steamship companies into providing the vessels they manufactured with all possible safety measures, among them adequate numbers of lifeboats. At the end of his fable of disaster, he warned: "This is exactly what might take place, and what will take place, if liners are sent to sea short of boats."

In 1892, Stead wrote another article about a shipwreck, this time describing an imaginary collision between an ocean liner and an iceberg in the Atlantic. This account was even more graphic. Almost two decades passed, but Stead did not abandon his theme. In 1910, he gave a lecture in which he developed his point about the necessity for sufficient lifeboats, adding a harrowing picture of himself as a shipwreck victim floundering in icy water and calling in vain for help.

By this time, a New York author, Morgan Robertson, had produced a novel about a terrible disaster at sea. Robertson had been a sailor for most of his life, and although he was a natural storyteller, he found the process of writing very difficult. He sat at his desk and waited for the mood to come to him; when it did, he went into a kind of trance, and from there the story seemed to flow through his fingers.

The story that came to Robertson began with the scene of a mid-Atlantic fog on an icy April evening. A great luxury liner, a beauty of a ship, sliced through the murk at twenty-three knots, much too fast for the weather conditions. Its length, he reckoned, was around 800 feet; its top speed was twenty-five knots; and its horse-power, 75,000. Robertson stared at the paper before him. In his mind, the ocean liner drew abreast and passed him, and on its bow he saw the name *Titan*. He saw the lifeboats, also: There were only twenty-four of them, not nearly enough for the ship's enormous size and the some 3,000 people aboard. Ahead, in the fog, the tip of an iceberg showed above the water. "She was the largest craft afloat and the greatest of the works of men," he wrote. "Unsinkable, indestructible, she carried as few boats as would satisfy the laws." And then: "Forty-five-thousand tons—deadweight—rushing through the fog at the rate of fifty feet a second . . . hurled itself at an iceberg . . . nearly 3,000 human voices, raised in agonized screams."

In 1898 Robertson published his novel, *Futility.* A little more than a decade later, around the time Stead was giving his London audience a vivid word picture of him-

The Titanic *on her maiden voyage in 1912*

self as a shipwreck victim, work began on a White Star liner to be called the *Titanic*. She was to be the biggest, sleekest, fastest ship afloat: 882.5 feet long, with a displacement tonnage of 66,000, a top speed of twenty-five knots, and a passenger capacity of 3,000. Also, with a double bottom and sixteen watertight compartments, the ship was designed to be unsinkable.

While the ship was being built, something he could not explain impelled Stead to visit first one psychic and then another. The first, Count Louis Hamon, warned him that there was danger for him at sea and followed up his prediction several months later with a note warning him that "travel would be dangerous in the month of April, 1912." The second psychic, one W. de Kerlor, told Stead that he would go on a trip to America, which Stead at that time had no intention of doing; de Kerlor subsequently dreamed that Stead was "in the midst of a catastrophe on the water," in which more than a thousand people were struggling and crying for help.

At much the same time, an American woman heard a voice which, as she wrote to *Light* magazine, gave her a message about Stead. "The time is soon coming when he will be called home," said the voice; "in the first half of 1912." A few months later, when the *Titanic* was in the final stages of construction and looking incredibly like the elegant ship that Robertson had portrayed in his novel, a respected clergyman wrote a letter to Stead, predicting that the new ocean liner would sink. In spite of these many warnings, including his own unconscious messages to himself, Stead booked passage on the *Titanic*'s maiden voyage across the Atlantic, which was scheduled to get under way on April 10, 1912.

Others acted on their premonitions. As the sailing date drew near, a Mr. Colin Macdonald declined the position of second engineer on the *Titanic* because he had a hunch some sort of disaster lay ahead. The banker J. Pierpont Morgan and a number of other ticket holders canceled passage, some of them with the belated excuse that they were superstitious about sailing on a ship's maiden voyage. A London businessman named J. Connon Middleton dreamed, two nights in a row, that he was looking down on the wreck of the *Titanic* and seeing "her passengers and crew swimming around her." Feeling uneasy and oppressed, he told friends and family about his dreams but did not cancel passage to America until a few days later, when he received a cable from New York urging him to delay his journey and take passage on another ship.

On Wednesday, April 10, those who had not canceled were assembled on the decks of the world's most celebrated steamship as she cast off from the Southampton dock. On that same day, a psychic named V. N. Turvey divined that "a great liner would be lost," and in a letter to an acquaintance he predicted that she would sink within two days.

As the *Titanic* steamed majestically past the Isle of Wight, people living along the coast stood on rooftops to watch her passage through an unruffled sea. Jack Marshall and his family, like their neighbors, cheered and waved from the roof of their home, thrilled by the magnificent sight. Then, suddenly, Mrs. Marshall screamed and grabbled her husband's arm. "It's going to sink!" she cried hysterically. "That ship is going to sink!" In her mind she saw a vivid image of the *Titanic* plunging beneath the waters of the Atlantic and its passengers struggling and dying by the hundreds in the icy sea. "Do something!" she screamed. "Are you so blind that you are going to let them drown? Save them! Save them!"

Four days later, on the evening of April 14, 1912, the *Titanic* entered a thick fog. Nevertheless, she sped ahead at twenty-two and a half knots. The captain had been warned of icebergs in his path, but he thought his ship was invulnerable and he took no heed—not even when the lookout in the crow's nest rang the signal bell and telephoned the bridge. "Iceberg right ahead," the lookout said. It was 11:40 P.M. Moments later, the ship slammed into a floating island of ice.

The blow was a sideswipe that to many of the people on board felt like a minor impact. But the great body of the iceberg struck the starboard side of the ship below the waterline, tearing open and flooding five of the supposedly watertight compartments. Soon, spillover would pour into the rest.

Only gradually did the scope of the disaster become clear. As the *Titanic* began to list, passengers who had never had a boat drill tried in vain to find places on the lifeboats. Many did not even have that opportunity. They were trapped inside or fell or jumped or were washed into the sea.

For the 2,206 people aboard the *Titanic,* there were a mere twenty lifeboats—with room for no more than 1,178 people. But only about 700 were able to scramble into them before the boats were lowered into the sea. W. T. Stead, splashing hopelessly around in the water among hundreds of others who were struggling and screaming for help, may or may not have had a chance to remember his own warning about what would occur if liners were sent to sea with a shortage of boats. He did not survive to tell.

No one who did survive would ever forget what one described as "the agonizing cries of death from over a thousand throats, the wails and groans of the suffering, the shrieks of the terrror-stricken and the awful gaspings for breath of those in the last throes of drowning"—exactly the scene of horror that had been predicted.

In all, more than 1,500 lives were lost.

In the decades following the sinking of the supposedly unsinkable ship, many investigators attempted to analyze the multiplicity of premonitions. Discarding all vague forebodings and after-the-fact claims of prescience, at least nineteen impressive cases of precognition through dreams, trances, visions, and voices remained. To be sure, skeptics offered nonpsychic explanations for such seeming foreknowledge. But the uncanny accuracy of the collective predictions suggested to some investigators that a sort of early-warning system, in the form of a central clearinghouse for prophecies and premonitions, might help prevent future disasters or at least reduce their magnitude. Such a central bureau would not materialize until 1967, however, following another cataclysm that had been widely predicted—this time in the little South Wales mining village of Aberfan.

On the morning of October 20, 1966, ten-year-old Eryl Mai Jones woke up at her home in Aberfan and told her mother what she had dreamed during the night. "I dreamed I went to school," she said, "and there was no school there. Something black had come down all over it."

A waking vision of something black had already appeared on October 14 to Alexander Venn, a retired Cunard Line employee and an amateur artist who lived in southwestern England. He kept feeling that some sort of disaster was imminent, something to do with coal dust, and he said to his wife: "Something terrible is going to happen, and it won't be far from here." With a deepening sense of foreboding, he took up his sketch pad and proceeded to draw a human head engulfed in blackness. On Wednesday night, October 19, reported dreams and forebodings began to snowball. An Englishwoman had a dreadful nightmare of suffocating in "deep blackness." Several other people in various parts of England also had frightening dreams of enveloping blackness, and one woman dreamed of a small child running, screaming, from a mountainside that appeared to be flowing downward.

On the evening of Thursday the twentieth, Mrs. C. Milden of Plymouth, England, was at a spiritualists' meeting when a vision came to her. Strangely enough, it seemed to be on film. She saw a schoolhouse in a valley and a terrified small boy with a long fringe of hair; she saw an avalanche of coal thundering down a mountainside, at the bottom of which a number of rescue workers were digging for bodies under mounds of slag and other debris; and she noticed that one of the workers was wearing an unusual-looking peaked cap.

In the early morning hours of Friday, October 21, Mrs. Sybil Brown of Brighton, south of London, awoke from a ghastly dream. A child in the confined space of a telephone booth was screaming with fear, while another child walking toward the dreamer was followed by—as Mrs. Brown described it—"a black, billowing mass." At the same time, a London woman woke up from a stifling dream and felt that the walls of her bedroom were caving in on her. An elderly gentleman in northwestern England was puzzled by his dream: He saw, spelled out in dazzling light, the letters *A-B-E-R-F-A-N*.

Rescue workers search for survivors in the aftermath of the coal-waste avalanche in Aberfan, Wales

At shortly after nine o'clock that morning, Eryl Mai Jones joined her classmates at the Pantglas Junior School. Looming overhead was the mountain that dominated the village of Aberfan. Its peak, a 600-foot mass of coal waste from the adjacent mines, glistened with the heavy rains that had fallen over the previous two days.

By 9:14, the morning prayer session was over, and the children were in their classrooms waiting for roll call. At the same time, in an aircraft plant not many miles away, a secretary, Mrs. Monica McBean, was overwhelmed by a sense that "something drastic" was going to happen. A horrible image flashed through her mind: "a black mountain moving and children buried under it."

Above the schoolhouse, the mountain moved. Half a million tons of black waste, dislodged by pounding rain, began to slither, then billow, then thunder down the mountainside in a gathering bulk of blackness that reached forty feet high. Houses were swept away; trees were torn up by their roots. Eryl Mai Jones and more than one hundred of her fellow pupils were buried under the suffocating black mass. Pantlas Junior School was gone, just as Eryl Mai Jones had dreamed. Rescue workers dug all day and all night to recover the bodies. The final count was 144 dead: twenty-eight adults and 116 children, most of them the schoolmates of Eryl Mai Jones.

During the day of disaster and the weekend, news spread throughout the British Isles and reached people who felt they had known something of it before it happened. Mrs. C. Milden, for instance, saw a television broadcast on Sunday in which she recognized the digging-out operation of her filmlike vision, complete with the terrified small boy with the long fringe of hair and the worker wearing the unusual peaked cap. What she had seen was an apparent preview of the broadcast.

Other predictions surfaced as the days went by, largely because of the efforts of a London psychiatrist named J. C. Barker, who was writing a book about psychic predictions. Wondering if there had been any premonitions of the coal slide, he launched a newspaper appeal to those who might have experienced foreshadowings. Two other organizations undertook similar investigations. The three surveys received a total of 200 replies, seventy-six of which were directed to Dr. Barker—who discarded sixteen that seemed to be obviously suspect and conducted a thorough investigation of the remaining sixty responses.

To more than half of the respondents, the premonitions had occurred in vivid dreams. Most of the others had experienced visions in a drowsy or trancelike state; some, like the retired Cunard employee, had sensed the forthcoming event while fully awake. A total of twenty-four precognitive episodes were attested to either by a letter or diary note written at the time by the respondents or by others who had been told of them before the coal slide.

To Dr. Barker, the evidence he had seen for what he viewed as some kind of seismic sense of impending events was, if far from conclusive, at least suggestive. "I realized," he wrote in a letter published by the London *Medical News-Tribune* on January 20, 1967, "that the time had surely come to call a halt to attempts to prove or disprove precognition. We should instead set about trying to harness

Eryl Mai Jones, who died in the Aberfan disaster after dreaming "something black" had obliterated her school

and utilize it with a view to preventing future disasters."

To that end, Dr. Barker created an information exchange, called the British Premonitions Bureau, to receive and analyze predictions from recognized psychics and individuals among the general public who just "knew" that something terrible—or even, perhaps, something wonderful—was going to happen. A similar agency, known as the Central Premonitions Registry, was founded in the United States shortly after its British counterpart was formed.

Even the most enthusiastic investigators of psychic phenomena will admit that a great many premonitions do not come true. The hits are remembered; the misses are not. Indeed, there are no reports that any disasters have been averted—or even foreseen—as a result of predictions filed with premonition exchanges. Nevertheless, the paranormal has generated such widespread interest that in some scholarly circles the question is no longer whether it deserves to be studied but instead how the subject may be dealt with in a scientific and rational manner.

Professional Mediums

*The American Society for Psychical Research
today, on New York's Upper West Side*

THE MID-NINETEENTH century marked one of those historic junctures when faith and reason threatened to run afoul of each other to the detriment of both. The Industrial Revolution had brought with it social upheaval and confusion, as well as a full flood of interest in science. Sometimes old truths withstood the torrent. Sometimes they were swamped. Against this tumultuous backdrop, spiritualism—belief that the dead survive discarnate and, often through mediums, can communicate with the living—raged across America and parts of Europe. Eventually it even came to intrigue the intelligentsia, some of whom saw a rare chance to wed rationalism to belief. What if, they thought, the newest methods of science could be brought to bear on the oldest riddles of metaphysics?

The Society for Psychical Research (SPR) was organized in London in 1882 with an agenda that included not only mediumship but hypnotism, telepathy, clairvoyance, and any other area where the mind seemed to transcend its boundaries. An American SPR (ASPR) was organized in Boston some three years later. More fractious than its British counterpart, the ASPR went through several disruptions caused by disputes over aims and methods. Nevertheless, its persists today, headquartered in New York. Recently, the organization began to restructure its jumbled archives and make them available for researchers and historians. From those archives come many of the photographs on the following pages. They represent some of the earliest steps, stumbling but venturesome, toward documenting the paranormal.

The ASPR studied mediums in two categories: mental and physical. Mental mediums bring only spoken or written messages from the spirits. The more spectacular (if less plausible) physical mediums produce spectral manifestations: rappings, tooting trumpets, trembling tables, and sometimes even ectoplasm—eerily diaphanous matter said by some to be the very substance of materialized spirits.

If not the most convincing, Boston's Mina Crandon was easily the most controversial medium the American Society for Psychical Research ever studied. She was better known as Margery—a *nom de séance* given her by a psychic investigator—and her exploits during the 1920s helped occasion a major rift within the ASPR.

Margery was a physical medium, and ectoplasm was her specialty. Phantom limbs seemed to sprout from her body. Spectral hands groped across tables. Moreover, Margery's ectoplasm was not the usual vaporous stuff but more solid material not unlike custard. Some investigators thought if looked like lung tissue. Margery was married to the eminent surgeon Le Roi Goddard Crandon, who was his wife's biggest booster, but skeptics could only ponder the tissue's possible origin. In any event, she clearly relied on one source of family help: Her chief spirit guide was her dead brother, Walter.

In 1922, a *Scientific American* contest offered $2,500 to any medium who could produce a "visible psychic manifestation," and Margery was an entry. Judges included *Scientific American* associate editor J. Malcolm Bird, ASPR researcher Walter F. Prince, and the magician Houdini. Bird became convinced of Margery's legitimacy and wrote rave reviews in his magazine. Newspapers embellished the story, saying the medium had even stumped Houdini. So incensed by this was Houdini, who had yet to investigate the medium, that he broke off a tour and rushed to Boston. After a few séances, he concluded Margery was an arrant fraud. Prince, who had made his own probe, could not have agreed more. He even suggested snidely that more credulous

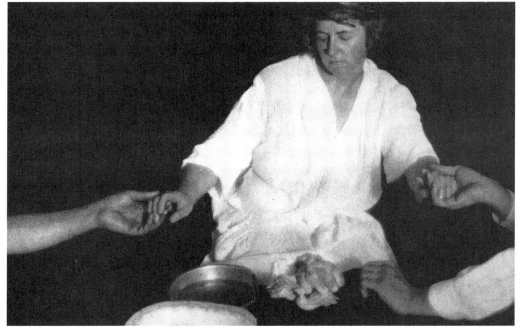

Medium Margery, a.k.a. Mina Crandon

Courtesy ASPR

Courtesy ASPR

Mary M. exuding ectoplasm at a 1929 séance

investigators were being swayed by the lady's personal charms. He and Bird had a bitter falling out, and when Bird joined the ASPR, Prince resigned. He became research officer for a new organization, the Boston Society for Psychic Research. The more scientifically minded ASPR members followed his lead, and the original organization was thus split into warring pro-Margery and anti-Margery factions. The breach healed some years later.

Although Margery was a wonder with ectoplasm, she by no means had a corner on the market. In spiritualism's heyday, ectoplasm was all the rage. It was variously semisolid, vaporous, or even liquid, and it might emerge in forms ranging from spidery tendrils to spectacular full-figure manifestations. But it almost always seemed to come from the medium's body, usually emanating from the mouth or some other bodily orifice.

An early and famed extruder of ectoplasm was a Frenchwoman named Marthe Beraud, known in psychic circles as Eva C. Her emanations were said to begin with a flow that resembled thick saliva and end up with a consistency akin to cream cheese. In 1905, Eva astounded the psychic researcher Charles Richet by producing a robed and bearded full figure who identified himself as Bien Boa, a long-dead Hindu. Eva later confessed that Bien Boa was in fact an Arab servant who was very much alive, but Richet would have none of it. He could not have been tricked, he insisted. Eva's confession merely denoted that she was mentally unstable, which, he said, was typical of mediums.

A Canadian medium who went by the name of Mary M. was notable for the human faces that sometimes appeared on the ectoplasm that she extruded. Her ectoplasm was variously described as looking like cotton wool, dough, or paste.

Theories about ectoplasm abounded. Some had it that spirits formed themselves from the substance of the medium's body or soul—or both. Allegedly for this reason, séance etiquette forbade touching the ectoplasm lest the medium be harmed or even killed. Few such casualties were ever reported, however, and violators of the taboo sometimes found that ectoplasm felt very much like cloth. Indeed, one medium who finally declared himself a fraud reported that chiffon was the ectoplasm of choice for him and his colleagues. Sometimes the fabric would be treated with a phosphorescent substance to give it a ghostly glow in the dim light of séance rooms. The material could be manipulated with a variety of mechanical contrivances. Or, it could be concealed inside the medium's body—even swallowed, in some cases—and extruded at will.

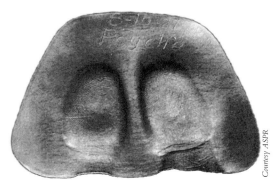

One expert claimed that these prints, allegedly left by "Walter," belonged to Margery's dentist

Generally, the ASPR was dubious of photographs purporting to show spirits of the dead. But when Marguerite Du Pont Lee declared she was taking such pictures, the society paid attention.

Lee, a daughter of the Delaware Du Ponts, was of impeccable lineage, spotless repute, philanthropic impulse, and apparent good sense. Her friend Episcopal minister Kemper Bocock died in 1904. Thereafter, Lee began having episodes of automatic writing, possibly communications from Bocock. The writing told her to take up photography; she did, usually putting an oil portrait of either herself or Bocock on a chair and taking pictures of it. Some of them showed inexplicable blobs of light and spectral faces, some amorphous, some distinct. Some looked like the dead pastor. About the same time, Lee was having her own picture taken by William M. Keeler. He was expert in spirit photography, snapping supposed discarnate entities who coalesced around loved ones for portraits. With Keeler's involvement, Bocock's appearances proliferated. There were pictures of Bocock dancing, preaching, sightseeing, and so on.

Lee confided in the ASPR's James H. Hyslop, a philosopher and psychic investigator, in 1919. Declaring that in Lee's case there could be no question of fraud, Hyslop undertook an investigation, only to conclude that he could not say exactly what was going on. But by 1920, Hyslop was dead, Walter F. Prince was the ASPR's head researcher, and the Keeler-Lee pictures had numbered some four thousand. After studying the case himself, Prince had little doubt about the forces at work.

Although deferential to Lee, Prince clearly regarded Keeler as a humbug and an exploitive cad. Prince noted that in all the Bocock photographs, the minister's head appeared facing about one-third off center, right or left, or almost in profile, right or left. The two poses were amazingly like those in the only two extant pictures of Bocock while he was alive. Whatever post-mortem pursuit was pictured, Prince noted, the minister "smiles not, exults not, wonders not, grieves not, nor ever once opens his lips, but is as if fixed in the calm of Buddha forever." Prince also observed that the static Bocock heads were at odds with an alarmingly plastic Bocock body, which appeared variously as fat, thin, short, tall, swan-necked, no-necked. The photos, Prince thought, were faked.

Courtesy ASPR

*ASPR researcher Walter Prince declared this photo of a ghostly Reverend
Kemper Bocock and Marguerite Du Pont Lee an obvious fake*

TWO RECENT giants of psychism are Eileen Garrett and Edgar Cayce. They
operated quite differently, but each seemed able—while unconscious—to gain
access to information not available to the waking mind. Garrett functioned mostly as
a medium—a conduit for spirits of the dead. Cayce was renowned as a psychic healer
and a prophet. Firm conclusions about the nature of their apparent powers eluded
both of these two people, though others theorized that clairvoyance, or telepathy, or
both, figured in their work. Garrett was born Eileen Jeanette Vancho in mist-
shrouded County Meath in Ireland. She spent her childhood near the mystical Hill of
Tara, a fey countryside where, she said later, "the 'little people' were universally accepted as an everyday part of normal existence." This myth-laden landscape was one
of two factors she credited for the possible origin of her psychic gifts. The other was
what she called "the almost equally universal acceptance of death as an intimate element of the daily round." She granted the possibility that the dead could communi-

cate with the living and was fairly comfortable serving as a vehicle for the dialogue.

Certainly, death was an intimate specter in Garrett's personal life. Both her parents committed suicide while she was still an infant; one of her three husbands was killed in World War I, and only one of her four children survived into adulthood. But for all the death surrounding her, Garrett was anything but morbid.

"She hated to be deprived of any experience within her grasp—or even slightly beyond it," Garrett's daughter, Eileen Coley, has said. "She was such an entertaining personality—interested in so many things, so many people. If I could be fascinated by waking up at 7 A.M. to exchange funny stories with her, you can imagine what sort of person she was. A lot of people likened her to Auntie Mame." Indeed, according to Coley, novelist Patrick Dennis knew Garrett and used her as a prototype for his zany, globe-trotting heroine in *Auntie Mame*. It was Garrett's sheer force of personality, at least as much as her alleged psychic gifts, that made such an impact on the many people she influenced.

Garrett left her native Ireland as a young woman and lived in London and the south of France before settling down in New York, becoming an American citizen, and undertaking a successful career in publishing. This was a reasonable enough direction for her life to take. From her youth, she had been something of a pet among the British literati, and her friends and acquaintances included D. H. Lawrence, William Butler Yeats, George Bernard Shaw, Thomas Mann, Aldous Huxley, Robert Graves, and H. G. Wells.

In 1951, Garrett founded the Parapsychology Foundation, which supported scholarly and scientific research. Through the organization, she funded expeditions to many parts of the world, spreading her passion to define and explain psychic powers. Garrett's fascination with the mysterious and arcane seemed inbred and inexhaustible. She took an interest in voodoo, which she studied in Haiti and Jamaica. As a young woman Garrett even investigated the practice of devil worship, though more in a spirit of curiosity than commitment. She also submitted herself to the scrutiny of psychiatrists, psychologists, and neurologists, as well as to J. B. Rhine and other serious parapsychologists.

One famous experiment in 1931 tested Garrett's supposed ability to leave her body while in a trance and report on distant scenes she saw in her astral state. In a New York apartment, a psychiatrist and a secretary looked on while the medium tried to see into a doctor's office in Reykjavik, Iceland. In preparation for the experiment, the doctor had placed a number of items on an office table. Garrett was supposed to describe them. While in a trance, she did so, and then went on to repeat verbatim a passage from a book the physician was reading while the test took place. In addition, she reported that the doctor's head was bandaged. The doctor confirmed later that she had identified the objects correctly, quoted the book accurately, and, because of a slight accident that happened just before the experiment, his head had indeed been bandaged. He also reported sensing Garrett's presence in his office during the test.

Along with participating in experiments, Garrett tried to advance research by

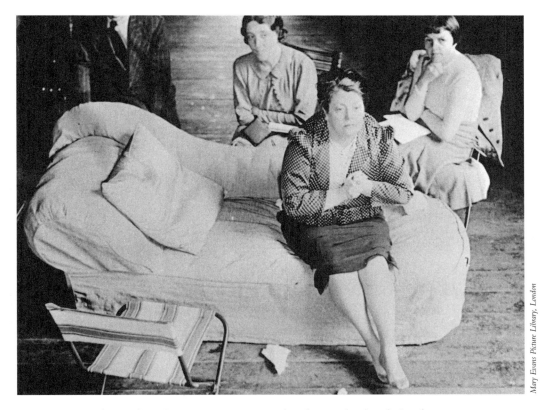

Mary Evans Picture Library, London

Medium Eileen Garrett enters a trance in this photograph taken during the 1930s

traveling widely to lecture on psychic phenomena—to Switzerland, Spain, the Scandinavian countries, Austria, Germany, Italy, Greece, India, Japan, and parts of South America. In the course of her travels, she would, if asked, conduct séances. But these meetings were not public events. Rather, they consisted of only small groups, often of only one or two friends.

As a medium, Garrett purportedly worked with several spirit guides, or controls, who identified themselves as long-dead individuals. Chief among the controls was an Oriental personage called Uvani. Seeming to act as a sort of doorkeeper, Uvani controlled access for the other spirits seeking to speak through Garrett.

A hallmark of Garrett's fifty-year career as a medium was a reputation for honesty. She never took money for her séances. And, though she worked in a time when spiritualism was under attack and many mediums were exposed as frauds, she remained beyond reproach. This is not to say, however, that her accuracy was beyond question. In fact, the results of one of her most famous mediumistic triumphs were subject to considerable debate.

The séance took place in London on October 7, 1930. It was organized by Harry Price, director of the National Laboratory of Psychic Research, who was one of three people seated at the séance table. By his side his secretary, Miss Ethel Beenham, edged forward on her chair, her notebook poised, while an Australian newspaperman named Ian Coster nervously twined and unlaced his fingers. The evening began with talk about the British dirigible R-101, the largest and costliest airship built to date, which had crashed in northern France during its maiden voyage. In the ensuing explosions and fire, all but six of the fifty-four people on board perished. Among the dead was Flight Lieutenant Carmichael Irwin, the dirigible's commander. Newspapers bulged with accounts of the disaster, the worst in British aviation history at the time, and controversy raged over whether England's ambitious airship program should be jettisoned altogether.

The three séance participants discussed the subject at some length, then were silent, staring expectantly at the stylish woman slumped in an armchair. If her companions were almost feverishly anticipatory, she seemed unaware of it—or perhaps even bored by it. She was, as Coster later wrote, "yawning her head off."

The séance followed by three months the death of Sir Arthur Conan Doyle, the creator of Sherlock Holmes. A devout spiritualist, Conan Doyle was convinced that the living could commune with those who had crossed to the other side, as his fellow believers were wont to say. Thus it did not seem unreasonable to expect that he himself might be accessible postmortem. So thinking, and sensing a possible sensational story, journalist Coster had asked Price to find the most reliable and respected medium in England to summon Conan Doyle's spirit. Price chose Eileen Garrett, the lady in the armchair.

Settling deeper into her cushion, Garrett breathed heavily and evenly, seeming to drift toward deep sleep. But no sooner had she closed her blue-green eyes than they began to gush tears, to the onlookers' astonishment. Uvani made only a brief appearance before an urgent voice interrupted him. "The whole bulk of the dirigible was . . . too much for her engine capacity," the male voice stuttered. The startled observers could see the psychic speaking, but the voice coming from her mouth certainly was not Garrett's, nor was it Uvani's, nor was it the restrained delivery of Conan Doyle. The speaker was agitated, panicky. "Useful lift too small," he said. "Gross lift computed badly . . . elevator jammed. Oil pipe plugged." On and on he went. Miss Beenham scribbled shorthand notes, her eyes glassy with amazement. Along with the others, she had read with horrified fascination the newspaper accounts of the R-101 disaster. No one had any trouble recognizing the man who was speaking through the medium. It seemed that Flight Lieutenant Irwin was describing in great technical detail the crash that had killed him two days before.

Sometime after Irwin finished his account, Conan Doyle did impart a message through Mrs. Garrett. At that point, however, the séance attendees regarded his contribution as a distinct anticlimax.

Garrett knew nothing about the mechanics of dirigibles, yet somehow she—or whoever was speaking through her—had spouted all sorts of technical aerodynamic details. Price rushed a transcript of the performance to the R-101's builders at the Royal Airship Works in Cardington. It was directed to a man named Charlton, described by Price as an "acclaimed expert" on the majestic zeppelin. The alleged expert declared himself astounded by the accuracy of Garrett's technical descriptions and her revelations of secret details about the airship. In fact, however, Charlton was not an engineer or an aviator, but one of 400 members of the Cardington ground crew. His expertise was thus much in question, as was his objectivity: He was, as it turned out, a spiritualist. When the same document Charlton had reviewed was shown to two high-ranking, well-qualified members of the airship team, they adjudged that most of the vaunted technical details that Garrett had spouted were dead wrong.

In addition, Charlton's contention that secret details came out at the séance was hard to credit, since virtually nothing about the R-101 was secret. The dirigible was a pet project of Britain's Labour party, then in power. The government, competing with a private company that was building a similar craft, was anxious to get the ship airborne to prove the superiority of state ownership over private enterprise. Thus bureaucrats were constantly dismissing objections from scientists that numerous technical problems had to be resolved before the zeppelin could safely fly. The whole matter became a subject of great public debate, and most anyone who cared to follow it in the newspapers knew almost all there was to know about the ill-fated R-101.

Nevertheless, Garrett's R-101 séance gained instant fame and easily outstripped the facts on its way to becoming legend. At the time, not even skeptics cared to call the lady a liar; her reputation was far too pristine. Rather, it was suggested that the medium had somehow picked up telepathic emanations from Coster, who, being a journalist, probably would have been familiar with at least some specifics about the dirigible and its problems. As was her habit, Garrett herself offered no assessment of the matter and left the debate about the séance to others.

Although her purported psychic gifts centered on mediumship, Garrett commonly experienced more straightforward psychic episodes as well. She was dining with friends at the Savoy Hotel in London one night during World War I when she suddenly felt herself surrounded by reeking fumes and the sounds of war. At the same time, she had a horrifying clairvoyant vision of her young husband and several other men being blown up on a battlefield. A few days later, the British War Office advised her that her husband was among the missing. He had gone on a wire-cutting mission and not returned, and the War Office was never able to supply details of his death. "Only I knew the manner in which he had died," the psychic wrote at a later date.

Eileen Coley has said that her mother considered her unusual talents more a burden than a blessing, and her long search to explain them was a way of exorcising the affliction and trying to turn it to good use. "Why should she be stuck with this business, she felt, unless she could find out some way it could be used for the good of other human beings?" the daughter said. Garrett encouraged the laboratory approach to unraveling the mystery, as she encouraged all inquiry. But she observed that "any attempt to explain the psyche and its manifold patterns in terms of language gets bogged down. The answer may well come from other aspects of science as yet not heard from officially." Finally, her quest was as inconclusive as it was thorough.

It was not the habit of most mediums to doubt the utter veracity of their spirit guides, but Garrett, a lifelong skeptic despite her seeming gifts, was always dubious about the true nature of hers. In her autobiography, she theorized that the controls might have been no more than manifestations from her own subconscious. Beyond that, she knew of them only what she was told, she said, since she had never met them. Necessarily, they were present only when she was unconscious.

As to her purported powers of clairvoyance, telepathy, and precognition, Garrett was certain only that there was nothing supernatural, or even paranormal, about them. She speculated that they might have originated in the hypothalamus gland, or in the vestigial animal brain at the base of the skull. Animals seemed able to sense danger in ways unrelated to the five senses, she posited, while in most humans that knack might have atrophied beneath the weight of prodigious forebrains. Secure in her powers but still unsure of their origins, Garrett died in France, on September 15, 1970, at the age of seventy-seven.

Garrett and Edgar Cayce were contemporaries and had in common the apparent ability to transcend their own psyches, but they could scarcely have been more different. Garrett was a brilliant, sophisticated, much traveled, and worldly woman. Cayce was an unlettered rustic from rural Kentucky. Garrett spent a lifetime seeking to explore and develop her talents. Cayce was a somewhat reluctant seer, troubled through much of his life by his strange gifts. Cayce and Garrett met once, in the 1930s, and did readings for each other. Although associates of both said the psychics had great respect for each other, the single meeting did not produce a close friendship. Whatever the two may have had in common in matters of spirit, they were worlds apart in matters of style.

According to his biographers, Cayce's psychic turning point came on a fine May afternoon in 1890 when he was thirteen years old. He was sitting in the woods on the family farm near Hopkinsville, Kentucky, enjoying a favorite pastime—reading the Bible. Suddenly, he realized he was not alone. He looked up to see a woman standing before him. At first he thought it was his mother: The sun was bright behind her, and it was difficult to see. But when she spoke, he realized she was not anyone that he knew. Her voice was uncommonly soft and musical.

"Your prayers have been heard," she said. "Tell me what you would like most of all, so that I may give it to you."

Though frightened, the teenager stammered an answer: "Most of all I would like to be helpful to others, especially to children when they are sick."

Without reply the woman vanished into the sunbeams. Edgar's first reaction was to fear he might be going crazy. But following on the heels of the vision was an indication that, indeed, he had been given some special power.

Edgar had never done well in school. His teachers complained that he was dreamy and inattentive. These failings much displeased his father, a no-nonsense fellow called Squire Cayce by his neighbors because he was the local justice of the peace. The night after the vision, Edgar was studying his spelling primer—as usual,

Corbis-Bettmann

Edgar Cayce

without much luck—when the elder Cayce decided to take matters in hand. Father and son sat at a table with the book between them. Over the course of a long evening, the father intoned one word after another, and the son spelled most of them incorrectly. At half past ten, the boy heard the lady in the woods saying, "If you can sleep a little, we can help you." Begging the squire for a short respite, Edgar curled up in a chair with the spelling book under his head and fell asleep instantly.

When the lesson resumed a few minutes after he woke, Edgar's answers were rapid and correct. To his father's astonishment, he went on to spell words from future lessons and even to specify which words were on which page and what illustrations went with them. For the rest of his life, Edgar Cayce allegedly maintained this clairvoyant ability to absorb near-photographic images of printed matter when, literally, he slept on it.

Not long after the spelling incident, young Edgar had an accident when a pitched ball hit him near the base of the spine. There was no apparent serious injury, but for the rest of the day he behaved oddly. At dinner that night, the normally reserved boy threw things at his three sisters and taunted his father. Stranger yet, when he went to bed and fell asleep, he began to talk. He told his parents he was in shock. To cure it, he said, they should make a poultice of cornmeal, onions, and herbs, and apply it to the back of his head. They did. The next morning he remembered nothing at all of the day before, but he was back to normal. It seemed that he had just delivered his first psychic reading.

During the eleven years following these two curious episodes, Cayce made scant use of his apparent psychic power. He was ill at ease with it. A deeply religious fundamentalist Christian, he was unsure whether his gift came from God or the devil or why, in either case, it should have devolved on him. It is possible he might have continued trying to ignore his talents indefinitely had he not, in 1900, lost his voice.

It was a peculiar infirmity in that doctors found no apparent physical cause for it, yet it persisted into 1901. This came at a particularly troublesome time. Cayce was just starting to make his way as an apprentice photographer, hoping to earn enough money to marry his fiancée, Gertrude Evans. Being unable to talk above a muffled rasp was interfering with both his career and his courtship, Near despair, Cayce turned for a cure to hypnotism, which was much in vogue in the United States at the time.

A local hypnotist named Al C. Layne, familiar with the squire's tale of Edgar's poultice cure, proposed putting the younger Cayce into a trance and having him diagnose himself. Edgar agreed to try. On a Sunday afternoon in March, Layne was ushered into the parlor of the Cayce farmhouse, where the squire and Edgar waited. Layne began talking softly, trying to induce a trance, but his patient interrupted. There was no need for such an effort, Edgar said. He often put himself "to sleep." It was no trouble at all. Layne should just concentrate on making the proper suggestions once Edgar was under. With that, the young man sighed deeply and slipped instantly into what appeared to be profound slumber. Layne then suggested that Edgar look inside his own body and pinpoint the trouble with his throat.

As his biographers would have it later, the entranced Cayce began to mumble at first, and then the young man began to speak in a clear voice. "Yes," he said, "we can see the body. In the normal state this body is unable to speak due to a partial paralysis of the inferior muscles of the vocal cords, produced by nerve strain. This is a psychological condition producing a physical effect. This may be removed by increasing the circulation to the affected parts by suggestion while in this unconscious condition."

The squire and the hypnotist were amazed. Edgar did not ordinarily talk that way. Awake, he might not have been able to pronounce some of those words, let alone understand them. Nevertheless, Layne gave the instructed suggestion. He and the squire looked on for the next twenty minutes while the skin over Edgar's throat and upper chest turned pink, then rose, then crimson with heightened blood flow. Finally, the sleeping man spoke.

"It is all right now," he said. "The condition is removed. Make the suggestion that the circulation return to normal, and that after that the body awaken." When Cayce awoke, his voice was fully restored.

Layne, who dabbled in osteopathy, argued that Cayce should use his apparent gift for psychic healing to help others. At first, Cayce resisted. He knew nothing about his unconscious pronouncements except what he was told, and certainly he had no conscious control over them. He feared he might harm the very people he was trying to help. But finally, reluctantly, he agreed it was his duty to try.

Over the next twenty-two years, Cayce did thousands of medical readings. Twice a day he would lie down and "sleep" as he regarded it. In this altered state, which resembled a self-induced hypnotic trance, he would answer requests for psychic healing. As newspapers began spreading reports of his work, those requests began coming in from throughout the United States. Cayce dealt with as many of these requests as time permitted. Apparently, distance was no barrier to his alleged mental probes, since he often did readings for clients who were hundreds of miles away. In time he came to have thousands of enthusiastic supporters. But, of course, there were detractors as well.

A very private man, Cayce suffered under the notoriety his work occasioned, and he was mortified by the inevitable accusations of fraud. In November of 1931, during a brief visit to meet with admirers in New York, he ran afoul of the law. He had acceded to two women's request for a reading, but the women turned out to be police officers and Cayce was arrested. He was charged under a 1927 New York statute making it a misdemeanor to tell fortunes for money or with intent to defraud. At a hearing before a magistrate, Cayce was asked about claims that he was a psychic. "I make no claims whatever," he answered. "For thirty-one years I have been told I was a psychic. It first began as a child. I didn't know what it was. After it had gone on for years, a company was formed to study my work."

The company in question was the Association for Research and Enlightenment (ARE), founded by Cayce adherents earlier in 1931 to study and preserve his work. The magistrate, deciding that the ARE was an "incorporated ecclesiastical body," threw the case out of court. The police had no right, the magistrate stated, to tamper with the beliefs of an ecclesiastical body. Besides, he did not believe Cayce intended any fraud.

Despite the favorable outcome, the case was enough to exacerbate the psychic's considerable self-doubt and send him into a depression. As he had several times during his career, he wondered if his apparent psychic gifts were either valid or useful, and he considered giving up the work.

Some analysts of Cayce's work have categorized his power as clairvoyance—an ability to see into bodies at a distance to diagnose ailments, as well as a talent for peering into the past and future. However, Cayce and his family saw it more as telepathy—mind-to-mind communication—but on a subconscious level. In addition, Cayce seemed to be saying that he could telepathically tap into the knowledge of some transcendental mind, perhaps akin to what psychologist Carl Jung called the collective unconscious.

Cayce himself described this cosmic mind pool as God's book of remembrance or the universal consciousness. He also used a term that would eventually be popularized by New Age psychics who came after him—the akashic records. The term was derived from the Hindu theosophical word akasa, refering to a primary creative principle of nature. The authoritative *Encyclopedia of Occultism and Parapsychology* gives the definition of the akashic records as "a kind of central filing system of all events, thoughts and actions impressed upon an astral plane, which may be consulted in certain conditions of consciousness." Events so recorded on the astral ether were thought to be "reanimated by mystics like a celestial television set."

It was Cayce's habit to have someone take notes during his readings. In the early years, the transcriptionist would be his father or his wife, but in 1923, he hired Gladys Davis as a full-time secretary. Thereafter, there was a verbatim record of all his work. When Edgar Cayce died in 1945, he left behind more than 14,000 recorded readings, the great majority dealing either with physical ailments or with past lives of his clients. All remain on file in Virginia Beach, Virginia, at the headquarters of the ARE, which continues to flourish under the aegis of his two sons.

The ARE today claims a membership of more than 30,000 people. Thousands more belong to many "Search for God" study groups that pursue Cayce's work.

These are located on every continent in the world except Antarctica. Some one hundred dred books have been written about the sleeping prophet, and collectively they have sold more than twelve million copies. No psychic, not even Eileen Garrett, has ever approached Edgar Cayce in popular appeal.

That appeal cannot be explained fully in terms of the knowledge he claimed to tap, phenomenal though it was. Rather, his enduring influence seems more a product of the man himself, the waking Cayce—gentle, unassuming, much beleaguered, and perfectly ordinary. If Garrett was the grande doyenne of the psychic world, Cayce was its quintessential common man. He was, as his chief biographer, Thomas Sugrue, once commented, "just an American guy." Precisely because of his ordinariness, hundreds of thousands of people who were not rich or famous or well connected could identify with him. They believed that if a man like Cayce could somehow enter a mysterious world that was finer, loftier, and saner than this one, and if a powerless man could call on great power, then maybe anybody could. Certainly, in his wake, many have tried.

Psychic Sleuths

Illinois psychic detective Greta Alexander has aided law enforcement agencies across the country with her abilities, which she claims developed after she was struck by lightning in 1961

In recent times, a new breed of psychic has emerged, one that attempts to reconcile the mysterious world of extrasensory perception with the logic of the modern age. These psychics, many of whom consider their talent a simple fact of nature, have found ways to adapt, and even thrive, in a skeptical environment. They consult with law enforcement agencies on murders and disappearances, often sharing the thoughts and sensations of the criminal or the victim. They work in espionage, sometimes pitting their paranormal skills against the cunning of wartime enemies. Psychics have also entered the corporate arena, predicting the ups and downs of the stock market, charting a company's future, even teaching employees how to be more intuitive themselves. By finding applications for extrasensory powers, these modern psychics may one day draw back the veil of the unknown and reveal the hidden potential of the human mind.

Although most modern police investigators are slow to grasp the potential of professional psychics, the practice boasts a venerable tradition. When faced with the greatest challenge of its long history, Britain's celebrated Scotland Yard may have relied on the counsel of a psychic consultant. In 1888, a gruesome series of murders was carried out in the seedy Whitechapel district of London. Five women, many of them prostitutes, were found slain and dismembered by the demented killer known only as Jack the Ripper, whose apparent relish for his crimes shocked the city and frustrated the detectives assigned to the case. Many students of the Ripper case now believe that the beleaguered Scotland Yard was aided in its investigation by a well-known London psychic named Robert James Lees.

The author of several books on spiritualism, Lees frequently offered psychic

Mary Evans Picture Library, London

Robert James Lees

consultations to some of London's most prominent citizens and even enjoyed the patronage of Queen Victoria herself on one occasion. He maintained an unblemished reputation as a man of integrity. Even so, Scotland Yard was reluctant to take his offers of assistance seriously. Shortly after the murders began, Lees experienced a premonition of the Ripper's next attack. Upon reporting his impressions to Scotland Yard, he was promptly turned away as a crank. When the Ripper next struck, in a pattern similar to the one anticipated by Lees, the detectives quickly dismissed the matter as a coincidence.

Nevertheless, Lees returned to Scotland Yard after having a second precognitive vision, this one involving a victim whose ears had been sliced off. This time, the Scotland Yard detectives took him more seriously; they had already received a boastful note, signed by the Ripper, in which he promised to remove the ears of his next victim.

Though Lees's warning failed to prevent the next Ripper slaying, which occurred much as the psychic had foreseen, Scotland Yard was now ready to involve him in the investigation. When Lees had a third premonition, a team of constables escorted him to the location of the Ripper's latest crime. There, in the words of one witness, Lees reacted "almost like a bloodhound"; soon he was off on a chase, as if tracking a fox, through the maze of London's back streets and alleys. A short time later, Lees and his escorts found themselves standing before the door of a noted London physician. This man, declared Lees, was Jack the Ripper.

With no evidence to link the physician to the crimes of the Ripper, Scotland

Yard began to make discreet inquiries. The suspect, it was learned, had been mysteriously absent from home during each of the Ripper slayings, and often displayed radical extremes of temperament—his wife described him as alternately gentle and sadistic. In time, the physician, whose identity was never revealed, was judged to be mentally incompetent by a panel of doctors and committed to an asylum for the insane. Whether or not he was guilty of any crime may never be known, but the vicious killer known as Jack the Ripper never struck again.

Although the Ripper case may never be fully laid bare, it marked a turning point in the use of professional psychics by law enforcement agencies. One man who saw great potential for psychic sleuths was Sir Arthur Conan Doyle, the creator of the fictional detective Sherlock Holmes. Conan Doyle put his beliefs to the ultimate test when fellow crime novelist Agatha Christie mysteriously disappeared in December 1926. The episode began when Christie's car was found abandoned at the edge of a chalk pit with its motor running. The disappearance touched off a nationwide search and a flood of lurid speculation in the press. Many feared that the author had been abducted or even murdered. Scotland Yard, as it had been in so many of Christie's novels, was baffled.

Conan Doyle firmly believed that he could locate the missing author by psychic means. For years he had been fascinated with an extrasensory talent known as psychometry, in which a physical object such as a photograph or an article of clothing is thought to serve as a conduit for psychic vibrations and energies. Conan Doyle had

London "blue bottles" (policemen) discover another victim of Jack the Ripper in this 1891 illustration

studied earlier cases in which psychometrists, upon handling an object from a crime scene, had been able to provide startlingly accurate reconstructions of the actual crimes. "It is," wrote Conan Doyle, "a power which is elusive and uncertain, but occasionally it is remarkable in its efficiency."

Such was the case with the disappearance of Agatha Christie. With the cooperation of Christie's husband, Conan Doyle obtained a glove that belonged to the novelist and placed it in the hands of a psychic known for his psychometric talent. "I gave him no clue at all as to what I wanted or to whom the article belonged," explained Conan Doyle. "There was nothing to connect either it or me with the Christie case." Nevertheless, the psychic appears to have drawn a prompt impression. "There is trouble connected with this article," he told Conan Doyle. "The person who owns it is half dazed and half purposeful. She is not dead as many think. She is alive. You will hear of her, I think, next Wednesday." Conan Doyle did, in fact, receive word of Christie the following Wednesday. The missing writer, who claimed to have suffered amnesia, had been found at a hotel spa, registered under an assumed name. Although the circumstances of the disappearance soon sparked controversy—some claimed that Christie had staged the affair to gain publicity—Conan Doyle was convinced of the accuracy of the psychometrist's impressions. "Everything in the reading," he concluded, "proved to be true."

Given the arbitrary nature of most psychic phenomena, the more recent case of Chicago psychic Irene Hughes seems all the more extraordinary. Not only did she test her talent against a highly volatile political intrigue, she did so before a live radio audience. On October 5, 1970, the whole of Canada was shocked when a pair of high-ranking government officials—British Trade Commissioner James Jasper Cross and Quebec Labor Minister Pierre LaPorte—were kidnapped by a radical terrorist group known as the FLQ, or Front de Liberation du Quebec. The terrorists, who had previously bombed several public buildings, demanded the immediate release from jail of twenty-three members of their group, whom they termed "political prisoners." Canadian officials quickly entered into negotiations, but they held out little hope of reaching a peaceful solution. The prospects for the captured men appeared bleak.

On October 14, Canadian broadcast-journalist Robert Cummings, the

Chicago psychic Irene Hughes

host of a radio talk show called "Afterthought," placed an on-air telephone call to American psychic Irene Hughes at her home in Chicago. Hughes, who had previously gained notoriety for predicting the launch-pad explosion of the Apollo 1 spacecraft, was unfamiliar with the details of the kidnapping when she received Cummings's call. Nevertheless, following a brief explanation of the situation, Hughes made an astonishingly precise and decisive series of predictions. James Cross, she told the audience, was

Canadian Labor Minister Pierre LaPorte

alive and unharmed, and would remain so. She was less optimistic regarding Pierre La-Porte. When pressed repeatedly, Irene Hughes admitted that she believed LaPorte's life was in jeopardy. Before concluding the interview, Hughes also predicted that an arrest would come quickly, and that on November 6, there would be a "striking and unusual" development in the case.

On October 17, the body of Pierre LaPorte was discovered in the trunk of a green Chevrolet abandoned at a military base. He had been both strangled and stabbed. The following day, Robert Cummings again called Irene Hughes. After expressing her dismay over the death of LaPorte, the psychic rebuked herself. During their earlier conversation, she said, she had experienced an odd impression of a green automobile, but thought it unimportant. She then repeated her conviction that James Cross was still alive.

Cummings, impressed by the uncanny accuracy of the psychic's earlier predictions, pressed her to reveal the exact location where James Cross was being held. Once again, Hughes gave a startlingly detailed answer. "I will say five miles northwest of Montreal," she said. "It seems that the place he is in is about three stories high. I feel that it is red brick, a kind of old place, and it actually could be an apartment building.

British Trade Commissioner James Cross survived the kidnapping incident

No sooner had Cummings completed his broadcast than he contacted the authorities, but their response was lukewarm. Not only were the officials involved in the case reluctant to ally themselves with a psychic, they went so far as to instruct Cummings to discontinue his live broadcasts, presumably because they posed a threat to the investigation. Cummings complied, but he continued to record his private conversations with Irene Hughes and to make transcripts available to the authorities.

On November 6—the date on which Hughes had predicted "striking and unusual news"—police arrested one of the kidnappers in West Montreal. The same day, authorities confirmed that they had received an authentic recent photograph of James Cross seated on a box of explosives.

Hughes accurately described the terrorists' Montreal hideout

Following the arrest, the kidnapping plot quickly came unraveled. Within a month, James Cross was freed by his captors. Upon Cross's release, the remarkable accuracy of Hughes's predictions soon became a matter of public record. Cross had been held for sixty days in a three-story, red-brick apartment building in a northwest suburb of Montreal, exactly as Hughes had stated.

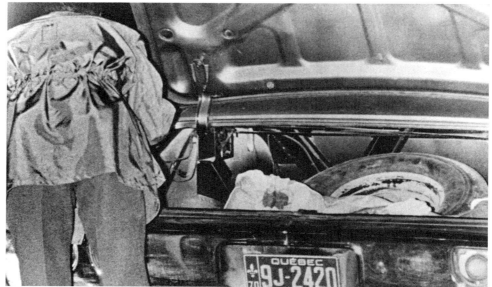

Pierre LaPorte was found in this green Chevrolet on October 17, 1970.
Irene Hughes had felt that a green automobile was involved.

"My mind almost boggles when I consider the remarkable accuracy and detail of Irene's many psychic evaluations," said Robert Cummings at the conclusion of the case. "There were predictions of major consequence, such as the events of November 6 and Cross's release; her accurate description of the LaPorte kidnappers' automobile and the three-story brick duplex northwest of Montreal where Cross was held. Undoubtedly, this endeavor represents an impressive documentation of ESP at work in a 'now' manner in modern history."

3
OUT-OF-BODY EXPERIENCES

Out of the Shell

Mary Evans Picture Library, London

ONE AUTUMN EVENING in 1910, Caroline Larsen lay in bed in Burlington, Vermont, drowsily listening to her husband rehearse a Beethoven string quartet downstairs with three other amateur musicians when suddenly she was seized by a feeling of apprehension, as though she were about to faint.

"I braced myself against it, but to no avail," she related later. "The overpowering oppression deepened and soon numbness crept over me until every muscle became paralyzed. . . . At first I heard the music plainly . . . until finally everything became a blank. . . . The next thing I knew was that I, I myself, was standing on the floor beside my bed looking down attentively at my own physical body lying in it."

As Mrs. Larsen gazed down at her face, pale and still as death, the eyes closed and the mouth partly open, she felt no horror or shock but instead a calm sort of curiosity. She looked around the room; everything appeared to be in perfect order—the table

Marilyn Krauss

A sleeping traveler

with books and trinkets, the bureau, dresser, chairs, the green carpet and red wallpaper with its pattern of urns and flowers, figures that she had so often counted when she lay sleepless. She glanced once more at her body in the bed, then walked slowly out the door and down the hall to the bathroom, where there was a large mirror. "Through force of habit," she recalled, "I went through the motions of turning on the electric light, which of course I did not actually turn on." But there was no need: From her face and body emanated a strong whitish light that illuminated the room brilliantly.

"Looking into the mirror I became aware for the first time of the astonishing transformation I had undergone," she continued. "Instead of seeing a middle-aged woman, I beheld the figure of a girl about eighteen years age. I recognized the form and features of my girlhood. But I was now infinitely more beautiful. My face appeared as if it were chiseled out of the finest alabaster and it seemed transparent, as did my arms and hands when I raised them to touch my hair. . . . But they were not entirely translucent for in the center of the arms and hands and fingers there was a darker, more compact substance, as in X-ray photographs. My eyes, quite strong in the physical body, were piercingly keen now. . . . My hair, no longer gray, was now, as in my youth, dark brown and it fell in waves over my shoulders and down my back. And, to my delight, I was dressed in the loveliest white shining garment imaginable— a sleeveless one-piece dress, cut low at the neck and reaching almost to the ankles."

Mrs. Larsen had lost track of the music while studying herself in the mirror. But now she heard the discordant strains of a Mendelssohn violin concerto being played badly. "I knew at once that the Frenchman was playing the solo," she recounted. "It was a habit he always indulged while the music was being changed on the stands. But, as always, he played it out of tune. As usual I felt disgusted and for the moment forgetting all about myself I muttered angrily 'Oh! I wish my husband would tell that Frenchman to play that concerto in tune or not to play at all.'" Fortunately, the quartet soon resumed its Beethoven. The music soothed Mrs. Larsen, and she was stuck by a splendid idea. She would go downstairs and show off her youthful beauty before the men. How admiring they would be.

"Turning away from the mirror I walked out into the hall," she continued. "Enjoying in anticipation the success of my plan, I stepped on gaily. I reveled in the feeling of bodily lightness. . . . I moved with the freedom of thought." The music sounded lovelier than ever as Mrs. Larsen started down the stairs. But her hopes were soon dashed: "Just as I came to the little platform which divides the stairway into two flights, I saw, standing before me, a woman spirit in shining clothes with arms outstretched and with forefinger pointing upwards. . . . She spoke to me sternly, 'Where are you going? Go back to your body!'. . . . I knew instinctively—that from this spirit's command and authority there was no appeal."

Reluctantly heeding the command of the unknown spirit, Mrs. Larsen turned and ascended the stairs to her bedroom. "My physical body lay there," she said, "as still and lifeless as when I left it. I viewed it with feelings of loathing and disappointment. I knew that I would soon have to enter it again, no matter how ugly it seemed to me or how much I shrank from it." But there was no time for reflection. "In another instant I had again joined with my physical form. With a gasp and a start, I woke up in it."

Caroline Larsen was by no means the first, and will certainly not be the last, person to feel the core of his or her self split off from the physical body. Such out-of-body experiences—or OBEs, as they are familiarly called—have been recorded since the beginnings of history by many people in all manner of cultures in every part of the world.

No PARTICULAR ETHNIC GROUP or nationality seems greatly more prone to OBEs than others. They occur among Tibetans as well as Icelanders; as commonly among the French as among the Russians, Britons, and Americans; and they have been widely recorded among the primitive peoples of Borneo, Africa, and Oceania. Nor does any individual occupation appear to bring forth many more OBEs than another—though numerous creative writers claim to have undergone OBEs and have described them vividly. The German poet Goethe, for example, underwent a number of out-of-body experiences, as did D. H. Lawrence, Aldous Huxley, Arthur Koestler, Emily Brontë, Guy de Maupassant, and Jack London, to name only a few.

Yet for every well-known person who has been involved in an OBE, there are thousands of ordinary men and women—like Caroline Larsen—who have felt themselves carried along on some sort of fantastic psychic voyage. Certain circumstances seem to favor OBEs: sleep and dreaming, hallucinogenic drugs and general anesthetics, and very serious illnesses or close encounters with death itself. People who have been on the brink of death or even clinically dead, only to return to life, often claim to have experienced a type of OBE that is referred to as a near-death experience, or

NDE. And then there is reincarnation.

One might speculate, if the soul can voyage outside the body in life and survive death, then could it not be reborn in another body? The idea of reincarnation, as ancient as civilization, is being pursued by ardent researchers using the techniques of twentieth-century science. Indeed, the whole phenomenon of psychic voyages is today the subject of scientific scrutiny, though there are many members of the academic community who recoil at the very mention of the word science in connection with such things.

The critics dismiss psychic voyages—OBEs, NDEs, reincarnation, and the rest— as dreams or hallucinations or even fraud. Proponents, on the other hand, firmly hold that genuine out-of-body experiences entail a far greater sense of reality than has been demonstrated by ordinary dreams or hallucinations, both at the time of the experience and in retrospect. Moreover, say the advocates, the patterns of psychic mind-travel are all so amazingly similar and occur among so many completely unrelated people in such diverse places and walks of life that the phenomenon is unlikely to be the mere dreams or hallucinations of a relatively few susceptible people. One student of OBEs, Dr. Eugene E. Barnard, has estimated that one out of every hundred people experiences an actual OBE at some time during his or her lifetime. Others suggest that the incidence might be as high as fifteen or twenty percent.

Another psychic researcher, Dr. Charles T. Tart, has written: "Because of its apparently universal distribution across cultures and throughout history, out-of-the-body experiences constitute what the psychiatrist Carl Jung termed an 'archetypal' experience—an experience potentially available to many members of the human race simply by virtue of being human."

IN THE NINETEENTH CENTURY, the entire range of OBEs became the focus of what was known as spiritualism, a religion that explored communication with the deceased. The basic tenet of spiritualism was that all people survive death as ghostly entities who evolve toward spiritual perfection in a world of inconceivable beauty and pleasure, from which they communicate their experiences to the living through mediums in séances. Spiritualism offered ready explanations for OBEs, which fit loosely within traditional Christian theology, but other enthusiasts in the late nineteenth and early twentieth centuries developed entirely new religious systems in order to explain them. One of the most famous—and assuredly most controversial—of these systems was Theosophy. Its founder, Madame Helena Petrovna Blavatsky, was a Russian spiritualist who had wandered around the world and through a number of bigamous marriages before arriving destitute in New York in 1873. She found her life's calling through a chance meeting with Colonel Henry Olcott, a lawyer and journalist who was also a spiritualist. Olcott was greatly impressed with Madame Blavatsky's apparent powers; with his financial backing the two of them launched the Theosophical Society in 1875.

The term Theosophy was taken from the Greek words for god and wisdom.

The society would be composed, wrote Madame Blavatsky, "of learned occultists . . . and of passionate antiquaries and Egyptologists generally. We want to make an experimental comparison between Spiritualism and the magic of the ancients."

The Theosophical Society attracted few followers in its first years. In 1877, Madame Blavatsky published *Isis Unveiled*, which painted its author as a woman of tremendous learning, versed in a vast body of ancient spiritual truths. She suggested that she had access to unseen but powerful disembodied spirits and that she had been chosen by them to mount a revival of primal truths in the modern world.

Among these alleged truths was a central tenet of Theosophy: that human beings exist on many planes besides the purely physical one. One of these levels is the astral body, a ghostly reproduction of the physical self that can travel far and wide outside the physical body. Everyone's astral body journeys during sleep, according to Madame Blavatsky, but the truly adept can will their astral bodies out of their physical selves by means of what she called astral projection. Moreover, those who are expert in the astral arts are able to see other people's astral bodies in plain daylight. They appear as multicolored halos around the physical body and reveal the essence of each personality through a range of colors.

The book achieved a modest success, but hostile critics incessantly scoffed and published accusations of fraud, along with unpleasant stories about Madame Blavatsky's background. She and the colonel decided to take the movement to India, where, as she put it, "no one will know my name."

Mary Evans Picture Library, London

Madame Helena Petrovna Blavatsky founded the Theosophical Society in 1875

But once in India, so intriguing were her ideas and so hypnotic was her personality that Theosophy gained a considerable following among both Indians and British colonials. Before long, her movement had spread back westward, with branches sprinkled throughout England, France, and other European countries. In the year 1884, Blavatsky and Olcott traveled to Europe to meet their new disciples; while they were there, they went before the Society for Psychical Research in order to present evidence of the marvels they had observed.

Whether favorably disposed or skeptical, the SPR dispatched an investigator to India. His report was devastating. The lady, he concluded, could be described "neither as the mouthpiece of the hidden seers, nor as a mere vulgar adventuress; we think she has achieved title to permanent remembrance as one of the most accomplished, ingenious and interesting impostors of history."

Whether or not Madame Blavatsky was a charlatan, the essence of her system—that there was a psychic self which could travel outside the body—was remarkably consistent with the mass of OBE testimony. Whatever her faults, she provided welcome explanations to many psychic voyagers bewildered by their alleged experiences.

Most of those experiences appeared to be spontaneous, once-in-a-lifetime events. But there were a few individuals who claimed that they traveled out of their physical bodies on a regular basis and that they could evoke such experiences at will.

BORN AROUND 1903, Sylvan Joseph Muldoon was an avid student of the occult. By his own account, his introduction to out-of-body experiences had occurred when he was twelve years old. His mother, who was an active spiritualist, had taken her young son with her to a Spiritualist Association camp in Clinton, Iowa. In the dead of his first night there, Muldoon awoke with a start. "I was powerless," he recalled. "My entire rigid body (I thought it was my physical, but it was my astral) commenced vibrating at a great rate of speed, in an up-and-down direction, and I could feel a tremendous pressure being exerted in the back of my head. . . . Then the sense of hearing began to function, and that of sight followed. When able to see, I was more than astonished: I was floating in the air, rigidly horizontal a few feet above the bed. . . . Involuntarily, at about six feet above the bed . . . I was uprighted and placed standing upon the floor of the room. . . . Then I managed to turn around. There was another 'me' lying quietly on the bed. My two identical bodies were joined by means of an elastic-like cable which extended across the space of probably six feet which separated us. . . . My first thought was that I had died during sleep."

The disembodied Muldoon drifted into the room where his mother was sleeping and tried to shake her awake. But his hands passed right through her—and through the bodies of other people he attempted to rouse. The child began weeping and wandered around for another quarter of a hour until he was pulled back in to his body by his cable, or cord. "At the moment of coincidence," he later wrote, "every muscle in the physical body jerked, and a penetrating pain, as if I had been split open from head to foot, shot through me. I was physically alive again, as amazed as fearful.

Mary Evans Picture Library, London

Psychic voyager Sylvan Joseph Muldoon

I had been conscious throughout the entire occurrence."

After recovering from his initial shock, Muldoon went on to experience literally hundreds of projections, he said. The most remarkable took place in 1924, when he was twenty-one. He had gone out for a walk after supper, feeling listless and lonely, and had soon returned home, where he went to his room, locked the door, and threw himself on his bed. Soon his body began to turn numb, and he knew that a projection was coming on.

Moments later he felt his body rise up, at first horizontally off the bed, then rotate into a vertical position, which enabled him to move around freely. After he roamed through his house for a bit, he went outside and was suddenly carried away at fantastic speed to a strange place, a farmhouse, where he found four people together in a room. One of them was a pretty young girl of about seventeen; she was sewing something and Muldoon saw that it was a black dress. He moved forward until he was directly in front of the girl. He watched her sew for a short while, then went around the room looking at the furnishings. At that point, it occurred to Muldoon that he had no legitimate reason to be there, so he took one last glance around and left, shortly afterward reentering his body back home.

Some weeks later, according to Muldoon, he encountered the girl of his projection. He asked her where she lived, and when she told him it was none of his business, young Muldoon described her home in precise detail, both outside and in. She and Muldoon became fast friends, and he visited her home, which was fifteen miles away, a number of times; Muldoon claimed that he recognized everything he had seen on his astral excursion.

In his writings, Muldoon urged readers to attempt out-of-body travel. His suggested techniques for inducing OBEs included trying to be fully conscious at the moment of falling asleep and seeking to invoke a dream that involved rising, flying, or ascending in an elevator. Muldoon also believed that most people experience subtle OBEs without ever realizing it: Actions like fainting or twitching when on the verge of sleep he regarded as examples of partial separation of the double from the body.

SINCE WORLD WAR II, the best known of the putative astral travelers has been Robert Monroe, a former advertising executive who claims to have experienced his first out-of-body experience in 1958, at the relatively advanced age of forty-three. In every respect, Monroe was a perfectly normal and unexceptional American businessman: college educated and married, with children, a level-headed man with no serious vices or peculiarities. His only "unorthodox activity," as he put it, was "my experimentation with techniques of data learning during sleep—with myself as the chief subject."

Monroe suspects that these learning experiments—which involved listening to audiotapes while he slept—might have had something to do with his first OBEs. His first inkling that something unusual was happening came one Sunday after brunch, when he was seized by what he described as "a severe, iron-hard cramp, which extended across my diaphragm or solar plexus area just under my rib cage. It was a solid band of unyielding ache." Monroe thought it might be food poisoning, but none of the other family members felt ill. The cramp lasted from 1:30 in the afternoon until about midnight, when Monroe fell asleep from pure exhaustion. It was gone the next morning, and except for some soreness, there were no aftereffects. "In retrospect," said Monroe wryly, "perhaps it was the touch of a magic wand—or a sledge hammer."

Three weeks later, according to Monroe, again on a Sunday afternoon, he experienced another touch of that magic wand—or whatever it was. He was reclining comfortably when a ray, a beam of some sort, seemed to come out of the sky and strike his body, causing it to vibrate violently. "I was utterly powerless to move," reported Monroe of the incident. "It was as if I were being held in a vise." The vibration lasted only a few seconds, then faded.

Nine times during the next six weeks the same vibration returned—always when Monroe was lying down to rest or sleep—and faded away when he fought himself to a sitting position. On one occasion, he claimed, the vibrations developed into a ring of sparks, with Monroe's body being the axis in the center of the ring. "The ring would start at the head and slowly sweep down to my toes and back to the head, keeping this up in regular oscillation," said Monroe. "When the ring passed over my head, a great roaring surged with it, and I felt the vibrations in my brain."

Monroe anxiously consulted his family doctor, who assured him that he was not entering the first stages of schizophrenia. On the chance that some physical ailment might be at the root of his singular symptoms, Monroe underwent a thorough medical examination; he was not an epileptic, showed no signs of brain tumor, and was in fact perfectly healthy. The doctor suggested that he ease off working so hard, get more sleep, and lose some weight.

The vibrations continued. One night, as Monroe lay in bed, waiting for them to pass, his arm brushed the floor, and he pressed his fingers against the rug. They went right through to the floor; Monroe pushed harder and his fingers penetrated the floor to the area below, where he felt a small chip of wood, a bent nail, and some sawdust. Next, Monroe found that his whole arm was through the floor and that he was splashing his hand in water.

To put it mildly, Monroe was perplexed. "I was wide awake," he would recall. "I could see the moon-lit landscape through the window. I could feel myself lying on the bed, the covers over my body, the pillow under my head, my chest rising and falling as I breathed. The vibrations were still present, but to a lesser degree." Monroe wondered in awe, "How could I be awake in all other respects and still 'dream' that my arm was stuck down through the floor?"

Monroe mentioned his experience to a psychologist friend, who agreed that it was a pretty convincing daydream—if that was what it was. Half jokingly, he suggested that Monroe cut a hole in the floor to find out what was down there.

About a month later, the vibrations came again, and after a moment, Monroe became aware of something pressing against his shoulder; it was smooth and he thought that it was the wall. But as he looked around him, he realized that it had no windows, no furniture against it, no doors. "It was the ceiling," said Monroe. "I was floating against the ceiling, bouncing gently with any movement I made. I rolled in the air, startled, and looked down. There, in the dim light below me, was the bed. There were two figures lying in the bed. To the right was my wife. Beside her was someone else. . . . I looked more closely, and the shock was intense. I was the someone on the bed!"

Monroe was stunned. "Here I was, there was my body. I was dying, this was death and I wasn't ready to die. Desperately, like a diver, I swooped down to my body and dove in. I then felt the bed and the covers, and when I opened my eyes, I was looking at the room from the perspective of my bed."

The next time he saw his psychologist friend, a concerned Monroe told him about his latest experience and said that he was not ready to die. "Oh, I don't think you'll do that," the psychologist reassured him calmly. "Some of the fellows who practice yoga and those Eastern religions claim that they can do it whenever they want." "Do what?" inquired Monroe. "Why, get out of their physical body for a while," the doctor replied. "They claim they can go all over the place. You ought to try it."

I N THE YEARS TO COME, Monroe would dedicate himself to exploring OBEs as thoroughly and systematically as he could. He claimed to have traveled in three different dimensions, which he designated as Locales I, II, and III. Locale I was the world as everyone knows it, and Monroe's travels usually took him to relatively familiar places close to home. Locale II was a different story altogether.

Monroe had some difficulty describing it, and chose his words carefully. He began by stating, "The best introduction to Locale II is to suggest a room with a sign over the door saying, 'Please Check All Physical Concepts Here.'" He went on to describe its immensity: "Locale II is a non-material environment with laws of motion and matter only remotely related to the physical world. It . . . has depth and dimensions incomprehensible to the finite, conscious mind. In this vastness lie all of the aspects we attribute to heaven and hell, which are but part of Locale II. It is inhabited, if that is the word, by entities with various degrees of intelligence with whom communication is possible."

Monroe continued, "Superseding all appears to be one prime law. Locale II is a state of being where that which we label thought is the wellspring of existence. It is the vital creative force that produces energy, assembles 'matter' into form, and provides channels of perception and communication. . . . in this environment, no mechanical supplements are found. . . . You *think* movement and it is fact."

Locale III, which Monroe supposedly visited a number of times on what he called "intrusions," seemed almost mundane in comparison with the others. This third dimension was, said Monroe, "a physical-matter world almost identical to our own. There are trees, houses, cities, people, artifacts and all the appurtenances of a reasonably civilized society." However, Monroe noted, Locale III had evolved on a somewhat different technological basis; there was no electricity or fossil fuels; its inhabitants relied instead on a sort of nuclear power.

And here, said Monroe, his disembodied double "met and 'merged' temporarily and involuntarily with one who can only be described as the 'I' who lives 'there.' I, fully conscious of living and being 'here,' was attracted to and began momentarily to inhabit the body of a person 'there,' much like myself." Monroe's counterpart in Locale III—Monroe called him his "I" There—was an architect who lived in a boarding house and rode a bus to work; reasonably well-educated, he was a rather introspective person, and not notably prosperous. Monroe's adventures in Locale III included his counterpart's eventual marriage to Lea, a rich but depressed young woman with two children from a previous marriage. The union was not very successful, and they separated. Monroe's "I" There was unhappy over the alienation and promised to visit Lea, but he somehow lost the address. Shortly thereafter, Monroe's "intrusions" into the world of Locale III ceased.

What did Monroe make of all this? In view of the less-than-idyllic circumstances, he thought it unlikely to be an escape from reality via the unconscious. "One can only speculate," he said, "and such speculation of itself must consider concepts unacceptable to present-day science." Far different from the here and now of Locale

MONROE'S TIPS FOR ASTRAL TRAVELERS

According to Robert Monroe, anyone can travel outside the body—all it takes is practice and the desire to do it. For those attempting OBEs, Monroe suggests the following guidelines:

1. In a warm, dark room where you will not be disturbed, lie in a comfortable position with your head pointing north. Loosen clothes and remove any jewelry.
2. Relax your mind and body. Close your eyes and breathe rhythmically, keeping your mouth slightly open.
3. Focus on a single image as you drift toward sleep. When you reach the state bordering wakefulness and sleep, deepen your relaxation by concentrating on the blackness beyond your eyelids.
4. To induce the vibrations that allegedly herald the onset of an OBE, focus on a point about twelve inches from your forehead. Gradually extend the point of focus to a distance of six feet, and draw an imaginary line parallel to your body. Focusing on that plane, imagine the vibrations and bring them down into your head.
5. Gain control of the vibrations by consciously guiding them through your body—from your head to your toes and back again. Once these vibratory waves can be produced on mental command, you are ready to attempt separation from the body.
6. To leave the body, concentrate on how pleasant it would be to float upward. Maintain these thoughts, and your astral form should begin to rise.
7. To return to the physical self, simply focus on reengaging the two entities.

I, Locale III was "neither the known past nor the present, and not the probable future." Monroe thought that "it might be a memory, racial or otherwise, of a physical earth civilization that pre-dates known history. It might be another earth-type world located in another part of the universe which is somehow accessible through mental manipulation. It might be an antimatter duplicate of this physical earth-world where we are the same but different, bonded together unit for unit by a force beyond our present comprehension."

In the 1970s, Monroe made OBEs and other parapsychological phenomena his full-time occupation. He founded the Monroe Institute for Applied Sciences in rural Virginia to teach techniques for achieving OBEs and other altered states of consciousness. Although Monroe is not without his detractors—one investigator who sought to verify Monroe's out-of-body visits to friends found no one who could corroborate his claims—in 1982, the Monroe Institute, in conjunction with the University of Kansas Medical Center, was invited to present three papers on out-of-body experiences at a meeting of the American Psychiatric Association. Monroe contended that his appearance before the assembled psychiatrists somehow validated the whole notion of astral travel. "For them even to schedule and permit such papers to be read," he averred, "was an acknowledgment that such phenomena do exist."

According to American anthropologist Dean Sheils, who has studied OBEs in sixty-seven different cultures around the world, sleep is regarded as the most important source of OBEs in about eighty percent of those cultures. Psychologist Stephen

LaBerge, of the Stanford Sleep Research Center, goes on to hypothesize that since most OBEs occur during sleep, they are actually variant interpretations of lucid dreams. And he supports his conclusion with his own experience: "In about one percent of the lucid dreams in my record, I felt I was in some sense out of my body. In every case, when examining the experience after awakening, I noted some deficiency in either my memory or my critical thinking during the experience. In one such situation, I tried to memorize the serial number of a dollar bill to verify later whether I really had been out of my body or not. When I awoke, I couldn't recall the number, but it hardly mattered. I remembered that I hadn't lived in the house I thought I was asleep in for several years."

Another researcher, a psychiatrist by the name of Glen Gabbard, speculates that out-of-body experiences may, in fact, be what he calls hypnagogic images—images that occur during the time one hovers between wakefulness and sleep. He concludes that the hypnagogic image is experienced as extremely real, and this causes it to be confused with an actual experience outside the body.

Whatever they are, supposed OBEs often exert a profound impact on those who have experienced them. Many people emerge with entirely new values and beliefs, often convinced of the reality of life after death and a world beyond the senses.

Back from the Dead

Corbis-Bettmann

EARLY IN DECEMBER 1943, as American troops fought the Japanese in the Solomon Islands, and as the Allies prepared to invade Normandy, a twenty-year-old army private named George Ritchie celebrated his good luck. He could hardly believe that, after finishing basic training in Abilene, Texas, he was to go to the Medical College of Virginia, where he would become a doctor at government expense.

Seven days before he was to leave for medical school, Private Ritchie developed a bad chest cold. It turned into influenza, and he was hospitalized. Over the next few days he seemed to recover. But the night before he was scheduled to leave for Richmond, his temperature soared to a life-threatening 106.5 degrees Fahrenheit. His surroundings became a dizzy blur. He heard the click and whir of the X-ray machine—and then silence.

The young soldier woke up on a strange bed in a small, dimly lit, unfamiliar room. His head was clear. In a panic that he might miss the train to Richmond, Private Ritchie jumped out of bed. "My uniform wasn't on the chair," he remembered later. "I looked beneath it. Behind it. No duffel bag either. . . . Under the bed maybe? I turned around, then froze."

Ritchie was shocked to see that a young man was lying in the bed that he had just vacated. "The thing was impossible," he recalled. "I myself had just gotten out of that bed. For a moment I wrestled with the mystery of it. It was too strange to think about—and anyway, I didn't have time."

Private Ritchie shivered and ran from the room. The only thing he could think about was getting to Richmond. Out in the hall a sergeant walked toward him carrying an instrument tray. "Excuse me, Sergeant," Ritchie said. "You haven't seen the ward boy for this unit, have you?" The sergeant did not answer or even slow down. At the last minute Ritchie yelled, "Look out!" but the man walked right past him. The next minute he was behind him, walking away without even looking back at Ritchie.

Before he had time to wonder if he was delirious or dreaming, Ritchie found himself outside the hospital. It was dark and he was moving fast as though flying through the air. He still wore only his army hospital pajamas but had no sensation of cold. After willing himself to slow down, Ritchie landed on a street corner in a town by a large river. People walked by without seeing him. He leaned up against a thick guy wire bracing a telephone pole, but his body passed right through it. "In some unimaginable way," George Ritchie wrote later, "I had lost my firmness of flesh, the body that other people saw."

Oddly, given the bizarre circumstances, the young man's most pressing concern was that he was not going to be able to study medicine in his present disembodied form. He knew he had to get back to his physical body as fast as he could. The return to the hospital was quick, even faster than his voyage away from it had been. Running from ward to ward and room to room, Ritchie searched the faces of sleeping soldiers. It was not easy to distinguish them in the dim light, so he decided to look for his identifying onyx and gold fraternity ring on their hands instead.

After what seemed an eternity, Private Ritchie found a left hand with the correct ring on the third finger, but the body was covered with a sheet. For the first time he thought, "This is what we human beings call 'death,' this splitting up of one's self." At the same time, he wondered how he could be dead and still be awake, thinking and experiencing.

Suddenly, the room was filled with an intense illumination, and Ritchie saw that a man made of light had appeared. From inside himself he heard the words, "You are in the presence of the son of God." Simultaneously, his whole life, "every event and thought and conversation, as palpable as a series of pictures," he said later, passed before him in review.

Then Private Ritchie woke up in his own body, to the astonishment of the physician who had just signed his death certificate. An orderly who had been preparing the body for the morgue noticed feeble signs of life in the corpse and called the doctor, who hastily injected adrenaline directly into the heart. Although Ritchie had not taken a breath for nine full minutes, he showed no symptoms of brain damage. The commanding officer at the hospital called the Ritchie case "the most amazing circumstance" of his career and signed an affidavit that George Ritchie had indeed made a miraculous return from virtual death on the night of December 20, 1943.

Private George Ritchie went on to become Dr. George Ritchie, a psychiatrist who had ample opportunity to study dreams and hallucinations. Such work convinced him that his own extraordinary experience was no delusion—that he had, in fact, seen over the threshold of death. Nor, it appears, was his mystic journey unique. No less a realist than the author Ernest Hemingway, after he was wounded in Italy in

Apparitions of the deceased rise out of the water in The Bay of the Dead

World War I, felt his soul leave his body; he later used some of his memories of it in the novel *A Farewell to Arms.* Famed aviator Edward V. (Eddie) Rickenbacker, rescued after three weeks on a raft in the Pacific Ocean in 1942, recounted in his autobiography how he had faced death: "Then I began to die, I felt the presence of death, and I knew that I was going. . . . All was serene and calm. How wonderful it would be simply to float out of this world. It is easy to die."

Such anecdotal evidence, available from sources throughout the world and throughout history, has attracted scientific notice since Victorian times. However, it was not until the twentieth century, when advances in medical technology made it possible to revive people who were apparently dead, that this research received much in the way of popular notice. During recent decades the medical profession has been unable to ignore the accounts of those who, when threatened with death, apparently had experiences in which they felt as if their spirits were somehow moving toward an afterlife. In the 1970s and 1980s, these near-death experiences, or NDEs, as they came to be called, were brought to public attention in books and lectures by such investigators as Raymond A. Moody, Jr., Kenneth Ring, and Elisabeth Kübler-Ross.

Increasingly rigorous analysis of these stories has shown many of them to be remarkably consistent. Furthermore, those who recount them are almost always sincere people whose experiences do not appear to be delusions or dreams. Still, researchers have been unable to demonstrate the objective reality of near-death experiences, and the jury is still out on their significance. Most people who are facing death do not report such occurrences. Are those who do merely suffering from stress-induced hallucinations? Or are their real-seeming experiences real in fact, thereby demonstrating the separate existence of the consciousness and the presence of a world beyond death?

WESTERN PHILOSOPHERS AND VISIONARIES often describe a separation of body and soul at death. Christian mystics have described how, when near death from illness or accident, their spirits were guided by angels through a tour of hell and heaven and their actions were weighed. Their journeys often ended in a realm of light.

These visionaries interpreted their near-death experiences as religious events. Beginning in the late nineteenth century, however, a few researchers, many of them with impeccable scientific credentials, began to investigate the existence of ghosts and apparitions. In the process, some of them became interested in deathbed visions.

Once such investigator was Sir William Barrett, a physicist at the Royal College of Science in Dublin. He began collecting deathbed visions in the 1920s after his wife, an obstetrician, reported an unusual case to him.

On the night of January 12, 1924, Lady Barrett delivered the baby of a woman named Doris. (The Barretts withheld her last name when reporting the story.) After the difficult birth, as the woman lay dying, she looked toward one part of the room with a radiant smile. "Oh, lovely, lovely," she said. When asked what was lovely, Doris replied, "What I see." She spoke in a low, intense voice. "Lovely brightness—wonderful beings."

Then, Lady Barrett reported, Doris seemed to focus on one spot in the room and cried out, "Why, it's Father! Oh, he's so glad I'm coming; he is so glad. It would be perfect if only W. [her husband, his name also concealed by the Barretts] would come too."

Doris's baby was brought for her to see. She looked at it with concern, and then said, "Do you think I ought to stay for baby's sake?" Turning toward her vision, she cried, "I can't—I can't stay; if you could see what I do, you would know I can't stay." Speaking presumably to her father, she said, "I am coming" and then, puzzled, commented to the bystanders, "He has Vida with him." Looking back to her vision, she said: "You do want me, Dad; I am coming."

The woman died shortly afterward. Aside from the sheer intensity of Doris's feelings and speech, what made the greatest impression on Sir William and Lady Barrett was the fact that Vida, Doris's sister, had died three weeks earlier—but Doris had not been told because of her precarious health. Doris, it seems, had had a vision of someone she could not have expected to see.

This episode, and a number of others like it, appeared in the book *Death-Bed Visions,* written by Sir William Barrett in 1926. Familiar with the medical belief that dying patients see only hallucinations, Barrett pointed out that deathbed visions often occur when the patient's mind is clear and rational. Furthermore, the dying are often astonished by what they see; for example, Barrett wrote, dying children were surprised to see angels without wings. If their visions were hallucinations, he noted, they would be more likely to conform to popular stereotypes.

TRAINED AS A PSYCHIATRIST, Dr. Elisabeth Kübler-Ross lifted the virtual public taboo on discussions of death and dying with her best-selling books in the late 1960s and afterward; her name would ever after be linked with the subject in the public mind. And while her books dealt primarily with the stages of acceptance of death, Kübler-Ross's work led her to believe in an afterlife. "Before I started working with dying patients," said Kübler-Ross in 1974, "I did not believe in life after death. I now believe in it beyond a shadow of a doubt."

Born in Zurich in 1926, the first of triplets, young Elisabeth Kübler had a closer acquaintance than most young women with death and suffering. Stubborn and independent, as a teenager she defied her father's wishes in order to nurse refugees from countries that had been devastated by World War II; later, she volunteered to treat survivors of the Holocaust in Poland. The horrors she saw there haunted her dreams for years.

After taking her medical degree at the University of Zurich (again, against her father's wishes), Kübler married an American doctor, Emanuel Ross, in 1958 and moved to the United States to specialize in psychiatry. Her work with terminally ill patients in Chicago persuaded her that the whole subject of death should be confronted and discussed much more openly. Having identified what she believed were the five emotional stages of dying—denial, anger, bargaining, depression, and acceptance—Kübler-Ross published her first book, *On Death and Dying*, in 1969 to widespread acclaim.

Yet even as she was gathering praise and writing sequels to her successful volume, Kübler-Ross's life was taking a turn away from the mainstream of the medical profession. Some of the patients she had worked with reported mystical experiences as they neared death—and soon Kübler-Ross had some of her own. Not the least of them, by Kübler-Ross's account, came in the late 1960s, after she heard an unusual story from a dying woman by the name of Mrs. Schwartz.

Mrs. Schwartz told Kübler-Ross how, when she lay unconscious from internal bleeding, she regained awareness and found herself floating above her body. She could see everything in the room—the doctors, the nurses, their attempts to resuscitate her—but she could not speak to them. Mrs. Schwartz said she reentered her body as it was being wheeled to the morgue, and she startled the attendants by pulling the sheet away from her body.

Shortly after recounting this incident to Kübler-Ross, Mrs. Schwartz died. Around this time, the psychiatrist said, the stress of working with the dying was telling on her, and she decided to give up her specialty. As she stood in a hospital corridor, having just made her decision, she turned to see none other than Mrs. Schwartz beside her. The dead woman looked solid and real.

Kübler-Ross says she led her visitor to her office and asked her to write and sign a note as evidence of her visit. The smiling woman did so, then walked out of the room. Later, according to Kübler-Ross, the handwriting was compared with other samples of the dead woman's hand and identified as hers.

Psychiatrist Elizabeth Kübler-Ross (left)

After studying such experiences, says Kübler-Ross, she learned to induce her own out-of-body experiences whenever she wanted. Combining her studies of death and dying with such personal episodes, the psychiatrist started to speak out publicly on the separate existence of the spirit and the reality of the afterlife. "When people die," she said, "they very simply shed their body, much as a butterfly comes out of its cocoon."

Kübler-Ross's work set the stage for what may have been the most influential book on near-death experience, Raymond Moody's *Life After Life,* published in 1975. It was he who first categorized the common features of many near-death experiences (a phrase he coined) and who clarified the concept for the public. His book, as well as Kübler-Ross's studies, has given the average person the clearest picture yet of what it is like to die.

Raymond Moody was first exposed to the subject in the middle of the 1960s, when he was a philosophy student at the University of Virginia and heard Dr. George Ritchie, a professor of psychiatry at the school, describe his own near-death experience as a soldier in Texas during World War II. After receiving his doctorate in philosophy, Moody went on to teach in North Carolina, where he heard his second account of a near-death experience from a student whose story was remarkably similar to Ritchie's. By the time he entered medical school in 1972, Moody had begun to gather an informal collection of such reports. He found them to be so widespread and yet so little studied that he decided to conduct his own survey and interviews as he was beginning his medical career.

Moody collected about 150 tales. Some of them came from people who were resuscitated after having been declared dead. Others were the accounts of people who, through accident or severe illness, had come very close to death. After studying these firsthand stories, Moody identified fifteen elements that recurred among the NDEs. Not all of them were present in any one case, nor did they necessarily occur in the same sequence. However, a theoretically ideal or complete near-death experience would, in Moody's words, run something like this:

"A man is dying and, as he reaches the point of greatest physical distress, he hears himself pronounced dead by his doctor. He begins to hear an uncomfortable noise, a loud ringing or buzzing, and at the same time feels himself moving very rapidly through a long dark tunnel. After this, he suddenly finds himself outside of his own physical body, but still in the immediate physical environment, and he sees his own body from a distance, as though he is a spectator. He watches the resuscitation attempt from this unusual vantage point and is in a state of emotional upheaval.

"After a while, he collects himself and becomes more accustomed to his odd condition. He notices that he still has a 'body,' but one of a very different nature and with very different powers from the physical body he has left behind. Soon other things begin to happen. Others come to meet and to help him. He glimpses the spirits of relatives and friends who have already died, and a loving, warm spirit of a kind he has never encountered before—a being of light—appears before him. This being asks him a question, non-verbally, to make him evaluate his life and helps him along by showing him a panoramic, instantaneous playback of the major events of his life. At some point he finds himself approaching some sort of barrier or border, apparently representing the limit between earthly life and the next life. Yet, he finds that he must go back to the earth, that the time for his death has not yet come. At this point he resists, for by now he is taken up with his experiences in the afterlife and does not want to return. He is overwhelmed by intense feelings of joy, love, and peace. Despite his attitude, though, he somehow reunites with his physical body and lives.

"Later he tries to tell others, but he has trouble doing so. In the first place, he can find no human words adequate to describe these unearthly episodes. He also finds that others scoff, so he stops telling other people. Still, the experience affects his life profoundly, especially his views about death and its relationship to life."

Moody also described each of the characteristic elements of the NDEs he heard. The main features are:

Ineffability. Moody found that those who reported NDEs uniformly believe them to be inexpressible in ordinary language. As one woman put it, "Our world—the one we're living in now—is three-dimensional, but the next one definitely isn't. And that's why it's so hard to tell you this. I have to describe it to you in words that are three-dimensional. That's as close as I can get to it, but it's not really adequate. I can't really give you a complete picture."

Hearing the news of one's own death. Many of Moody's respondents tell of hearing their doctors or others pronounce them dead. Said one survivor: "First, they tested this drug they were going to use on my arm, since I had a lot of drug allergies. But

Scala/Art Resource, New York

The deceased pass through a long, dark tunnel in The Ascent into the Empyrean, *by Hieronymus Bosch*

there was no reaction, so they went ahead. When they used it this time, I arrested on them. I heard the radiologist who was working on me go over to the telephone, and I heard very clearly as he dialed it. I heard him say, 'Dr. James, I've killed your patient, Mrs. Martin,' And I knew I wasn't dead. I tried to move or let them know, but I couldn't. When they were trying to resuscitate me, I could hear them telling how many cc's of something to give me, but I didn't feel the needles going in." Almost everyone who reports hearing of his or her death tries in vain to deny it. The person can see and hear and think but is unable to move or speak.

Feelings of serenity. For those studied, the early stages of an NDE often involve extremely pleasant feelings and sensations. Any pain that the person may have been feeling has disappeared. After one man received a severe head injury, his vital signs were undetectable. He said later: "At the point of injury there was a momentary flash of pain, but then all the pain vanished. I had the feeling of floating in a dark space. The day was bitterly cold, yet while I was in that blackness all I felt was warmth and the most extreme comfort I have ever experienced. . . . I remember thinking, 'I must be dead.'"

Noise. Those experiencing NDEs often hear unusual sounds, sometimes of a very unpleasant nature. A man who "died" for twenty minutes during an abdominal operation reported "a really bad buzzing noise coming from inside my head. It made me very uncomfortable." On the other hand, the sound can be magnificent. A young woman who had suffered from internal bleeding said that at the instant she collapsed she "began to hear music of some sort, a majestic, really beautiful sort of music."

The dark tunnel. As they hear the noise, many subjects report the sensation of being pulled rapidly through a dark tunnel, valley, cave, well, cylinder, or other elongated space. One informant stopped breathing because of an allergic reaction to a local anesthetic: "The first thing that happened—it was real quick—was that I went through this dark, black vacuum at super speed. You could compare it to a tunnel, I guess. I felt like I was riding on a roller coaster train at an amusement park, going through this tunnel at a tremendous speed."

Leaving the body. Often what people find to be the most surprising and affecting part of the near-death experience is an apparent out-of-body episode. This awareness of separation from one's body frequently follows the trip through the dark tunnel.

One woman who underwent such an experience recalled: "I was admitted to the hospital with heart trouble, and the next morning, lying in the hospital bed, I began to have a very severe pain in my chest. I pushed the button beside the bed to call for the nurses, and they came in and started working on me. I was quite uncomfortable lying on my back so I turned over, and as I did I quit breathing and my heart stopped beating. Just then, I heard the nurses shout, 'Code pink! Code pink!' As they were saying this, I could feel myself moving out of my body and sliding down between the mattress and the rail on the side of the bed—actually it seemed as if I went *through* the rail—on down to the floor. Then I started rising upward, slowly. On my way up, I saw more nurses come running into the room—there must have been a dozen of them. . . . I drifted on up past the light fixture—I saw it from the side and very distinctly—and then I stopped, floating right below the ceiling, looking down. I felt almost as though I were a piece of paper that someone had blown up to the ceiling."

Meeting others. Spirits of dead relatives, friends, or guardian beings seem to appear in order to ease the loneliness of the transition into death. A woman who underwent a very difficult childbirth heard the doctors tell her relatives that she was dying. "Even as I heard him saying this I felt myself coming to," she recounted. "As I did, I realized that all these people were there, almost in multitudes it seems, hovering around the ceiling of the room. They were all people I had known in my past life, but who had passed on before. I recognized my grandmother and a girl I had known when I was in school, and many other relatives and friends. It seems that I mainly saw their faces and felt their presence. They all seemed pleased. It was a very happy occasion, and I felt that they had come to protect or to guide me. It was almost as if I was coming home."

Corbis-Bettmann

*A mysterious apparition appears to a young woman
in this nineteenth-century etching*

The being of light. The most amazing element in the accounts that Moody studied, and the one that has the most profound effect on the individual, is the encounter with the being of light. Typically, the light is dim at first but then waxes brighter and brighter until it reaches an unearthly or indescribable brilliance. At the same time, those who have seen the light say that it does not hurt their eyes or keep them from being able to see other things. Perhaps, Moody notes, this is because the dying do not have the physical eyes to be dazzled.

In every case that Moody recorded, those who saw the light as part of a near-death experience knew that it was a being, one who emanated love and warmth beyond description. The identification of this being varies with the religious background of the dying person. Most Christians see the light as Christ, whereas Jews have identified it as an angel. The being may communicate with the dying person, seemingly by thought transference. Usually it asks a question that is understood as "Are you prepared to die?" or "What have you done with your life to show me" or "Is it worth it?" None of the subjects felt that the questions were judgmental or condemning.

One person remembered the experience this way: "It was just a tremendous amount of light. . . . I just can't describe it. It seemed that it covered everything. . . . At first, when the light came, I wasn't sure what was happening, but then, it asked, it kind of asked me if I was ready to die. It was like talking to a person, but a person wasn't there. The light's what was talking to me, but in a voice. Now, I think that the voice that was talking to me actually realized that I wasn't ready to die. You know, it was just kind of testing me more than anything else. Yet, from the moment the light spoke to me, I felt really good—secure and loved."

The review. The appearance of the being of light and its probing questions may precede a moment of startling intensity during which the being presents the person with an overview of his or her life. The review is very fast, like a movie shown at high speed, although some respondents said that they saw everything at once and were able to take it all in at a glance.

One woman recalled her experience: "When the light appeared, the first thing he said to me was 'What do you have to show me that you've done with your life?' or something to this effect. And that's when these flashbacks started. I thought, 'Gee, what is going on? Because all of a sudden, I was back early in my childhood. And from then on, it was like I was walking from the time of my early life, on through each year of my life, right up to the present.'"

The border. In a few cases, people feel themselves approaching a border or limit of some kind. It has been described as a door, a fence, a body of water, a gray mist, or simply a line. They may see the border as the threshold between life and death. A man dying of kidney disease first saw the being of light. Next, the "thoughts or words came into my mind: 'Do you want to die?' And I replied that I didn't know since I knew nothing about death. Then the white light said, 'Come over this line and you will learn.'"

Coming back. Obviously, the people that Raymond Moody talked with had come back from the apparent threshold of death, or there would have been no material for *Life After Life.* The return represents an important element in the near-death experience. It comes at the end of the experience and at a time when many of the dying have lost any desire to reenter their bodies. Once a dying person reaches a certain depth in the experience, respondents have said, he or she rarely wants to return. This is especially true for those who go so far into an NDE that they encounter the being of light.

Several mothers of young children said they would have preferred to stay in the spiritual world but felt an obligation to go back and raise their children. Others said they returned because of unfinished tasks on earth.

Coming back quite often involves another trip through the dark tunnel, though few of Moody's respondents experienced an actual reentry into their physical bodies. Most said they simply lapsed into unconsciousness at the end of the experience and woke later to find themselves back in their flesh-and-blood bodies.

Moody named four other characteristic elements of NDEs, all of which could fall under the heading "beginning again": telling others, corroboration of the experience, changed lives, and new views of death. People who undergo near-death experiences have no doubts about the reality and importance of their NDEs, says Moody, but few are willing to discuss them openly. They usually find that a skeptical society is simply not ready to receive NDE reports with sympathy and understanding. One survivor commented, "I tried to tell my minister, but he told me that I had been hallucinating, so I shut up."

Finally, Moody found that the near-death experience almost always alters one's attitude toward death, especially for those who before their NDE thought that death meant complete extinction—of the spirit as well as the body. According to one person, "Some people I have known are so afraid, so scared. I always smile to myself when I hear people doubt that there is an afterlife, or say, 'When you're dead, you're gone.' I think to myself, 'They really don't know.'"

Few of Moody's respondents had experiences containing all of these elements. And for some, the NDE was even unpleasant. One woman remarked, "If you leave here a tormented soul, you will be a tormented soul over there, too." A widower who tried to commit suicide said, "I didn't go where [my wife] was. I went to an awful place. . . . I immediately saw what a mistake I had made." Such cases were a small minority of Moody's sample, however.

AS NDE RESEARCH CONTINUES, so too does the debate. The phenomenon itself is widely accepted as real—almost no one questions that people are honestly reporting their experiences—but its meaning is still controversial. Despite a century of active investigation, the crucial issue remains very much as it was in the 1880s: Do NDEs prove the existence of life after death? Or is there a psychological or physiological explanation for them?

Skeptics raise a number of objections to a survivalist interpretation of NDEs. For instance, most people who have been close to death simply do not have NDEs. Some return with nightmarish experiences. Moreover, the primary Moody-type NDE sometimes happens to people who are not in danger of death at all, so the experience could not always be related to dying. And finally, the evidence for NDEs comes only from the living. "Clinically dead" is an ambiguous term often used by those who tell of such experiences, but the fact is that the person did not really die. For obvious reasons, there is no evidence about what happens to people who actually die.

Nonsurvivalist explanations for near-death experiences generally fall into two camps: One, NDEs are psychological constructs, illusions triggered by the stressful occasion of approaching death, or two, NDEs are hallucinations produced by chemical changes in the dying brain. The depersonalization theory of Russell Noyes is one such psychological explanation, although even Noyes admits that it does not cover all facets of mystical consciousness. Some observers have also suggested that the near-death experience is an archetype, a kind of universal myth stored in everyone's unconscious mind and brought forth only in extreme situations. Others prefer a physiological explanation, noting similarities between near-death experiences and drug-induced hallucinations. (For instance, LSD visions often include a trip through a tunnel.) Perhaps, they say, hospital anesthesia could account for such experiences. Or, it is possible that the overstressed brain is itself suffering a chemical disorder or reacting to oxygen deprivation (common in dying people), which might cause vivid visions. Clearly, near-death experiences remain an enigma.

Twice Around

THE LITTLE BOY called Sujith had not yet reached his second birthday in 1971 when, according to his family, he began to talk about an earlier life. Expressing himself in the limited speech of a child so young, adding sounds and gestures when vocabulary failed, Sujith said that his name in his past life had been Sammy and that he had been a railroad worker and later a seller of bootleg arrack, a potent liquor distilled from rice, molasses, or other ingredients. He said that as Sammy he had lived in the village of Gorakana, about eight miles south of his present home in the suburbs of Colombo, Sri Lanka (formerly Ceylon). He went on to relate that his—or Sammy's—wife was named Maggie and that one day, when he was drunk and they had quarreled, he had set out on foot along the busy highway in front of their house, only to be struck and killed by a passing truck. Repeatedly, the toddler demanded to be taken to Gorakana. He also had a precocious taste for cigarettes and arrack.

Sujith's mother, Nandanie, who had been divorced from the boy's father soon after the child's birth, was not entirely mystified by such behavior. She and other members of her family knew no one in Gorakana, nor did they know if a bootlegger named Sammy had ever existed. But like most Sri Lankans, they were Buddhists and accepted the idea of reincarnation, which holds that every human has a soul or psychic essence separate from the physical self, and that this psychic entity survives death to reappear, usually anonymously, in another body at some later time. The fact that little Sujith might contain the spirit of a quarrelsome drunkard from a neighboring town and be able to give witness to it was hardly unimaginable. Thus Nandanie expressed no objection when a monk in a nearby temple, having heard about the boy, asked if he could investigate.

The monk interviewed Sujith at length, wrote down significant details of his story, and selected sixteen items about his past life that could be checked for accuracy. He then visited Gorakana on several occasions and managed to verify nearly all of them. He discovered, for example, that a man named Sammy Fernando had lived in Gorakana until six months before Sujith's birth. This Sammy had been a former railway worker and an arrack dealer. He also had a wife named Maggie and a father named Jamis. People in Gorakana confirmed that Sammy Fernando had been killed by a truck outside his home shortly after quarreling with his wife; the dead man was, they added, a hard-drinking, violent, and impulsively generous man who had had repeated brushes with the police. He was a cigarette smoker.

It was not long before a newspaper article about Sujith found its way to Ian Stevenson, a professor of psychiatry at the University of Virginia and director of the division of personality studies at the university medical center. Stevenson traveled to Sri Lanka in 1973 and conducted a series of interviews with everyone involved, including Sujith, who was by then three-and-one-half years old, and Sammy's widow, Maggilin Fernando. In so doing, he was able to find corroboration for fifty-nine of Sujith's statements about his earlier life. Stevenson discovered additional behavior parallels between the child and the person whose life he claimed to remember—including a taste for spicy food and a preference for wearing a certain type of shirt and sarong not commonly found among young children. Both persons shared an enthusiasm for singing, used profanity freely, were given to physical violence, and were notably generous with their meager possessions. The toddler even displayed a peculiar wariness around policemen and a pronounced fear of trucks that seemed to have parallels in Sammy's life. Sujith also showed what seemed to be instant recognition of a number of people in Sammy's family when they were brought together. He called Maggilin "Maggie" and other pet names that Sammy used, and made her cry by proclaiming "I love you Maggie" and then blaming her for his death.

Stevenson's fieldwork turned up no evidence that Sujith's family and the Fernandos had previously known each other. The closest connection was a former drinking companion of Sammy's who was casually acquainted with Sujith's family, but both this man and Sujith's mother and grandmother denied ever having discussed Sammy. Likewise, Sujith's eccentric behavior and his easy recognition of Sammy's relatives seemed to rule out the possibility that the child was pretending or fantasizing, or that anyone else was using him as part of an elaborate deception, even assuming that he could memorize all the facts he seemed to know at ages two and three. The only other explanation, from Stevenson's vantage, was reincarnation.

ONLY RECENTLY has reincarnation been subjected to any sort of systematic study. But the possibility of multiple lives has been accepted on faith since ancient times. Indeed, belief in reincarnation may date back to the Stone Age, some 12,000 years ago or earlier. Archaeologists, noting that it was common practice at the time to bury the dead in the fetal position, have speculated that prehistoric peoples may have been preparing the bodies for a literal rebirth of the spirit. And the phenomenon of reincarnation has played—and continues to play—a part in countless primitive cultures around the world, among peoples who were and are living in remote regions of Africa, Asia, Australia, and the Americas.

Reincarnation has also been incorporated into the formal beliefs of more civilized cultures, extending back as far as the beginnings of recorded history. The ancient Egyptians, for example, enclosed in the coffins of their dead texts that attested to the deceased's virtues, in the hopes of persuading the god Osiris to grant them further lives. Herodotus, the Greek historian who wrote extensively on Egyptian customs, reported that Egyptians believed that it took 3,000 years for a spirit to complete the full cycle of lives through which it had to go.

And reincarnation figured in the teachings of many ancient Greek philosopher-mystics. Pythagoras, the sixth-century B.C. mathematician and mystic, claimed to have lived many other lives, including that of a Trojan warrior, a prophet, a peasant, a prostitute, and a shopkeeper. Once, he reportedly stopped a man from beating a puppy, saying: "Do not hit him, it is the soul of a friend of mine. I recognized it when I heard it cry out." Plato, the fifth-century B.C. sage, was fully persuaded of reincarnation, and he offered a theory on how the soul gradually ascends (or descends) through nine degrees of righteousness in a series of rebirth experiences. Describing the process in the *Phaedrus*, he depicted the lowest rank as that of tyrants and others of extreme unrighteousness. However, he said, those who live righteously gradually journey upward to ever higher levels, the soul eventually entering the body of a gymnast or physician (fourth rank), a politician or economist (third rank), and a righteous king or warrior (second level). Finally, when the soul has shown itself worthy of true enlightenment and is divorced completely from subservience to the material world, it may be born into the body of a philosopher, artist, musician, or lover. Only then, according to Plato, is the soul ready to cease its rebirth and find unending peace in a heavenly realm of sublime knowledge.

The classical version of reincarnation had a subversive influence on early Christian thought. Then, as now, the idea of rebirth was regarded by most churchmen as heretical; orthodox Christian doctrine, after all, declares that the souls of the departed pass directly to heaven, hell, or purgatory, and not into another physical being.

Notable among Christians with differing views was Origen, a third-century philosopher from Alexandria, Egypt. Origen devoted his life to writing and teaching a kind of neoplatonic Christianity that included belief in reincarnation. In one of the few fragments of his writing that has survived, he described how he understood rebirth to work: "Everyone, therefore, of those who descend to the earth is, according to his deserts or to the position that he had there, ordained to be born in this world either in a different place, or in a different nation, or in a different occupation, or with different infirmities, or to be descended from religious or at least less pious parents; so as sometimes to bring about that an Israelite descends among the Scythians, and a poor Egyptian is brought down to Judaea."

Origen was posthumously condemned for such "blasphemous opinions" by Pope Anastasius in 400. But his influence lingered on with sufficient power that the sixth-century council of Constantinople issued a decree of anathema against him and all who accepted his concept of "monstrous restoration."

Apparently, the council's reach did not extend very far. By the eleventh century a diverse collection of some seventy or more heretical sects, many of them stressing reincarnation, were flourishing throughout Christendom. Perhaps the most influential was a group of dissidents known as the Albigenses (for the French town of Albi) or Cathars ("purified ones"), who believed that human souls were fallen spirits for whom a human incarnation was a period of probation and expiation. Good lives were rewarded with rebirth into a body capable of still greater spiritual development. Bad lives could only lead to rebirth into a body full of pain, suffering, and still more evil. The Cathars, who also would tolerate little of this world, including music, papal wealth, and the high standard of living of much of the clergy, ultimately were put down by the Church, and reincarnation was once again declared outside of Christian doctrine.

I N THE EAST, the concept of reincarnation can also be traced to ancient times— and it has remained a central tenet of mainstream religious beliefs and practices. It was probably first articulated in a formal sense in the Upanishads, the concluding section of a vast body of traditional hymns or vedas preserved by the high priests of the Aryan peoples who invaded India sometime around 1500 B.C. According to the Upanishads, the individual ego or spirit (atman) has its origin in a transcendent spiritual essence. The atman begins its existence in an immature state, and in order to grow in wisdom and reach spiritual maturity, it must undergo an endless cycle of rebirth, suffering, and death. With each new life it assumes a new physical form: human, animal, or even vegetable. That form, whether higher or lower than the preceding one, is determined by the karma or ethical conduct followed in the previous life. The law of karma presumes that there is an inevitable punishment or reward which follows every act, thought, attitude, and aspiration and that the atman thus generates its own favorable or unfavorable destiny in the next life.

Acts of hostility or acts that in any way harm other creatures are believed to have a particularly negative effect on karma, as does passive ignorance that leads to such destructive behavior. By the same token, acts of mental and physical self-discipline, such as the system of exercises known as yoga, can contribute positive karma; through them the atman can eliminate human error and sensuality. When the atman finally develops all the capacities latent in human nature, and thus reaches complete spiritual insight, its journey ends in a final transcendent union with the world spirit.

This new metaphysic was shared in its basic outlines by most of the major formal religions that arose in ancient India—by Brahmanism, or Hinduism, which embraced it virtually whole, and by Buddhism and Jainism, which came along some-

Twins Gillian and Jennifer Pollock hold a photo of their deceased sisters, Joanna and Jacqueline

what later and recast the idea of rebirth in slightly different forms. Buddhists, for example, reject the idea of the soul that persists unchanged from one life to the next. Rather, they believe that when people die they are survived by a dynamic complex of personality and character traits and memories that are always changing, much as genetic material passes on from generation to generation in a continuous flow, each time expressed differently. A person may be reborn into any of five classes of living beings: gods, human beings, animals, hungry ghosts, or the damned. Buddhists hold that rebirth ends when the three "fires"—craving, ill-will, and ignorance—are ultimately extinguished, a condition and place signified in the word Nirvana.

ANOTHER FREQUENTLY cited example of allegedly spontaneous past-life memories involves a set of British twin girls. Born to Florence and John Pollock on October 4, 1958, Jennifer and Gillian were believed by their father and mother to be the reincarnated spirits of older daughters Joanna and Jacqueline, who had been killed by an automobile while walking to church one Sunday morning in 1957. What made the case particularly unusual is the fact that both parents were Roman Catholics, ordinarily not the sort of people to give credence to reincarnation. But John, a convert to Catholicism at the age of nineteen, had always held a personal, if slightly clandestine, belief in reincarnation—so much so that he repeatedly prayed to God for some proof. When Joanna and Jacqueline died, he feared that their loss was intended as some kind of punishment for his heresy, but when he learned soon after that he was about to become a father again, he saw the event as God's favorable answer to his prayers. He told his wife that she would bear not one child, as the doctor assured her, but two and that they would be girls.

After the twins' births, their father noted many curious similarities between them and their deceased older sisters: a scarlike mark on Jennifer's forehead that seemed to match one on Jacqueline's forehead, instances in which the twins claimed to recognize landmarks of which they could not reasonably have had any knowledge, a shared fear of a car under circumstances matching that of their sisters' death. But researchers like Ian Wilson, the British author of *All in the Mind*, a skeptical book about reincarnation, hold the opinion that the simplest explanation is probably the best—that the twins were sensitized to their father's feelings and convictions from a very early age and that they thereby unconsciously gathered all sorts of messages from him. As such, his wishes literally became father to their deeds.

VISIONS OF SUPPOSED previous lives sometimes appear to be triggered by visits to sites that were frequented by a person during some earlier incarnation. For example, George S. Patton, the great American general of World War II, never doubted what he called the "subconscious memories" in which he saw himself as a warrior who had fought and died in battle many times throughout history: He believed, for example, that he had served as a soldier under Alexander the Great, with the Roman legions, and with Napoleon, among others. Of course, Patton's visions may have been traceable to nothing more than a wide knowledge of military history and a self-dramatizing imagination, but he himself sometimes appeared to be surprised by them. His first such experience occurred when he was a young officer in France during World War I. Another took place in 1943, after Patton had defeated the Axis forces in Sicily. Given a tour of the island, the general repeatedly interrupted his astonished guide by pointing out the sites and details of obscure historical events. Finally, the guide asked him if had been there before. "I suppose so," Patton replied, though this was in fact his first visit to Sicily.

Patton's seeming remembrances of scenes from the past were in a way similar to the almost universal experience of déjà vu, the momentary sensation of witnessing a scene or an event we have seen before but have no clear recollection of and cannot explain. Researchers believe that most déjà vu incidents are either genuine memories that we have forgotten or recollections of things that have been learned secondhand but have become tangled or confused in our minds as personal experiences. Other déjà vu sensations can be explained physiologically: The brain sometimes produces what amounts to a double exposure, two glimpses—a fraction of a second apart—of a remembered scene, which the mind mistakenly takes to be widely separated in time; blinking at the right moment can have a similar effect.

But some reports, if true, seem to indicate something beyond forgotten memories. One such story tells of a British youth who was touring caves formerly used as prisons on the isle of Guernsey when he claimed to remember watching, in a former life, a prisoner being sealed in a cavern at the site. Officials denied any such incident, but when the boy persisted, they launched a search; behind a bricked-up entrance they found a skeleton. According to the boy's mother, who reported the incident to a reincarnation researcher nearly twenty-five years after her son's death in 1935, a search of the old prison's archives revealed an inmate with the same name as the one given by her son for the walled-in prisoner.

Equally intriguing is the case of a young woman who told her story to the paranormal researcher D. Scott Rogo. In the 1970s, she claimed, she was driving on the New Jersey Turnpike when she suddenly had the feeling that everything she was seeing was familiar, even though she knew for a fact that she had never been there before. She told her driving companion that "about a mile or so down the road is a house I used to live in," and went on to predict what other sights lay ahead. She then exited from the highway and approached a small town, which she described in advance; there she saw the very porch where, perhaps eighty years earlier, she had sat with her grandmother. Rogo's informant went on to claim that she then described a certain drugstore, with a high marble counter, where her grandmother would take her for lemonade. "The building was still there, much the same as it used to look, but it was boarded up, and we could not look inside. . . . I 'knew' that I had died when I was about six or seven years old." She wanted to try to find her grave, which she said was in a cemetery just over the hill, but her friend, too frightened to continue, insisted on getting back in the car and leaving.

OTHER INVESTIGATORS probe the alleged past-life memories of their subjects through hypnotic regression. For purposes of reincarnation study, a hypnotist typically uses suggestion to regress subjects back to childhood and then induce them to leap the void to a time before their present lives. Often enough the images thus triggered are intense and detailed, although most subjects cannot remember subsequently what they said while in a trance.

One problem with hypnotic regression in reincarnation research is that it is extremely difficult, if not impossible, to screen out the subject's conscious or unconscious adoption of clues that are suggested by the hypnotist. Studies have shown that hypnotic subjects are often eager to give a hypnotist whatever they think he or she wants to hear and that their stories become more elaborate as their sessions progress. Stevenson maintains that suggestibility is at the root of most past-life regressions and compares the resultant tales to dreams. "Nearly all hypnotically evoked previous personalities are entirely imaginary," he declares, "just as are the contents of most dreams."

A second problem falls in the general category of abnormal memory—often termed cryptomnesia—a phenomenon that can reveal itself when the subject is undergoing hypnotic regression. In cases of cryptomnesia, subjects tap into a detailed memory of something of which, when they are in a normal state of consciousness, they are unaware. Although it may appear to be information gathered in an earlier life, and thus evidence of reincarnation, the possibility that subjects are calling up from their subconscious mind material that was gathered in a long-forgotten book,

A doctor works with a patient to produce the hypnotic state in this nineteenth-century French etching

movie, or television show cannot be ruled out easily.

A classic example of cryptomnesia was recounted by a Canadian psychologist, who described putting one of his patients under hypnotic regression, only to have him begin to write at length in a strange language. When the patient came out of his trance, he was unable to recognize what he had written or explain its origin. The doctor, fascinated by this curious occurrence, sought the help of linguists, who eventually identified the writing as Oscan, a precursor of classic Latin. The patient swore he knew nothing of the language, but after extensive questioning, the doctor was able to trace the source to an occasion many years earlier when his subject had spent an afternoon in a library, sitting next to someone engaged in research. That individual, it turned out, had his book open to a page on which an ancient Oscan curse was recorded. The doctor's patient had merely glanced over at his neighbor's work, but in the process had taken a mental snapshot of the open page. The image of the esoteric writing registered so strongly on his unconscious memory that it remained there ready to be called up again when the right circumstances—the heightened concentration of the trance state—presented themselves.

Another favorite example of cryptomnesia is the story of one Countess Maud, allegedly a fourteenth-century Englishwoman, who played a starring role in the persuasively detailed recollections of a hypnotic subject in England in 1906. The portrait of Maud was exquisitely rounded; it included what she ate, how she dressed, her friends—a veritable treasure of medieval trivia that turned out to be correct in almost every particular. And with good reason: As a sleuth for the British Society for Psychical Research proved, the historical details were all from a little-known story the subject eventually remembered having read. Its title was "Countess Maud."

Acknowledging the potential for contamination by suggestion and cryptomnesia, the more scrupulous hypnotic regressionists look for alternative explanations for their subjects' stories before accepting them as evidence of reincarnation. At the same time, the colorful stories that unreel under hypnosis are the most exciting and dramatic in the literature of reincarnation. And they can exert an extraordinary power over those relating them, regardless of the source or the validity of the outpourings.

The all-time superstar among past-life subjects is Virginia Tighe. The wife of a Pueblo, Colorado, businessman, she proclaimed while under hypnosis that she had lived in Ireland more than a century earlier as one Bridget (Bridey) Murphy. And the name of Bridey Murphy would be forever enshrined in the public mind as the quintessential example of a previous life revealed by hypnotic regression.

The Tighe/Murphy story was first brought to light by Morey Bernstein, an experienced hypnotist living in Pueblo who detailed his conversations with her in a 1956 book titled *The Search for Bridey Murphy*, which became an international sensation, propelling the subject of reincarnation onto front pages over the world.

Bernstein called Tighe by the pseudonym of Ruth Simmons to preserve her privacy, for she feared that her in-laws would look askance at a respectable Christian woman who dabbled in hypnosis and reincarnation. At the time of the hypnosis sessions, she was a twenty-nine-year-old mother of three. Born in Madison, Wisconsin, and a resident of Chicago for several of her formative years, she would later claim never to have visited Ireland or to have had any special association with Irish people. (Bernstein also insisted that he had no personal knowledge of Ireland.) Yet, she was able to give a wonderfully detailed account of Bridey's life in nineteenth-century Ireland.

Bridey appeared after Bernstein had first regressed Mrs. Tighe to childhood and then encouraged her to "go to some other place in some other time" (critics later accused him of leading her). "Scratched the paint off all my bed . . . " were her first words, referring to an incident in her alleged earlier childhood. Speaking in an Irish brogue, she said that she grew up in the city of Cork in a Protestant family that consisted of her father, Duncan, a barrister, her mother, Kathleen, and a brother also named Duncan. Constantly probing for verifiable details, Bernstein elicited a birth date in 1798 and a description of her death sixty-six years later, after breaking a hip. Bridey "just sort of withered away," she said, and after her funeral, at which a man played the "uilleann pipes," she was "ditched," or buried.

Specifics of all kinds—names, dates, places, events, customs, songs, shops—tumbled out of her as Bernstein's tape recorder rolled through six separate sessions. Bridey said she was married in a Protestant ceremony at the age of twenty to Sean Brian Joseph McCarthy, a Catholic and son of a Cork barrister. Brian, as she called him, had also studied law, and after they were wed they moved to Belfast, where he taught at Queen's University. To satisfy Brian's family, they were married a second time in a

© June 6, 1965, Chicago American, courtesy the Chicago Tribune

Virginia Tighe, who shrank from her Bridey Murphy notoriety

Catholic service at Belfast's Saint Theresa's Church, by Father John Joseph Gorman. On another occasion she described the cliffs of Antrim that she had seen as a child ("the streams run down real fast and make little rivulets in the ground"), the stores where she shopped in Belfast (Farr's for food, John Carrigan's greengrocery), and her favorite meal (potato cakes, which she called by their colloquial name, "platters"). At one point she said she could dance the "morning jig," and under a posthypnotic suggestion from Bernstein, Virginia Tighe performed a lively little dance.

Much of the appeal of Bridey's story lay in just such ordinary detail, the accumulation of commonplace facts and incidents. And when Tighe returned to consciousness after each session, she was invariably surprised. She could not account for the source of any of the information played back to her on tape.

When Bernstein probed further and asked Bridey about the interval between one life and the next, she mentioned "a place of waiting . . . where everybody waits," a realm without day or night or death or disease or families. There, she told him, she could travel by merely willing herself to be somewhere else. In time she learned of her imminent rebirth from "some women," and then she simply "passed to another existence."

Bridey's story proved so intriguing, and touched such a receptive chord in people's imagination, that it was published in thirty countries and serialized in dozens of newspapers. Bartenders concocted Bridey Murphy cocktails, disc jockeys played "The Ballad of Bridey Murphy," comedians told reincarnation jokes ("I've changed my will—I'm leaving everything to myself," quipped one), and in California a self-described "Mr. Hypnosis" offered clients a tour of their prior lives at twenty-five dollars per life. "Come as you were" parties enjoyed a brief vogue, too. On a darker note, however, a Shawnee, Oklahoma, youth shot himself to death because, as he said in the suicide note he left: "They say that curiosity kills a cat. I'm a cat and I'm very curious about this Bridey Murphy story so I'm going to investigate the theory in person."

Meanwhile, journalists pawed through dusty Irish records in an effort to confirm or contradict the numerous details in Bridey's tale. The results of their search were mixed. Many of her statements proved to be correct, or at least they were consistent with the earlier time and place. Among these were her description of the Antrim cliffs, her identification of merchants Farr and Carrigan, and the uilleann pipes that she said were played at her funeral. Bridey also seemed to know things that could only have been learned in Ireland, and with difficulty even there.

Those eager to debunk her story took comfort in the reporters' failure to find any specific traces of Bridey or her family. Indeed, no records corroborated her account of her birth, marriage, or death, but that could just as well have been because the government's vital statistics records did not go back that far; only a family Bible was likely to contain the kinds of data wanted, and finding that in a country with literally tens of thousands of Murphys was a task too great even for the swarms of self-appointed investigators crawling over the Irish countryside.

On the other hand, some of Bridey's memories were found on examination to be just plain wrong, and her language was not always reliable either. Sometimes spiced with Irish vernacular ("linen" for handkerchief), her speech also contained glaring examples of twentieth-century American speech ("downtown," for example). A Chicago newspaper, which looked into Virginia Tighe's early years in the city, claimed that the source of Bridey's information was actually an Irish-born woman that Tighe had known as a child, but this exposé all but evaporated on investigation. The woman in question was never shown to have spent time in Virginia's company, much less to have regaled her with Irish dialect stories, and the fact that she was the mother of one of the very editors involved in writing the debunking articles in the first place would seem to cast even further doubt on the newspaper's objectivity.

The final judgment on Bridey Murphy is yet to be delivered. Mrs. Tighe rejected nightclub offers and other opportunities to capitalize on her transitory celebrity. Bernstein's earnest openness and what *Life* magazine called his awed "what-have-I-wrought style" helped his credibility. The best reporter on Bridey's trail, William Barker of the *Denver Post*, came away persuaded that her story had "the ring of truth, whatever that truth ultimately means." Ian Wilson, surely no advocate of reincarnation, saw "evidence for something as yet unexplained" in Bridey's saga. And Ian Stevenson counts the Bridey Murphy phenomenon as a rare exception to his general dismissal of hypnotic regression cases. Virginia Tighe's remembrance of her life as Bridey could still turn out to be a subconscious fantasy rooted in an unfound book or a forgotten childhood experience, but Stevenson does not think so. He believes her memories were "somehow acquired paranormally."

4
MIND OVER MATTER

Psychokinesis

*Barbara Scheid of West Germany held PK responsible for
the mysterious bending of her cutlery in the early 1970s*

P SYCHOKINESIS—OR PK, as it is commonly known—refers to the
alleged ability of the human mind to influence objects and events without
physical contact. Literally translated from its Greek roots, psychokinesis
means "motion produced by the mind"; in its more popular interpretation,
it is nothing less than "mind over matter."

PK can supposedly be directed either consciously or unconsciously, with results
that may or may not be obvious to an observer. Some instances of reported PK, like
metal bending and clock starting, are played out on what investigators term a
"macro" scale, their seeming results readily appreciated by the naked eye. According
to current theory, another example of macro-PK at work might be poltergeists, those
unruly racketing spirits that are believed to erupt in households, causing all manner
of noises and hurling objects throughout the air.

Other forms of alleged psychokinesis, however, may be so subtle as to be detectable only in the laboratory by application of statistics or scientific measuring devices or both. Termed "micro-PK," these phenomena include effects on target systems, such as random number or event generators and dice-rolling machines, where results that should conform to the normal laws of probability are thought by some to have been altered significantly by PK. The ability to influence air temperature and magnetic fields is also considered an example of micropsychokinesis.

Those who study the field of parapsychology generally regard psychokinesis as related to extrasensory perception, or ESP, the supposed ability to acquire or transmit information through means other than known sensory channels. PK and ESP are often referred to collectively as psi phenomena, or simply psi, after the first letter in the Greek word psyche, meaning "mind or spirit." As the professionals explain it, both ESP and PK involve some kind of interaction between the mind and the material world. ESP, it is said, is a demonstration of a mental exchange with another person's brain or with the physical world; PK is a physical influence. Both forms of psi appear to share a fine disregard for physical barriers of any sort—their energies can reportedly penetrate locked doors and steel walls and travel long distances with no diminution of effect.

But if there is relative agreement in parapsychological circles as to what constitutes psi phenomena, there is nothing but controversy and speculation regarding how any alleged mental force might actually be translated into physical action. Some psi researchers, among them psychologist John Beloff of the University of Edinburgh, contend that PK simply exists. "Under certain conditions, still to be established," Beloff has written, "an idea or intention in the mind can automatically constrain a physical system to act in such a way as to express the idea or intention. That this is, in the last resort, [is] an ultimate fact about the world." Others believe that PK is a type of reordered cosmic energy, a life force that can, at times, be channeled through the human mind. Still others believe that psychokinetic energy is a force within all humankind, just waiting to be tapped.

THE NOTION that the mind might have occult influence over matter appears to go far back in human history, though it was apparently not until the seventeenth century that anyone went on record to say that psychokinesis deserved serious philosophic investigation. Sir Francis Bacon, perhaps the greatest intellect of the Elizabethan age and a man singularly devoted to the idea of inductive reasoning and the experimental method, theorized in his 1627 collection of essays, *Sylva Sylvarum: Or a Natural History,* that there may be an occult force within one's being that is capable through the "binding of thoughts" of influencing the material world. He proposed that the existence of this binding force might be tested "upon things that have the lightest and easiest motions," among them the "shuffling of cards, or casting of dice." It was not until the mid-nineteenth century, however, that any consistent efforts were made to explore the truth or falsity behind alleged psi phenomena.

The advent of spiritualism in the mid-1800s spurred an enormous amount of popular interest in all sorts of psychic matters, both in the United States and Europe. This quasi-religious movement held as its fundamental premise that the dead survive discarnate in a world beyond, as spirits or intelligences that are able to communicate with the living through "sensitives," or "mediums." Of particular interest to both scientists and savants were the so-called physical mediums, who reportedly relayed the messages of otherworldly spirits to the living in the form of rappings, table tiltings, or other séance effects.

Not surprisingly, most members of the scientific community were loath to cross the boundary into psychic research. Indeed, the majority of them expressed contempt for—and perhaps some underlying fear of—any phenomena that could not be readily explained by current science. There were some, however, who theorized that the mysterious séance happenings were not signals from the spirit world, but psychokinetic phenomena emanating from the mediums themselves—perhaps produced by the "binding of thoughts," a conscious or subconscious act of will.

One of the first to attempt an in-depth study of such events was the respected

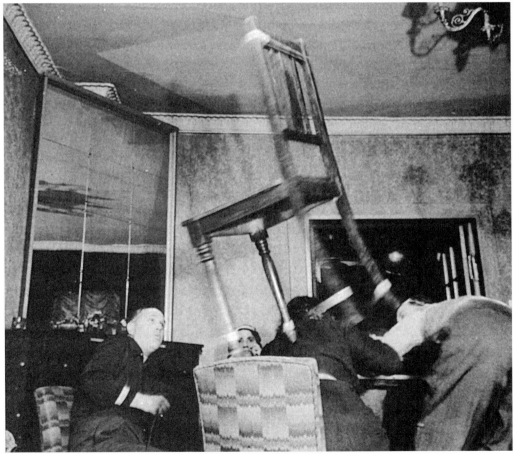

Nordfoto, Denmark

Many modern psychical researchers regard bizarre occurrences like the one above, in which a chair sailed over the heads of sitters at a 1940s séance in Denmark, not as messages from the dead, but as examples of psychokinesis

British physicist Michael Faraday. In 1853, Faraday engaged several "successful table-movers" in an investigation of the table-turning effect common at séances. He created a number of ingenious devices that he placed on the tabletop during various experiments; all were designed to reveal whether any table movements were somehow initiated by the object itself or by the sitters. Faraday came away from his efforts convinced that, although the sitters believed themselves to be only pressing down on the tabletop with their fingertips, they were actually unconsciously pushing it in the direction they expected it to rotate.

As some skilled investigators discovered at the time, many of the purported psychics of the golden age of spiritualism were nothing more than rank charlatans or stage magicians pulling the wool over the eyes of a gullible public. Others, however, demonstrated apparent PK effects that are difficult to explain even today. One of them was Eusapia Palladino. Born in southern Italy in 1854 and orphaned at the age of twelve, Palladino, too, allegedly became the center of spontaneous psychokinetic events as a young child. But it was not until the girl's late teens, when she came under the tutelage of a psychic investigator named Damiani, that the full extent of her alleged powers began to manifest itself.

Precisely what Damiani taught his rustic, uneducated, and rather indelicately mannered subject may never be known. But one thing seems clear—if Palladino truly had psychic gifts, she did not regard them as a precious trust. Whenever she sensed that she could get away with simple fraud, she was only too eager to take the easy route. And when caught cheating, the medium was quick to blame the non-believers in the audience who, she claimed, willed her to play tricks; in her trance-like state, she explained, she was incapable of defending herself against such dishonest suggestions. Nevertheless, occasions abounded when Palladino's paranormal effects—by one count she could call up thirty-nine different phenomena—seemed to defy all reason.

In time Palladino came to the attention of Dr. Cesare Lombroso, a prominent Italian psychiatrist and criminal anthropologist with an avowed skepticism toward the paranormal. Lombroso went to Naples in 1890 to observe the young woman in action and, to his great surprise, came away a convert. Based on Lombroso's favorable report, an international team of scientists and intellectuals invited Palladino to display her talents before them in Milan. The Milan Commission, as they were known, supervised a series of seventeen séances in 1892, and although Palladino seems to have had less than her usual success in the presence of these hoary heads, she was able to confound them with several partial materializations. According to the participants, she somehow had caused disembodied hands to float around the room and to touch the observers.

At the completion of their study the savants of the commission declared, "It is impossible to count the number of times that a hand appeared and was touched by one of us. Suffice it to say that doubt was no longer possible. It was indeed a living, human hand which we saw and touched, while at the same time the bust and arms

Leif Geiges, courtesy Verena Geiges, Germany

*Italian medium Eusapia Palladino apparently causes a
small table to float at an 1892 séance in Naples*

of the medium remained visible and her hands were held by those on either side of
her." (These manifestations reportedly occurred even when Palladino's hands were
tied to the chair in which she sat.)

It would appear that the only mildly dissenting voice among the commission-
ers was that of Charles Richet, professor of physiology at the Sorbonne, in Paris. "It
seems to me," Richet later wrote, "very difficult to attribute the phenomena produced
to deception, conscious or unconscious, or to a series of deceptions. Nevertheless,
conclusive and indisputable proof that there was no fraud on Eusapia's part, or illusion
on our part, is wanting: we must therefore renew our efforts to obtain such proof."

No less an authority than Dr. Julien Ochorowicz, director of the Institut
Général Psychologique in Paris, studied Palladino from November 1893 to January
1894. Ochorowicz ruled out the theory that spirits were behind the medium's alleged
effects, concluding instead that the phenomena were the work of Palladino's "fluidic

double." Taking Count Agénor de Gasparin's concept of "psychic fluid" one step further, Ochorowicz proposed that Palladino could summon up from this fluid a type of psychic twin that could, under certain circumstances, detach itself from the medium and act independently.

Colleagues from as far away as London and St. Petersburg, Russia, also took up Richet's challenge, and Eusapia Palladino found herself shuttling all over Europe to be examined further. But Richet, who would earn the Nobel Prize for Physiology and Medicine in 1913, was the most thorough of the researchers. In 1894, he invited the peripatetic medium to join him on the Ile Roubaud, his private island off the coast of France; there, he reasoned, any possibility of accomplices or fraudulent devices could be removed. As an additional precaution, Richet invited two well-known psychical investigators, Frederic W. H. Myers and Sir Oliver Lodge, early members of the British Society for Psychical Research. Organized in 1882 by an eminent group of scholars in and around Cambridge University, the society's mandate was "to investigate that large body of debatable phenomena designated by such terms as mesmeric, psychical and spiritualistic."

As table tilting featured prominently in Palladino's psychokinetic effects, Richet had a sturdy table specially made for her. "The legs were pointed so that it would be difficult to raise it with the foot. . . . We thought . . . it much too heavy (forty-four pounds), but we tried it the same evening. As soon as Eusapia touched this heavy table with the tips of her fingers, it tilted, swaying about, and without the legs being touched at all, it rose up completely with all four feet off the ground."

After a series of séances, Richet and his British colleagues pronounced Palladino's powers genuine, and the SPR representatives invited her to Cambridge to perform before a full meeting of their organization. At the gathering, however, Palladino was caught cheating by one of her hosts, who had deliberately sought to entrap her, and she was sent packing in disgrace.

Back on the Continent, though, the more pragmatic European investigators, who had acknowledged that the medium would always take shortcuts if given the chance, denounced the SPR and resumed their own investigations. One French researcher, M. Arthur Lévy, was thoroughly persuaded of Palladino's telekinetic skills after viewing a particularly unruly séance in which "the sofa came forward when she looked at it, then recoiled before her breath; all the instruments were thrown pell-mell upon the table; the tambourine rose almost to the height of the ceiling; the cushions took part in the sport, overturning everything on the table." One observer, Lévy noted, "was thrown from his chair. This chair—a heavy dining-room chair of black walnut—rose into the air, came up on the table with a great clatter, then was pushed off."

Before the séances, Palladino was usually undressed by female attendants and examined for any hidden implements that would aid in trickery. By the turn of the century, however, researchers were also using rather sophisticated electrical devices to evaluate psychic phenomena. And as reputable physicists at several of Europe's leading universities continued to record positive results from investigations of Palladino, the SPR decided to take another look.

In 1908, the organization sent three of its best—and most skeptical—investigators, including one who was a practiced conjurer, to meet Palladino in Naples. The British delegation produced a 263-page report detailing eleven separate séances and confessed that they had seen 470 events for which they could uncover no earthly explanation. One of the experts, F. H. Everard Feilding, concluded that "for the first time I have the absolute conviction that our observation is not mistaken. I realize as an appreciable fact of life that from an empty curtain I have seen hands and heads come forth, and that behind the empty curtain I have been seized by living fingers, the existence and position of the nails of which were perceptible. I have seen this extraordinary woman, sitting outside the curtain, held hand and foot, visible to myself, by my colleagues, immobile, except for the occasional straining of a limb while some entity within the curtain has over and over pressed my hand in a position clearly beyond her reach."

But Palladino's flush of success paled within a year; on a subsequent tour of the United States, she was caught cheating once again, and the effectively discredited medium all but disappeared from the séance scene. Nevertheless, in the minds of many investigators, an intriguing question still remained unanswered: How, they wondered, short of having genuine psychokinetic powers, did Palladino manage to achieve her many extraordinary feats without having some of Europe's most skilled investigators detect fraud?

DESPITE THE EARNEST EFFORTS of the SPR and its American counterpart—the ASPR, founded in 1885—to throw some light on the mysteries of levitation, table tilting, spirit rappings, and materializations, by the beginning of World War I most formal scientists had once again turned their backs on physical mediumship and psychokinesis. The discovery of numerous frauds among the self-proclaimed sensitives bred a mistrust difficult to overcome, and many who valued their reputations were reluctant to court the ridicule that was often heaped on serious students of PK. Then, in the 1920s, along came two discoveries that were sufficiently provocative to revive a lively interest in all quarters.

At the center of all the excitement was a rather flamboyant figure named Harry Price, the self-styled founder, director, and sole proprietor of the National Laboratory of Psychical Research in London. Price was by all accounts a kind of puckish gadfly within the field of psychic studies. He had none of the formal training or academic titles so generously represented at the SPR and was a consummate self-promoter. But Price had certain advantages over his more learned colleagues—he was a skilled magician, adept at detecting fraud, and he was not particularly burdened with scientific methods of investigation.

It was only by chance that Price, making his daily train commute between London and his country home near Pulborough, met Stella Cranshaw. The two hap-

Mary Evans Picture Library, London

Harry Price in 1927, in his London laboratory

pened to strike up a conversation about matters psychic, during which Cranshaw, a rather modest young hospital nurse, told the investigator that she had been experiencing some very unsettling phenomena for several years—everything from odd rapping noises and "cold breezes" to household objects inexplicably taking flight. Price, excited by the prospect of a new research subject, identified himself as a specialist in the paranormal and invited her to his laboratory for testing; she reluctantly agreed.

Price was also an inventor and immediately set about designing an array of experimental equipment that he hoped would authenticate the young woman's claims. He built a special table for the séances; in addition, he placed thermometers around the séance room in his laboratory, each near a camera so that temperature changes could be recorded periodically. Most ingenious of all, however, was his "telekinetoscope," a clever device consisting of a telegraph key that, when depressed, completed an electrical circuit and caused a red light to flash. The key was both surrounded by an impermanent soap-and-glycerine bubble and covered by a bell jar; according to Price, only psychic energy directed toward the key could activate the device without disturbing the protective glass jar and breaking the delicate bubble.

During thirteen séances conducted between March and October of 1923—and always in the presence of several witnesses—Cranshaw went into ever-deeper trances as she ran through a spectacular repertoire of psychokinesis. On the third meeting, for example, Price reported that she managed to levitate the table so high that some of the observers at the séance were forced to rise out of their chairs in order to keep their hands on the tabletop. Then, the researcher continued, two of the table's three legs broke away "with a percussion-like noise" as the fracture occurred. But still more feats were to come. "Suddenly, and without warning, the tabletop snapped violently into two parts, and, simultaneously, the remaining leg and other supports of the table *crumpled up*, the whole being reduced to little more than matchwood. The sitting then concluded."

Price kept meticulous records of the gatherings and noted in his journal the temperature fluctuations during each séance—a drop of more than twenty degrees on one occasion—and the fact that Cranshaw had managed to activate his telekinetoscope. But she was usually exhausted by the end of each session and eventually called a halt to the proceedings, claiming that the séances were causing her emotional as well as physical distress. (However, evidence uncovered after Price's death in 1948 suggests foul play. It appears that the investigator may have paid the young woman to abet him in an elaborate scheme to promote psychic research and, of course, himself.)

Mary Evans Picture Library, London

Stella Cranshaw

THEN, IN THE 1960s, a new crop of PK practitioners began to emerge. But they were not mediums; these men and women did not confine their talents to the shadows of the séance room but displayed them in the unforgiving light of laboratories all over the world. One of the most important of this new generation was a Leningrad housewife named Nina Kulagina. Kulagina—also known as Nelya Mikhailova—first came to the attention of Leonid L. Vasiliev in the early 1960s, while Vasiliev was testing volunteers for "dermo-optic vision," the purported ESP ability to sense specific colors through the fingertips. Vasiliev, the Soviet Union's leading figure in parapsychology at the time, reported that when Kulagina was concentrating intensely, small objects on the table would sometimes move on their own when she placed her hands over them. This discovery led to extended studies of Kulagina's presumed psi powers, which were found to range from the original "eyeless sight" to the ability to deflect compass needles and levitate small objects.

Soviet psychic Nina Kulagina attempts to move an object inside a glass jar during a 1960s test

© Leif Geiges, courtesy Verena Geiges, Germany

With Vasiliev's death in 1966, other scientists took on Kulagina's case. Zdenek Rejdak, a Czech psychical researcher, filmed several controlled tests conducted with Kulagina in 1968. Rejdak reported—although the film did not confirm it—that Kulagina was first searched and x-rayed for concealed magnets or other devices that might affect results. Then, in full light and with several skilled observers seated around a table, she produced a series of effects using small objects, provided by Rejdak, that she had neither seen nor touched before the tests had begun.

One particularly impressive display involved a collection of wooden matches that were placed before her by the scientist. "We asked her to make the matches move not only toward her but also away from her," Rejdak explained. "We also asked her to move only one match, specified by us, from the whole group of matches." These PK effects, and many others, Kulagina completed to the observers' satisfaction. Rejdak concluded, "It appears therefore that the exteriorized energy can be directed by the subject's will."

Other investigators gradually developed a fuller description of Kulagina's supposed psychokinetic powers, finding that she could equally affect objects of metal, plastic, wood, and fabric; that when working with new materials she could move them away from her with ease, but toward her only with practice; that shielding objects with paper, acrylic, lead-impregnated glass, or even metal had no discernible effect on her performance; and that the greater the distance an object lay from her, the more energy was apparently required to move it.

Researchers also noted that when objects began to move, the direction paralleled Kulagina's own body movements. As she gained psychic control over the objects, however, they moved more freely in the requested manner. It was also reported that sparks sometimes emanated from her hands during PK and that her influence lingered on in the motion of target objects even after she had ceased willing them, as though some residual energy in the object had to be exhausted. About the only limitation anyone discovered in Kulagina's powers was that she could not move objects that been placed in a vacuum.

Not surprisingly, when the provocative articles and films of Kulagina's activities began circulating in the West, every psi researcher wanted to witness this marvel firsthand. Beginning in 1968, many succeeded, though under conditions that were often complicated by the rigors of the Soviet Union's closed society. Although the government barred full-scale controlled experiments of Kulagina, it permitted informal, impromptu demonstrations, either at her apartment or at the visitor's hotel.

All but a handful of the investigators came away convinced that they had witnessed genuine PK. Benson Herbert, a British parapsychologist, even claimed to have had the marks on his skin to prove it. He described having been gripped on his left forearm by Kulagina: "For two minutes, I felt nothing whatever, save only a natural increase of warmth under her hands. Then, quite abruptly, I experienced a new sensation . . . akin to a mild electric shock." After about two minutes, he reported, "I could not endure the sensation a moment longer, and disengaged my arm." For eight days thereafter, according to Herbert, he had a burnlike mark where the woman's hand had rested.

True to form, the critics—particularly in the United States—have dismissed Kulagina as a charlatan, maintaining that she manages her feats of alleged PK through the use of gossamer threads and cleverly concealed magnets. And while it is doubtful that the controversy will ever be settled to the satisfaction of all, Kulagina's supporters were considerably cheered in early 1988 when the Moscow newspaper *Pravda* reported the outcome of a legal action brought by Kulagina against a publication that had accused her of trickery. Two members of the Soviet Academy of Sciences testified on the plaintiff's behalf, swearing that her powers did not involve deception. The court ruled in Kulagina's favor and ordered the offending journal, *Man and Law*, to publish a retraction.

PK in the Lab

*An experiment at J. B. Rhine's Duke University
parapsychology laboratory*

ROM ITS BEGINNING, the primary purpose of research into the field of mind over matter was to provide definitive proof that the phenomenon being investigated was real. Along with other early psychical researchers, most members of the SPR and the ASPR tended more toward anecdote gathering than experimentation. They collected stories of the feats of mediums and offered rational explanations, but they did not investigate methodically or establish the conditions under which a particular event could be expected to occur. They did not, in proper scientific fashion, look for general principles, but tended instead to focus on the supposed uniqueness of each event. Their work generally took place on the mediums' home turf, often a darkened room where close observation was all but impossible.

It remained for J. B. Rhine—frequently in collaboration with his wife, Louisa—to develop what most observers consider to be the first systematic, experimental approach to psychokinetic phenomena. Born in 1895 and schooled as a botanist, Rhine was nudged toward parapsychology in 1922, when he attended a lecture by the British author Sir Arthur Conan Doyle, an avid dabbler in spiritualism. His interest was further piqued when he read a book by the British-born Harvard psychologist William McDougall, who contended that a full understanding of human nature required the study of psychic matters. In 1927, when McDougall was asked to set up a department of psychology at Duke, Rhine jumped at the chance to join him there to engage in psychic research.

AT THE TIME, such study was a wide-open field in the academic world. Rhine and McDougall were swimming against the tide of behaviorism, which accepted only strictly observable events as a proper subject for psychologists to study. The Duke investigators, however, shared with the psychic research societies an interest in the decidedly nonbehaviorist phenomenon of telepathy—the supposed ability of minds to communicate directly through channels other than the generally recognized senses.

Rhine decided to use his scientific training to investigate telepathy and the closely related phenomenon of precognition—the supposed capacity of an individual to foresee future events. Later, he would coin the term extrasensory perception, or ESP, to describe such abilities. The new name, he hoped, would help diminish the prejudice against his research in academic circles.

Conceptually, it was an easy transition for him from ESP to PK. If the mind could bypass the senses and know the world by some other mode of perception, he reasoned, it could conceivably bypass nerves and muscles to act on the physical world with some other sort of power. Rhine had long been fascinated by the idea of mind over matter but was unsure of how it could be tested. He was intrigued by the investigative possibilities of dice throwing, which could easily and inexpensively be adapted to laboratory experimentation and statistical analysis.

For his first experiments, Rhine recruited students as subjects, who simply shook a pair of dice in cupped hands, threw them onto the floor, and let them rebound from a corner—all the while concentrating on rolling high numbers, which Rhine defined as any combination of the dots on the two upper die faces adding up to eight or more. Six of the thirty-six possible combinations add up to seven, which he declared a neutral number. The remaining thirty combinations are evenly divided between high and low numbers. According to the laws of chance, fifteen out of every thirty-six throws, or five out of twelve, should come up high. For statistical convenience, Rhine divided his experimental sessions into twelve-throw units, which he called runs.

To eliminate any effect of throwing techniques, Rhine designed a crude but serviceable dice chute. Somewhat to his surprise, the scores of the first 108 runs conducted with the dice board were just as high as those of the hand-tossed series. Rhine followed up with another device for testing the influence of throwing skills: a "dice machine," composed of a motorized rotating cage. Rhine and two assistants took turns operating the machine and serving as subjects, trying to achieve a high score. When playing the subject role, they chose the speed at which the cage turned but were not allowed to touch either the dice or the machine. Once again, Rhine was surprised by the results: Scores in machine-thrown runs were slightly higher than runs in which subjects used a dice cup. Perhaps, he speculated, the novelty of the machine, or the fact that subjects had nothing to do but concentrate on making a hit, gave the scores a boost.

Rhine also had to screen out "dice bias"—an uneven distribution of weight in

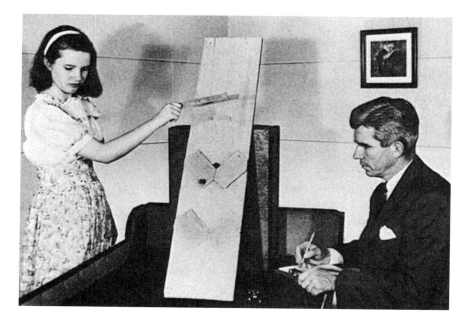

J. B. Rhine, with subject, in a dice-toppling experiment

a die, possibly due to the indentations on each side, that could cause a particular side to land faceup more often than the rest. After testing for bias by using differently constructed dice—one type with smooth surfaces and painted dots, another with inlaid dots—Rhine concluded that dice bias was not a significant problem in the research.

But one effort to screen for dice bias produced curious results. When Rhine changed the target combination from high numbers to low numbers, the overall scores actually lowered. Subjects had done worse than chance would have dictated. It seemed to Rhine that a prejudice against low numbers had developed during the first experiments, when high numbers were always the desired target. Their inner feeling about the target, it appeared, had caused PK to operate in a negative way. Mood was apparently a factor with Rhine's laboratory subjects as well. Gamelike, informal conditions and enthusiastic subjects produced good results, while negative feelings produced chance or worse-than-chance results.

More evidence that PK could be altered by psychological factors came when one of Rhine's research assistants, Margaret Price, bet Joseph L. Woodruff, a star PK subject, that she could sabotage his scores if she made negative comments in the room as he sought to influence the fall of dice in the machine. Woodruff's scores, which had been extraordinarily good the previous day, plummeted to an abysmal below-chance level.

The test was far from airtight. For one thing, no one except Woodruff and Price was present at the time. But it suggested a fascinating implication for psychic research: Anyone present at any experiment, particularly a negative observer, might be at least partially responsible for the outcome. If PK were subject to both conscious and unconscious control, it would be extremely difficult to prove who, if anyone, was actually determining the events in an experimental setting. This inherent ambiguity made it difficult to answer criticism that no experiment could ever show conclusively where the supposed force originated. In the future, every PK researcher would try to overcome this stumbling block by clever experimental design.

WITH WORLD WAR II, when many members of the psychology department joined the armed forces or left for war-related civilian jobs, Rhine decided in 1942 that the time was ripe to review and analyze his eight years of research on PK. Psychologists had concluded that performance declines when a subject begins to get bored with the experimental task. Rhine speculated that similar patterns would appear in the records of his PK research. And as he and his one remaining wartime graduate student, Elizabeth Humphrey, sorted through the old experiment reports, it did not take them long to discover a position effect. In each of eighteen reports they compared, the subjects made more hits early in a run than they did later, and the earliest runs in a test sequence also showed higher scores than later runs. Another analysis yielded a U curve in nine of the eighteen reports. Rhine's wife and frequent research associate, Louisa Rhine, later compared the effect to a "gardener hoeing long rows, who would find the end of a row endowed with added interest just because it was the end." To the Rhines, the results were persuasive evidence that PK was a genuine mental process.

And J. B. Rhine was ready to respond to whatever barbs the critics of parapsychology might hurl at him or his work. In March 1943, the Rhines jointly published the results of the early high-dice experiments in the *Journal of Parapsychology*, which Rhine had cofounded with his colleague William McDougall in 1937, a year before McDougall's death. Over the next three years he published the rest of his PK research. To his amazement, he was not greeted by an immediate outcry from conventional psychologists. Perhaps, he thought, the critics did not know—at least for the moment—how to respond to the quantitative and statistical approach he had used to study a subject that had historically been the stuff of breathless anecdote. Indeed, his work drew numerous positive responses, scientific and otherwise. In a letter to Rhine, Aldous Huxley wrote, "I admire you for not going mad under the strain of devising scientific experiments in a field where there is no really satisfactory hypothesis!" More muted praise came from English criminologist and psychic researcher D. J. West. While noting that Rhine's procedures were rather informal and doubting that his results could be repeated by other experimenters, West conceded that the American's statistics were the most conclusive evidence to date for the existence of PK.

And just as West suspected, Rhine's apparent successes proved difficult to repeat in experiments conducted by other researchers. In England, a series of similar dice-throwing studies failed to yield any indication of PK in action. Another set of experiments, conducted by a Philadelphia biophysicist in 1944, also showed no evidence of PK. While few critics have gone so far as to charge researchers such as Rhine with

John Beckett

Magicians Michael Edwards, James Randi, and Steven Shaw in 1979

outright fraud, others have questioned their methods. The Brooklyn College psychologist Edward Girden carefully assessed Rhine's dice studies and faulted them for, among other things, their informal nature and lack of accurate record keeping.

IN 1979 TWO YOUNG MEN offered to test their claimed psychic powers at the McDonnell Laboratory at Washington University. Over the next three years, researchers at the laboratory—which had recently been established with a bequest from aviation pioneer James McDonnell to investigate psychic phenomena—spent about 120 hours and $10,000 working with the pair, and amassed impressive results. The only trouble was that their subjects—Steven Shaw, then eighteen years old, and Michael Edwards, seventeen—were no more than talented magicians. They had insinuated themselves into the experiments at the urging of James Randi, magician and crusader against the paranormal.

For years Randi has maintained that psychic research is carried out so casually that hoaxers go undetected. He offers $10,000 to anyone who performs one paranormal feat "under the proper observing conditions." And researchers have sometimes found to their chagrin that purported psychics may take advantage of poor supervision. At the University of Bath in England, for example, children who had said they could bend metal were caught cheating in 1975 when they were observed through one-way mirrors.

At McDonnell, Edwards and Shaw put on a good show. They bent metal by

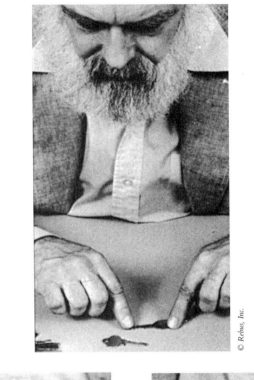

© Rebus, Inc.

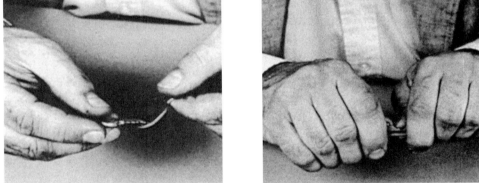

*Magician James Randi shows how a hoaxer might bend keys through sleight of hand,
either inserting the tip of one key into the slotted head of another and exerting pressure (left),
or bending a lightweight key with both thumbs (right)*

stroking it, caused a clock to fall off a table, advanced the hands of a watch, and super-imposed images on photographs. In fact, as Randi would later disclose, Shaw had previously bent the metal wire that appeared to bow upward under his hand. He edged the clock off a table with a virtually invisible thread stretched between his thumbs. Another clock, a digital model whose readings seem to have been turned into gibberish, had been placed in a microwave oven. To create streaks or blotches on photographs, the young men had exposed individual frames of film without removing them from the camera. For one series of alleged thoughtographs (for which a subject supposedly uses PK to "think" an image onto film) in which a psychiatrist discerned parts of a woman's body, Shaw explained, "I spat on the lens."

Not everybody was fooled by the young conjurors; when the videotapes of Shaw's and Edward's handiwork were presented at a Parapsychological Association meeting in 1981, many in the audience complained about the evident lack of controls. But Randi lost no opportunity to gloat when he announced the hoax at a press conference in early 1983. And a few months later the association formally agreed to invite magicians into experiments to mitigate fraud.

IN THE 1960s, the concept of micro-PK came onto the scene. Previous dice and cube studies had suggested that randomly moving objects were more susceptible to the influence of psychokinesis than were stationary ones. Now, some researchers proposed that the more random and unpredictable the movement, the more powerful a PK effect would be.

To test their notions, they turned to the principles of atomic physics to investigate the most random of movements—those of subatomic particles emitted during the process of radioactive decay. German-born physicist Helmut Schmidt designed ingenious high-speed electronic devices, like his random event generator, or REG—essentially an electronic coin-flipper. The switch is driven by the completely random—and, presumably, uncontrollable—emission of electrons from a bit of strontium 90 as the unstable element decays. For one series of experiments, Schmidt connected the generator to a display panel with nine lights. At any given moment, only one light would be on. If the generator relayed a "heads" signal to the panel, the next light in a clockwise direction would light up; a "tails" signal would prompt a move counterclockwise. Electrons moving in a purely random way would theoretically make the lights flash on and off in an equally random pattern. But if PK could influence the way the radioactive material emitted electrons, the lights would display a discernible pattern. All of his early subjects did only a bit better than pure chance would predict, but one, who believed herself to be psychic, was so good that the odds against her performance being the result of pure chance were a billion to one.

In a variation of this test, Schmidt substituted sound for light. Through headphones, subjects listened to clicks produced by electron emissions. They were instructed to concentrate on "hearing" more clicks in their right ear. The results were well above chance.

Schmidt's findings were intriguing, and his testing process seemed to eliminate some of the ambiguities that tainted earlier investigations of PK. His data could be automatically recorded and analyzed, reducing the chance for human error, bias, or fraud. On the other hand, some observers have maintained that these factors cannot be completely ruled out in the case of Schmidt's studies. They have further noted that some of the researcher's target generators could well have shown natural deviations from random patterns, deviations that could have been interpreted as evidence of PK. Moreover, the British psychologist and psi critic C. E. M. Hansel has pointed out that earlier tests by the U.S. Air Force, using a random target generator called VERITAC, turned up no evidence that the experimental subjects were exercising any kind of psi powers. Whatever its flaws, Schmidt's work was part of a new direction in parapsychology.

In the mid-1970s, Schmidt devised a series of experiments to search for evidence of "retro-PK"—that is, a form of supposed psychokinesis that could move backward across the barriers of time and, in effect, influence events that had already occurred. This intriguing research had its beginnings in a more conventional PK experiment in which Schmidt used one of his random generators to produce a random sequence of barely audible clicks to subjects through their headphones. By chance alone, subjects could expect to hear a click once in about 6.4 seconds.

Schmidt, speculating that some of his subjects might be able to speed up the clicks through PK, instructed them only to listen very carefully and to imagine a vaguely analogous real-life experience, such as walking in a forest and listening for soft bird calls. Schmidt hoped to create a mood of eager anticipation, a condition that Rhine and other researchers had maintained is conducive to PK success. Apparently, it worked. Schmidt reported that his subjects heard clicks every 5.42 seconds—almost a full second ahead of the chance schedule. Without even consciously trying, it seemed, his subjects had somehow altered the timing of the hits.

Now came Schmidt's move into retro-PK. He activated his equipment to record the clicks on audio cassettes. Neither he nor anyone else was present when the recordings were made, and, he reported, no one listened to the tapes until the subjects heard them during the experiment. According to observation theory, the recordings were at that point unmeasured, since no one had heard them, and their characteristics were only probabilities and not certainties—although it could be argued that the clicks were, in fact, measured and set in reality when they were taped. Schmidt selected half the recordings as targets for the subjects and designated the other half as controls.

He then assembled his subjects and described the same procedure used for the first experiment. He did not tell them that they were listening to prerecorded sequences, since conventional ideas of time would make ridiculous the notion that they could change past events. But when he compared the experimental tapes with the control tapes, he discovered that the ones that the subjects had listened to had significantly shorter intervals between clicks. It appeared that his subjects had achieved the impossible: They apparently exercised PK to alter events—in this case, recorded sounds—that had already taken place. For observation theorists, the experiment seemed a major triumph, although critics would maintain that the results, like so many findings reported by parapsychologists, were inconclusive and unrepeatable by other researchers.

A NUMBER OF INDIVIDUALS with seemingly sensational psychokinetic abilities burst onto the scene in the 1970s. Decades of scientific advances had shattered forever the credibility of the traditional darkened séance room, and self-proclaimed psychics were expected to perform in the bright light of the laboratory. One of the first of the new psychics to submit to scientific appraisal was Ingo Swann, a Colorado-born artist, writer, and purported astral traveler. In the early 1970s Swann, curious about the then-current idea of affecting plant growth through prayer, purchased a cheap unhealthy-looking *Dracaena massangeana* and took it to his New York office. At the plant's request, Swann said, he called it Lucifer and talked to it reassuringly. Lucifer responded forcefully, sending mental pictures to make its wants known.

Courtesy Time-Life Inc. Collection

Psychic Ingo Swann

Once, over-watered by the office staff in Swann's absence, Lucifer fell into a sorry state. When Swann returned, the wilting plant seemed to demand a sign, Do Not Water. Within a couple of hours after the sign had been posted, Swann reported, Lucifer had perked up, although its soil remained sodden. On another occasion, a droopy Lucifer seemed to be saying something about wanting a penny for its pot. A coworker with a green thumb cleared up Swann's confusion: Lucifer needed the nutrient copper oxide. Five pennies and a few hours later, the plant had made a full recovery.

October of 1972 found Swann attempting to upset a philodendron by sending it messages about mistreatment, such as having acid poured on its leaves. This plant was in the midtown Manhattan lie-detection school of Cleve Backster, a former CIA interrogations specialist who had become well known in parapsychological circles for using polygraph technology to study the supposed ESP capabilities of plants. Backster had hooked the plant up to a machine that measures changes in electrical resistance. At first, alterations in the plant's electrical resistance corresponded to Swann's threats, but then the responses subsided; Swann concluded that the plant perceived his threats as idle.

SWANN PERSUADED Gertrude R. Schmeidler, a psychology professor at City College in New York, to test his purported ability to change the temperatures of remote objects through PK. The essential equipment included very sensitive thermometers called thermistors and a polygraph device to record temperature changes. Schmeidler gave Swann a series of commands that ran, "Hotter, rest, colder, rest, colder, rest, hotter," and so on. This procedure was designed to eliminate any distortions from progressive or cyclical changes in room temperature. In seven out of ten series, Schmeidler reported small but significant temperature changes—even when the target thermistors were sealed in vacuum bottles and placed as much as twenty-five feet away from Swann. During a pause in one experiment, the polygraph suddenly registered a temperature change. Swann reported that he had begun to wonder about the thermistor's exact location inside the vacuum bottle and had "probed" the interior psychically to find it. He thought that his psychic musing must have inadvertently caused a temperature rise.

From Schmeidler's laboratory Swann went west, to what was then the Stanford Research Institute in Menlo Park, California, to give a demonstration at the invitation of physicist and parapsychologist Harold Puthoff. A harder test than Puthoff devised could scarcely be imagined: He had arranged with Stanford University physicist Arthur Hebard to experiment with a highly sensitive magnetometer designed for measuring magnetic fields and detecting quarks, believed to the smallest units of matter.

Swann's task would be to alter the magnetic field in the magnetometer's core. The magnetometer was encased in an eight-ton iron vault that was set in concrete beneath the laboratory floor; four separate shields, including a supercooled electrical coil, surrounded the core and kept its magnetic field safe from outside influence. Signals from the field were picked up by a small probe and relayed to a chart recorder. If Swann succeeded, any changes in the field would show up in the lines traced by the recorder.

Swann was astounded by the difficulty of the assignment. But he later credited his shock with altering his state of consciousness to a point where he was equal to the Herculean task. With Puthoff, the dubious Hebard, and a third physicist, Martin Lee, looking on, Swann set about his supposed mental probing of the magnetometer's core. Suddenly, Puthoff recounted afterward, the steady waves that the chart recorder had been tracing doubled their frequency for half a minute.

The still-skeptical Hebard, whose apparatus was supposedly impenetrable, suggested that something might be wrong with it. Swann would be more convincing, he said, if he could stop the magnetic changes completely. To the amazement of the observers, the wavy lines on the chart recorder flattened out. After about forty-five seconds, Swann told the men that he could no longer "hold it"; he had to let go. The lines on the chart recorder immediately took on their former undulating pattern, indicating that magnetic activity had resumed.

Puthoff, Hebard, and Lee were stunned. Swann explained that he had peered psychically into the interior of the magnetometer and then made a sketch of what he had seen, including a plate of gold alloy that the physicists had not mentioned to him. As he described the magnetometer, the chart recorder registered still more changes. Puthoff asked Swann not to think about the magnetometer. While they chatted about other matters, the waves remained stable. But when talk once more turned to the apparatus, their frequency increased again. Puthoff could not be completely sure whether Swann had induced a change in the magnetometer itself or merely in the chart recorder. However, Swann's sketch of the magnetometer's interior seemed to provide circumstantial evidence that he had somehow penetrated its defenses, and the three California physicists said they were convinced of his powers.

But for all the apparent advances in laboratory techniques that PK researchers have made since J. B. Rhine's early dice-throwing experiments, they have yet to produce experimental results that are repeatable. So, even after many decades of laboratory investigation, PK remains a mystery. If it exists, it must be, from a scientific point of view, a physical force comparable to gravity, electromagnetism, or the special forces governing nuclear particles. But no one has ever produced any evidence that PK is another natural force. And, despite much research, none of the forces already known has been proven to account for PK. Some parapsychologists join J. B. Rhine in the belief that it is a mistake to treat psychokinesis as a physical force. They firmly maintain that it is an aspect of will, of soul, of consciousness, and that it is not bound by any of the physical laws.

It is difficult to imagine what common theoretical ground researchers will ever be able to find. But while theorists argue, the more pragmatic are eager to make use of the supposed force of psychokinesis, no matter what its nature and mechanics may be, because if it is truly an operative phenomenon, the implications—from medical uses to agriculture to psychic warfare—would be staggering.

Poltergeists

Photographs taken in Harry Price's National Laboratory of Psychical Research show the results of alleged attacks on Eleonora Zugun in the 1920s. Welts on her face and bite marks on her hands and arms appeared as Price and his assistants observed.

I N 1851 THE QUIET VILLAGE of Cideville, eighty miles northwest of Paris, was the site of a witch trial. Almost by definition, such events tend to be more than a trifle bizarre, but this one was even stranger than most. For the case was brought by the alleged witch, a shepherd named Felix Thorel, and the defendant was none other than the village priest, Father Tinel.

The chain of events leading to this improbable case began the previous year, when Father Tinel paid a call on an ailing parishioner. The patient, the priest discovered, had been treated with the medicines of a local charlatan who claimed to be a practicing sorcerer. When the parishioner died soon afterward, Father Tinel had the so-called sorcerer arrested and thrown into jail. From his cell, the sorcerer vowed to take revenge.

The revenge, if such it was, took a strange and roundabout form. At the time, two young boys were living in Father Tinel's parsonage. One day at an auction in Cideville, the shepherd Thorel—who was a disciple of the jailed sorcerer—stopped the boys, placed his hands upon their heads, and murmured a mysterious incantation. In the months that followed, Cideville ceased to be a quiet village for the priest and his pupils.

According to the trial records, no sooner had the boys returned to their room in the parsonage than a fearsome gust of wind rocked the building. That night, a loud and persistent rapping noise disturbed their sleep; no cause could be found. Over the next two months, a series of increasingly freakish events transformed the once restful parsonage into a scene of nightmarish madness. Tables skittered across the floor, candlesticks and fireplace tongs danced in the air, and chairs and carpets hovered over the heads of astonished visitors.

By far the most unrelenting of the many reported disturbances was the loud rapping, which sounded as though someone were striking the wainscoting of the room with a hammer. In time, Father Tinel and the marquis de Mirville, a nobleman who had come from Paris to investigate the well-publicized incidents, initiated a crude form of communication through these rappings. The marquis was able to deduce that the entity that was wreaking havoc at the parsonage had a paralyzing fear of nails, spikes, and other sharp points.

Immediately, he and Father Tinel began driving nails into the floor and walls of the room wherever the strange manifestations had occurred. It is said that the first of the nails instantly glowed red-hot and that the floor crackled and smoked. When another nail was driven into a cupboard, Father Tinel's elder pupil reported a fleeting vision of a nail tearing a man's cheek. The following day that vision appeared in the flesh: The shepherd Thorel was seen with an ugly gash on his cheek that looked as though it had been made by the sharp point of a nail. As far as Father Tinel was concerned, that proved the man's guilt. He accused the shepherd of witchcraft and knocked him to the ground with his walking stick. Unexpectedly, Thorel responded by suing the clergyman for libel.

Thorel not only lost the suit, but he was compelled to pay court costs. Still, he had one victory. Father Tinel reluctantly agreed to let his pupils leave the parsonage. Only then was peace restored.

Although the events in Cideville were thought at the time to be witchcraft, in later years some students of the paranormal have suspected the presence of a poltergeist. The term poltergeist—from the German words *poltern*, meaning to make noise, and *Geist*, meaning ghost or spirit—describes a curious kind of allegedly psychic phenomenon characterized by strangely mischievous, almost teasing events that defy easy explanation.

If there was a poltergeist in the parsonage, it behaved true to form. Typically, when a poltergeist is said to be at hand, there are mysterious rappings and bangings and gusts of cold air. Objects move about inexplicably: Crockery tumbles to the floor and furniture flies through the air. Sometimes doors and windows fling open by themselves, items disappear only to be found in the next room, stones and rocks mysteriously bombard buildings, and in a few rare cases, people are physically attacked. Often, these events take place in the presence of a child or adolescent.

SKEPTICS POINT OUT that many so-called paranormal rappings and creakings could have far more mundane explanations, such as shrinking timbers or the effects of underground streams. Still, a number of modern psychical investigators take a more serious view of poltergeists, but reject the long-held notion that they are discarnate, or noncorporeal beings. The poltergeist, in their view, has little or no independent existence. Rather, it is a "person-centered" phenomenon, triggered within the subconscious of a living, human agent.

In many cases the presumed agent seems to be experiencing great personal unhappiness or frustration, which may, in some unknown fashion, be expressed as a powerful psychokinetic force. Some theorists have even suggested that the onset of puberty, with all its attendant anxieties, may trigger a poltergeist.

Although researchers still seek to understand the genesis of poltergeist activity, they have detected certain patterns over the years. Foremost of these is that the occurrences are never single, isolated incidents. Rather, the poltergeist tends to stretch out its visits over weeks and months, sometimes even a period of years. For this reason, many psychical researchers use the phrase "recurrent spontaneous psychokinesis" (RSPK) to describe poltergeist phenomena.

In the best fairy-tale tradition, the story of Eleonora Zugun begins with a little girl going to visit her grandmother. In February 1925, Eleonora, a twelve-year-old peasant living in the northern Rumanian village of Talpa, set out to see her grandmother, who lived in a village nearby. The girl found some money by the road and bought candy with her windfall. But when she told her grandmother of her lucky find, the old lady flew into a rage. The money had been left there by malicious spirits, she declared, and Eleonora, having eaten the candy, had absorbed the devil, too.

The devil, or whatever it was, reportedly made itself known the next day. In Eleonora's presence, small objects began to jump up and fly through the air; stones showered down on the grandmother's cottage, shattering windows. When villagers learned of the strange happenings, Eleonora was sent home to Talpa. There, not three days later, the phenomena resumed with even greater violence.

In despair, Eleanora's parents took her to a priest to be exorcized of evil spirits. But far from being put to rest, the poltergeist proceeded to put on its most impressive show yet. Bystanders, including the stunned priest, watched in amazement as a water-filled jug sailed through the air without spilling a drop and a trunk began to rock. One observer even received a blow across the face from a flying kitchen cutting board. Eyewitnesses agreed that Eleonora could not physically have been responsible for such events.

Perhaps not, but as the poltergeist persisted, Eleanora was ostracized even by her parents. The girl found temporary refuge in a local monastery; when the violent activities continued even there, she was moved to a lunatic asylum. By then the case had been the subject of considerable newspaper coverage, and the publicity had attracted the attention of psychical investigators. Among them was a Viennese countess named Zo Wassilko-Serecki, who said she was convinced that Eleonora was the victim of a poltergeist. In January 1926 the countess removed the girl, by now dirty and frightened, from the asylum and brought her to live in Vienna.

For the first time since she had eaten the "tainted" candy, Eleonora appeared happy—but the phenomena grew even more horrible. Within two months of moving in with the countess, Eleonora seemed to be under physical attack by an unseen tormenter. Scratches and welts appeared on her face, neck, and arms. On one occasion her hands and arms turned purple from as many as twenty-five apparent bites.

In her diary, the countess wrote that she had seen the painful marks emerge "exactly as though [Eleonora] had been bitten by somebody," even as she held the girl's hands.

Harry Price, the noted British psychical researcher, came to Vienna to observe Eleonora and was equally impressed by the vivid bite and scratch marks and by such events as a seat cushion floating through the air. "Some of the telekinetic phenomena witnessed by me were not the work of normal forces," he stated. And that September, Price invited Eleonora and the countess to his National Laboratory of Psychical Research in London, then a leading force in the investigation of the spirit world.

For two weeks, Eleonora was subjected to every manner of psychic test available. Although much of the phenomena—notably the movement and disappearance of various objects—was less impressive than it had been in Vienna, Price managed to record a graphic series of photographs of the bites and scratches that kept appearing on the girl's face and hands.

While Price was convinced of their authenticity, others were dubious. The following year, when Eleonora and her patron were on a visit to Munich, a medical doctor accused the countess of inflicting the wounds on the girl, under the guise of tidying her hair or examining a scratch. The countess angrily denied the charges, noting that even if she had accidentally scratched the girl, she could not have bitten her without being detected.

Whatever the truth, the supposed poltergeist attacks stopped a few months later when Eleonora began to menstruate for the first time. Then, after two years of fear and pain, Eleonora resumed a normal life in Rumania.

Eleonora Zugun's case proved to be a milestone in the study of poltergeists, ushering in a new era of research and prompting a reappraisal of a number of cases, with a greater emphasis on the human focus. Perhaps the most significant new theory advanced during this period was that of the British parapsychologist Hereward Carrington, who was one of the first to discern a connection between human biology and reports of poltergeist activity. Writing in 1930, Carrington theorized that the onset of puberty in adolescents, together with additional, unknown factors, might bring on poltergeist phenomena. "An energy seems to be radiated from the body," the researcher speculated. "It would almost seem as if these energies instead of taking the normal course . . . find this curious means of externalization."

ALAN R. G. OWEN, a British geneticist and mathematician with an abiding interest in the paranormal, later expanded on Carrington's thesis. While pointing out

Irma Schrey with her lopped-off braid

that a number of poltergeist cases apparently center exclusively on adults, Owen acknowledged that many poltergeist agents have ranged in age from ten to twenty years old. "It is by no means clear," he wrote in 1970, "that the poltergeist disturbances coincide at all precisely with pubertal changes. However, there may be something to be said for a modified form of Carrington's theory in which we think not of physiological energy but of emotional tension which can occur both before and after puberty."

Certainly, emotions ran high in the case of Carola and Otto Schrey and their two daughters. The Schreys' troubles had their roots in the upheaval of World War II. Having fled Allied bombardment in western Germany, the Schreys settled down in a small apartment in the Bavarian village of Lauter. During their relocation, they became foster parents to a thirteen-year-old girl named Irma, who had lost her real parents a few months earlier. Later the couple took in yet another orphan, a three-year-old named Edith. The Schreys eventually adopted Edith, a beautiful, well-mannered little girl, but not Irma, who was frequently truculent and withdrawn.

In June of 1946, Edith, whose nickname was Ditti, underwent an alarming personality change. The once placid girl became unruly and even spiteful, and her constant tantrums terrorized the family. When confronted about her behavior, the child would say only, "Ditti did it because I am not allowed."

Though a rebellious child is hardly the stuff of the supernatural, Edith's black moods reportedly marked the beginning of months of horror. Soon the child sank regularly into trancelike states. During these periods, according to Carola Schrey, the household became a virtual sewer. Piles of human excrement and pools of urine materialized in every corner of the small apartment—under the furniture, on the kitchen floor, even in the beds. At first Carola Schrey assumed that one of her daughters was responsible and went so far as to withhold liquids from the girls. But the foul messes persisted.

Things continued to deteriorate for the Schreys. Irma began to fall into the same trancelike lethargy that plagued little Edith. Ink pens, iron files, and razor blades broke into fragments. Religious pictures were spattered with tomatoes; liverwurst flew out of the frying pan and into the cleaning supplies. Indecipherable messages were typed on Carola Schrey's portable typewriter, although the machine was securely locked in its carrying case.

The disorder turned to violence one day as Irma was carrying a box of firewood into the house. As the girl entered the kitchen, in full view of her foster parents, one of her long braids fell to the ground as if lopped off by an invisible blade. Later, the rest of her hair would be viciously hacked away, leaving her scalp bloody and raw. One cut penetrated the skull.

At this point, there appeared on the scene Hans Bender, the parapsychologist who was founder and director of Freiburg University's Institute for Border Areas of Psychology and Mental Hygiene. In previous investigations, Bender had found that his presence had a dampening effect on poltergeist activity, as though the noisy spirits shrank from scrutiny by outsiders.

But whatever entity was troubling the Schreys displayed no such reticence, according to Bender. He was interviewing the Schrey couple during one of his first visits to their apartment when the presumed poltergeist announced itself in no uncertain terms. Moments after Irma came into the room, closing the door behind her, the adults heard loud noises coming from the hallway. Throwing open the door, they found that a heavy rug stored there had been twisted so wildly that it took all three of them several minutes to straighten it out.

Bender came away convinced that the Schreys were the victims of a genuine poltergeist—and he thought he knew the source. Although both Schrey girls had been caught up in the disturbances, Irma, the adolescent, seemed the likelier focus. That she, unlike Edith, had not been officially adopted by the Schreys might have been a source of resentment—or "emotional tension," as Alan Owen would call it. And that, in turn, reasoned Bender, may have triggered the poltergeist's unwelcome visit.

A SIMILAR NIGHTMARE reportedly was experienced by the Plach family, only a few miles away in the mountain village of Vachendorf. On March 16, 1947, Maria and Franz Plach were playing cards in their living room with their fourteen-year-old adopted daughter, Mitzi. As the game went on, all the players found that they were holding fewer and fewer cards. When some of the missing cards reappeared under the table, the Plachs naturally assumed that someone had dropped them there and dismissed the incident. But when they dealt a new hand, the cards vanished once again. And this time, they did not resurface. By the end of the evening there were just nineteen cards remaining from the fifty-two-card deck.

Forced to abandon their game, the Plachs

Franz Plach gazes at a group of whirling dinner rolls in this photographic reconstruction

© Leif Geiges, courtesy Verena Geiges, Germany

140

*Laundry is flung over Maria Plach's head in photographer
Leif Geiges's re-creation of the event*

© Leif Geiges, courtesy Verena Geiges, Germany

shrugged and went to bed—only to confront a greater mystery. Because the Plachs' home was small, Mitzi slept in the same room with her parents. That night, however, no one slept. No sooner had the lights been turned off than the Plachs found themselves pelted by a hailstorm of hammers, knives, coal, water, stones, and dirt. Shielding his face with his hands, Franz Plach leaped out of bed to turn on the light, but the bulbs had somehow been loosened in their sockets. When the family attempted to flee from the bedroom, they discovered the door was locked. Later, after neighbors had broken down the door and released the terrified family, the missing key was spotted hanging from a clock in another room.

Unfortunately for the Plachs, the night of the flying objects was only a prelude to days of continuing aerial mischief. Laundry left hanging in the attic would float and cavort about the house. Dishes would come sailing out of a cupboard and crash against the opposite wall, falling unbroken to the floor. A bowl of soup skated along the table and emptied its contents into Franz Plach's lap. Rolls that Mitzi had brought home flew about the kitchen like "so many swallows," Maria Plach wrote in her diary, while the butter moved incautiously toward the oven and melted.

The Plachs fought back, but to little avail. When Maria gathered up all the loose objects in the house, put them in a box, and locked the box in a closet, the items simply flew out again, apparently penetrating both boxes and locked door. "It was no use," Maria wrote, "I grabbed everything, put it into the box and sat on it, but it all came out again."

Once again Hans Bender arrived on the scene, with a photographer, Leif Geiges, in hopes of capturing the strange manifestations on film. One of the more baffling and violent episodes took place in the presence of the intruding investigator.

A bowl of the Plachs' soup inexplicably topples over

As Franz Plach worked absorbedly on a wood carving, a heavy wooden shoe flew across the room and struck him in the head with a resounding smack. Bender's photographer caught the somewhat rueful expression on the victim's face seconds after the blow. When Plach recovered, he pointed out that the shoe had been kept in a glassed-in cabinet that was still intact. The bizarre incident, according to the researcher, was "a clear case of telekinesis and a case of matter penetrating matter."

Just as Bender had zeroed in on the sullen Irma Schrey, this time his attention was drawn to teenaged Mitzi Plach. When Bender learned that the poltergeist activity had ceased while Mitzi made a brief trip away from home, his suspicions were confirmed. Once again, a girl in the early stages of puberty appeared to be the focus of a poltergeist visitation. Although the sources of emotional tension were not quite as obvious in the Plach family, the parallels to the Schrey case seemed to be clear. Happily the Plachs' apparent haunting, like the Schreys', soon stopped as abruptly as it had begun.

For the troubled human agents who are its focus, Alan Owen has suggested, the poltergeist is like a fever that runs its course. "We might guess that poltergeistery starts but eventually terminates," the researcher wrote, "because it is not a disease but a cure."

5

UFOs AND ALIENS

Missed Time: The Alien Abduction

Raymond E. Fowler, The Allagash Abductions, Wildflower Press, OR, 1993

Chuck Rak's sketch of the "tunnel of light" up which he and his three companions were drawn in 1976

WHEN HE finally talked to a doctor about his problem in 1988, Jim Weiner was at the end of his rope. For years the Boston man's sleep had been plagued by strange and terrifying dreams about creatures not of this world. Worse yet, he was often jerked out of slumber by a feeling that he was in the throes of a struggle against an unearthly force he could not see.

Unable to bear the strain any longer, Weiner told his troubles to a physician who had been treating him for epilepsy stemming from an accident ten years earlier. Weiner mentioned that the scenes in his nightmares reminded him of things he had read in a book about a man who claimed to have been abducted by a UFO. The doctor suggested that he attend a conference on UFOs soon to be held in a Boston suburb. Weiner took the advice, and at the conference he introduced himself to Raymond Fowler, a UFO investigator. As they talked, Weiner began to tell Fowler about an inci-

HAVE YOU BEEN ABDUCTED?
The Signs to Look For

Abduction investigators say these telltale symptoms are common to people who purportedly have been kidnapped by aliens. But the same symptoms can indicate earthly problems requiring medical attention. ◆ MISSING TIME. A memory gap, say believers, could mean a person has been abducted and was compelled by alien captors to forget the experience. ◆ CONFUSED MEMORY. Alleged victims often struggle to make sense of fragmentary recollections of mysterious lights, odd beings, invasive medical procedures, and other related phenomena. ◆ IRRATIONAL TERROR. A panicky fear is said to overcome abductees whenever they approach a particular location, see a helicopter hovering overhead, or find themselves in other situations with similarities to the repressed trauma. And they may react with anxiety to movies, magazine articles, and books that deal with UFOs and alien encounters. ◆ NIGHTTIME DISORDERS. Supposed abductees may have trouble falling asleep and then doze only lightly. Many dream of spaceships or bizarre creatures with oversize eyes, and some inexplicably wake up at the same moment night after night. In the morning, they feel disoriented and have short bouts of dizziness, numbness, tingling, and paralysis. ◆ BLEEDING. Upon waking, some find blood on their pillows—an aftereffect, they believe, of the surgical implantation or removal of alien tracking devices in the nose or ears. ◆ PHYSICAL DAMAGE. Abductees also discover puzzling marks on their bodies—pinpricks, puncture wounds, scrapes, straight-line scars, small craterlike depressions, and bruises that they say are evidence of the physical examinations they endured.

dent from his past that riveted the investigator's attention.

In August 1976 Jim Weiner, his twin brother Jack, and their friends Chuck Rak and Charlie Foltz had taken a camping and canoe trip in northern Maine. The outing began as a fun-filled adventure, including a stirring flight in a pontoon plane to the deep pine woods of the remote Allagash River country. But there, Jim related, something happened that cast a pall over the rest of the trip.

The men, he said, were out in their canoe on the night of August 26 when Chuck, in the rear position, suddenly got the feeling that he was being watched. He looked back over his shoulder and saw a large ball of bright light hovering noiselessly several hundred feet above the water. "That's a hell of a case of swamp gas," he exclaimed.

The other three turned to look; all were transfixed by the strange sight. They ceased paddling, and the canoe slowed to a stop. The sphere was as big as a two-story house, Jim Weiner later reckoned, and it seemed to have a liquid surface over which changing colors of light—red, green, and yellow—pulsated and swirled as it floated silently above the trees about two or three hundred yards away.

Charlie Foltz, who had been in the navy, began signaling to the object with a powerful flashlight the group had brought along, flashing the Morse code for SOS.

The ball of light instantly began moving toward them, and suddenly what had been a mysterious sight to wonder at became a terrifying apparition. Three of the four started paddling desperately toward shore, the two in the middle, who had no paddles, slashing at the water with their bare hands. Chuck Rak alone remained curious and unconcerned, even when a cone-shaped beam of light shot out of the bottom of the UFO and traveled across the water toward them. "Swamp gas doesn't have beams!" yelled Charlie.

As the canoe neared shore, Jack Weiner thought, "This is it! We'll never get away." Then abruptly, Chuck Rak was sitting serenely in the beached canoe and the others were standing on the shore, quietly watching as the glowing sphere seemed to curl in on itself and accelerate out of sight at dazzling speed. The men felt dazed; they were unable to speak for a few minutes. As the feeling wore off, Chuck got out of the canoe, and the group slowly went back to their campsite.

What the men saw there shocked them, even in their befuddled state. Before going out in the canoe, they had placed several huge logs on their campfire—enough, they knew, to burn bright for two to three hours and help them find their way back in the inky night. Now, after they had been gone for what seemed no more than fifteen to twenty minutes, only embers and ashes remained of the fire. None of the men had checked his watch when the UFO appeared, but the evidence of the fire was unmistakable—and deeply disturbing. Someone or something that night had stolen two or three hours out of their lives.

Raymond E. Fowler, The Allagash Abductions, Wildflower Press, OR, 1993

Fourteen years after their alleged abduction by aliens on Maine's Allagash River, (from left) Jack Weiner, Jim Weiner, Chuck Rak, and Charlie Foltz are photographed together in September 1990

For the rest of the trip, the men just went through the motions, scarcely remembering anything they did. And in the years to follow, the mystery of their missing time would remain unsolved. But not forgotten. After a number of years all four began to have the kinds of frightening dreams Jim Weiner told his doctor about, and all felt that their troubled sleep had something to do with that night in Maine.

Raymond Fowler, struck by Jim's mention of the missing time, soon got in touch with the other three men and by January 1989 had arranged for all four to undergo hypnotic regression, a technique by which a subject is encouraged, under hypnosis, to relive traumatic past experiences that are otherwise inaccessible to the conscious mind.

The story that the Allagash campers told while hypnotized was an extraordinary one. The men revealed that their memory of paddling toward shore in a state of extreme agitation, then suddenly standing calmly on the shore, had glossed over a long and terrifying ordeal. The beam of light they had tried to escape had actually caught them within its circle and drawn them up into the spacecraft. There they were confronted with alien creatures, who communicated instructions to them telepathically. As Jack Weiner related in halting speech while under hypnosis, "They're saying things . . . with their eyes . . . in my head. They're saying, 'Don't be afraid. . . . We won't harm you. . . . Do what we say.'"

All four were made to undress, lie on a table, and undergo a painful and frightening physical examination. Then, the next thing any of them knew, they were back on the Allagash—Chuck in the canoe, the others on shore—and the UFO was departing the scene.

If the four men had told such a story twenty-five years earlier, it would probably not have been taken seriously. Even UFO enthusiasts would most likely have dismissed it as a fantastic dream. But by 1989, what the Allagash four revealed under hypnosis struck several familiar chords. In particular, the phenomenon of missing time—an inexplicable gap in a person's life, typically of an hour or two, sometimes longer—had become well established as a common element in similar reports from all parts of the United States, as well as Europe, Asia, Australia, and Latin America. The theme linking the stories was the narrators' conviction, sometimes after hypnotic recall, that they had been abducted by aliens.

THERE WAS nothing new about the idea of alien contact in itself. Ever since the postwar UFO wave was touched off by the first reports of flying saucers in 1947, there had been speculation about the creatures that might be riding inside the supposed spaceships, and in the decade that followed, several individuals would claim to have been contacted by these extraterrestrial voyagers.

The best known of the "contactees," as the 1950s observers were later named, was George Adamski, a Polish-born odd-job man from California who wrote books describing his encounters with the visitors. The beings he claims to have seen were generally tall, blond, and stately. They had come to Earth from their home on Venus, he said, to deliver a warning about the dangers of nuclear weapons testing. Adamski asserted that the aliens took him on flying-saucer rides to the far side of the Moon, where he saw great cities—a statement that considerably deflated his already tenuous credibility, particularly when, in 1959, Soviet satellite photographs showed the far side to be the barren wasteland astronomers had always assumed it was.

The derision rubbed off on other contactees of the time, who, like Adamski, tended to encounter handsome, human-looking beings prone to rambling philosophical discourses. Their loquacious concern for the Earth's well-being won these first-generation aliens the appellation "Space Brothers" among early observers of the UFO phenomenon. For some years, the scant credence accorded Space Brothers stories effectively discouraged serious investigation of any purported contacts with aliens, even by flying-saucer enthusiasts. Attention focused instead on attempts—most notably by the U.S. Air Force's Project Blue Book—to verify any of the continuing stream of reported UFO sightings, and on the hardware and technology of the new field of investigation called ufology.

What changed the situation was the now-famous story of Barney and Betty Hill. The 1966 publication of *The Interrupted Journey,* a book recounting the New Hampshire couple's alleged abduction by aliens five years earlier, and later the broadcast of the widely seen television movie based on the book, brought to public notice a fascinating sequence of events unlike anything to be found at that time in the growing literature of extraterrestrial contact. The Hills' account of being snatched from their car by a UFO, subjected to terrifying physical examinations, and returned to the car with no conscious memory of the ordeal had most of the characteristics that investigators would later class as typical of abduction stories. Once the Hills' saga hit the mass media, the era of the alien abduction experience—or more properly, of abduction reporting—was under way.

Betty Hill, age forty-one, and her thirty-nine-year-old husband, Barney, were returning to their Portsmouth, New Hampshire, home from a vacation in Canada on the night of September 19, 1961. While their car was traveling along U.S. Route 3, the couple noticed a bright, starlike object moving through the southwestern sky. Barney Hill stopped the car several times so his wife could gaze at the object through 7 x 50 binoculars. He thought it was a small airplane until it changed course and curved toward them. They were a little more than two miles from North Woodstock when the UFO slid around in front of the car and hovered to the right of the highway "eight or ten stories" (as the husband estimated) above the ground.

Barney Hill took the binoculars from his wife and stepped out onto the deserted highway for a closer look. The saucer-shaped UFO silently shifted to the left and approached the stopped car head on. Then Barney got an enormous shock: Through the binoculars he could make out lit portholes along the side of the craft, and behind the portholes he could see the illuminated interior where from five to eleven human-like figures were busily working. To Hill, the humanoids appeared to be wearing some kind of shiny black uniforms with billed caps. Their movements reminded him of German soldiers executing a military drill. From inside the car, Betty could hear her husband exclaiming, "I don't believe it! I don't believe it! This is ridiculous!"

The Hills claimed that the craft came so close to them that it filled the field of view of the binoculars. Barney dashed back to the waiting car in a state of hysteria, as his wife remembered, and they took off down the highway. As they drove, a series of inexplicable beeps seemed to come from the trunk, sounds that caused the car to vibrate. The couple made it home without further incident, but those few minutes of fright and excitement were to haunt them for years.

Betty and Barney Hill holding a copy of The Interrupted Journey, *an account of their alleged abduction by aliens in New Hampshire in 1961*

Betty began to dream nightly of a terrifying UFO experience. Barney suffered from apprehension, insomnia, and a worsening of his duodenal ulcer. In reliving the incident in his own mind, Hill was disturbed when he realized that he was unable to account for more than two hours between the time they first encountered the UFO and the time they reached home. Where had the seemingly missing time gone? What had happened?

As their anxieties grew, the couple decided to get medical help. A local doctor recommended that they consult a prominent Boston psychiatrist, Dr. Benjamin Simon, to see if hypnotic regression could unravel the mystery surrounding the night of September 19 and allow them to pick up their lives again. The psychiatric treatments began in December 1963, more than two years after the alleged UFO encounter. It was while under deep hypnosis that Barney and Betty Hill narrated a tale much stranger than the one apparently lodged in their conscious minds. Dr. Simon kept his tape recorder going while Barney described his abduction by alien captors.

Hill recounted being led up a ramp to the alien craft and ushered into an examination room. "I could feel them examining me with their hands. . . . They looked at my back, and I could feel them touching my skin . . . , as if they were counting my spinal column . . . and then I was turned over, and again I was looked at. My mouth was opened, and I could feel two fingers pulling it back. Then I heard as if some more men came in, and I could feel them rustling around on the left side of the table I was lying on. Something scratched very lightly, like a stick against my left arm. And then these men left.

"Then my shoes were put back on, and I stepped down. I think I felt very good because I knew it was over. . . . I went down [the ramp] and opened my eyes and kept walking. I saw my car . . . and Betty was coming down the road, and she came around and opened the door."

Betty told a similar story of physical examination. It seemed to her that the aliens were taking samples for later analysis. "I go into this room," she began, "and some of the men come in the room with this man who speaks English. They stay a minute—I don't know who they are; I guess maybe they're the crew . . . and another man comes in. I haven't seen him before. I think he's a doctor. They bring the machine over . . . it's something like a microscope, only a microscope with a big lens. I had an idea they were taking a picture of my skin. Then they took something like a letter opener—only it wasn't—and they scratched my arm here . . . there was something like a piece of cellophane or plastic, or something like that, they scraped, and they put this that came off on this plastic."

Betty said she asked the apparent leader where his ship had come from, and he showed her the location on a star map. Then she was escorted back down the ramp so she could return to the car.

The psychiatric examination of Betty and Barney Hill lasted six months; at the end of that time, Dr. Simon delivered his professional opinion: "The charisma of hypnosis has tended to foster the belief that hypnosis is the magical and royal road to TRUTH. In one sense, this is so, but it must be understood that hypnosis is a pathway to the truth as it is felt and understood by the patient. The truth is what he believes to be the truth, and this may or may not be consonant with the ultimate nonpersonal truth." Simon concluded that the abduction part of the Hills' story was a fantasy, absorbed by Barney from Betty's retelling of her dreams following the encounter along the lonely New Hampshire road.

Barney Hill recovered his health but died at the age of forty-six from natural causes. Years afterward, Betty Hill claimed to see UFOs again, sometimes as many as fifty to one hundred a night in what she called "a special area" of New Hampshire. But she never again claimed to be the target of kidnappers from other planets.

The elements in the Hill story, and in a similar tale told by a young Brazilian by the name of Antonio Villas Boas, who claimed to have been abducted in 1957, soon started to show up in a growing number of other accounts reaching UFO investigators and, sometimes, the media. A number of the stories detailed events that purportedly had happened well before the Hills's and Villas Boas's experiences but that had been kept secret by the abductees. Only after observing the publicity surrounding the Hills' ordeal did the individuals involved feel confident enough to admit publicly their own experiences. Some of the victims, like Villas Boas, had conscious recall of what had happened to them; others, like the Hills and the Allagash four, were aware only of a sense of missing time until much later, when their traumatic memories of abduction were retrieved by hypnosis.

VILLAS BOAS claimed to have been plowing a field by the lights of his tractor one night in 1957, when an egg-shaped UFO landed about fifteen yards away from him. The tractor's engine failed, and although Villas Boas attempted to run away, four humanoids managed to seize him and drag him struggling into their spacecraft. The creatures spoke to each other with odd barking noises while they took a blood sample and removed the young man's clothes. Villas Boas, who was already disoriented by these invasive procedures, was further astonished when the humanoids departed and another creature, who was described as a small, naked, and beautifully blond "woman" entered the room.

After some encouragement by the speechless alien, the student reported, he felt compelled to have sex with her; following this she pointed to her belly and then to the sky, leading Villas Boas to believe that she would bear his child. The humanoids then allowed him to dress, gave him a tour of the craft, and finally deposited him back in his fields as dawn was approaching.

Villas Boas felt increasingly nauseous over the next few days, and he discovered unusual wounds on his body. The doctor who examined him a few months later recorded a number of strange scars as well as symptoms resembling those typical of radiation poisoning. This medical evidence, together with the young man's reputation for honesty, has led some researchers to study the case seriously, despite the fact that its details sound incredible.

A triple abduction in 1976 threw the limelight on three Liberty, Kentucky, women, whose drive home late one night was interrupted in a terrifying fashion. Louise Smith and Elaine Thomas had taken their friend Mona Stafford out to dinner in nearby Lancaster to celebrate her thirty-sixth birthday. Near the town of Stanford, they said, they saw a reddish, disk-shaped UFO with a white, glowing dome. The craft followed their car, illuminating it with a blue light. Louise Smith, who was driving, lost control of the vehicle, which accelerated to eighty-five miles per hour, and the women felt burning sensations in their eyes. They experienced hallucinations of being dragged backward in the car along a bumpy road, and then they saw a wide, brilliantly lit highway that was unfamiliar to them, although they knew the area well. The women eventually reentered normal reality at a point eight miles from the original encounter site and drove home without further incident, but with a mysterious time gap of more than an hour.

The women all subsequently suffered severe anxiety symptoms and drastic

Louise Smith, Elaine Thomas, and Mona Stafford

weight loss. Persuaded to undergo hypnotic regression, they each related a similar story of abduction by four-foot-tall aliens, followed by painful physical examinations. In the weeks and months after the event, all of them claimed to be experiencing various psychic phenomena, which they associated with the abduction. After the incident, Elaine Thomas suffered ill health and eventually died three years later at the age of fifty-two. Oddly enough, of the three victims she alone had claimed to have experienced beneficial personality changes, asserting that the alien encounter had somehow made her more self-confident and outgoing.

THE PERIOD from the mid-1970s to the early 1980s proved to be banner years for abduction reports. Twenty-five cases emerged in 1975 alone. In 1979, twenty-seven cases came to light, and more than forty were logged in each of the two following years. To deal with the growing number of cases that needed investigating, several new volunteer ufologists' organizations came into being. The J. Allen Hynek Center for UFO Studies (CUFOS), the Fund for UFO Research (FUFOR), and the Mutual UFO Network (MUFON) joined the ranks of such venerable groups as the Aerial Phenomena Research Organization (APRO) and the National Investigations Committee on Aerial Phenomena (NICAP), which were both founded during the 1950s.

In 1987 an abduction story shot to the top of the best-seller lists. In *Communion,* popular horror-story writer Whitley Strieber recounted experiences that he said had happened to him in his isolated cabin in upstate New York. According to the book, he was abducted from his bed by an alien while his wife lay sleeping at his side. Taken aboard a craft, he encountered other aliens of differing shapes and sizes; one, whom he took to be female, inserted a needlelike probe into his brain. His account of the hor-

Members of a support group for people who believe they have been abducted meet with
ufologists at the home of UFO investigator Budd Hopkins (third from left)

rific experience, recalled with the aid of hypnotic regression, would make *Communion*
an even bigger seller than his earlier, fictional works, *The Wolfen* and *The Hunger*.

By the time of the book's publication, so many Americans were claiming to
have experienced abduction that the event was approaching the level of a psycho-
social phenomenon. Support groups, in which people who claim to have been
abducted shared therapeutic discussions about their problems, sprang up in several
parts of the country. There was even an annual conference for abductees, first convened in 1980 at the University of Wyoming by a longtime UFO consultant to
APRO. In 1991, 137 people attended the conference.

To impose some order on the welter of extraterrestrial incidents being reported,
one noted researcher, J. Allen Hynek, had developed in the early 1970s a hierarchy
of types of contacts. His system began with three low-ranking categories of distant
UFO sightings—the lowest being lights in the night sky, followed by disks seen in
daylight and sightings backed by radar readings. Of greater moment were his three
groupings of more direct contacts, which he named close encounters.

A close encounter of the first kind was a sighting of a UFO from no farther away
than 500 feet—but without any interaction between the UFO and the observer or
the environment. Discernible physical effects attributable to UFOs, such as patterns
of crushed or burned vegetation in cultivated fields, or shutdowns of electrical systems, were close encounters of the second kind. A close encounter of the third kind,
in this typology, was one in which alien beings were seen in or near a craft.

Hynek, founder of CUFOS, went no further with his ranking system. But the
growing numbers of abduction claims from the mid-1970s onward made it clear that
the close encounters of the third kind category—abbreviated CEIII by ufologists—

The Tower of London, pictured here, is reputed to be haunted by the ghosts of victims who were confined or murdered within its walls

Rare lenticular clouds such as these, seen here drifting over São Paulo, Brazil, are often mistaken for UFOs

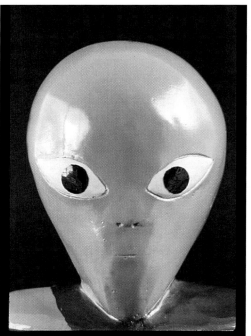

MUFON (Mutual UFO Network) investigator Fred Youngren constructed this representation of an alien head based on Betty Andreasson's descriptions of her unearthly visitors

In this eighteenth-century T. H. Matteson painting, Examination of a Witch, *a woman is stripped and searched for identifying marks*

Chaos ensues in the Salem courts in The Trial of George Jacobs, *an eighteenth-century painting by T. H. Matteson. Jacobs' indicters included his own granddaughter, who later recanted and confessed she had been blackmailed by the other girls into testifying.*

Sorcerers perform a ritual to raise up the dead in The Magic Mirror,
an eighteenth-century French print

Petrus Gonsalvus, a sixteenth-century "wolfman," actually suffered from the rare congenital condition hypertrichosis, which is marked by a thick coating of fine body hair. After marrying an attractive Parisienne, he passed the disease on to their two children (above).

Historians have recently concluded it is unlikely that the "Blood Countess" Elizabeth Báthory—here in a seventeenth-century portrait by an unknown master—actually bathed in the blood of her victims to preserve her youthful good looks

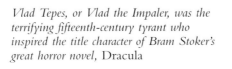

Vlad Tepes, or Vlad the Impaler, was the terrifying fifteenth-century tyrant who inspired the title character of Bram Stoker's great horror novel, Dracula

Sandra Marnsi took this photograph of the creature known as "Champ" from the shores of Lake Champlain in July of 1977. Since Marnsi's negative was lost, skeptics have not ruled out a hoax, although the creature has been sighted over two hundred times and supposedly captured on film.

Five centuries of records at Urquhart Castle, on the banks of Loch Ness, contain no mention of any sightings of the lake's legendary monster

James Sugar/Black Star

Stonehenge looms over Salisbury Plain in southwestern England

Alongside an ice ax for scale, this snowy Himalayan track was allegedly left by a Yeti. Although scientists claimed melting snow had distorted and magnified the print, they were unable to cite any known animal that could have left such tracks.

Eric Shipton, courtesy Royal Geographical Society Picture Collection failed to accommodate an increasingly important phenomenon. A CEIV has since been added: abduction of humans by aliens.

Although the bulk of abduction reports still came from the United States, similar stories were also being uncovered in other countries where organized groups of UFO observers were active, notably in Argentina, Brazil, the United Kingdom, and Australia. One account even told of a woman parachutist who vanished during free fall, only to reappear three days later claiming to have been intercepted by a flying saucer in midair.

There were by the late 1980s enough self-proclaimed abductees for investigators to attempt demographic analyses of their backgrounds and personalities. The victims were shown to have come from all walks of life, although their overall educational level was slightly higher than the general average. About two-thirds were male, with a slight preponderance of individuals involved in work that took them out-of-doors on their own at night—police officers, farmers, truckers, traveling salespeople. Abduction was for the most part a solo experience.

The aliens' only obvious predilection seemed to be for young adults. A disproportionate number of victims were in their twenties and thirties; a seventy-seven-year-old Englishman claimed to have been abducted in August 1983 but then released after only a cursory examination by his captors, apparently because he did not fill the bill.

There was much less uniformity when it came to reporting what the aliens themselves looked like. Abductees described almost every conceivable kind of creature, from giants to dwarfs, from the humanoid to the bizarre. The majority of the reports, however, were of humanoids, somewhat shorter than the average Earthling, with large heads, large eyes, and spindly frames. Typical were the beings who appeared to Betty Andreasson, a New England mother of seven whose reported series of abductions, stretching over almost four decades, furnished the material for three separate books.

Like many abductees, Betty Andreasson claimed to have only a fragmentary memory of her experience until the whole story emerged under hypnosis, many years later. According to this subsequent recollection, during the winter of 1967 Andreasson, her parents, and her seven children were going through trying times in their home in South Ashburnham, Massachusetts, since her husband had been badly hurt in an automobile accident the previous month.

On January 25, the warm air of an early thaw wrapped the little town in fog. That night, the lights in the Andreasson house flickered and went out. At the same time, a pink glow pulsed into the house through a kitchen window. Betty's father, looking into the backyard, witnessed something amazing. According to his signed statement: "These creature that I saw through the window of Betty's house were just like Halloween freaks. I thought they had put on a funny kind of headdress imitating a moon man . . . the one in front looked at me and I felt kind of queer. That's all I know."

At that point, Andreasson said later, her entire family fell into a sort of suspended animation. But she remained awake to see small alien beings enter her house, passing right through a closed door. She described the intruding creatures as short and gray skinned, with huge, slanted, catlike eyes. Their hands each had only three fingers, and their bodies were clothed in shiny, form-fitting uniforms.

The aliens communicated with the woman telepathically. They asked her, she said, to follow them so she could help the world. When she reluctantly agreed, feeling as though she was being hypnotized, the creatures led her to their oval craft in her backyard.

Like Betty and Barney Hill, Betty Andreasson reported being subjected to an unpleasant medical examination on board the craft. At one point the aliens inserted needle-like wires into her nose and navel, relieving some of the ensuing pain merely by placing

Betty Andreasson

their hands on her forehead. When they were finished with the exam, she said, her captors led her through a long black tunnel and into a room where she was encased in a glassy canopy. A gray fluid flowed into the canopy, covering Andreasson and apparently protecting her while she and the aliens traveled to another world.

When they arrived, more tunnels led the woman and two aliens from the vehicle into an eerie, lifeless landscape. Shimmering red light surrounded them as they glided along a floating track between square buildings. Andreasson was horrified to see headless creatures that resembled lemurs swarming over some of the structures—but she and her captors passed safely among them.

After moving through a circular membrane, the woman found herself amid new scenery: The atmosphere was now green, and the travelers were flanked on either side by misty bodies of water. Ahead of the party appeared a pyramid and an array of airborne crystals, which were reflecting a brilliant light. The light source lay at the end of the path, but blocking their view of it was an even more astonishing sight. A huge bird that looked like an eagle but was twice as tall as a human loomed in front of her, radiating an intense heat. Even as the woman watched, half blinded by the light, the bird vanished. In its place was a small fire, dying down to ashes; from the ashes crawled a thick gray worm.

A loud voice to her right called Andreasson's name. It told her that she had been chosen, although her mission was not to be revealed to her then. When the woman proclaimed her faith in God, the voice told her that was the reason why she was chosen. No more information was given to her, and the woman's alien companions brought her back through the green and red realms to the room with the glass canopies. The apparent leader of the creatures, whose name seemed to be Quazgaa, told her that he would impart to her certain formulas that could help humanity, but only when people learned to look with the spirit.

The return voyage, if such it was, resembled the first trip, and Andreasson and her captors soon emerged into her fog-shrouded backyard. It was still nighttime, and Andreasson's family was still frozen in position inside her house. The aliens led them all to their beds and departed. In the morning, the woman said later, she remembered little of the experience. It was not until eight years afterward, when she saw an article about J. Allen Hynek's studies of unidentified flying objects, that she wrote to investigators.

Betty Andreasson could provide no corroborating evidence for her story other than the fleeting impressions of her family. She was unable to explain her phoenix-like vision or relate the message that had supposedly been implanted in her memory. Voice-stress tests and psychiatric examinations confirmed both her sanity and her sincerity, however, and those looking into her case could conclude only that she appeared to be a reliable person who believed in the truth of her experience.

Similar descriptions of aliens regularly cropped up in other reports. There was less variety in descriptions of the crafts in which the aliens traveled. As might have been expected, they were usually saucer shaped, although reports of oval or oblong ships were also common. Inside, the principal chamber was usually round domed. For psychologically minded skeptics, the absence of corners in the descriptions suggested that the victims were subconsciously recalling images of the womb.

Given the sheer number of claimed abductions, more than 300 by 1985, wide variety in the stories might have been expected, but in fact the victims' reports tended to follow a regular pattern. Although they often differed a great deal in details, there was a sequence of abduction, examination in a brightly lit room, and return to the familiar world that appeared again and again.

When a folklorist, Thomas E. Bullard, analyzed the 300-plus abduction reports, he was able to distinguish eight typical stages in the process. The first, of course, was *capture*. Next came *examination;* followed by *conference,* a phase in which the aliens held a telephatic conversation with the abductee; a *tour* of the spacecraft; an *otherworldly journey,* in which the abductee was sometimes transported over great distances; then the rarest event of the sequence, a religious experience labeled by Bullard a *theophany.* A *return* to the normal world marked the conclusion of the abduction itself. Bullard's last stage was the often damaging *aftermath,* in which the victims continued to be troubled, sometimes for long periods following the abduction experience. Although only one of Bullard's cases included all eight stages, virtually all featured several of them, usually in the same order of occurrence.

In the first stage, capture, light played a crucial part. The abductee was often first alerted to the presence of something abnormal by the sight of a strange illumination; in other cases a beam of light was instrumental in drawing the captive up into the alien craft. Many victims described a sensation of floating as they moved toward the UFO, although the feeling may have been deceptive; Barney Hill thought he had floated into the spacecraft, but his wife, who was watching, reported that he was actually walking, half-supported by his captors. One of the oddest features of the capture was that very few abductees seemed to retain any recollection—even under hypnosis—of the moment of entry into the craft, a circumstance that Bullard characterized as "doorway amnesia."

In the domed interior of the vessel, the central drama of the abduction experience was played out. Here, in 133 of Bullard's cases, the abductees underwent an often painful physical examination. This episode loomed so large in so many accounts, and was so consistently the first thing the victims were subjected to upon entering the spacecraft, that those who accept the reality of the abductees' claims have little doubt that the examination is the primary purpose of the entire abduction phenomenon. The aliens' long-term goals, they believe, are somehow inextricably connected with the detailed investigation of human biology.

Often the examination fell into separate parts. Initially the victim, laid full length upon a table, might be scanned by a device similar to an x-ray camera. One abductee, Sara Shaw, tried to describe the one she saw: "It's like the other half of the table. But, you know, upside down, sandwichlike. It's not scorching me or coming anywhere near me. It's just hanging over me."

After the scan, the aliens generally examined the abductee directly, sometimes using instruments to take samples of skin and other tissue, as in the Hill case, or even gouging out tiny scoops of flesh, leaving lasting indentations in the skin of their victims. New York artist and ufologist Budd Hopkins particularly noted this phenomenon, stating that the operation could leave scars of two different types: round, shallow scoops or long, thin, scalpel-like cuts.

The examination was often a terrifying ordeal. The victim usually felt a devastating sense of loss of control; he or she was completely at the mercy of the aliens, whose interest in the proceedings generally appeared to be as clinical and objective as that of human scientists working on laboratory animals—and often as devoid of warmth or consideration. A twenty-seven-year-old woman who relived an abduction experience under hypnotic regression said: "I was so scared. I knew they were so strong. I think I gave up. . . . I just laid there. . . . It was a terrible thing."

In the Allagash case, where four victims at once were held in the spacecraft, the aliens used some covert form of behavior control to maintain order. Jim Weiner testified that while his twin brother Jack was being examined, the other two members of the party sat on a bench with a "dumb, expressionless look" on their faces, while he himself could only look straight ahead. Since the others independently reported under hypnosis the same vacant look on Jim's face, the investigators concluded that they all had been put in a state of suspended animation.

After the rigors of the examination, Bullard noted, the atmosphere often lightened as the phase he described as the conference got under way. "The beings relax, slow down and warm to their captive," he wrote, "often taking him out of the exam-

Betty Andreasson's depiction of the alien beings that allegedly visited her in 1967 shows beings vanishing and reappearing, each time "leaving a vapory image behind"

ination room with its unhappy memories to another part of the ship. This change to a friendlier, more considerate atmosphere is striking, since the beings suddenly begin to treat their captive like a human being and even a guest, instead of like a guinea pig."

BETTY ANDREASSON's abductors told her that they were "the watchers," caretakers of nature and natural forms. "They love mankind," she asserted. "They love the planet Earth and they have been caring for it and Man since Man's beginning. They watch the spirit in all things. . . . Man is destroying much of nature. They are curious about the emotions of mankind."

According to other abductees, their captors evinced a similar curiosity about earthly matters but seemed to be motivated more by self-interest. A fifty-three-year-old California businessman reported that his aliens were interested in humans because their own society, though technologically highly advanced, had lost qualities they still saw among humans.

In some reports, the abductors offered more specific information, including hints as to their place of origin. Betty Hill was allowed to see a star map containing the home planet of her captors, but—as the being who showed it to her pointed out—the knowledge was of little use to her as she had no way of orienting it to Earth.

Betty Andreasson under hypnosis during an interview with a MUFON investigator

Nonetheless she was subsequently able, under hypnosis, to sketch an approximation of what she saw.

An Ohio schoolteacher named Marjorie Fish was later to spend five years attempting to correlate the sketch with known star locations, eventually suggesting that the aliens' home planet might have been located in the neighborhood of Zeta 2 Reticuli, one half of a twin-star system in a small constellation visible in the Southern Hemisphere, thirty-six light-years from Earth. Other astronomers were less convinced. Astrophysicist Carl Sagan subsequently used a computer to plot Fish's star positions and concluded that they bore little similarity to those in Hill's drawing.

After the conference stage, sixteen of the abductees covered in Bullard's study were given a tour of the craft. Accounts of such tours were normally less informative than investigators hoped, because the witnesses lacked the knowledge or even the words to explain what exactly they were seeing. The craft they described resembled for the most part standard movie images of spaceships, with engine rooms, control rooms featuring computers and star charts, and, sometimes, living quarters. Few included details as striking as the vivarium that Betty Andreasson reported having seen during one of her abductions. It seemed as she entered it to be a separate world of woods and water, where she saw a pond with fish swimming in it. Only when a door opened and light flooded in did it become apparent that this pastoral environment had somehow been created on board the spacecraft.

An even more spectacular appeal to the imagination was provided by Bullard's fifth stage, the otherworldly journey, a feature he found in fifty-four of the reports that he categorized. He used the term to describe all voyages, some of them merely terrestrial, made by abductees aboard their captors' craft. Among reported destinations were New York City, the pyramids of Egypt, a U.S. Navy destroyer, and a supposed UFO landing field at the North Pole.

The most interesting reports of otherworldly journeys, however, featured travel to entirely unearthly realms. Some witnesses described bare, lifeless scenes, with stunted trees rising against empty skylines. Other abductees saw lush landscapes rich in alien plant life. There were descriptions of futuristic cities with suspended roadways, and of factories manufacturing UFOs or crystals, apparently used for the production of energy.

Probably no accounts were more extraordinary than the descriptions Betty Andreasson gave of her travels with aliens. When hypnotized in 1977 and 1980, she recalled that she had been abducted from her home twice: in 1950, when she was thirteen, and again in 1967. During one hypnotic regression devoted to Andreasson's 1950 abduction, her recollections provided a memorable example of the mystical experience that Bullard called a theophany, the sixth of the stages he listed, although it appeared in no more than six of the 300-plus cases he logged. On this occasion Andreasson spoke of passing through a subsurface tunnel to a glass wall with a great door. Beyond this door, she was told, was a being called simply the One; Andreasson, a religious woman, seemingly identified the being with God. She then saw a twin image of herself, perhaps representing her spirit, passing through the door, to reemerge later with a look of radiant joy on its face.

At the time, her hypnotist repeatedly asked her to describe what she saw behind the door, but she insisted that she could not do so. A further attempt to unlock her memory eight years later also failed, even though the hypnotist, in a attempt to lessen the emotional content of the experience, suggested that she observe it as though it were projected on a television screen. "There's a bright light coming out of the television," Andreasson responded. "This is weird! There's rays of light, bright white light, just like they've got a spotlight coming out of the television. . . . It's too bright! It's hurting my eyes!" Recognizing that she was in pain, the hypnotist brought the session to a close, and Andreasson reported headaches and aching eyes for several days afterward.

In comparison with the wonders of the otherworldly journey, Bullard noted a sense of anticlimax in descriptions of the return, the seventh of his categories and the last extraterrestrial stage of the abduction experience. "This episode gets slighted in many reports," he wrote, "because it simply reverses capture without adding much that is new to the story."

A notable exception, however, was the testimony under hypnosis of Chuck Rak, one of the Allagash four. Rak reported that when it came time to return to Earth, he and his companions were led to the wall of the spacecraft where, in the manner of movie or television science fiction, a portal somehow appeared. "It's almost like a place in the wall where something happens," said Rak. "And it's like we're penetrating a membrane."

The Allagash exception notwithstanding, the usual experience is for the abductors to bid farewell to their captive, perhaps enjoining secrecy or inducing memory loss. Then the victim is returned to the normal earthly world—although after the abduction experience, normality may seem a dubious state to the returnee.

Evidence and Incredulity

Betty Andreasson's drawing of one of the aliens who
allegedly abducted her in 1967

THE CENTRAL PROBLEM of the abduction accounts remains the absence of hard evidence. For the most part investigators trying to assess the objective reality of the experience have nothing to go on but the abductee's word as to what happened.

One phase of Thomas E. Bullard's abduction sequence, however, did have obvious manifestations. That was the phenomenon he labeled the aftermath. It was undeniable that in many cases individuals reporting abductions presented physical and psychological symptoms suggestive of highly stressful experiences. Sometimes these effects rapidly wore away, but in other cases they left lasting scars.

Some aftereffects were physical. Many victims reported persistent nausea and headaches as well as heightened sensitivity to touch. Abductees might show burn marks; in some cases they developed rashes. A claim by one abductee that a bruise took abnormally long to heal after his abduction suggested to some that his immune system might have been affected. Barney Hill developed a circle of warts in the genital area; in his testimony under hypnosis he had claimed that his abductors had placed a cuplike device over his groin.

Many victims mentioned suffering burning or bloodshot eyes. The three women abducted in the 1976 Kentucky case all subsequently reported eye problems. One went on to develop severe conjunctivitis; because she alone of the three had not been wearing glasses, some investigators speculated that the lenses might have afforded some degree of protection to the others, perhaps by partially blocking ultraviolet radiation.

The emotional havoc wrought by the abductions could be even more devastating than the physical effects. At the very least, abductees generally suffered from depression, reporting such effects as sleeplessness, anxiety, and occasional panic attacks. Some developed temporary amnesia. Recurrent dreams in which aspects of the abduction returned to haunt the sleeper were also frequently mentioned.

Psychologists reading through such lists quickly noted a familiar pattern. The symptoms displayed were markedly similar to those shown by combat veterans and by the victims of airplane hijackings, near-fatal accidents, and other deeply disturbing experiences. In those cases the resultant condition—marked by recurrent flashbacks to the original cause of the distress, inability to concentrate, extreme jumpiness, and a general sense of alienation and detachment—was normally diagnosed as post-traumatic stress disorder (PTSD).

A complicating factor for abduction victims was the fact that the root of their complaint was not as immediately evident as, say, rape or military combat. One psychologist writing in the *Journal of UFO Studies* attempted to address this fact by suggesting that abductees should be categorized differently from other PTSD sufferers. He proposed grouping them instead with victims of such other hidden injuries as childhood sexual abuse and psychological torture, under a separate label: experienced anomalous trauma (EAT). He pointed out that because EAT victims have a hard time convincing others of the reality of their condition, some might even develop psychosomatic symptoms as a way of validating the authenticity of their pain.

In fact, few people who investigate alleged abductees have any doubts as to the traumatic nature of the experiences described, regardless of whether the investigators are prepared to accept that an abduction really happened. This is particularly true of the events connected with the examination—the episode in the abduction experience that seemed to leave the most enduring memories and rouse the deepest fears.

A common element among many of the stories was the insertion of needlelike devices into the captive's body. In this respect, Betty Hill's account was to be the prototype for experiences reported by many subsequent abductees. In 1987, for example, a thirty-four-year-old Californian remembered under hypnosis an abduction that had occurred at the hands of five-foot-tall aliens three years earlier as he was preparing for bed in his parents' home in the San Fernando Valley: "I looked up and they were putting this needle into my stomach. It was really long, maybe two feet long, and it looked too fat to put into me. As it went in, I started to panic." The victim was calmed by his abductors, however, and a dark fluid was injected into his navel without his experiencing pain. Because such reports so closely resemble Betty Hill's story, some observers speculate that the accounts may reflect subconscious memories of the film version of *The Interrupted Journey*.

Other aspects of the examination have a disturbingly sexual orientation that lead critics to see in them an expression of the victims' normally repressed psychosexual anxieties. Some accounts seem to hint at deep fears of sexual invasion; victims talked of large wire objects being used to probe the rectum or of wires being inserted into the urethral tube. One abductee claimed that he turned his head from the examination table and found himself watching a replay of his past sexual encounters on something that resembled a television screen. At least two females said they were raped by their abductors.

There is, however, another interpretation of the marked sexual emphasis of such accounts. Those who assert the objective reality of the abductions see in it evidence of the aliens' fascination with the workings of the human reproductive system. In the words of Budd Hopkins, a leading proponent of this view: "The central focus of the entire UFO phenomenon is the 'study and laboratory use' of human beings with special attention to our physical, genetic and reproductive properties. . . . Apparently the center of this ongoing genetic experiment is a systematic attempt to create a hybrid species, a mix of human and alien characteristics." In Hopkins's view, men have been abducted primarily so that sperm samples could be taken from them, women to be made pregnant. The resulting embryos have been removed during subsequent abductions. Hopkins cites in support of this fantastic-sounding thesis the evidence of his own case studies, as reported in his books.

In Hopkins's 1987 work, *Intruders,* he details just such a case over a span of three generations. Its principal subject, an Indianapolis woman to whom he has given the pseudonym Kathie Davis, claimed to have experienced a phantom pregnancy that ended mysteriously. Under hypnosis she recalled not only that the baby was removed from her body by alien beings but that she was given a baby to hold as an apparent exercise in bonding.

As unlikely as Hopkins's theory might sound, it has been supported in the accounts of other abductees. A California artist expressed under hypnosis the conviction that her abductors were trying to extract her ova: "Oh! That's what they did. The probing was taking the egg. They're going to try and reproduce us," she cried. A gynecologist identified the surgical procedures described in some abductees' reports as laparoscopy, a process of ova removal used in the conception of test-tube babies.

Betty Andreasson even claims to have been an eyewitness to the aliens' breeding program in action. In one of her many regressions under hypnosis, Andreasson recounted seeing large-headed aliens removing a small, strange-looking fetus from an apparently human woman. They then gagged its mouth and inserted needles into its cranium and ears, explaining that they could not allow it to take a breath of air. For reasons they did

Kathie Davis drew this photo of an alien while under hypnosis. She claims that in 1978 aliens removed a fetus from her womb.

Kathie Davis, courtesy Budd Hopkins

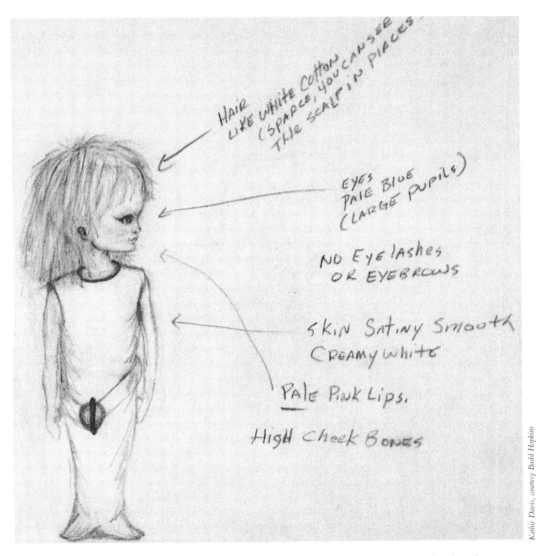

HAIR LIKE WHITE COTTON (SPARSE, YOU CAN SEE THE SCALP IN PLACES

EYES PALE BLUE (LARGE PUPILS)

NO EYELASHES OR EYEBROWS

SKIN SATINY SMOOTH CREAMY WHITE

PALE PINK LIPS,

HIGH CHEEK BONES

Kathie Davis, courtesy Budd Hopkins

Kathie Davis's drawing of the hybrid child she claims aliens bred using an egg stolen from her ovaries. During a later abduction, she reported, aliens presented the child to her.

not elucidate, they also cut its eyelids, then placed it in a glass jar filled with liquid, the jar's cap sprouting tiny, hairlike filaments illuminated by sparks of light. The aliens referred to the process by which the baby had been born as "splicing." Subsequently Andreasson was to describe seeing eighteen-inch-long infants playing in the vivarium she visited aboard the spacecraft.

Another feature linked by Hopkins and other investigators to genetic experimentation is the implanting of small devices in the abductee's body or brain. Victims typically state that a tiny metal bead or burr was inserted into one of their nostrils with the aid of a wire probe. Andreasson claims to have memories of the aliens retrieving from her body one such object, which had tiny wires implanted in it. But an attempt to have her describe the original implantation under hypnosis failed,

UFO SIGHTING QUESTIONNAIRE · PSYCHOLOGICAL/PHYSIOLOGICAL CASES (FORM 5)

PERSONAL ACCOUNT (Include on Form 1)
In your own words, describe any psychological/physiological effects experienced.

PSYCHOLOGICAL EFFECTS

(Circle the D and/or A beside each item checked to denote whether the effect was noted during or after the UFO sighting. Additional information, including the time duration of each effect, should be clearly stated on the reverse side of this questionnaire. Use additional numbered sheets, if necessary.)

PHYSIOLOGICAL EFFECTS
(Use same instructions as for above)

RELATIONSHIP OF UFO OR ENTITY TO AFFECTED PERSON

PSYCHIC INTERESTS AND ABILITIES

UFO QUESTIONNAIRE · ANIMAL EFFECT CASES (FORM 4)

PERSONAL ACCOUNT (Include on Form 1)
In your own words, describe the apparent Animal Reaction to the UFO and/or Entities.

ANIMAL EFFECT "DURING" UFO ENCOUNTER
(Please elaborate on items checked below, where applicable, by using a separate sheet.)

ANIMAL EFFECT "AFTER" UFO ENCOUNTER
(Please elaborate on items checked below, where applicable, by using a separate sheet.)

RELATIONSHIP OF UFO OR ENTITY TO AFFECTED ANIMAL

MUFON, Texas

apparently because she found the experience too painful to relive.

Adherents to the genetic-experiment theory consider such devices a means by which the abductors can keep in regular contact with their victim, who thereby becomes, in Hopkins's expressive phrase, a "tagged animal." An obvious implication of the tagging concept is that victims will be visited again by those who originally marked them out. Investigators found individuals who believe they were singled out in just that way.

One such is a businesswoman named Susan Ramstead. Her first UFO experience came in 1973. While driving to a conference, she noticed a craft that had landed in a field. Four years later, she recounted the story to an investigator, who suggested that she undergo hypnosis. Hypnotic regression subsequently revealed that she had been abducted and had been strapped naked to a table and subjected to a physical examination.

Six more years passed before the investigator heard from Ramstead again. This time she reported recurrent dreams of her earlier abductors. She saw them coming for her in her bedroom, floating her out of the house and back to the spacecraft and the examination table. Now, though, she was assailed by vivid images of metallic probes entering her nostrils.

Further hypnotic sessions revealed that Ramstead had experienced a pattern of repeated abduction in which just such incidents occurred. Ramstead's conclusion was

UFO SIGHTING QUESTIONNAIRE - RADAR CASES (FORM 9)

UFO SIGHTING QUESTIONNAIRE - ENTITY CASES (FORM 7)

MUFON, Texas

The MUFON (Mutual UFO Network) questionnaires enable field investigators to collect data on sightings in a consistent and thorough manner

that the aliens choose certain individuals to be human guinea pigs and then return periodically to review their progress. The homing device in her case was a tiny metallic object placed in her nose.

The story has a happy ending, for Ramstead believes that in the course of a final abduction the implant was removed. She woke up the morning after this abduction with a massive nosebleed, which she believes resulted from the removal, and it was the nosebleed that persuaded her to contact the investigator again. She claims to feel physically better since the object's removal; headaches that had periodically troubled her no longer do so, and she has lost the sensation of having a permanently blocked nose. She does not think that the aliens will trouble her again.

As the abductees' claims became more pressing, the question of their veracity became one of the most urgent issues in the abduction debate. The first serious psychological study of abductees was made by psychologist Elizabeth Slater between 1981 and 1983. The survey was financed by the Fund for UFO Research, and the nine individuals surveyed were in no way a random sample; they had been selected as "credible" by Budd Hopkins and his colleagues. But Slater herself was not made aware that they had any connections with UFOs until after she had completed her test-

A UFO photographed in March 1975 by Patric McCarthy in Hamilton, Ontario

ing. She was merely asked to "evaluate the similarities and differences in personality structure" of the subjects and to measure their psychological strengths and weaknesses. The subjects themselves were told not to mention any UFO connection to her.

Using a battery of standard psychological tests, she determined that the subjects as a group were above average in intelligence, were sensitive to fantasy, showed indications of narcissistic identity disturbance, and suffered some impairment in personal relationships. She also mentioned that some of the subjects were "simply flooded" with anxiety. At least six of the nine, she reported, were potentially capable of psychotic episodes; they might temporarily lose touch with reality and display confused, even bizarre behavior that was highly emotionally charged.

The puzzle is this: Did the subjects' psychological problems cause them to imagine that they had been abducted by aliens? Or did their abduction experiences bring about their psychological problems? Slater seemed convinced that the first alternative was not a viable one. Informed of the UFO connection after submitting her report, she wrote an addendum stating, "The first and most critical question is whether our subjects' reported experiences could be accounted for strictly on the basis of psychopathology, i.e., mental disorder. The answer is a firm no."

Along with witness reliability, the role of hypnotism in bringing to light many of the abduction stories has also been challenged. Regression techniques have played a particularly important role in missing-time accounts. Before the hypnosis sessions began, subjects have often been unaware of anything more specific than a momentary sense of discontinuity in their lives. Some critics claim that the technique increases witnesses' suggestibility and might enable the investigator to steer their recollections in desired directions. Even proponents of hypnosis admit that there is a danger of confabulation—the process by which hypnotized people sometimes fill in gaps in their recall by inventing additional detail.

In an attempt to answer these criticisms, two ufologists in California staged an experiment. They advertised in a local college's student newspaper for "creative, verbal types" to volunteer for "an interesting experience in hypnosis and imagination." They selected eight subjects, taking care to screen out any obvious UFO enthusiasts from the sample. Under hypnosis the volunteers were told to imagine that they had been taken on board a flying saucer and given a physical examination; then they were asked to describe the experience. The investigators were astonished—and no doubt distressed—by the fluency and detail of the imagined abduction tales. Their finding: "The imaginary subjects under hypnosis report UFO experiences which seem identical to those of 'real' witnesses." The experiment showed that detailed accounts under hypnosis are not the exclusive province of abductees, and they therefore do not establish the truth of abductees' stories.

Those convinced of the reality of the UFO abductions retort that hypnosis in fact occurred in only a minority of all abduction reports, that the circumstances of the imagined-abduction interviews were different from those of "real" cases, and that mere imagination could not explain away such phenomena as multiple-witness abductions and physical traces left on victims or their surroundings.

A PHYSICAL phenomenon that lately has attracted increasing attention from ufologists—as well as from researchers with other special fields of interest—is crop circles, those puzzling, often complex, patterns of flattened and swirled wheat or other grain plants that have appeared inexplicably on farms all over the world. Some ufologists believe the circles may be traces of alien activity. Most attention has been focused on British examples, since they have seemed to be most numerous— appearing at the rate of hundreds a year—and often spectacular in dimension and design.

Serious crop circle researchers—they call themselves cereologists—have turned up information that lays waste to any hoax explanation. Marshall Dudley, for instance, a systems engineer at Tennelec/Nucleus in Oak Ridge, Tennessee, used highly accurate radiation measuring devices to compare soil samples from several crop circles with control samples collected outside the circles. What he found was both fascinating and puzzling. Some soil from circles gave off considerably less alpha and beta radiation than their controls, while samples from other circles emitted significantly higher levels of radiation than soil collected nearby. The alpha and beta elevations were steep

*These crop circles (above and below) appeared in July 1986 in an area called the
Devil's Punchbowl in Hampshire, England*

enough to occasion a health caution from Dudley: Anyone who actually sees a crop
circle form should stay out of the immediate area for several hours.

Dr. W. C. Levengood, a Michigan biophysicist, compared wheat plants from
circles with control plants taken from the same fields but outside the circles. He found
that the growth nodes in the stalks of the circle plants were swollen, as if they had
been heated or otherwise subjected to a quick burst of intense energy. Under micro-
scopic examination the cell walls of the circle plants were seen to be stretched and
distorted, again as if heated rapidly, enlarging the tiny apertures through which ions

Jerome Wyckoff

*Light-refracting ice crystals can project a mock sun, or sun dog (right),
that can be mistaken for a UFO*

and electrolytes pass into and out of cells. And up to forty percent of the seeds from the circle plants were malformed, versus no malformed seeds in the control wheat. The same tests were run on plants taken from crop circles known to be created by hoaxers; none of the anomalous effects were present.

Researchers like Dudley and Levengood do not necessarily look for UFOs as an explanation for crop circles, but their work is of great interest to ufologists who do make a connection. And so are the many field studies of crop circles during which investigators have observed strange lights and heard weird noises, much like those reported by people who say they have seen UFOs.

Nothing excites ufologists as much as physical traces associated with a full-fledged allegation of a UFO sighting. Such was the case in Delphos, Kansas, a small prairie town devoted to wheat and livestock, according to the following account related by a sixteen-year-old farm boy named Ronald Johnson and his parents. The young Johnson said that at dusk on November 2, 1971, he was startled to see an illuminated object hovering near a tree seventy-five feet away. The thing seemed to be about nine feet in diameter and ten feet high; it glowed red, orange, and blue, while giving off a rumbling noise that Ronald later described as "like an old washing machine that vibrates." The UFO seemed to be suspended about two feet off the ground, which was lit by a bright glare emanating from the object's underside. He said the light was so intense that it hurt his eyes.

The teenager stood transfixed for some minutes. Then, the UFO started to move off, and Ronald ran to get his parents. They saw the object receding into the distance, and where it had hovered over the ground there remained a brightly glowing ring of soil. Mrs. Johnson hurried to the house for a Polaroid camera and photographed the luminescent ring. The Johnsons then touched the ring. It felt cool, but they immediately experienced a numbing effect in their fingers, something akin to a local anesthetic. They described the soil as having "a slick, crust-like" texture, as though "crystallized," and it seemed to be blistered.

The next day, the sheriff came out to collect soil samples and photograph the ring, which had stopped glowing by then. A month later, MUFON investigator Ted Phillips, Jr., arrived in Delphos to interview the Johnsons and examine the site. It had snowed and thawed, and the ring exhibited an extremely odd characteristic—a hydrophobicity, or aversion to water, that left it covered with unmelted snow in contrast to the muddy earth all around. This hydrophobicity lasted all through the winter.

In the course of the investigation, both photographs proved inconclusive. On analysis, Mrs. Johnson's Polaroid showed considerable reflected moonlight that could be taken for an internal glow; the sheriff's photo, shot nineteen hours after the event, showed a whitish surface to the earth that would reflect moonlight. Nevertheless, researcher Phillips was highly impressed with the credibility of the Johnson family and sent off soil samples to Erol A. Faruk, an English soil analyst.

In his published report, Faruk concluded that while deception was possible, the

According to retired NASA research scientist Richard F. Haines, Hannah McRoberts's 1981 photograph, taken on Canada's Vancouver Island, is one of the few genuine photographs of a UFO

presence in the soil of an unidentified compound with "unusual characteristics" made a hoax "the least plausible of explanations." The puzzling compound appeared to be highly unstable silver salt, which, when exposed to air, would oxidize to produce a fluorescent substance.

Faruk speculated that a "hovering object of presently unknown origin" possibly did appear over the Johnson farm that November evening. He argued that it could have "contained within its periphery an aqueous solution of an unstable compound whose sole function would be for light emission"; that "some of the solution was deposited into the ground" while the object hovered low; and that "the rumbling noise heard at the same time might be associated with the manner in which the deposition occurred. Once enough of this essentially expendable solution was ejected the object departed while Mr. and Mrs. Johnson approached the ring area."

Faruk offered no suggestions as to what the reason for such an event might have been. He simply said his research indicated that it could have happened just as the Johnsons described. Further study "should provide a conclusive answer, not the least of which is the identity of the soil compound," Faruk wrote.

UFOs in the '60s:
The Government Investigates

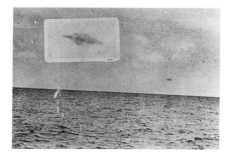

THE 1960s WERE, to say the least, a turbulent time for the United States. There was unprecedented prosperity—never had an economic boom gone on so long—yet at the same time violent protests against poverty and racial segregation convulsed such major cities as Los Angeles and Detroit. The perceived threat of nuclear war with the Soviet Union eased, but America's entanglement in Vietnam was costing more in money and blood than anyone had intended, and seemingly could not be controlled. Science progressed dramatically as humankind reached for the moon, while a lengthening list of political leaders fell victim to assassins' bullets. Along with it all, beginning in 1965, came one of the great waves of UFO sightings. Since 1958, the number of cases reported to Project Blue Book had been averaging 514 per year; there were nearly that many in the summer alone of 1965.

The air force had long demonstrated that it did not want this job. The entire national program was being run out of Wright-Patterson Air Force Base in Ohio by an officer, a sergeant, and a secretary. Its usual response to a sighting was to dispatch an officer from the nearest air force base to take a cursory look around, then issue an immediate explanation—one that often had little or no credibility even with the casually interested—or refuse to comment. UFO enthusiasts continued to mutter darkly of a massive cover-up on the part of the U.S. government.

Far larger numbers of people thought the subject deserved better research. With astronauts virtually commuting to outer space, and the moon about to become a landing field for human explorers, public expectations of a complete explanation of the stubborn mystery of UFOs steadily escalated.

The pressure could not be bottled up indefinitely. During the next few years, matters seemed to come to a head: The U.S. Congress, sensitive to the growing public dissatisfaction, responded with two separate investigations; the air force contracted with the University of Colorado for an impartial, scientific review of the whole subject; and American journalists, finding all this irresistible, wrote copiously about the sightings, the investigators, and the investigations of the investigators. Surely no mystery, even one as intractable as UFOs, could withstand such sophisticated attention.

The flurry began early on the morning of September 3, 1965, in southeastern New Hampshire, not far from that state's minuscule share of the Atlantic shore. Norman J. Muscarello, eighteen, was hitchhiking home to the small town of Exeter from Amesbury, Massachusetts, about twelve miles away. Few cars were traveling Route 150 through the countryside after midnight; Muscarello had to walk most of the way. He had only about two miles to go when he saw it.

An enormous sphere rose like a red moon from behind some trees. But it was no moon. It pitched forward and hovered over a nearby house belonging to Clyde Russell, illuminating it with brilliant red light. Muscarello reckoned the thing was eighty or ninety feet long, much bigger than Russell's house, and noted a belt of blinking red lights around its girth. He had no idea what it was, but he knew it was no ordinary aircraft, for it yawed and careened clumsily and generated no engine noise. Suddenly, it appeared to lurch toward him, and Muscarello dived into the ditch for cover. But the craft disappeared behind the trees.

Muscarello got up, ran to the Russell house, and pounded on the front door,

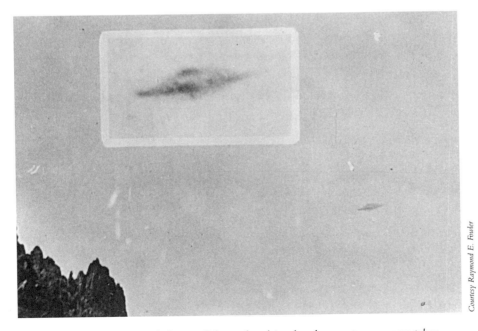

Courtesy Raymond E. Fowler

These two photographs of a dark gray disk enveloped in phosphorescent vapor were taken on January 16, 1958, by Almiro Barauna, a photographer aboard a Brazilian navy ship. Over one hundred crew members witnessed the incident.

screaming for help. There was no response. He saw headlights coming up the road, dashed out, and flagged down the car. It stopped, and the couple in it gave him a ride into Exeter. At 2:25 A.M., a badly shaken Muscarello stumbled into the Exeter police station and began babbling about having seen a UFO.

The patrolman on desk duty, Reginald Toland, listened to the scrambled story and asked the youth how many beers he had had to drink. "Look," Muscarello pleaded, "I know you don't believe me. I don't blame you. But you got to send somebody back out there with me!" Toland put no stock in the story but could see that the boy was genuinely scared, and it was a slow night. He called in a patrol car.

Minutes later, officer Eugene Bertrand arrived at the station. And it turned out that he had something to add to Muscarello's story. An hour or so earlier, while patrolling the outskirts of Exeter, he had spotted a car parked alongside a highway. Upon checking, he found a woman sitting in it, too distraught to drive. She told Bertrand she had been followed for about twelve miles from Epping, New Hampshire, by a glowing red object. It hovered over her car until she reached Exeter, then shot straight up and disappeared. Bertrand had dismissed her story, not even bothering to report it to the station. Now, listening to Muscarello, he began to wonder. Bertrand drove Muscarello back to the field where the boy claimed to have seen the UFO. It was a clear night with very little wind. The moon had gone down sometime before midnight, and the stars shone brightly. Bertrand parked the cruiser near a telephone pole and told Toland by radio that he could not see anything unusual. But Muscarello was still upset.

The patrol officer walked with him toward the woods, across a farm field owned by Carl Dining. When they reached a horse corral, Bertrand flicked his flashlight around and tried to persuade Muscarello that he had probably seen a helicopter. Muscarello protested that he knew aircraft and how they flew, and that what he had seen was definitely not a helicopter or one of the aircraft stationed at Pease Air Force Base about ten miles to the northeast. Then, as Bertrand told it later, the horses in the corral began kicking and whinnying, dogs in the nearby yards began howling, and Muscarello screamed, "I see it! I see it!"

Bertrand whirled and saw, rising slowly from behind the trees, a brilliant, round object. Silently, it wobbled toward them as a leaf flutters from a tree, bathing the landscape in crimson light. Bertrand, an air force veteran who had served aboard KC-97 tankers, was so frightened that he reflexively grabbed for his revolver. Then he thought better of that and ran with Muscarello back to the cruiser.

"My God!" Bertrand yelled into his radio, "I see the damn thing myself!" Then he and Muscarello watched, enthralled, as the object hovered eerily about one hundred feet above the ground, 300 feet away from them. It rocked silently back and forth, its brilliant red lights flashing sequentially. They were so bright, Bertrand said later, that he could not determine the exact shape of the object; it was, he said, "like trying to describe a car with its headlights coming at you."

Another patrolman, David Hunt, had been listening to the radio traffic and had decided to have a look. As he pulled up and jumped out of his car, he said later, "I

Courtesy Raymond E. Fowler

Highway Inspector Rex Heflin took these three photographs of a domed disc on August 3, 1965, in Santa Ana, California. Numerous investigators and ufologists pronounced the photographs genuine.

could see those pulsating lights. I could hear those horses kicking out in the barn there. Those dogs were really howling. Then it started moving, slow-like, across the tops of the trees, just above the trees. It was rocking when it did this. A creepy type of look. Airplanes don't do this."

Bertrand was unwilling to believe his eyes. "Your mind is telling you this can't be true, and yet you're seeing it," he said later. "I kept telling Dave, What is that, Dave? What do you think? He'd say, I don't know. I have never seen an aircraft like that before, and I know damn well they haven't changed that much since I was in the service." The object finally moved out toward the ocean. "We waited a while," said Hunt. "A B-47 came over. You could tell the difference. There was no comparison."

Shortly after the overwrought message from Bertrand, Officer Toland received another call back at the station—this one from a night telephone operator in Exeter. "Some man had just called her," Toland reported later, "and he was so hysterical he could hardly talk straight. He told her that a flying saucer came right at him, but before he could finish, he was cut off." The caller had been at a pay phone in Hampton, about seven miles east of Exeter. Toland notified the Hampton police and Pease Air Force Base.

The hysterical man was never located, but that night and for several days afterward, other people reported similar sightings. The next day two air force officers interviewed Muscarello, Bertrand, and Hunt, then returned, tight-lipped, to the base. Under air force regulations, official comment could be made only from the office of the secretary of the air force in Washington. No one knew when that might come.

But because of the number of witnesses involved, their credibility, and the convincing detail of their reports, the story could not be ignored. It was picked up by the national news services, and among the people intrigued by it was John Fuller, a columnist for the magazine *Saturday Review*. Fuller published his own carefully researched version of what came to be known as the "Exeter incident," then decided to investigate even more extensively.

He was hardly alone. The National Investigations Committee on Aerial Phenomena (NICAP), headquartered in Washington, D.C., had already assigned one of its investigators to the case. Despite its imposing name, NICAP had no official status; it was an organization of private citizens who were convinced that UFO sightings were not being properly studied. A volunteer NICAP investigator from Massachusetts, Raymond E. Fowler, visited Exeter, collected signed statements from the witnesses, and compiled a thorough eighteen-page report. Fowler was impressed by the quality of the sighting. He told Fuller that "both the officers are intelligent, capable, and seem to know what they're talking about." Others were not so impressed. A local reporter who knew that a pilot often flew around the Exeter area towing an illuminated advertising sign suggested that that was what everyone had been seeing. Aside from the fact that there was no resemblance between the sign and the descriptions of the object, it was later confirmed that the aircraft and the sign had been on the ground when the sightings occurred.

Then there was the air force. It took its usual uninterested stance, despite the proximity of these reported aerial phenomena to Pease Air Force Base—a Strategic Air Command bomber base, home to B-47s and B-52s. Several witnesses reported having observed, in addition to the big red UFO, a number of jet fighters in the sky that night. Area residents were used to seeing bombers but not fighters; the presence of interceptors suggested that they had been sent up from other bases to investigate the UFOs, although the air force emphatically denied this.

There was other evidence, however, that the air force was intensely interested in the incident at Exeter. Air force officers were seen for a time prowling the roads where the sightings had taken place. Two of them—a colonel and a major—got into an angry exchange with some local residents when the colonel insisted that what everyone had taken for a UFO was just the glare of landing lights at the base. In the face of vociferous denials, the colonel sent the major off to have the runway marker lights and approach strobes (which provide visual assistance to pilots in all kinds of weather) turned on and off for a fifteen-minute period. Neither the colonel nor anyone else present saw a thing. In due course, the air force issued its official pronouncement on the Exeter sightings. In fact, the statement made at the Pentagon on October 27, 1965, offered several explanations, all of them natural. To begin with, said a spokesman, multiple aircraft had been in the area because of a Strategic Air Command training exercise. Moreover, there had been a weather inversion, in which cold air is trapped between warm layers of air, causing stars and planets to "dance and twinkle." In conclusion, he said, "We believe what people saw that night were stars and planets in unusual formations." He offered no specifics about these so-called unusual formations.

Later checking revealed that the training exercise, which had been run out of Westover Air Force Base at Springfield, Massachusetts, more than one hundred air miles from Exeter, was over by 2:00 A.M., well before officers Bertrand and Hunt had observed the UFO. As to the dancing planets in unusual formations, there was nothing to check. Patrolmen Bertrand and Hunt, deeply embarrassed by the belittling official explanation of their frightening experience, wrote a letter of protest to the air force. Approximately three months later, they received an apology of sorts. Signed by a lieutenant colonel in an air force public-information office, it said: "Based on additional information you submitted to our UFO investigation office at Wright-Patterson Air Force Base, Ohio, we have been unable to identify the object you observed on September 3, 1965."

But, it went on to say, virtually all such reports in the past had turned out to be man-made objects, or the product of atmospheric conditions, or meteors. And, in conclusion, "Thank you for reporting your observation to the Air Force." John Fuller's book *Incident at Exeter* stimulated a third and more serious attempt to explain what all those people had seen. The book was read carefully by, among many others, Philip J. Klass—an electrical engineer and senior editor of the technical journal *Aviation Week & Space Technology*. He was preparing to debunk UFOs at a 1966 symposium sponsored by the Institute of Electrical and Electronics Engineers.

Klass was struck by several prominent themes present in most of the Exeter sightings—the spherical shape, erratic flight, bright glow, and humming or hissing sound of the objects. Klass knew of something in nature that had all these characteristics: ball lightning. This little-known kind of lightning is usually oval in shape and an intense red, is often heard to sizzle, and moves around with unpredictable vigor, sometimes hanging motionless, at other times darting about at high speeds with instantaneous changes in direction. Of course, Klass had problems trying to make a complete match between the Exeter UFO sightings and ball lightning. The objects seen around Exeter were larger, and remained visible longer, than any confirmed examples of ball lightning. And, of course, the big objection was that ball lightning is a product of thunderstorms, and the Exeter sightings were not accompanied by any. Unwilling to give up on a promising line of research, Klass delved deeper. Ball lightning is one example of what physicists call a plasma—a region of ionized gas (in this case, air) created by a strong electrical charge.

Plasmas, which behave differently from ordinary gases, are regarded as a fourth state of matter; their study has become a separate branch of physics. They are being researched for use in controlling thermonuclear reactions and as the potential driving force for interstellar travel. Saint Elmo's fire, often seen on ships and aircraft during thunderstorms, is a plasma. But it is not only static electricity that produces plasmas; high-voltage power lines are sometimes spangled with moving globes of light called coronas—another form of plasma. And many of the Exeter UFO reports included references to nearby electric transmission lines.

Perhaps, Klass said, the corona of the high-tension lines had somehow produced a special, previously unknown kind of luminous plasma—a larger, more long-lived form of ball lightning originating from power lines instead of thunderstorms. No such phenomenon had ever been witnessed or produced in a laboratory, but it seemed far more plausible—to Klass, at least—than the alternate explanation that the objects were alien spaceships.

Klass extended his study to 746 other sightings documented by NICAP. In every case, he found the reported UFOs displayed the characteristics typical of plasmas: color, shape, erratic movement, hissing. The strong electrical charge of a plasma could also explain the frequent reports of interference with radios, lights, and automobile electrical systems in the vicinity of UFOs. Since a plasma has little mass and is responsive to electromagnetic fields, its erratic flight and high-speed reversals of direction posed no theoretical problem. Moreover, plasmas reflect radio waves, so they cannot be ruled out when UFOs appear on radar screens. Klass made limited, but insistent, claims for his hypothesis. It may, he wrote, "explain many sightings of lower-altitude 'unidentified flying objects.'" Another writer quoted him as believing his explanation was "susceptible to confirmation by scientific experiment." After examining the NICAP literature, Klass made a stronger statement of his belief: "Hundreds of 'unidentified flying objects' exhibit characteristics that clearly identify them as plasmas."

Klass received scant encouragement. Traditional scientists had little reason to pursue his hypothesis; those who had already made up their minds about UFOs were uninterested or openly hostile. *Newsweek* called his theory "one of the most persuasive explanations of all" but added that the air force was "noncommittal" and that UFO buffs were "unimpressed." One skeptic sarcastically described Klass's theory as "a freak of nature—hitherto unknown to science: a clear-weather plasma, akin to 'ball lightning,' caused by an electrical discharge from nearby high-tension power lines, which was somehow able to detach itself, grow to tremendous size, and cavort about the countryside under its own power." As Klass put it, somewhat ruefully, a few UFO buffs "seemed to appreciate my attempt to explain the UFO mystery rationally, but most of them acted as though I had shot Santa Claus or spat upon my country's flag."

Whatever he had done, he had not answered all the questions about the Exeter incident, which would remain classified as unexplained. Meanwhile, another rash of sightings of mysterious objects in the sky occurred, prompting another less-than-convincing explanation.

The next widely publicized cluster of UFO sightings—around Ann Arbor, Michigan, during March 1966—gained notoriety as the "swamp gas affair" and embroiled the Congress of the United States in the UFO controversy.

The first episode to gain national attention took place on March 14, when citizens and police officers in three counties reported that they had seen lit objects flashing across the predawn skies. According to one deputy sheriff, "these objects could move at fantastic speeds, make very sharp turns, dive and climb and hover with great maneuverability." Three days later, a similar display of aerobatics was widely reported in the same area. On Sunday, March 20, near the town of Dexter, twelve miles from Ann Arbor, Frank Mannor, a forty-seven-year-old truck driver, went outside at about 7:30 P.M. to quiet his dogs. "When I turned back I saw this meteor," he said later. "It stopped and settled to the ground, then rose again. It was about a half mile away. I called my wife and my kids out, and we watched it for fifteen minutes."

Then Mannor and his son, Ronnie, walked toward the object. "We got to about 500 yards of the thing. It was sort of shaped like a pyramid, with a blue-green light on the right-hand side and on the left a white light. I didn't see no antenna or porthole. The body was like a yellowish coral rock and looked like it had holes in it—sort of like if you took a piece of cardboard box and split it open. You couldn't see it too good, because it was surrounded with heat waves, like you see on the desert. The white light turned to a blood red as we got close to it, and Ron said, 'Look at that horrible thing.'" At that point the object disappeared.

In the meantime, Mannor's wife, Leona, had called the police, using the family's multiparty telephone line. "We've got an object out here that looks like what they call a flying saucer," she reported while several neighbors listened in. "It's got lights on it down in the swamp." By the time six cruisers arrived, the road past the Mannor house was jammed with sight-seers' cars. More than fifty people reported they had seen the object in the swamp that Sunday evening, including several police officers. And later, on the way back to Ann Arbor, police in one squad car spotted a

UFO in the sky and pursued it at high speed, fruitlessly.

The next day, another fifty people, including twelve policemen, saw an object near Ann Arbor that resembled the one the Mannors had described. That evening, eighty-seven female students at Hillsdale College, sixty-five miles southwest of Ann Arbor, watched an object flying around and flashing bright lights in a swampland for a period of about four hours. With them was a local civil defense director and a college dean, who was also a former newspaper reporter. They said that the object was shaped like a football; that it swayed, wobbled, and glowed in flight; and that it once darted straight toward a dormitory window before stopping suddenly. The entire area, indeed much of the state of Michigan, was in a frenzy that was magnified by the national news media. Beseeched by state and local officials to do something, the air force dispatched Project Blue Book's consultant, J. Allen Hynek, to Ann Arbor to investigate the sightings.

"The situation was so charged with emotion," Hynek said, "that it was impossible for me to do any really serious investigation." Even when he decided to focus only on the sightings of March 20 and 21, Hynek found that his work was obstructed by "clusters of reporters," and he received no assistance whatsoever from the air force.

Though he was a scientist and a skeptic, Hynek found himself caught up in what he described as the "near hysteria" that gripped the area. He was with the police one night when a sighting was reported; several squad cars converged on the spot, radios crackling with such excited messages as, "I see it!" or "There it is!" or "It's east of the river near Dexter!" Hynek later confessed that "occasionally even I thought I glimpsed 'it.'"

Finally the squad cars met at an intersection and officers spilled out, pointing excitedly at the sky and saying, "See—there it is! It's moving." But, Hynek wrote later, "it wasn't moving. 'It' was the star Arcturus, undeniably identified by its position in relation to the handle of the Big Dipper. A sobering demonstration for me."

Then, to add to this already chaotic situation, peremptory orders were issued by the air force: Hynek was to hold a news conference on March 25—only four days after the sighting. As he recalled, his instructions were to release "a statement about the cause of the sights. It did me no good to protest, to say that as yet I had no real idea what had caused the reported sightings in the swamps. I was to have a press conference, ready or not."

Hynek had nothing to go on until he remembered a phone call from a botanist at the University of Michigan who had "called to my attention the phenomenon of burning 'swamp gas.'" This was a substance better known to folklore and legend—as jack-o'-lantern, fox fire, or will-o'-the-wisp—than to science. It is a gas caused by decaying vegetation, consisting mainly of methane; under certain circumstances it can ignite spontaneously and cast a brief, flickering light. Little else was known about it, but it suited Hynek's need perfectly: "After learning more about swamp gas from other Michigan scientists, I decided that it was a 'possible' explanation that I could offer to the reporters."

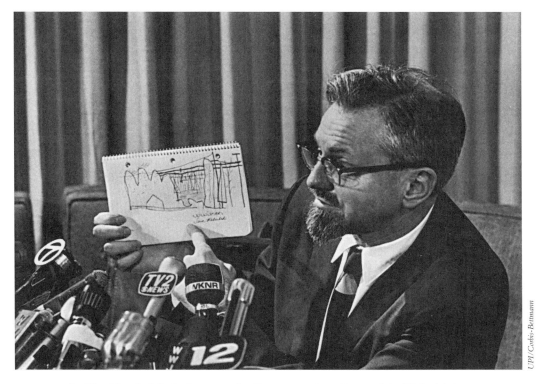

*J. Allen Hynek defends the unpopular "swamp gas theory" to explain UFO sightings
at a news conference in Michigan in March 1966*

To his credit, Hynek made repeated, strenuous qualifications in his statement. "I am not making a blanket statement to cover the entire UFO phenomenon," he wrote; "I emphasize in conclusion that I cannot prove in a Court of Law that this is the full explanation of these sightings."

But most of his statement was an exposition of swamp gas as the probable cause of the sightings at Dexter and Hillsdale: "The flames go out in one place and suddenly appear in another place, giving the illusion of motion. No heat is felt, and the lights do not burn or char the ground. They can appear for hours at a time and sometimes for a whole night. Generally there is no smell, and usually no sound, except the popping sound of little explosions." To Hynek's dismay, however, the news conference "turned out to be no place for scholarly discussion; it was a circus. The TV cameramen wanted me in one spot, the newspaper men wanted me in another, and for a while, both groups were actually tugging at me. Everyone was clamoring for a single, spectacular explanation of the sightings. They wanted little green men. When I handed out a statement that discussed swamp gas, many of the men simply ignored the fact that I said it was a 'possible' reason. I watched with horror as one reporter scanned the page, found the phrase 'swamp gas,' underlined it, and rushed for a telephone.

"Too many of the stories the next day not only said that swamp gas was definitely the cause of the Michigan lights but implied that it was the cause of other UFO sightings as well. I got out of town as quickly and as quietly as I could."

One of Michigan's representatives in Congress, House minority leader Gerald Ford, returned to Washington in late March to issue a call for a "full-blown" congressional investigation. At about the same time, there were calls for action from respected publications and observers not previously heard from on this issue. *The Christian Science Monitor,* for one, said in an editorial that the Michigan sightings had "deepened the mystery" of UFOs, adding, "It is time for the scientific community to conduct a thorough and objective study of the 'unexplainable.'" Syndicated columnist Roscoe Drummond called on Congress to "take charge" and order an investigation. If the air force believed it could ignore such demands, Congress was under no such illusion. Like it or not, it would have to act.

Thus it was that the first congressional hearing on UFOs began as a closed session of the House Committee on Armed Services, chaired by Representative L. Mendel Rivers of South Carolina, on April 5, 1966. The previous week, Rivers had received a letter from Congressman Ford, who cited widespread dissatisfaction with the official response to the Ann Arbor sightings and concluded: "In the firm belief that the American public deserves a better explanation than that thus far given by the Air Force, I strongly recommend that there be a committee investigation" of the UFO phenomenon. Ford did not get the wide-ranging inquiry that he had hope for. He had asked that members of the executive branch of government and people who had seen UFOs be invited to testify; instead, Rivers summoned just three men to brief the committee: Secretary of the Air Force Harold Brown; the director of Project Blue Book, Major Hector Quintanilla, Jr.; and Blue Book's scientific consultant, J. Allen Hynek. "See if you can shed some light on these highly illuminated objects," drawled Rivers. "We can't just write them off. There are too many responsible people who are concerned." Secretary Brown responded with pride that of 10,147 UFOs investigated since 1947 by the air force, 9,501 had been identified as "bright stars and planets, comets and meteors," and the like by "carefully selected and highly qualified scientists, engineers, technicians and consultants"—implied experts—using "the finest Air Force laboratories, test centers, scientific instrumentation and technical equipment." In the other 646 cases, he said, "the information available does not provide an adequate basis for analysis."

He had reached a confident conclusion: "The past 18 years of investigating UFOs have not yet identified any threat to our national security, or evidence that the unidentified objects represent developments or principles beyond present-day scientific knowledge, or any evidence of extraterrestrial vehicles." But despite the utter lack of results thus far, the air force would remain steadfast and, he said, "continue to investigate such phenomena with an open mind." Congressman Rivers was apparently reassured by Brown's stance; he suddenly saw no reason to continue in executive session and admitted the crowd of reporters that had gathered in the halls. Brown repeated his testimony for their benefit; then Rivers asked Hynek for his views. Hynek was a good deal more ambivalent than Brown, and in fact, more so than he had been in the past. In 1948, when he was first involved with Project Blue Book, he had stated that "the whole subject seemed utterly ridiculous" and had expected the fad to pass quickly. Instead, UFO sightings had become more widespread and frequent. The attention of the national news media waxed and waned, he said, but "the underlying concern about UFOs, fed by a continuous trickle of reports, is indeed growing in the mind and sight of the public." It was time, asserted Hynek, for a thorough, scholarly approach to what he called the "UFO problem." The air force had approached all UFO reports, he continued, with the assumption "that a conventional explanation existed, either as a misidentification or as an otherwise well-known object or phenomenon, a hallucination, or a hoax. This has been a very successful and productive hypothesis." Yet there were incidents for which that approach did not work; Hynek had collected twenty that he could not explain.

"In dealing with the truly puzzling cases, we have tended either to say that, if an investigation had been pursued long enough, the misidentified object would have been recognized, or that the sighting had no validity to begin with." Hynek admitted to being increasingly uncomfortable with the air force's confident approach. "As a scientist, I must be mindful of the lessons of the past; all too often it has happened that matters of great value to science were overlooked because the new phenomenon simply did not fit the accepted scientific outlook of the time." During a brief, rambling discussion peppered with jokes about Martians, committee members asked about a particularly spectacular sighting that had been covered by *Life* magazine. Major Quintanilla, who spoke only when directly questioned, said Project Blue Book had not investigated that case. And then, just an hour and twenty minutes after commencing, the congressional investigation was over.

Virtually nothing had been accomplished, except that some additional impetus was given to a proposal for a different kind of study. In an attempt to patch its badly frayed credibility on the subject, the air force had already convened what it called a scientific advisory board ad hoc committee to review Project Blue Book. After a one-day examination of Blue Book, the advisory committee reported in February 1966; Secretary Brown used some of its findings in his statement to Rivers's House committee. The full advisory report, however, directly contradicted Brown on one point. Whereas he had noted that highly qualified experts and sophisticated equipment had been brought to bear on UFO investigations, the advisory committee concluded that the resources assigned to Blue Book "(only one officer, a sergeant and secretary) have been quite limited." The committee recommended that skilled teams, including clinical psychologists and physical scientists, be recruited from various universities to investigate selected UFO sightings.

Congress also decided to take another, expanded look at the subject of UFOs. This was in the form of a symposium conducted by the House Committee on Science and Astronautics. One of its members, Representative J. Edward Roush of Indiana, had become impressed with the arguments of University of Arizona atmospheric physicist James McDonald, who was emerging as a leading advocate of the alien-spacecraft hypothesis.

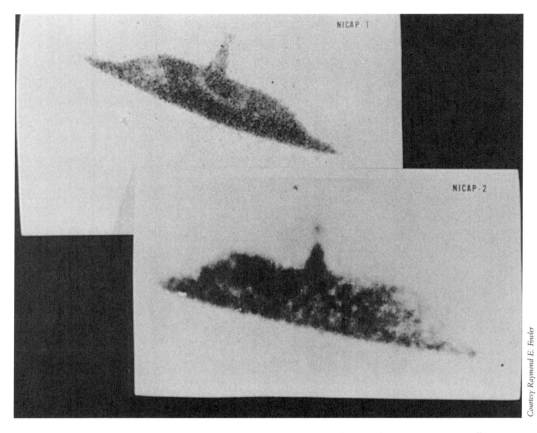

Courtesy Raymond E. Fowler

Two similar UFOs in different parts of the world, photographed by Paul Trent in McMinnville, Oregon, on May 11, 1950, and by a French Air Marshal in March 1954

McDonald was a tireless UFO investigator who lectured continually about his conclusions. After studying thousands of cases and interviewing hundreds of witnesses, he wrote, he had concluded that "the extraterrestrial hypothesis is the least unlikely hypothesis to account for the UFO." Influenced by McDonald's credentials and reasoning, Congressman Roush scheduled the symposium for July 29, 1968, and asked McDonald to select the witnesses.

As a result, the tone of the symposium was far different from that of the 1966 hearing. It was addressed by six distinguished scientists and academics associated with major universities: astronomer J. Allen Hynek, physicist James McDonald, sociologist Robert L. Hall, engineers James A. Harder and Robert M. Baker, and astrophysicist Carl Sagan.

Hynek, the veteran UFO debunker and Blue Book apologist, led off with a statement that confirmed his continuing change of attitude. The UFO problem, he said, "has been made immensely more difficult by the supposition held by most scientists, on the basis of the poor data available to them, that there couldn't possibly be anything substantial to UFO reports in the first place, and hence that there is no point to wasting time or money investigating." This, of course, was precisely the position that had been held by the air force, and by Hynek, for the previous twenty years.

But this attitude, Hynek now said, was no longer acceptable: "Can we afford not to look toward UFO skies; can we afford to overlook a potential breakthrough of great significance? And even apart from that, the public is growing impatient. The public does not want another twenty years of UFO confusion. They want to know whether there really is something to this whole UFO business—and I can tell you definitely that they are not satisfied with the answers they have been getting." Nor was Hynek. He confessed that he had been forced to a reluctant conclusion by "the cumulative weight of continued reports from groups of people around the world whose competence and sanity I have no reason to doubt, reports involving unexplainable craft with physical effects on animals, motor vehicles, growing plants and on the ground." The choice, he now believed, was clear: "Either there is a scientifically valuable subset of reports on the UFO phenomenon or we have a world society containing people who are articulate, sane and reputable in all matters save UFO reports."

Hynek's call for more serious research was echoed by McDonald: "My position is that UFOs are entirely real and we do not know what they are, because we have laughed them out of court. The possibility that these are extraterrestrial devices, that we are dealing with surveillance from some advanced technology, is a possibility I take very seriously." McDonald pleaded for a more strenuous scientific approach to the subject, with the involvement of the National Aeronautics and Space Administration.

James Harder, an engineering professor from the University of California at Berkeley, was even more blunt in his opinion: "On the basis of the data and the ordinary rules of evidence, as would be applied in civil or criminal courts, the physical reality of UFOs has been proved beyond a reasonable doubt."

There was, of course, dissent. Donald H. Menzel, the distinguished astronomer, former director to the Harvard College Observatory, and relentless UFO debunker, submitted a written statement that fairly dripped scorn. "The believers," he declared, "are too eager to reach a decision. Having no real logic on their side, they resort to innuendo as a weapon and try to discredit those who fail to support their view."

Menzel's logic was that if alien pilots had been "bugging us for centuries," as he put it, "why should one not have landed and shown himself to the President of the United States, to a member of the National Academy of Sciences, or at least to some member of Congress?" Menzel's conclusion about unidentified flying objects was unequivocal: "Natural explanations exist for the unexplained sightings."

But the consensus of the symposium was clearly that UFOs merited serious study and should be given closer, more objective attention. The proceedings, however, had been merely a discussion, not a prelude to any congressional action, and had little impact. And five months later the symposium sank even further into obscurity as the country turned its attention to the formal report of an academic committee headed by Edward U. Condon, a professor of physics. The Air Force had contracted the University of Colorado to form a committee that would be outside of its jurisdiction, and gave them access to the files of Project Blue Book.

Their report appeared to be an exhaustive review of the whole subject of UFOs

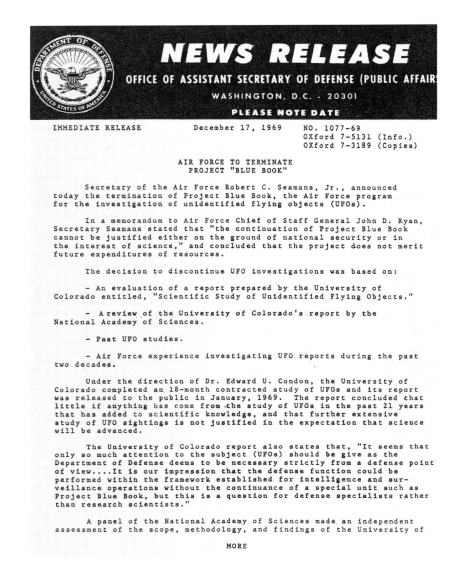

NEWS RELEASE

OFFICE OF ASSISTANT SECRETARY OF DEFENSE (PUBLIC AFFAIR

WASHINGTON, D.C. - 20301

PLEASE NOTE DATE

IMMEDIATE RELEASE   December 17, 1969   NO. 1077-69
                                                    OXford 7-5131 (Info.)
                                                    OXford 7-3189 (Copies)

AIR FORCE TO TERMINATE
PROJECT "BLUE BOOK"

Secretary of the Air Force Robert C. Seamans, Jr., announced today the termination of Project Blue Book, the Air Force program for the investigation of unidentified flying objects (UFOs).

In a memorandum to Air Force Chief of Staff General John D. Ryan, Secretary Seamans stated that "the continuation of Project Blue Book cannot be justified either on the ground of national security or in the interest of science," and concluded that the project does not merit future expenditures of resources.

The decision to discontinue UFO investigations was based on:

- An evaluation of a report prepared by the University of Colorado entitled, "Scientific Study of Unidentified Flying Objects."

- A review of the University of Colorado's report by the National Academy of Sciences.

- Past UFO studies.

- Air Force experience investigating UFO reports during the past two decades.

Under the direction of Dr. Edward U. Condon, the University of Colorado completed an 18-month contracted study of UFOs and its report was released to the public in January, 1969. The report concluded that little if anything has come from the study of UFOs in the past 21 years that has added to scientific knowledge, and that further extensive study of UFO sightings is not justified in the expectation that science will be advanced.

The University of Colorado report also states that, "It seems that only so much attention to the subject (UFOs) should be give as the Department of Defense deems to be necessary strictly from a defense point of view....It is our impression that the defense function could be performed within the framework established for intelligence and sur-veillance operations without the continuance of a special unit such as Project Blue Book, but this is a question for defense specialists rather than research scientists."

A panel of the National Academy of Sciences made an independent assessment of the scope, methodology, and findings of the University of

MORE

A news release issued in December 1969 stating that the Defense Department was officially disbanding Project Blue Book, which ended formal government investigations of UFOs

by first-rate scientists. It was physically impressive: 1,465 pages crammed with charts, photographs, and dense academic exposition. It seemed that no effort had been spared; thirty-six authors had contributed analyses and explanations, and the cost had exceeded half a million dollars.

The National Academy of Sciences had reviewed the report and announced its approval. Walter Sullivan, the respected science reporter for *The New York Times*, wrote an admiring introduction in which he said: "The report is a memorable doc-ument. While the case histories read like detective stories, it is also a scientific study." Few people, however, waded through the hundreds of pages of analysis. Most read only the first section, titled "Conclusions and Recommendations," and the second, "Summary of the Report." Both were written by Condon himself.

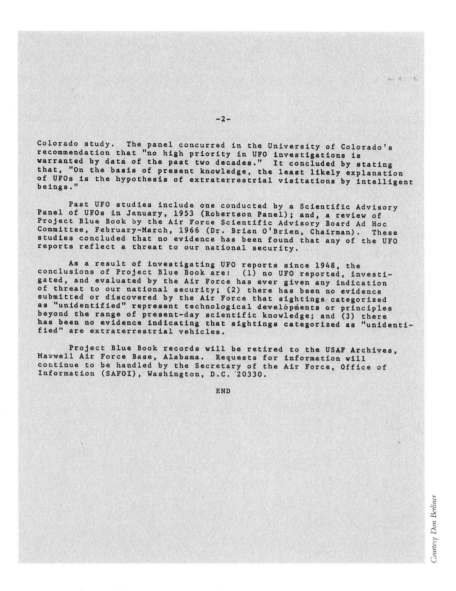

-2-

Colorado study. The panel concurred in the University of Colorado's recommendation that "no high priority in UFO investigations is warranted by data of the past two decades." It concluded by stating that, "On the basis of present knowledge, the least likely explanation of UFOs is the hypothesis of extraterrestrial visitations by intelligent beings."

Past UFO studies include one conducted by a Scientific Advisory Panel of UFOs in January, 1953 (Robertson Panel); and, a review of Project Blue Book by the Air Force Scientific Advisory Board Ad Hoc Committee, February-March, 1966 (Dr. Brian O'Brien, Chairman). These studies concluded that no evidence has been found that any of the UFO reports reflect a threat to our national security.

As a result of investigating UFO reports since 1948, the conclusions of Project Blue Book are: (1) no UFO reported, investigated, and evaluated by the Air Force has ever given any indication of threat to our national security; (2) there has been no evidence submitted or discovered by the Air Force that sightings categorized as "unidentified" represent technological developments or principles beyond the range of present-day scientific knowledge; and (3) there has been no evidence indicating that sightings categorized as "unidentified" are extraterrestrial vehicles.

Project Blue Book records will be retired to the USAF Archives, Maxwell Air Force Base, Alabama. Requests for information will continue to be handled by the Secretary of the Air Force, Office of Information (SAFOI), Washington, D.C. 20330.

END

Courtesy Don Berliner

"Our general conclusion," declared the committee chairman, "is that nothing has come from the study of UFOs in the past twenty-one years that has added to scientific knowledge. Careful consideration of the record leads us to conclude that further extensive study of UFOs probably cannot be justified in the expectation that science will be advanced thereby."

The air force, Condon continued, had been correct in its handling of UFO reports and had never attempted to conceal its findings. "It has been contended that the subject has been shrouded in official secrecy. We conclude otherwise. We have no evidence of secrecy concerning UFO reports. What has been miscalled secrecy has been no more than an intelligent policy of delay in releasing data so that the public does not become confused by premature publication of incomplete studies of reports."

In general, the report—or, more accurately, Condon's summary of the report—was greeted as the authoritative final word on the entire UFO controversy. Headlines proclaimed that "Flying Saucers Do Not Exist—Official" or, more bluntly, "UFOs are Bunk." But critics pointed out that what Condon had written was a summary not of the findings of the committee but of his own preexisting beliefs. Among other things, Condon ignored the fact that some thirty percent of the ninety-one cases his committee analyzed remained unsolved. This was a jarring statistic in view of the fact that Project Blue Book had classified as "unidentified" only about five percent of reported sightings. Moreover, the ninety-one cases had been selected from among thousands of possibilities, presumably with the intention of giving each one of them intensive—and conclusive—study.

Thus the massive "Scientific Study of Unidentified Flying Objects," in the end, gave skeptics the ammunition they wanted to dismiss UFO reports altogether. At the same time, it contained enough loose ends and mysteries for enthusiasts of the UFO phenomenon to continue to proclaim that there had been bias at best or, at worst, a cover-up.

Apparently, the air force—which, after all, had paid for the study—got what it wanted as well. In December 1969 it announced that it was disbanding Project Blue Book and, as Condon had recommended at the very beginning of his effort, was getting out of the UFO business. The very determined would be able to discover thereafter that the Department of Defense had given responsibility for future UFO reports to something called the Aerospace Defense Command. But to the general public, it seemed that the government wanted nothing more to do with UFO reports.

6
WITCHCRAFT

The Witch-Hunt

THERE WAS a time when belief in *maleficium,* the doing of harm by occult means, was a fact of everyday life. The average man was convinced that a deserted mistress who knew sorcery could take her revenge if he married another. The wronged woman had only to tie three knots in a string during his wedding; the knots would make him impotent. A herder could mutter a spell over a hunk of bread and conceal it in a tree to direct disease and injury away from his livestock and toward a neighbor's.

Documents of the medieval era chronicle a number of incidents involving lynch mobs that seized suspected witches and beat them, dunked them repeatedly, or burned them at the stake. But although the people dealt out their own rough justice now and again, more alleged witches were tolerated than attacked, especially those thought capable of healing ailing neighbors or helping fellow villagers fend off evil. Moreover, neither church nor secular authorities expended much energy in the pursuit of witches. Despite the fact that many forms of *maleficium* violated ecclesiastical or civil law, there were very few prosecutions for such offenses before the fourteenth century. Indeed, clergymen themselves were rumored to dabble in sorcery, at least in the higher-level occult practices that were known as ritual magic, since clerics were among the few who could read the old magic books.

But Europe's attitude toward witchcraft changed. Commencing in the fourteenth century, the Continent was to witness a frenzy of hatred and homicidal witch-baiting that would cost the lives of many thousands of innocent people over the next 300 years. Like brush fires spread by wind-borne sparks, the fury would erupt first in one place, then in another, searing the civilized life of France, Italy, Germany, the Low Countries, Spain, England, Scotland, Austria, Norway, Finland, and Sweden, and for one brief period, leaping the Atlantic to flare up even in the New World.

THE CHURCH was primarily responsible for the great witch-hunt. After the fall of the Roman Empire, the Church had been the only institution strong enough to maintain a kind of order and universality of culture in western Europe, and as time wore on, its influence became all-encompassing. Yet large numbers of nominal Christians in northern Europe still clung to certain pagan beliefs of their forebears. Particularly troublesome to Church authorities were the old fertility rites and other pagan feast days. In virtually every region, from late fall to early spring, there were days of celebration when people would hold feasts honoring Thor, Wotan, and the other gods; light bonfires; and perform various rituals intended to restore vigor to the low-lying sun. In some rites, male celebrants would don animal skins and headdresses, or disguise themselves as women, to join the ranks of the god and goddess Herne and Holda and their spirit retinues. Wine and beer would flow in copious amounts; dancers would work themselves into a frenzy and on occasion engage in sexual orgies reminiscent of the Roman Saturnalia and the Dionysian revels of ancient Greece.

The Church could not entirely suppress such activities, so it resorted to a shrewd expedient. The pagan feast days were incorporated into the Church calendar. For example, the Roman Saturnalia became Christmas Eve. The great Celtic festival of the dead, Samhain, which marked the beginning of winter and the Celtic new year, fell on October 31. In order to draw attention away from Samhain, the Church declared November 1 to be All Saints' Day, with masses sung to honor departed holy men and women.

But the Church's attempt to assimilate the old festivals was not entirely successful. The pre-Christian spirits that had roamed the earth since the dawn of time were too deeply embedded in the European psyche. Even today in some Western countries, people celebrate October 31—known in the Christian calendar as All Hallows' Eve, or Halloween—with activities that recall the ancient Samhain feast of the dead and by wearing costumes representing skeletons, ghosts, and witches. In those days, the tenacity of the old religious ideas was much more evident. As late as the eighth century, a backwoods Christian priest was found offering a sacrifice to Jupiter, and some isolated communities continued to worship trees and fountains. In a further effort to extinguish the pre-Christian loyalties, the Church declared the pagan gods to be demons.

The woodland sprites of northern climes, the elves, gnomes, ogres, and leprechauns, and the fauns and satyrs of the Mediterranean—all were condemned as enemies of the true Church. An act of homage to them was sacrilege, calling forth the gravest consequences. "If anyone sacrifices a human being to the Devil," declared an edict to the Saxons in 787, referring to a savage rite honoring the god Wotan, "and offers sacrifices to demons as is the custom of the pagans, he shall be put to death."

Sorcerers in particular were considered a danger to the realm, as a synod of bishops informed the emperor's son, Louis the Pious, in 829: "Their *maleficia* can disturb the air, bring down hail, foretell the future, remove the fruits and milk from one person and give them to another, and perform innumerable marvels." Witches must be routed out and punished, the bishops said, and "all the more severely because their wicked and overweening audacity does not shrink from serving the Devil."

The new concept of witchcraft, involving homage to demons, took inspiration from various arcane issues of Christian theology. The idea that a human could enter into a pact with Satan was nothing new. Some church fathers were having second thoughts about attributing so much power to the Devil's disciples, however. A document calculated to counteract this tendency called the *Canon Episcopi* was included in a guide for bishops. In sum, it said that witches and other sorcerers did not actually possess the occult abilities that had been credited to them, and that their sin was in *believing* that they did. For instance, the Canon addressed the popular belief that witches made airborne nocturnal journeys in the company of spirits. "Some wicked women, turning back to Satan and seduced by the illusions and phantoms of demons," it observed, "believe and openly avow that in the hours of night they ride upon certain beasts, together with Diana, goddess of the pagans, and a numberless multitude of other women."

Such supernatural goings-on simply did not occur, scoffed the document's author. But that so many people could be made to believe that they did constituted fresh evidence of the Devil's handiwork; such delusions could only have been put into people's heads by the archfiend himself. Priests were sternly enjoined to warn their congregations that Satan knew how to deceive ignorant women; he would indoctrinate them with all sorts of evil images while they were sleeping. Over time the Church gradually reversed this position, and theologians again began to subscribe to the idea that night flights, transformation into animals, and all the rest really did take place.

The Devil's business grew ever more depraved. Beyond the traditional forms of misconduct and *maleficium,* witches displayed the harpylike qualities of the ancient Roman *strigae,* Hecate's mortal-devouring companions. They would slip out at night, leaving their husbands asleep, pass wraithlike through the locked door if need be, and then roam over thousands of miles, killing and eating Christians or else plucking out their hearts and replacing them with nothing but straw. Sexually insatiable, a night-riding witch might transform herself into a beautiful phantom known as a succubus

in order to have unholy intercourse with men. One story, transcribed in England in the twelfth century, relates how a roisterous knight named Edric the Wild happened upon some maidens dancing in a forest cottage. Thoroughly enchanted, he seized one and made love to her—only to discover to his everlasting horror that the lovely maiden had turned into a hideous old witch. Most witches, the demonologists agreed, also engaged in coupling with sexually active male demons called incubi, and at times with the Devil himself. Indeed, amorous seduction by the Prince of Darkness was a common method of recruiting innocent females into his sinister coterie.

Equally abhorrent was the thought that large companies of witches would regularly gather to engage in profane rites of Devil worship. The English cleric Walter Map, writing in the late twelfth century, described how such an event might take place. The Satanic worshipers would meet in a secluded house with gates, doors, and windows securely fastened. After a period of silent meditation, the Devil himself would appear in the shape of a monstrous black cat, sliding down a rope from the ceiling. The congregation would snuff out the candles, hum evil chants, and gather

This seventeenth-century series of woodcuts by R. P. Guaccius depicts a group of innocents joining with the Devil to become sorcerers. Satan rebaptizes and reclothes them and obliges them to stomp on the cross and exchange a Bible for a book of black magic.

around the cat to kiss it in the most obscene places—its filthy feet, its genitals, even under its tail. Then everyone would grab his or her neighbor for a communal orgy of unbridled lust.

This blasphemous parody of Christian rites would later be termed a sabbat, apparently for the Jewish sabbath, which inspired only slightly less revulsion in the popular mind of Christian Europe. The witches' sabbat was regarded as the very apex of Satanism. Subsequent writers would embroider the scene with ghastly details. They would claim that the Devil might reveal himself as a goat, or a toad, or an enormous black man; that male celebrants might copulate with their mothers, or with their daughters, or with other men; and that women made no distinction as to the age, sex, or familial relationship between themselves and their partners. Along with such sexual license there would be frantic dancing and gluttonous feasting, as likely as not

In these seventeenth-century woodcuts by
R. P. Guaccius, sorcerers prostrate themselves
before Satan, who then addresses them and
ushers in a band of new initiates

on the roasted limbs of infants they had murdered.

Eventually, the profane rituals were expanded to include a reiteration of the Devil's pact. The communicants would defile the Christian sacraments, spit on the cross, denounce Christ, and swear fealty to Satan. And in a twisted parody of the Catholic confession, each individual would be called upon to relate all the evil deeds he or she had committed since the last meeting.

On the Continent, the Church set off a spate of witch trials—including some involving clerics who took too keen an interest in sorcery. At Agen, in southwestern France, a canon, another priest, and a layman were accused in 1326 of calling forth demons to kill people and make storms. The canon was allegedly caught in possession of books about magic as well as containers of peculiar powders and stinking liquids. His co-conspirators were said to have stolen limbs and heads from corpses on the local gallows for use in magic rituals. The layman was burned to death, while the clerics were turned over to Church authorities. Their fate is not known. Also undocumented is the fate of a prior and two other priests who were similarly charged that same year with practicing magic and summoning demons and who were handed over to a commission of three cardinals.

In 1323, the inquisitor of Paris hauled into court an abbot, several canons, and two laymen—the laymen being a magician and his assistant. The abbot had lost some valuables, and as would many of his contemporaries in an era when magical powers were often taken for granted, he turned to a sorcerer to help find them. Unfortunately for the abbot, he was not paying sufficient heed to the Church's new attitude about such matters. He and the other clerics were stripped of their priesthoods and imprisoned for the rest of their lives. The magician and his accomplice were burned to death.

A few years later a Carmelite brother in the southern French town of Carcassonne was brought before the Inquisition for allegedly using sorcery to satisfy his sexual appetite. The monk, named Pierre Recordi, confessed mixing blood from toads and his own saliva into wax puppets, then placing them under the thresholds of women's houses. Subsequently, if a woman did not comply with his advances, she would be persecuted by a demon. Recordi's confession was probably elicited by torture; during his long trial he several times recanted it. But nonetheless he was sentenced to life imprisonment, during which he was to be chained hand and foot and given nothing but bread and water.

In Switzerland, scores of accused witches were tried in secular courts. At Simmental, near Bern, an unspecified number of victims went to the stake convicted of boldly offering homage to Satan during Sunday church services. These witches also stole children, the charges read, and cooked and ate them for lunch, after first draining their blood to make magic ointments. Rubbed onto the body, the ointment could render the parishioners invisible, or transform them into animals, or allow them to fly through the air in proper witch style.

The secular courts of northern France also turned their attention to crimes of heretical witch-craft. In a Paris trial that began in 1390, a thirty-four-year-old female fortuneteller named Jehanne de Brigue, known for some reason as la Cordière, "the ropemaker," was accused of bewitching one Jeahn de Ruilly at the behest of de Ruilly's disaffected wife, Macette. The wife, it was charged, had fallen in love with a handsome young curate and in order to pursue her romance with him had employed the witch to turn off de Ruilly's affections. La Cordière obliged, but her incantations made the poor man so ill that the remorseful witch restored de Ruilly to health.

In the Paris criminal court, la Cordière first denied everything. Then, under severe questioning, she admitted casting spells by invoking the Holy Trinity, neglecting her regular prayers, and not wash-ing on Sunday. Pressed further, she confessed that her aunt had taught her how to call up a demon named Haussibut and that she sometimes worked magic by suckling toads and sticking pins in wax dolls. The trial

A witch prepares to depart into the night

dragged on through winter and spring, with occa-sional recesses. At one point in the proceedings, la Cordière was sentenced to burn-ing but was granted a reprieve because she was thought to be pregnant.

Eventually, the fortuneteller implicated Macette, who was arrested and charged. Tortured on the rack, Macette confessed to having played a part in the affair, and she, too, was found guilty. There were further delays. La Cordière's sentence had been reinstated, but she appealed to the Parliament of Paris, the nation's highest tribunal. Another set of judges reviewed the case. Finally, it confirmed both verdicts. On August 19, 1391, the two women were taken to the Pig Market. There they were burned at the stake.

Even among the upper reaches of Church hierarchy one was not safe from the lightning of the Inquisition. Father Guillaume Adeline, a prior of an important monastery at St.-Germain-en-Laye, was also a noted doctor of theology who for-merly had taught in Paris. In 1453, he was accused of witchcraft. Inquisitors alleged that a written compact with the Devil was found on his person. Almost certainly after

ABOMINATION DES SORCIERS

Est il rien qui soit plus damnable,   Ils tirent de leurs noirs mysteres   C'est la que ces maudites am
Ny plus digne du feu d'enfer,   L'horreur, la hayne le debat,   Se vont preparer leur tourm
Que cette engeance abominable   Et font de sanglans caracteres   Et qu'elles attisent les flamm
Des ministres de Lucifer: Dans leur execrable Sabat.   Qui bruslent eternellem,

A sixteenth-century depiction of the manifold abomination of a witches' revelry

extensive torture, he confessed to offenses that must have seemed ironically ludicrous: making love to a succubus, flying on a broomstick, and kissing a goat under its tail.

A single random accusation, if properly nurtured by the Inquisition's prosecutors and torturers, could lead to the netting of scores of victims. In 1459 in the northern French city of Arras, then a great manufacturing center, a poor hermit was condemned to be burned as a witch. Seeking to save himself and avoid further torture, he eagerly denounced a prostitute and an elderly poet hitherto best known for his celebrations of the Virgin Mary. Those two in turn accused others, and soon the burnings began.

The first of the executions took place in May 1460. Four pitiful creatures, including a half-witted woman and the old poet, were led onto a platform in front of the Episcopal Palace in Arras. Dressed in robes and miters emblazoned with the Devil's symbols, they listened to the charges of which they were convicted—that they had flown to sabbats on sticks, trampled the cross, and adored the Devil. (To protect the tender sensibilities of those who came to witness the witches being burned alive, authorities omitted from the reading the crime of having intercourse with Satan.) Then, as the fires were lighted, the victims proclaimed their innocence, screaming with their dying breaths that they had been promised they would be allowed to live if they confessed to the charges.

The arrests in and around Arras multiplied. Anyone who spoke out against the witch-hunt was soon among the prisoners. Inquisitors declared that only witches would oppose the burnings and that therefore any objectors should be burned also. According to the inquisitors, no less than a third of all people who claimed to be Christians, including many bishops and cardinals, were actually witches. Soon the entire city and surrounding region were in the grip of terror. Hundreds of people from all walks of life were implicated. Some of the richer folk managed to pay bribes in exchange for their freedom. Even so, several large estates were confiscated. The poor had no recourse; they filled the prisons and fueled the fires. Trade suffered and prosperity vanished.

Various tests were devised to confirm the suspect's guilt or innocence. Among the most common of these methods was trial by water, an ancient practice mentioned as early as 1750 B.C. in the Code of Hammurabi. Initially employed for all crimes, the water ordeal, or swimming, became a critical test for witches during the seventeenth century, particularly in England. If the accused floated when cast into water, she was deemed a witch and executed; if she sank, she was declared innocent. And if the suspect drowned in the process—a not unlikely outcome—at least her corpse enjoyed a proper burial. King James I gave the test royal approval, rationalizing that water would reject those who had "shaken off them the sacred water of baptism."

Eventually the authorities in Paris intervened. The chief inquisitor was summoned home, and anyone left in jail was set free. Finally, in 1491, the Paris Parliament declared that the Inquisition had acted "in error." Interrogation by torture was condemned. Those who had died at Arras were exonerated. A mass was said in their honor, and a cross was erected as a memorial on the spot where they were burned.

Unfortunately, in Germany a pair of ardent inquisitors, Heinrich Kramer and Jakob Sprenger, were incensed that large numbers of people, including clergymen, still felt that witchcraft was neither seriously evil nor particularly widespread. Kramer and Sprenger complained directly to Pope Innocent VIII, who reacted with anger and alarm to their reports of a lack of concern about witches. Thus encouraged, Kramer and Sprenger produced an exhaustive tome—*Malleus Maleficarum*, or "Hammer of Witches." In this impassioned screed of 250,000 words, Kramer and Sprenger detailed everything known or imagined about witches and witchcraft. The

Sixteenth-century depictions of witches spell-casting during a sabbat

work ranged from biblical times to the present moment, blending folk beliefs about sorcery with Church doctrine on heresy and demon worship. After theory came practice, with legal guidelines for conducting trials, examining witnesses, and obtaining confessions. In addition, there were some helpful suggestions on the most effective types of torture. The *Malleus* became a handbook for persecution, with a single goal in mind: To enforce the biblical injunction, in Exodus 22:18, that "thou shalt not suffer a witch to live."

Besides their abhorrence of demonic sin, the authors had an abiding disdain for the entire female gender. "What else is a woman but a foe to friendship," the writers asked, "an inescapable punishment, a necessary evil, a natural temptation?" Women were lustful, false, vain, vindictive, mean-minded, and weak-willed. Ever since Eve offered Adam the apple, they had lured men to perdition. No wonder the Devil sought them out. Although thousands of men would expire in the witch-hunt, the great majority of victims would be women. The *Malleus* was printed and reprinted again and again over the next two centuries. The work engraved on the European consciousness the indelible image of the devil-worshiping, night-flying, curse-spouting female witch.

ELSEWHERE IN Europe, the witch craze continued to flare up first in one place, then in another, often in the wake of drought, flood, or some other natural disaster, or as an outgrowth of a political or religious conflict, such as the sporadic clashes of Catholics versus Protestants. In Alsace and Lorraine and in the Rhineland states of western Germany, the trials multiplied until entire populations

*Anne Hendricks is burned at the stake in 1571 in Amsterdam in this
seventeenth-century illustration*

lived in mortal fear. In 1556, a woman at Bièvres in northern France was mistakenly
burned alive, instead of being garroted first as her sentence required. When it was discovered that she had suffered the agonizing punishment usually reserved for convicted
witches who recanted their confessions, inquisitors airily dismissed the error as God's
secret judgment. In 1579, the Church Council at Melun declared: "Every charlatan
and diviner, and others who practice necromancy, pyromancy, chiromancy, hydro-
mancy, will be punished by death."

Among the witch-hunt's most energetic practitioners was a grim zealot named
Nicholas Remy, who in 1591 became Lorraine's attorney general. As a youth, Remy
had been intrigued by the witchcraft trials and executions in the villages of his native
Vosges Mountains. He later became personally involved when, as a lawyer, he pros-
ecuted a beggar woman for bewitching his own son. It appears that Remy had refused
to give the woman alms, and he then considered her responsible some days afterward
when the boy took ill and died.

From then on he was a relentless demonologist—the term applied to lawyers,
judges, or theologians who specialized in witches and sorcery. He tracked down every
strange coincidence or event on the theory that since God must be rational, "whatever is not normal is due to the Devil." In a book he wrote on the subject, he declared
that "everything which is unknown lies, as far as I am concerned, in the cursed
domain of demonology; for there are no unexplained facts." When he published his

Witches offer up a baby to the Devil and feast and dance in this seventeenth-century series of woodcuts by R. P. Guaccius

book in 1595, he boasted on the title page that he had condemned some 900 witches in fifteen years. Remy continued to exterminate witches for almost two decades more, until he passed away in 1612.

Another who showed no qualms about the numbers he sent to their deaths was Henri Bouget, chief judge of Saint Claude in the French province of Burgundy. He employed the Inquisition's cruelest methods to wrest confessions from 600 people, ranging from elderly invalids to prepubescent children. It troubled him not at all to include children, believing that once they fell into the grip of Satan, they seldom could be reformed. All too many of Bouget's victims, young and old, were burned alive. One poor woman found the strength to burst her bonds at the stake three times and three times was tied up again and thrust back into the flames.

Despite the excesses of Remy and Bouget, they did not pursue their callings with more vigor and relish than did Pierre de Lancre, who was appointed special prosecutor in the Basque region of southwestern France in 1609. De Lancre probably stands alone for the very scale of his heinous vision. His investigations convinced him that *everybody,* the entire population of 30,000 souls in his district—including all the clergy—had been converted to witchcraft. The devils who had worked this wondrously wicked deed, he said, had arrived in the guise of refugees from Japan and the East Indies. Witnesses, he averred, had sighted flocks of Basque witches flying off to

A witch narrowly escapes the authorities in this 1570 woodcut from Geneva

sabbats as far away as Newfoundland. A more frequent venue was the main square at Bordeaux, where de Lancre claimed sabbat attendance reached as high as 100,000.

De Lancre worked swiftly, and in scarcely four months, he later boasted, he cremated 600 people. The numbers were great enough to inspire one of those rare instances when a community rose up in revolt against the witch-hunt. Mobs of howling protesters rioted and converged on his courthouse. Clearly, the Devil had urged them on—or so the prosecutor believed. And after de Lancre burned three priests, the bishop of Bayonne himself rescued five others from the prosecutor's jail and joined the opposition to the witch-hunt.

De Lancre's work apparently continued, however, because in 1612, he published a book describing it. For other would-be witch-hunters, the book provided rich details of the standard allegations that were the stuff of the trials. The Devil first appears as a black man and at midnight makes a pact with the accused. The witch finds himself or herself able to fly all over the world to Friday night sabbats, where the Devil—now in the shape of a huge black goat—copulates with the women. Then the participants fling themselves into indiscriminate sex, eat human infants, cook up poisonous plants and bits of corpses that they dug up from graveyards, and set forth to kill people and livestock and to destroy crops.

Despite de Lancre's grandiose ambitions, even in his district the persecution mania failed to reach the savage proportions it achieved in the German states. A series of calamities struck the region around the city of Trier in 1580—heavy rains, plagues of mice and grasshoppers, forays by Protestant mercenaries—and the troubles continued throughout the decade. Authorities blamed witchcraft and commenced trials in both civil and ecclesiastical courts. Convictions eliminated two villages, virtually wiping them from the map, and in another, only two members of the entire female population remained alive. The victims included some of the state's highest officials—burgomasters, counselors, judges.

Among the last was Trier's chief civil magistrate, Dietrich Flade, whose own moderation in handling trials had angered some authorities. His record of convictions was suspiciously meager. Could the judge be a witch himself? The Church inquisitors produced a befuddled boy who swore that he had seen Flade at a sabbat; and an old crone who was about to be executed gladly testified that Flade was a witch, in order to secure for herself the mercy of strangulation before roasting. Under torture, the judge confessed to plotting against the archbishop of Trier and to throwing clods of dirt into the air, which turned into crop-destroying slugs. Found guilty, he was strangled to death and his body burned.

The pyres of Trier were the initial sparks of conflagration that swept through many German states. In the Saxon town of Quedlinburg, the executioner burned 133 witches on a single day in 1589. A year later, a writer commented that in the town of Wolfenbuttel "the place of execution looked like a small wood from the number of stakes." At Fulda to the south, a sadistic judge named Balthasar Ross executed 300 people between 1603 and 1606, after first hoisting the women up on the pulley-and-rope device called the strappado, their wrists tied behind their backs, and jabbing hot skewers though their flesh. Ross met his own fate a few years later, when he was sent to the scaffold for embezzling state funds.

Sixteenth-century depictions of witches by Albrecht Dürer (above) and Israel van Mechelen (opposite page)

Among the most brutally efficient German witch-hunters were two cousins, each ruler of his own state. During the 1620s, Phillip Adolf von Ehrenberg, prince-bishop of Würzburg, burned 900 local witches; his cousin Johann Georg II, Fuchs von Dornheim, of Bamberg, did away with 600. Würzburg's horrified chancellor documented what it was like: "A third of the city is surely implicated. The rich-est, most attractive, most prominent of the clergy are already executed. A week ago, a girl of nineteen was burned, said everywhere to be the fairest in the whole city . . . there are 300 children of three and four years who are said to have intercourse with the Devil. I have seen children of seven put to death, and brave little scholars of ten, twelve, fourteen."

Confessions were still mandatory before an execution could take place, and the German inquisitors developed the process of extracting them to a high art. While imprisoned, the victims were force-fed herring cooked in salt to induce a raging thirst, then denied water. At the appointed hour, the victims were stripped—and in many cases, the women raped—before being led into the torture chamber, where notaries waited to take down their every agonized word. All the torture instruments had been blessed by a priest beforehand.

The torturers might begin with thumbscrews, followed by several dozen lashes from a whip. Then came leg vises, in which tightened metal bands crushed the shins and ankles, after which there might be a period of stretching on the rack or hanging from ropes to dislocate the shoulders. If these methods proved inadequate in securing a confession, the accused would be submerged in ice water or a scalding bath laced with lime, or have sulfur-dipped feathers burned under their groin and armpits. One or another horrifying device persuaded most suspects to say whatever was necessary to put an end to the suffering.

Once a confession was extracted, there was no going back. In one account, a woman named Margaret confessed to various crimes after being subjected to fiendish torture. The torturer then threatened her, saying, "You have now made your confession. Will you deny it? Tell me now, and if so, I will give you another going over. If you recant tomorrow or the day after tomorrow, or before the court, you will come back again into my hands, and then you will learn that up to now I have only been playing with you. I will plague you and torture you in such a way that even a stone would cry out in pity."

A few hardy souls resisted to the end. The judicial reports told of a remarkable sixty-nine-year-old German widow, Clara Geissler, who withstood the thumbscrews, but when "her feet were crushed and her body stretched" on the rack, confessed to everything she was accused of: that she drank the blood of infants she had stolen on night flights and that she had murdered sixty babies. Under prodding, she named twenty other women who had acted as accomplices and declared that the widow of a prominent burgomaster had presided over the night flights. Yet upon her release from the rack, Clara immediately retracted her confessions. She was then tortured a second time and confessed again, only to recant once more. The third time, she was tortured with "utmost severity," said the report. Her agony continued for several hours, at the end of which she collapsed and died. "The Devil would not let her reveal anything more and so wrung her neck," concluded the report, in tones of disappointment.

To fly through the air, the wisdom of the era held, witches had to be preternaturally light. Following that logic, weighing the accused became a popular method of witch detection in Europe. The tests varied from town to town. In one village, the suspect might be weighed against the big Bible in the parish church: If the scales tipped in her favor, she was deemed innocent. Elsewhere she might be required to balance the scales exactly against a set weight—a near-impossible feat ensuring a guilty verdict. There was one place, however, where a judgment of innocence was virtually guaranteed—the Dutch town of Oudewater. Under the watchful, honest eyes of the weightmasters, suspects were measured against their minimum nonflying weight. Since that number was determined by a simple formula based on height, everyone outweighed the minimum, and not one person was convicted of witchcraft in Oudewater.

And while the victims screamed and perished, their prosecutors and executioners grew rich. Not only did convicted witches and other heretics forfeit their estates, they had to pay all trial expenses, as well as fees for every torture inflicted upon them. At Trier, a chronicler noted, "the executioner rode a blooded horse, like a noble of the court, and went clad in gold and silver; his wife vied with noble dames in the richness of her array." If the witch had no money, as was often the case, the populace paid for the trial and torture through assessments.

THE HORROR of the witch trials and the calamitous effect they had on economies throughout Europe inevitably led to a reaction among those with the courage to speak out. One of the relatively few voices raised in protest in early-seventeenth-century Germany was the leading Jesuit official at Würzburg, Friedrich von Spee. Among Spee's priestly duties was hearing the last confessions of condemned prisoners, and he soon came to the realization that virtually all those accused

Archiv für Kunst und Geschichte/West Berlin

A woman is tested for witchery in the Dutch town of Oudewater

of demonic practices were in fact completely innocent. "Previously I never thought of doubting that there were many witches in the world," he wrote. "Now, however, when I examine the public record, I find myself believing that there are hardly any."

Among the dissenters was a German named Hermann Löher, who served as a law court official at Rheinbach, near Bonn, through two major witch-hunts, in 1631 and 1636. The toll was high. On average, every other family lost at least one person. His experiences convinced him that innocent people had been tortured and killed in the witch courts and that victims under torture would confess to anything. His opposition to the trials put his life and the lives of his family in jeopardy, so he sold most of his property and fled to Amsterdam in 1636.

Forty years later he published a book entitled *Most Pressing Humble Complaint of the Pious Innocents,* in which he described in scathing terms how one judge conducted a witch trial. The judge rants at the defendant cowering before him: "You apostate, you witch, you dumb dog! Confess your sin of witchery; reveal the names of your accomplices! You filthy whore, you devil's wanton, you sackcloth-maker, you dumb toad! Speak and confess in God's name! Swallow the holy salt! Drink the holy water! Tell who it was that taught you witchcraft, and whom you saw and recognized at the witches' sabbat. Then you will not be tortured any more but have eternal life."

Speaking for himself, Löher wrote that "the early Christian martyrs were falsely accused of grievous crimes; but in our day, Christian witches are far more unjustly accused of mortal sins that they have not committed—and that they could not possibly commit." Löher fervently urged local princes in Germany to examine the court records, to reduce the appalling fees levied against the hapless victims, and most important, to halt the torture.

In England, where the witch mania was never as severe as on the Continent, and death by hanging the strictest, albeit the most tragic, punishment a witch might face, a healthy skepticism had long been evident. As early as 1582, a Kentish squire by the name of Reginald Scot, whose passion in life was the growing of hops, was shocked by the hanging of two luckless women at St. Osyth. They had been convicted of casting spells and consorting with familiars based on the testimony of some overwrought children, aged six through nine. Scot was moved to write *Discovery of Witches,* published in 1584, in which he attacked the very notion of witchcraft as a monstrous delusion. "What abominable and devilish inventions, and what flat and plain knavery is practiced against these old women," he declared.

Still, sporadic outbursts of witch-baiting occurred in England every few years throughout the next century. The nation's most notorious witch-hunter was an East Anglia lawyer of mediocre skills named Matthew Hopkins, who realized that he could make a better living by preying on the credulity of local farm communities. He would offer to track down neighborhood witches by using various practical tests, torture being prohibited by English law. One of his favorite methods of verification was the aforementioned "swimming," in which a suspect was trussed up and dunked into a convenient pond. Another test favored by Hopkins was to stick a suspect with pins, on the theory that any spot insensitive to pain was a devil's mark. For these attentions Hopkins charged a healthy fee.

Although Hopkins's career as a witch-finder lasted only from March 1645 to late spring of 1646, in that brief time he was responsible for the hanging of perhaps several hundred harmless old women and other alleged witches. Often the most telling witnesses were undisciplined youngsters with overactive imaginations, who had been nurtured on ghost stories and fairy tales. Only when wiser heads prevailed was Hopkins forced into retirement.

By this time, the witch mania was abating throughout Europe. Businessmen and rulers viewed it as damaging to the economy. Intellectuals perceived it as irrational and inconsistent with the new scientific attitude that one day would cause the era now dawning to be called the Age of Enlightenment. By the century's turn, the rampant executions had ended in both France and Germany. In Spain, which had seen some witch burnings in Navarre and other northern provinces, the Inquisition had

Abraham Palingh, 1725

An accused witch is whipped, collared, and tortured until he dies

long since turned its attention to the pursuit of Jews, Moors, and other heretics. There was a sudden outbreak of witch-hunting in Sweden in 1669, at Mora, where eight-five elderly women were put to death at the stake after a number of hysterical children claimed to have flown with them to sabbats. But that was the end of the terror in Scandinavia.

The last convicted English witches died in 1682, three mistreated elderly women who wearily climbed the gallows steps at Exeter. After a lengthy trial at Lyons, Father Louis Debaraz was burned alive in 1745, accused of saying masses to the Devil in hopes of locating hidden treasure; he was the last person to die as a convicted witch in France. The last German trial, in Swabia in 1775, resulted in the execution of one Anna Maria Schwagel. After that, no further death sentences were handed down for witchcraft. The great European witch-hunt was over.

WITCHCRAFT HYSTERIA, however, came late to America. Although there were isolated witch trials throughout the colonies in the late 1600s, the phenomenon paled in comparison to the mass persecutions in Europe—until 1692, when a wave of witch madness engulfed the Massachusetts settlement of Salem. Before the year's end, nineteen men and women had been hanged and more than a hundred others arrested on charges of witchcraft.

For the people of Salem—as for most seventeenth-century New Englanders—witches and demons existed as surely as did the rocky land from which they scratched a living. Ruling this invisible world, as theologians of the time called it, was Satan himself. Odd incidents or coincidences and unaccountable illnesses were often attributed to the Devil and his followers.

So when the village physician, Dr. Griggs, could find no physical cause for the "strange and unusual" behavior exhibited by two local children in the early months of 1692, he suspected they might be under Satan's spell. What else could explain why Puritan children, taught to be quiet and obedient, would suffer convulsive fits and scream blasphemies as the Reverend Samuel Parris's nine-year-old daughter, Elizabeth, and her eleven-year-old cousin, Abigail Williams, were doing?

The probable real cause of the girls' bizarre behavior was to be found in the Reverend Mr. Parris's own kitchen. There, unbeknown to him, his West Indian slave woman, Tituba, regularly regaled a group of enthralled girls with vivid tales of voodoo spells and witchcraft. Some of the girls, aided by Tituba, had even tried their hand at fortunetelling. But when the horrified Parris learned of these activities, the revelation only served to confirm his darkest suspicions and the doctor's diagnosis: The two children were victims not of illness but of witchcraft.

In a short time, several other girls and young women in the village began displaying even more dramatic symptoms, clutching their necks as if choking, twisting their bodies into contorted positions, and claiming temporary loss of speech, sight, and hearing. The girls also said they experienced spells in which a specter—or the likeness of a witch—bit, pinched, pricked, or otherwise tormented them.

Alarmed that Satan's servants appeared to be operating in their midst, a group of village leaders questioned the girls. Under mounting pressure, they named three women as witches—Sarah Good and Sarah Osborne, both unpopular villagers, and the slave Tituba. Brought before the local magistrates, Good and Osborne righteously declared their innocence. Tituba, however, confessed with gusto to all manner of witchcraft and traffic with the Devil. Her enthusiastic testimony confirmed the villagers' worst fears of a demonic conspiracy. The three women were jailed to await formal trial.

Meanwhile, the girls warmed to their game and accused more people of witchcraft—men as well as women, the rich and respectable as well as the poor and despised. Salem plunged headlong into witch hysteria. Suspicion and fear thrived, and like an epidemic, the accusations and arrests spread to nearby settlements.

The witchcraft hearings began in May, when the colony's governor, Sir William Phips, set up a special court of oyer and terminer ("to hear and determine"). Ironi-

*Early-sixteenth- and late-fifteenth-century
depictions of a witches' gathering*

cally, the most incontrovertible type of evidence—a direct confession of witch-craft, such as Tituba's—was the one that virtually ensured the court's leniency. The self-declared guilty were forgiven and spared punishment, while those who refused to admit their transgressions were hanged. Thus the temptation to confess was great, and many of the accused took this route in order to save their lives. Others were persuaded to confess by tortures such as enforced sleeplessness or the binding of their necks and heels under increasing pressure until blood gushed from their noses.

If a reputed witch nonetheless continued to plead innocent, the judges sought other forms of evidence, such as telltale witch's marks. Supplying the court with its most decisive evidence, however—and transforming the proceedings into a near circus—were the afflicted girls. Their hysterical reactions as the judges questioned an accused witch were deemed valid proof of the defendant's guilt. All too typical were their actions during Martha Cory's trial. "When she wrung her hands," read one account, "they screamed that they were being pinched; when she bit her lips, they declared that they could feel teeth biting their own flesh." Even more damning was so-called spectral evidence, based on one girl's claim that an apparition of the accused had tormented her. On such questionable grounds, six men and thirteen women, Sarah Good among them, were hanged. Two other condemned witches, including Sarah Osborne, died in jail. And Giles Cory, Martha Cory's husband, was slowly crushed to death for refusing to plead either guilty or not guilty.

How the Salem witch trials ever reached such a violent pitch is still debated today. Certainly the belief of the villagers and the judges in a malevolent invisible world provided a receptive atmosphere for the girls' accusations. The court's reliance on such dubious proof as spectral evidence, however, is—and was even then—less easily justified.

Olaus Magnus, 1555

The Devil carries off a witch

Central to the whole affair, of course, were the girls. The fits of little Elizabeth Parris and Abigail Williams are thought by many to have been rooted in vivid, emotionally exciting fantasies provoked by Tituba's tales. The older girls may then have emulated the hysterics to gain attention themselves. Or perhaps the group was simply being mischievous, playing a childish prank that quickly spun out of control. The girls may have been loath to shame themselves by admitting the truth and perhaps were intoxicated by their unaccustomed power.

There is some evidence that a play-acting conspiracy of sorts existed. When twenty-year-old Mary Warren tried to retract her accusations, for instance, the other girls declared her to be a witch. Soon Mary was having fits and accusing others again. Some historians think the girls could have suffered true physical symptoms brought on by a hysterical, near-contagious reaction to the suggestion of bewitchment.

In such a suggestible state, the girls were probably easily influenced by the expectations of others; they probably implicated people based on negative impressions gleaned from adults. Moreover, the judges were not above proposing names to the girls, who more often than not confirmed their suggestions. Adult villagers joined in supporting the accusations, sometimes motivated by property squabbles or long-standing animosities.

Finally, one or two of the alleged witches may indeed have practiced the magic that everyone feared. Tituba's familiarity with West Indian voodoo and her immediate confession to witchcraft seemed to support that theory. And not only did tavern keeper Bridget Bishop's own husband accuse her of practicing the black arts, two laborers testified that they had found several needle-stuck rag dolls in her cellar wall.

Fortunately, by summer's end the public had become horrified by the death toll. In addition, local ministers had banded together to condemn the use of spectral evidence in the trials. One of the province's most respected clergymen, the Reverend Increase Mather, published a sermon signed by fourteen other pastors in which he said "it is better a guilty person should be absolved than that he should without ground of conviction be condemned." That fall Governor Phips forbade any more arrests and dismissed the court of oyer and terminer; the following spring the rest of the accused were acquitted or granted reprieves. Almost as suddenly as it had begun, the Salem witch mania had ended.

Modern Witchcraft

PARISHIONERS OF Boston's venerable Arlington Street Church have seen and heard many things over the years. Here in an earlier age of crisis, the abolitionist William Ellery Channing railed against the evils of slavery. And in this same church a century later, opponents of the American venture in Vietnam rallied in protest of that conflict.

However, even adventurous church members could hardly have conjured the improbable scene that occurred on an April Friday in 1976. At the chancel stood a high priestess of witchcraft, Morgan McFarland, the daughter of a Protestant minister. In a clear and steady voice, McFarland began a long and mystical-sounding incantation: "In the infinite moment before all Time began, the Goddess arose from Chaos and gave birth to Herself . . . before anything else had been born . . . not even Herself. And when She had separated the Skies from the Waters and had danced upon them, the Goddess in Her ecstasy created everything that is. Her movements made the wind, and the Element Air was born and did breathe."

The occasion was a three-day conference on women's spirituality, and this ceremony was as unorthodox an opening prayer as had ever echoed within the brownstone walls of the Arlington Street Church. It was also infectious, and by its end many in the audience were dancing in the aisles, and a thousand voices filled the stately old church with a single chant: "The Goddess is alive, magic is afoot. The Goddess is alive, magic is afoot."

To many scholars who have studied the history of witchcraft, the goddess being invoked at the ceremony—whose ecstatic dance is said to have woven wind and air and fire, and whose laughter, it is claimed, blew life into all women—could not have been around for the creation at all, because she was born and given form as well as character in some strictly modern imaginations. Her historical provenance, the skeptics say, is limited to a few traits culled from cloudy notions of the deities of pre-Christian

Europe, now overlaid with theatrical details that have been consciously devised to suit ceremonial needs.

But for many modern practitioners of witchcraft, their Great Goddess is indeed an ancient creator spirit who was worshiped in Europe and the Near East long before the Christian God was introduced there. They believe she survived centuries of persecution by hiding in the hearts of her secret adherents, spiritual daughters and sons who went to the rack and stake of the Inquisition because of their beliefs. And now, they say, the goddess moves abroad once more, openly, stirring celebrations in strongholds of the very same organized religion that once attempted to expunge every trace of her or her followers.

Today, thousands of otherwise ordinary men and women believe they are drawing on what author Theodore Roszak calls the "wellspring of human spiritual consciousness." In the process, these self-proclaimed neopagans are discovering—or as some of them put it, rediscovering—what they say is an age-old religion, one whose language is the language of myth and ritual, whose faith is as real as rapture and as difficult to define, and whose god is not one but many. These modern-day nature worshipers, like pagans of earlier eras, do not sift the natural from the supernatural, the ordinary from the extraordinary, the mundane from the spiritual. To a neopagan, all are one and the same.

Estimates of the number of neopagans run as high as 100,000 or more in the United States. This group comprises a cross section of society, including tattooists and tugboat captains as well as bankers, lawyers, and librarians, and a large number of computer professionals. Their religion is also known by the name of Wicca, an Old English word for a male witch; the term may also be related to the Indo-European roots *wic* and *weik,* meaning "to bend" or "to turn." Hence, in the eyes of modern Wiccans, witches were never the hags or seductresses that the populace purported them to be but those women and men who could bend reality by means of magic.

But stereotypes persist. To many people, a witch still is a devil worshiper. Under such an indictment, it is not surprising that the words "witch" and "witchcraft" continue to arouse revulsion. "Witchcraft is a word that frightens many people and confuses many others," observes a California-based writer and witch who goes by the name Starhawk. "In the popular imagination," she notes, witches of the past are "ugly old hags riding broomsticks, or evil Satanists performing obscene rites." Modern-day opinion has not shown them any more kindness, holding them to be, Starhawk points out, "members of a kooky cult, which lacks the depth, dignity and seriousness of purpose of true religion."

But a religion it is, both in the eyes of those witches who describe religion as "a human need for beauty," and when measured against the dictionary's definition of religion as an "institutionalized system of religious attitudes, beliefs and practices." Even the U.S. Department of Defense has given its imprimatur to Wicca's claim of being a valid religion, and in the mid-1970s, the Pentagon recruited a witch called Lady Theos to revise the chapter on witchcraft in the official U.S. Army chaplains' handbook. Lady Theos's contributions were updated in 1985 by a high-profile neo-

Popperfoto, London

*Gerald Gardner, one of Wicca's leading authors, blesses the marriage of two
British witches in 1960*

pagan named Selena Fox. Another sign of the times can be read on the dog tags worn
by members of the armed forces for identification, where the words "pagan" and
"Wiccan" now appear as routinely—though certainly not as frequently—as do the
names of other religious affiliations.

GIVEN THE difficulty of pinning down a concise list of beliefs common to all
Wiccans, a description of the characteristics that make a modern witch is necessarily an approximation. It can safely be said, however, that the vast majority of
witches believe in reincarnation, revere nature, worship a multifarious and all-perva-
sive deity, and incorporate ritual magic into that worship.

In addition, there are few witches who would dispute the encapsulation of basic
beliefs that author Margot Adler offered in *Drawing Down the Moon*. "The world is holy.
Sexuality is holy. The mind is holy. The imagination is holy. You are holy. A spiritual path
that is not stagnant ultimately leads one to the understanding of one's own divine nature. Thou art Goddess. Thou art God. Divinity is . . . as much within you as without."

Underlying such beliefs are three philosophical assumptions that link modern
witchcraft and neopaganism to corresponding practices in the ancient world. The first
assumption is animism, the idea that inanimate objects like rocks and trees are imbued
with spirits all their own. A second commonality holds that divinity is part and parcel of nature. And the third characteristic is polytheism, the conviction that divinity
is both multiple and diverse.

Taken together, these beliefs comprised a general outlook toward the divine that
animated the pre-Christian world. In the words of historian Arnold Toynbee, "divinity was inherent in all natural phenomena, including those that man had tamed and

domesticated. Divinity was present in springs and rivers and the sea; in trees, both the wild oak and the cultivated olive-tree; in corn and wines; in mountains; in earthquakes and lightning and thunder." God, or divinity, was felt to be everywhere, in everything; "plural, not singular; a pantheon, not a unique almighty superhuman person."

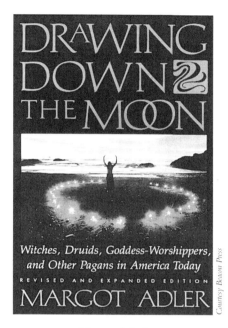

Margot Adler's
Drawing Down the Moon

Writer and witch Starhawk echoes much the same theme when she observes that witchcraft "is not based on dogma or a set of beliefs, nor on scriptures, or a sacred book revealed by a great man. Witchcraft takes its teachings from nature and reads inspiration in the movements of the sun, moon and stars, in the flight of birds, in the slow growth of trees and in the cycles of the seasons."

But Starhawk also acknowledges that it is the polytheistic aspect of Wicca—the worship of "the Triple Goddess of birth, love and death and of her Consort, the Hunter, who is Lord of the Dance of Life"—that most sets modern witchcraft apart from the mainstream of Western religion. Even so, many Wiccans disagree on whether their god and goddess are mere symbols, actual entities, or powerful primal images—what psychologist Carl Jung called archetypes—deeply rooted in the human subconscious. Witches are also equally divided on what appellations to give their deities. Names for the god and goddess abound, ranging from Cernunnos, Pan, and Herne for the male side of the godhead, to Cerridwen, Arianrhod, and Diana for the female side. As one priestess put it, "the goddess shall be called a million names."

MOST WITCHES, in writer Susan Roberts's estimation, are not the idle rich but "middle-class Americans who, on the surface, live quietly and unobtrusively in the mainstream of American life." Roberts also observes that while witches generally defy categorization, they do tend to be nonconformists and tend to have retained "that simple faith most of us believe to be the special province of children."

Other observers have reported similar findings. British anthropologist Tanya Luhrmann, for one, notes that a large number of witches she questioned regarding the allure of witchcraft cited such motivating forces as a "need to be childlike, to marvel at nature and to re-experience an imaginative intensity they had lost." Similarly, Margot Adler has noted that a sense of childlike wonder appears to be a common trait among the neopagans that she has observed, along with a calm acceptance of life and death and a desire to live in harmony with nature.

Despite the difficulties that arise when one tries to categorize witches, surveys of neopagans do provide some clues as to who is practicing what and why. One 1980 survey, for example, revealed that neopagans are, for the most part, white-collar, middle-class professionals. The same survey also showed that the religious backgrounds of these individuals closely parallel the national religious profile of all Americans, with former Protestants comprising nearly half of the group and former Catholics accounting for slightly more than 25 percent of the total.

A second survey, conducted by Margot Adler in 1985, found little change in these figures or in the kinds of jobs held by neopagans. It was Adler's survey that disclosed a surprisingly heavy proportion of computer programmers, analysts, and software developers. Asked to account for the apparent link between an interest in computers and an interest in neopaganism, one respondent to the survey pointed out that computers are similar to magic in that they "work in unseen ways to accomplish tasks." Another respondent observed that both the computer sciences and neopaganism "attract slightly unenculturated, solitary, creative thinkers."

Whatever the explanation, the relationship between the world of high-tech and the roots-and-berries sphere of the craft is not confined to one side of the Atlantic Ocean. In *Persuasions of the Witch's Craft,* her 1989 study of witchcraft in England, Luhrmann noted a similar concentration of computer professionals among the witches she met. She guessed that the attraction might reside in the fact that "both magic and computer science involve creating a world defined by chosen rules, and playing within their limits."

Another subgroup of the neopagans identified in the studies of Luhrmann and Adler consists of those who came to their practices and beliefs through an interest in science fiction and fantasy literature. The works of J. R. R. Tolkien, Ursula K. Le Guin, and Wiccan priestess Marion Zimmer Bradley are common on the bookshelves of Wiccans. Some Wiccans regard science fiction, in particular, as a form of religious literature, one that provides a new mythology for our age.

It is not surprising that many practitioners of a religion steeped in ritual and romance might be devotees of a literature that speaks of ancient power as well as timeless enchantment, or festering evil bested by noble good. As one witch told Margot Adler, "The Craft is a place for visionaries . . . a place where all of these things fit together: beauty, pageantry, music, dance, song, dream. It's necessary to me, somehow. It's almost like food and drink."

For some witches, the motivating force was a reverence for nature or a strong interest in mythology. Others discovered Wicca after rejecting Christianity and casting about for an alternative spiritual lifeline. Still others spoke of responding to a mysterious, vocation-like inner call, similar to that which induces young men to enter a seminary or impels young women to join a convent. Many Wiccans recalled that the primary attraction was the idea of a religion that has no intermediaries—one in which they could practice their beliefs in an entirely personal fashion. In the meantime, scholars rummaging for reasons to explain the upsurge of interest in Wicca suggest that witchcraft may offer its adherents meaning in a meaningless world, ritual in

Nathan Benn © 1979 National Geographic Society

Modern witches gather for a sabbat in Salem, Massachusetts

a ritual-starved society, or shelter from the pressures of rapid social and technological change. "There are a million paths to the Craft," concludes Margot Adler, "but the main thing is that no one 'converts' to Wicca—essentially everyone suddenly feels 'Oh! I always believed in that. I just never knew it had a name!'"

Most witches describe their introduction to the craft not as a conversion but as a kind of homecoming. As a result, few neopagans ever proselytize. The experience of Alison Harlow, a systems analyst at a large California medical research center, is typical of many and, in its telling, embraces several common Wiccan themes.

"It was Christmas Eve," she begins, "and I was singing in the choir of a lovely church at the edge of a lake, and the church was filled with beautiful decorations. It was full moon, and the moon was shining right through the glass windows of the church. I looked out and felt something very special happening, but it didn't seem to be happening inside the church." Once Mass was over, Harlow excused herself and retreated to the top of a nearby hill. As she was looking up at the moon and down again at the church, she suddenly felt a "presence."

Whatever it was, "it seemed very ancient and wise and definitely female," she recalls. "I can't describe it any closer than that, but I felt this presence, this being, was looking down on me, on this church and these people and saying, 'The poor little ones! They mean so well and they understand so little.'"

Harlow also sensed that whoever "she" was, "she was incredibly old and patient; she was exasperated with the way things were going on the planet, but she hadn't given up hope that we would start making some sense of the world." In the wake of that incident, Alison Harlow resolved to find out as much as she could about the female "presence," a decision that led her to the study of Wiccan literature, to contact with a number of craft traditions, to initiation as a Wiccan priestess, and ultimately to the creation of her own coven.

In this manner, the practice of witchcraft precedes belief, during what often becomes a protracted period of soul-searching. Particularly because the Wiccan creed flies in the face of convention, many newcomers need to take time for a gradual growth of belief. For many Wiccans, an important milestone along this path of growing belief is initiation as a witch. Some new practitioners perform a solitary ceremony of self-initiation, an affirmation of beliefs and of dedication to the goddess and god. Other Wiccans are inducted into the religion and into a coven at the same time, joining a group that may range in size from three to thirty members. Whether simple or elaborate, the attendant ritual is an outward signal of the novice's transition from explorer to devotee. Initiation often includes a blessing of the new witch's tools, and when the ritual is completed, a solemn oath of secrecy seals the ceremony—and the lips of its participants.

Secrecy is, in fact, a source of comfort to witches, for even today many of them still live in fear. Misconceptions about witchcraft and misinterpretation of its beliefs make the followers of Wicca targets of vandalism, discrimination, and job dismissals.

And if secular hassles are harsh reality for many modern-day Wiccans, the struggle to win legitimacy for the craft may have a price. The institutionalization of witchcraft raises in the minds of some practitioners the specter of a breakdown in craft values. Particularly troubling is the growing clamor for a paid clergy, which has risen in some factions of Wicca. Traditionalists feel that such a change would transgress the craft's own dictates against spreading the word for money. "One thing I don't want to see," says one high priestess, Doreen Valiente, "is Witchcraft becoming too much of an organized religion."

That prospect seems remote, despite the remarkable growth the craft has enjoyed in recent decades. As for the problems inherent in that growth, it is likely that a religion whose central invocation, the Charge of the Goddess, calls for "mirth and reverence" will be able to take in stride many real-world concerns. "Being alive is really rather funny," one priestess told anthropologist Tanya Luhrmann. "Wicca is the only religion that captures this."

The Wiccan Year

WICCANS SPEAK of the year as a wheel and their calendar is a circle, signifying that the cycle of seasons turns endlessly. Almost evenly spaced around the Wiccan Wheel of the Year are the eight Wiccan feast days, or sabbats. These are distinct from esbats, the twelve or thirteen occasions during a year when covens gather to celebrate the full moon. The four minor sabbats, in fact, are solar holidays, milestones in the sun's yearly journey around the skies. The four major sabbats celebrate the earth's agricultural cycle of seedtime, growth, harvest, and rest.

The sabbat cycle is a retelling and celebration of the age-old story of the Great Goddess and her son and consort, the Horned God. Wiccan sects cherish a host of variations on this myth; one traditional version follows, embodying many Wiccan beliefs about death, rebirth, and the faithful return of cycles.

Yule, a minor sabbat, is the feast of the winter solstice (about December 22), marking not only the longest night of the year but the start of the sun's return. At this time, the story goes, the goddess gives birth to the god, represented by the sun; she then rests through the cold months, which belong to the infant god. At Yule, Wiccans light fires or candles to welcome the sun, and they decorate with holly and mistletoe—red for the sun, green for eternal life, white for purity.

Imbolc (February 1), a major sabbat also called the Feast of Candles, celebrates the first stirrings of spring, the sprouting of seeds unseen under the ground. Longer days show the power of the boy god. Wiccans end winter's confinement with purification rites and light all manner of fires, from white candles to great bonfires.

At the minor sabbat of the spring equinox (about March 21), the exuberant goddess is awake and strewing the earth with fertility. Wiccans color eggs, plant seeds, and plan new enterprises.

At Beltane, or May Day (May 1), another major sabbat, the god attains manhood as the goddess's power to bring forth fruit peaks. Stirred by nature's energies, they mate and she conceives. Wiccans enjoy a flower festival, often including a dance around a maypole, a fertility symbol.

Midsummer (about June 21) is the longest day and calls for bonfires honoring the goddess and the god. It is also an occasion for handfastings, Wiccan weddings, at which the newlyweds jump over a broom. The season's major sabbat is Lugnasadh (pronounced "loon-sar"), on August 1, which marks the first harvest and the promise of ripening fruits and grains. Early grain is baked into sun-shaped loaves. As the days shorten, the god weakens, even as the goddess feels their child in her womb. At the autumn equinox (about September 22), the god prepares to die and the goddess is at her most bountiful. Wiccans give thanks for the harvest, symbolized by the cornucopia.

Just opposite the riotous flowering of Beltane on the Wheel of the Year stands the major sabbat of Samhain (pronounced "soe-en"), October 31, when all that flowered is dying or dormant. The sun grows fainter, and the god is dying. Aptly, this is the Wiccan New Year, embodying the faith that every death brings rebirth through the goddess. In fact the next feast, Yule, celebrates anew the birth of the god.

The coincidence of these festivals to Christian holidays, and the similarities between Wiccan and Christian symbols, say many anthropologists, are not accidental, but prove the preexistence of the pagan beliefs. For Christian authorities contending with older religions during Europe's Dark Ages, converting established holidays by giving them new Christian meanings eased the acceptance of the new faith.

Like adherents of more conventional religions, the followers of witchcraft, or Wicca, also use rituals to spiritually bind themselves to one another and to their deities. Wiccan rites differ from sect to sect. Some ceremonies are periodic, marking phases of the moon or the turning of the seasons. Some, such as initiation or the witches' marriage service, or handfasting, are performed when needed. Others are part of almost every coven meeting. Whatever their purpose, most Wiccan rituals—especially when celebrated in the outdoor settings long favored by witches—evoke a dreamlike mood that reaches across time to a more romantic era.

No Wiccan ceremony is more meaningful to a new witch than initiation. Some solitary witches initiate themselves, but more common is a group ritual that confers membership in a coven as well as entry to the Wiccan faith. It is a rite of symbolic death and rebirth.

The candidate is ritually bathed and then led to the magic circle nude, blindfolded, and with hands bound. These conditions are meant to test her trust in her companions. A challenger steps into her path, presses an athame (a dull, double-edged knife) to her chest, and demands to know her name and purpose. In symbolic rebirth, she answers with her new witch name, affirming that she embraces her new spiritual life and comes "in perfect love, in perfect trust."

An eighteenth-century depiction of a witches' Sabbat

As the ceremony concludes, the priest grasps her wrists to turn her in four directions, presenting her to the four compass points. She is then welcomed by the coven, and everyone celebrates with food and drink. As one says, "Pagans are very fond of merriment."

Wiccans identify the ever-changing moon—waxing, full, and waning—with their Great Goddess in her varied aspects as Maiden, Mother, and Crone. Thus it is that a ceremony intended to bring the moon's magical power to earth, called Drawing Down the Moon, is the essence of goddess worship and a key rite in the Wiccan liturgy.

When meeting for one of the year's twelve or thirteen esbats, or full-moon celebrations, members gather around the magic circle to direct their psychic energies through their high priest to their high priestess, who stands with arms upraised toward the night sky. The concentration of their energy will help the priestess, so they believe, to "draw the moon into herself" and become an embodiment of the goddess.

The cups in the priestess's hands hold water, the element that symbolizes and is ruled by the moon. Coven members say that this water becomes "psychically charged" with the power coursing through her. Each witch will drink some of it at the end of the ritual.

Many groups draw down the moon in its other phases as well as when it is full. They try to tap the power of the waxing moon to promote growth and beginnings, and that of the waning or dark moon to seal the endings of things that ought to end. And while most groups consider the ceremony a way to honor the Great Goddess, many forgo stylized ritual, simply taking a moment when the moon is full to meditate on the Wiccan deity.

Part of a witch's training is to learn to use psychic energy, and one primary technique, a ritual performed at almost every coven meeting, is Raising the Cone of Power. Like most other witch activities, it takes place within a magic circle. For this ritual especially, the magic circle is visualized as not just a circle but "a dome, or bubble, of psychic energy—a way to hold the power in before we do something with it."

In their efforts to generate energy for a cone of power, witches use many means, including dancing, meditating, and chanting. To "mold" the power they claim to produce, they gather around the magic circle, stretch their arms toward the earth, and gradually raise them toward a focal point above the circle's center. When the coven's leader feels that the group's energy is at a peak, she or he commands the members, "Send it now!" Then the witches all visualize the energy rising, as a cone, out of the circle and traveling onward to its previously determined destination.

Like other religious groups, Wiccan communities celebrate significant steps in individual and family life, including birth, death, marriage, which they call handfasting, and the naming of children. EarthSpirit is recognized as a church by the Commonwealth of Massachusetts and therefore its handfasting rite can confer legal marriage. Often, however, handfasting is used to create not a legal marriage but a bond recognized only by Wiccans. If a couple thus joined decide to separate, their bond can be undone by another Wiccan ceremony known as handparting.

Central to handfasting are the blessing of the couple's union and the ritual binding of their clasped hands—the step that gives the rite its name and long ago yielded the familiar phrase for marriage, "tying the knot." The colorful band that fastens the pair together is one they have created from three strands of fiber or leather, representing the bride, the groom, and their relationship. For weeks or months before this day, the couple have regularly taken time—at each new moon, perhaps—to sit together, braid part of the cord, and talk over the interweaving of their two lives, in love, work, friendship, sex, and children.

Children born to witches are presented to the coven in a naming ritual called a child blessing, or—in old Scots—saining. Many sainings include the planting of a tree, which may be fertilized by the child's placenta or umbilical cord. By a similar ceremony known as a magical saining, which usually comes before initiation, apprentice witches declare the names by which they choose to be known within the craft.

Wiccan rituals are not all somberness and solemnity. The eight sabbats that highlight the witches' year honoring the sun's yearly journey and the earth's rhythmic agricultural cycle are occasions for much joyous feasting. The most festive of sabbats is Beltane, a giddy salute to spring that takes place on the first of May. For Beltane the pagans of EarthSpirit gather to enjoy a traditional maypole frolic.

The maypole dance, an old fertility rite, begins as a ritualized game involving the kind of strong sexual symbolism that characterizes many witchcraft ceremonies.

The women of the coven dig a hole in which the obviously phallic maypole is to be planted. But when the men approach, carrying the pole, they are confronted by a ring of women surrounding the hole as if defending it. In a symbolic courtship, the women teasingly open and close the circle at different places as the males run around the outside with the pole, seeking a way in.

"Eventually" says a high priest, "the men are allowed to bring the pole in and plant it in the hole, and then both men and women cement it in place with earth." Finally, the witches perform their interweaving dance around the maypole, crossing and recrossing one another's paths so that the bright ribbons they hold are plaited around the pole. "The ritual binds female and male energy together," one explains, "so that fertility will abound."

7
TRANSFORMATIONS

Shapeshifters

S KIN BLACKENED, hair cropped short, and wearing only a leather loin-cloth, an Englishman named Frederick Kaigh settled on his perch in a tree as the dark shadows of the forest night gathered around him. He felt foolish. This was the 1930s, after all, and his getup would have been more suitable for a Victorian explorer on a romantic African adventure than for a twentieth-century man—a physician, in fact—even here in a remote region on the border of the Belgian Congo and Northern Rhodesia. But he knew that he must not be recognized; if the crowd assembling in the clearing near his tree became aware that a European was present, the secret dance that was about to begin would be halted.

With the appearance in the clearing of a *nyanga,* or witch doctor, the drums started beating "on a note and a rhythm I had not heard before," Kaigh later recalled. It was a rhythm that reverberated "inside one and tingled down the spine: a rhythm which seemed gradually to take on a bestial quality." To the accompaniment of the

*A fifteenth-century woodcut shows sorcerers transformed into
a donkey, a rooster, and a dog*

drums, the *nyanga* began a chant, answered by those seated in a ring on the ground. It grew louder and louder, fueled by the strong native beer being drunk by all present. Then rising to a high-pitched scream, the chant came suddenly to a halt, and an eerie silence filled the clearing.

The crouching *nyanga* was dressed as a jackal; skins of the animal hung from his body, which had been striped along the spine and across the ribs with white paint, and over his hair he wore the head of this doglike beast. Kaigh watched spellbound while the *nyanga* made medicine "in a little fire that burned with queer light as he threw his concoctions on the flames" and then drank a potion he had prepared. At the sound of a distant, faint jackal cry, the witch doctor stood up, jumped on the fire, and scattered the coals with his feet. From his mouth, "sudden as a gunshot," came the shrill, piercing howl of a beast, answered from the jungle by similar cries.

The witch doctor danced with ever increasing abandon, drawing upon an energy reserve that belied his advancing years, working himself into a frenzy and foaming at the mouth, until, exhausted, he dropped to the ground in an apparent trance. The hidden English spectator found the performance "brilliant, amazing, transcendental, depraved and bestial," but it was nothing compared with what was to follow.

While the *nyanga* lay in his trance, a young man and woman, both of whom were naked, leaped from the darkness into the inebriated circle and immediately threw themselves into the roles of mating jackals. "As the dance progressed, their imitations became more and more animal-like," Kaigh wrote later. "Then, in a twinkling, with incredulous amazement, I saw these two *turn into jackals before my eyes.*"

Kaigh had witnessed an occurrence as old as humankind, the seeming ability of some specially gifted—or cursed—men and women to transform themselves or others into animals. There is even a word for it: lycanthropy, from the Greek *lukos* for wolf and *anthropos* for man. It is a belief that has persisted for centuries around the world, in cultures as diverse as those of Europe, Africa, India, China, Japan, and pre-Columbian America, and is at the heart of many myths, legends, and fairy tales. Among those individuals who have claimed to have witnessed transformations or to have turned into a beast, the mystery defies analysis. For those who have studied the phenomenon, lycanthropy–commonly known as shapeshifting—is seen as a matter of illusion, delusion, or even madness, abetted often by the wearing of animal skins or the use of psychic stimulants, or both. Whatever its dynamics, lycanthropy was for so long so powerful a belief that it gave birth to two of the most fearsome of night creatures, the werewolf and the vampire.

THE ROOTS of lycanthropy stories reach all the way back to the prehistoric caves of the Cro-Magnons in Spain and southern France, where among the 20,000- to 30,000-year-old paintings of animals that cover the walls are found two of the earliest representations of Homo sapiens. Interestingly, these show the male not fully human, but as part animal. In one crudely drawn picture, a hunter lies on his back, perhaps in a trance like Kaigh's exhausted witch doctor, and his head is that of a bird and his hands are like claws. Close by is his spear, thought to be the implement that has just wounded a magnificent bison that stands on its last legs only inches away, its bowels hanging from its belly.

In the second image, a man with human beard, arms, and legs, but with the antlers and ears of a stag and the tail of a wolf or wild horse, appears to be taking a prancing step, perhaps a movement in a ritual dance. Located fifteen feet above the cave floor and at the end of a magnificently decorated chamber, this figure seems to preside over the assemblage of beasts that covers the walls. Why is he there? What purpose did the artists serve by showing men in animal guises? And what rites took place in these caves deep within the womb of the earth?

The answers can never be final, but thanks to information gathered over the years by a variety of researchers digging in the caves themselves, studying the artwork found there, and observing peoples in the wild, some informed guesses can be made. Curiously, the paintings and engravings often crop up in places that are inconvenient for viewing: in narrow niches, behind bulges in the rock, sometimes in areas that must have been not only difficult but also hazardous for the artists to work in. "It is simply impossible," says Johannes Maringer, a German archaeologist and student of prehistory, "that this art should have been invented, in these locations, to give pleasure to the eye of the beholder; the intention must always have been to veil it in mysterious secrecy."

What, then, were these ancient artists up to? According to numerous specialists, their art was a vehicle for magic—more specifically, for a form known as sympathetic hunting magic. Strong and intelligent, the Cro-Magnons—although well-equipped with all kinds of weapons, including stones and slings—lived in a primitive world, always in the shadow of unpredictable and incomprehensible forces. Doubtless the hunters felt it imperative, through whatever means, to stave off misfortune, injury, and death. Some of the animals they came up against were extremely dangerous, and, like many hunter-gatherers in remote parts of the earth today, they believed that magic could assist them in dodging misfortune and in gaining control over the beasts they wished to kill.

By painting pictures of their prey on the walls of the caves, these hunters in effect sought to strengthen their chances of dealing their prey a mortal wound during the hunt. Even today, many isolated peoples around the world believe that creating the likeness of someone or something gives the creator some supernatural power over the subject. This kind of art could also function as a kind of prayer, in which the artists sought to ensure that the beasts so vividly limned on the rock surface would remain fertile, mate, and produce game the hunters could then kill.

Hunting magic is also an explanation for the depictions of men dressed in the guise of beasts as well. Straightforward pictures of men dressed in animal skins may have been intended to guarantee successful stalking. They may also have been symbolic: projections of the hunters' feeling that a painting of a sorcerer disguised as a beast or partly transformed into one would work potent magic on a hunt. Or they may be depictions of the hunters themselves transformed: Around the figures of two bison discovered in one of the caves, for instance, the ghostly footprints of dancers turned up. But instead of pressing down on the soles of their feet as humans do, the dancers tripped around on their heels—in order to leave hooflike prints, experts believe. Some scholars think they were impersonating the bison in order to invoke the spirit of the animals, and perhaps acquire some well-admired traits: bullish strength and aggressiveness, attributes hunters need to be successful.

In the dawn of civilization, life for the human animal was brutish and short. Although at nature's mercy, our earliest ancestors doubtlessly felt themselves at one with the world, connected to all other living things. Most, if not all, probably did not see themselves as being superior to the animals, which, they recognized, possessed powers that they lacked. Nor did they see themselves as being at the center of the universe, as humankind does today, but rather saw themselves only as a part of mother earth, dependent upon all its other parts for their survival. They belonged to nature and venerated everything from weather and water to the spirits in plants and animals. Whatever they took from the earth for their own well-being, they felt they had to give back, through gifts and sacrifices of like worth. "Their priests and worshippers lived upon this planet as its child, and not as an enemy or occupying force" is how one writer has put it.

WITH THE spread of Christianity throughout pagan Europe, shapeshifting, whether genuine or imaginary, came under attack. The Church despised the notion of transformation, considering it the work of the devil. "No one must let himself think that a man can really be transformed into an animal, or an animal into a man," wrote one theologian. "These are magical portents and illusions, having the form but not the substance of those things which they present to our sight."

Despite such attacks on its credibility, the belief in shapeshifting survived. Superstition offered it fertile ground, and like some pale forest mushroom, it continued to proliferate for centuries in the shadowed crannies and outreaches of Europe. Church records down through the decades are filled with accounts of attempts by the pope and his missionaries to curtail the practice. In the eleventh century, the pope admonished the Danish king not only because there were still too many sorcerers worshiping pagan gods in an ostensibly Christian land but also because they had a reputation, whether deserved or not, for being able to turn themselves into cats and wolves.

People believed that in order to be transformed the shapeshifter had to do little more than rub his or her body with special ointment or salve, wear a belt or girdle made from the skin of the animal that individual wanted to become, consume some of the creature's brains, drink water from its footprint, or recite an incantation or cast a spell. Although the metamorphosis was generally seen as a voluntary act, it could also be triggered as a punishment, inflicted on an unsuspecting individual by a malevolent soul. According to some, the phenomenon was even contagious; brushing up against the shapeshifter's clothing or eating his food would be enough to damn an unwary innocent to a life of shapeshifting.

Shapeshifting was a belief as deeply rooted in the rest of the world as it was in Europe. The folklore of India, China, and Japan, among other countries, as well as that of the Indians of the Americas, is rich in tales of transformations. There exists a kind of universal protagonist of many of these tales, an animal that transforms itself into a human or possesses humanlike qualities, that enjoys outwitting people and often takes advantage of them sexually. Students of the genre of legend have labeled this character, whether it appears as a fox, or a *tanuki,* in Japan or as a coyote in the American Southwest, as the trickster. There is a good deal of humor in trickster stories, but these shapeshifters were also often seen as purveyors of evil.

In China, for example, it was told how during the first month of 1755, babies in what is now Beijing were dying of convulsions during the early hours of the morning. Wherever they struggled for life, an owl was observed flying into the death chamber. Hearing of the owl, an archer went to a room where an infant was dying and waited for the owl to enter. The moment it fluttered into view, he shot an arrow at the bird. Crying out in pain, the owl escaped, leaving a trail of blood that led to the kitchen of a military man. And there the archer discovered a servant woman with green eyes, incapacitated by a wound in her loin. Needless to say, the wound was enough to establish her connection to the bird and bring about her confession. She admitted leaving her abode

at midnight, in the guise of an owl, so that she might feed on the brains of babies. The woman was burned alive, and with her body reduced to ashes, the epidemic of convulsions allegedly came to an end.

The Navajo of the American Southwest also regard shapeshifters as evil beings. They see them as misusing their power in order to engage in incest, to harm individuals, and to steal from the dead. Acting out of self-protection, the Navajo have been known to track down and kill members of the tribe who they believe are lycanthropes.

Navajo shapeshifting lore centers on witches, male as well as female. While dressed in the skins of such fierce animals as the coyote, wolf, and bear, whose qualities they naturally assume, the witches are said to roam about at night, ready to drop a noxious powder through the smoke hole of a hogan or directly into the nostrils or mouths of their victims. This dusty substance, which resembles pollen, is prepared by grinding the flesh and bones of the dead, especially those of children—and is considered all the more effective for being made from the remains of twins. Particularly prized are the bones at the back of the neck and the skin of fingertips, with its characteristic pattern of whorls. When administered through any of the sinister means described above, or simply blown into the face of the intended target, or slipped into a cigarette, the preparation is believed to induce a variety of conditions, ranging from lockjaw and a black and swollen tongue, to unconsciousness. Sometimes the effects are not immediate, however, and the victim may be left to just slowly fade away.

The Navajo claim they can tell when a witch is close by. His or her presence is signaled by the sudden barking of dogs at night; a trickle of dirt descending into a hogan from the smoke hole, dislodged by the alien on the roof; or odd, unexplained noises outside. Invariably the transformed witch leaves tracks, which are generally bigger than the tracks of the actual animal whose skin the interloper wears. When the trail is followed, it often leads to the home of a tribe member previously unsuspected of practicing the black arts.

The Hopi, neighbors of the Navajo, take a kindlier view of shapeshifters. They feel there is no essential difference between humans and other forms of life. Only outward appearances separate the species from one another; and when the external is penetrated, their commonality emerges. The Hopi preserve their connection to the gods or nature spirits, and like the earliest humans, they consider themselves one with the earth and all its wonders. They find peace and stability through the cooperation and hard work their harsh desert environment continually demands of them. Believers in shapeshifting, they regard it as yet another manifestation of the close bond between the earth and the gods and see it as a power that, though given to certain individuals, belongs to the group as a whole and can be used for the good of all.

Werewolves

Jean-Loup Charmet, Paris

THROUGH MUCH of the last quarter of the sixteenth century, a large wolf rampaged the countryside around the German towns of Cologne and Bedburg. Its attacks on townsfolk and their animals were so frequent and its victims so numerous that people feared to travel from one place to another alone. "Oftentimes," recounted a lurid 1591 pamphlet, "the inhabitants found the Armes & legges of dead Men, Women, and Children scattered up and down the feelds to their great greefe and vexation of hart." But try as they might, they could not catch and kill "this greedy and cruell Woolfe."

Then, as chance would have it, a group of men spotted the wolf, surrounded him, "and most circumspectlye set their Dogges upon him, in such sort that there was no means to escape." To their astonishment the wolf turned out not to be an animal at all, but a man, one Peter Stubbe, well known to the very people whose friends and children he had murdered. Stubbe, according to the pamphlet, was the most feared of creatures, a werewolf, changed by magic from man to beast and driven to wantonly kill and feast on his human victims.

Stubbe's case contains so many classic elements of the werewolf phenomenon that it is worth examining in some detail. Tied by his captors to the torture device known as the wheel and fearing the punishment they would use to force his story out of him, he confessed to a series of villainies. He revealed how he achieved his transformation into ravener by strapping around his waist a magic girdle or belt, "procured of the Devill." Thus equipped, he became, as the pamphlet delighted in telling, "strong and mighty, with eyes great and large, which in the night sparkeled like unto brands of fire, a mouth great and wide, with most sharpe and cruell teeth,

Courtesy Art Resource, New York

This sixteenth-century woodcut shows the grisly punishment of Peter Stubbe. He was strapped to a wheel, torn apart with hot pincers, decapitated, and finally burned at the stake.

a huge body, and mightye pawes." Unable to find the girdle, the magistrates assumed that the devil had reclaimed it after abandoning Stubbe "to torments which his deedes deserved."

And heinous deeds they were. Among his reported victims were thirteen children and two pregnant women, from whose wombs he had torn their babies and eaten the "harts panting hot and rawe, which he accounted dainty morsells & best agreeing to his Appetite."

Dusty archives the world over contain records telling of pathetic werewolves such as Stubbe, compelled to abandon their humanity for the bestial appearance and behavior of the wolf. This animal—a creature of cunning, stealth, swiftness, and rapacity—was the one most often described in stories of lycanthropy.

From centuries of stories, a composite portrait can be assembled of the werewolf. In human form, it tended to have bushy eyebrows that met over the bridge of the nose; red teeth; a long third finger; long, almond-shaped fingernails, with a blood-red tinge to them; and ears that tended to be far back and low down on the head. The person's mouth and eyes were dry, and he was often thirsty. (According to one French judge who regularly attended torture sessions, werewolves, like witches, were unable to weep.) The skin was scabrous, much scratched and cut because of the brush through which the werewolf ran in animal form, and often of a yellowish, pinkish, or greenish cast, with a tendency to hairiness.

In addition to such physical features, the werewolf displayed certain pronounced psychological traits. Among these was a preference for night over day and solitude to company. Beset by deep melancholy ("very black and vehement," as the late-seventeenth-century French historian Simon Goulert describes it), the person was a habitué of graveyards and was known, on occasion, to dig up a corpse and feast on it. February was apparently the cruelest month for a lycanthrope, or at least so suggests Tommaso Garzoni in his *Hospitall of Incurable Fooles,* published in 1600. Garzoni tells how in the month of February the lycanthrope "will goe out of the house in the night like a wolfe, hunting about the graves of the dead with great howling, and plucke the dead men's bones out of the sepulchers, carrying them about the streets, to the great fears and astonishment of all them that meet him." Goulert describes running into one of his friends, a lycanthrope, who deep in a melancholy fit carried "upon his shoulders the whole thigh and legge of a dead man."

The transformation of the afflicted human into a beast was supposedly achieved in a number of ways. It was said that, like witches, werewolves rubbed their bodies with magic ointments and salves of various kinds. The composition of these differed, but many contained psychoactive alkaloids that had potent hallucinatory effects, which could lead to a belief that the body had changed. Indeed, two of the most commonly employed plant ingredients in lycanthropy's pharmacopoeia—nightshade and henbane—could produce in the person who had absorbed them through the skin or taken them by mouth the delusion that he or she had become a wolf. Pig fat, turpentine, and olive oil were among the substances used as a base for such a salve. Later, when the distillation of spirits was perfected, alcohol was used as a solvent for the herbs. Extracted into a potion, they became even more active.

Helping the delusion along was the wolf hide or the girdle or belt made from the animal's skin that the aspiring werewolf often wore. To further increase the efficacy of the ointments and potions, magical incantations were also frequently used. These medieval rituals, however, came late in werewolf lore. They were said to have been used by those who wished to become werewolves. In the earliest stories, lycanthropy was the result not of a wish but of a curse. Such a tale is the Greek myth of Lycaon. In one version of this legend, the great shapeshifter Zeus, disguised this time as a wayfarer, sought hospitality at the court of a vicious Arcadian king named Lycaon. Lycaon, recognizing the god and attempting to kill him, served a dish containing human flesh. But omnipotent Zeus recognized the terrible trick and did not eat. Outraged, he drove Lycaon from his palace, destroyed it, and as a final punishment, exiled the king to the countryside, damning him to live the rest of his life as a wolf, the animal he most resembled.

This sixteenth-century woodcut depicts two witches transformed into a wolf and a cat

A vivid description of his metamorphosis was given in later centuries by Ovid, the Roman poet. Lycaon's "clothes changed into bristling hairs, his arms to legs. His own savage nature showed in his rabid jaws, and he now directed against the flocks his innate lust for killing. He had a mania, even yet, for shedding blood. But though he was a wolf, he retained some traces of his original shape. The grayness of his hair was the same, his face showed the same violence, his eyes gleamed as before, and he presented the same picture of ferocity."

The tale was only one expression of a violent Arcadian tradition. According to ancient historians, transformations involving human sacrifices were carried out in the Arcadian temple on Mount Lycaeus, in whose holy precincts neither man nor woman was supposed ever to cast a shadow or to remain alive for more than a year. The sacrifices were the means by which cultists were transformed into wolves. It was said that such transformations lasted nine years only—unless the animals ate human flesh. Then they were doomed to remain beasts forever.

With Ovid's tale the werewolf tradition entered popular literature, which provided plenty of eerie accounts. The Roman Petronius, for instance, regaled his readers with the story of a former slave named Niceros. One night, this young man left Rome to visit his mistress, who lived on a farm some miles from the city. He persuaded a soldier—"as lusty a lad as the very devil"—to keep him company on the

Movie Star News

Actor Henry Hull peers at a caged wolf in a still from the 1935 film Werewolf of London

road. "Off we set about cockcrow," related Niceros, "and the moon was shining as bright as midday." When they passed a cemetery, the soldier turned off the road and walked among the monuments, apparently to relieve himself. But to Niceros's surprise, his companion took off all his clothes and left them in a pile by the roadside. Stranger still, he urinated in a circle, which held some magic import, for within minutes he turned into a wolf. Howling, the moonstruck soldier ran off into the woods. The startled Niceros tried to pick up the man's clothes but found that they had turned to stone.

"Half dead with fear," Niceros made his way in the darkness to the house of his mistress, whom he found in an agitated state of mind. If only he had come a little earlier, she said, he could have helped. A wolf had broken into the barnyard and wreaked havoc among the cows and sheep. But the marauder had not escaped unwounded, she was happy to say; one of the farmhands had managed to jab it in the neck with a pike.

After staying the night, Niceros started back to his master's. When he came to the spot where the rigidified clothes had lain, he found a pool of blood. And when he got home, he discovered the soldier lying in bed, attended by a doctor who was busy dressing a wound in his neck. Niceros needed no more confirmation than this of his friend's supernatural power, "and after that I could neither bite nor sup with him; no, not if you had killed me for it."

AMONG THE first of the French werewolf trials to gain widespread notoriety was that of Pierre Burgot and Michel Verdun, two peasants who were tried in 1521. Burgot told a strange tale. Nineteen years earlier, he had been tending his flock of sheep when a violent storm broke out. As he ran about trying to collect the frightened animals, he came upon three horsemen, dressed in black, on black steeds. One of them asked him what was wrong, and the breathless Burgot told him that some of his sheep were lost and that he feared they would fall prey to wolves. The stranger said not to worry, that if Burgot would agree to serve him as his lord and master, he would protect the sheep in the days and years ahead and give him money as well. Accepting the proposition, Burgot agreed to meet again with the stranger, who called himself Moyset.

When the meeting took place, Moyset announced the full terms of the deal: Burgot must do nothing less than renounce God, the Holy Virgin, the Company of Heaven, his baptism, and his confirmation. Burgot accepted, swearing also never to assist at mass or to use holy water. Then he kissed Moyset's hand; it was as cold, he said, as the hand of a dead man.

As the years passed, Burgot weakened in his resolve to obey Moyset, and for this he was called to task by Michel Verdun, who demanded that he strip naked and let himself be anointed with a magic salve. The unguent soon had its effect, convincing Burgot that he had metamorphosed into a wolf. He was amazed to see his arms and legs grow hairy and his hands and feet become paws. Rubbing himself with the salve, Verdun also changed shape, and together they ran amuck through the surrounding countryside.

As werewolves, Burgot and Verdun committed a variety of gruesome crimes. They attacked a seven-year-old boy and tore him to pieces, killed a woman who was picking peas, and abducted a four-year-old girl and consumed all of her but her arm. Impelled by a growing cannibalistic appetite, they took to lapping up the blood of their victims. They even mated with female wolves.

The trial of Burgot and Verdun before Maître Jean Bodin, the prior of a Dominican convent at Poligny in Franche-Comté, attracted large crowds. The so-called werewolves and their accomplice were convicted and duly put to death, and pictures of them were put up in the local church as a reminder to all of the evil deeds that men can commit under the influence of the devil.

In 1584, two alleged werewolves, Pierre Gandillon and his son George, were apprehended. They were accused of having murdered and eaten numerous youngsters, always under the narcotic influence of the salve with which they had covered their bodies. Their degeneracy had wrought a terrible change in their appearance: Scrambling about on all fours, they had thick, age-toughened nails as sharp as claws; dirty, unkempt hair; and as befitted werewolves, gleaming red eyes.

A similarly horrid impression was made in the Loire Valley by Jacques Rollet,

Jean-Loup Charmet, Paris

known as the werewolf of Caude, who in 1598 was tried for killing and eating a boy of fifteen. After having reportedly been scared off the corpse by townsmen, he was found in the woods, half-naked, with long, matted hair and beard, and blood-covered hands to which gobbets of flesh still clung. At his trial he told how he had slaughtered a variety of other people, including attorneys, lawyers, and bailiffs, the last of whom, he said, he had found tough and flavorless. Although he was given the death penalty by the court, he was later adjudged mentally incompetent and sent to the madhouse, there to remain for the surprisingly short period of two years.

Among the numerous other French werewolf cases, the villainy of a tailor, whose name the source does not provide, stands out. Whether he was under the influence of drugs or simply a psychotic is unclear. In any case, at dusk, and in the guise of a wolf, he would lope through the forests and leap out on those who passed by, ripping open their throats. Like so many other lycanthropes, he had a predilection for children, whom he would lure to his shop. There he molested them and then slit their throats, before carving them up like so much butcher's meat. In his cellars he kept barrels of bones and, in the words of a historian familiar with the case, "other foul and hideous things." The records accumulated during the trial were apparently so revolting in their content that the court thought better of preserving them and ordered them destroyed.

An equally horrendous case ostensibly involved a child werewolf, one Jean Grenier of Aquitaire, who was no more than thirteen or fourteen years of age when finally caught in 1603. Although physically retarded in his growth and mentally deficient, he was nevertheless said to have been responsible for a reign of terror, during which children, including an infant in his cradle, disappeared. When finally caught, Grenier—who admitted to eating fifty youngsters—had a tale as strange as Burgot's to tell. He claimed to be a priest's son but in fact was the offspring of a day laborer, who had often beaten him. To escape his father, he had run away. Shifting for himself, he tended cows, begged, and otherwise lived like the wild thing that he was.

One evening another boy, Pierre la Tilhaire, took him into the depths of the woods, into the presence, Grenier said, of the Lord of the Forest, a tall, dark man, dressed in black and mounted on a black horse—in appearance not unlike Burgot's Moyset. The so-called Lord got off his horse and kissed Grenier on the mouth, and his lips were icy. During a second meeting, Grenier and la Tilhaire gave themselves over to the Lord of the Forest, submitting to a kind of brand, which the master carved into their thighs with his sharp fingernail. To celebrate their bondage to him, he brought out a winebag from which the boys took swigs. He gave them both wolf skins and told them that they must always rub themselves with an ointment before donning the furs, if indeed the skins were to have their hideous effect. He had two stipulations, though—that they allow the nails of their left thumbs to grow long and that they come to him for the salve whenever the werewolf mood came upon them. On his subsequent journeys into the forest to obtain the ointment, Grenier several times came upon the so-called Lord in the company of four or five other men who seemed to adore him, members perhaps of a more extensive cult.

Taking into account his age and his limited mental capacity, the judge ordered that Grenier be confined to a cloister for life. Seven years later, when a man called Pierre de Lancre visited him, Grenier had grown gaunt and lean, and his deep-set black eyes burned intently. His hands were like claws, with bent nails, and his teeth were long and caninelike. Apparently he enjoyed hearing about wolves and readily imitated them, moving with agility on all fours. When he had first come to the cloister, he had refused to eat any regular food and devoured offal instead. One year after de Lancre visited him, the pathetic Grenier died, to be remembered forever in the annals of werewolves as the boy lycanthrope.

G RENIER'S CASE is among those that represent a shift in attitude toward the werewolf phenomenon. The head of the inquest committee that looked into his

A traveler is waylaid by a demon in the form of a three-headed wolf in this French etching

crimes found Grenier incapable of rational thought. "The change of shape existed only in the disorganized brain of the insane," the lawyer wrote. "Consequently, it was not a crime which could be punished." Whether enlightenment had truly come to the French courts or not, judges began to regard their werewolf cases with something approaching tolerance. This may have partly had to do with the werewolf hysteria that had overtaken the populace, prompting even some of France's leading citizens to confess to lycanthropy. Was the phenomenon real or more a matter of delusion—or of drug-induced madness?

There was no lack of effort down through the ages to explain werewolf behavior. Some thinkers asserted that it was caused by an excess of melancholy or, as the parlance of the day had it, an imbalance of the humors, the liquid or fluid part of the body. Many doctors believed that such melancholy could lead to hallucinations, delusions, and insanity. One physician recommended that the lycanthrope be treated with baths, purging, bleeding, dietary measures, and—to promote a state of calmness—opium rubbed into the nostrils. Robert Burton, the British clergyman and scholar, in his 1621 work entitled *Anatomy of Melancholy,* also considered lycanthropy to be a form of madness, and he blamed it on everything from sorcerers and witches to poor diet, bad air, sleeplessness, and even lack of exercise.

Such views were not widely adopted. Instead, a frightened populace preferred magical explanations. Thus, for some, the werewolf was the projection of a demon, who made its victim appear in his own eyes and to those around him as a wolf. For others, the werewolf was a direct manifestation of the devil. Early-seventeenth-century French author Henri Bouguet believed, as did a great many people of the day, that Satan would leave the lycanthrope asleep behind a bush, go forth as a wolf, and perform whatever evil might be in that person's mind. According to Bouguet, the devil could confuse the sleeper's imagination to such an extent "that he believes he has really been a wolf and has run about and killed men and beasts."

If wolves were a natural evil, comparable to plague or famine, werewolves apparently had to be considered a supernatural evil. Since the Bible offered no clues as to how the phenomenon should be regarded, it was up to the theorists in the Church to rationalize it. Some, noting that the devil was a master of delusion, came up with a theory. "God alone can perform real miracles," wrote Saint Thomas Aquinas in his *Summa theologica,* "but the demons are permitted to perform lying wonders, extraordinary to us, and they employ certain seeds that exist in the elements of the world by which operation they seem to effect transformations." Aquinas enumerated three ways in which such evil spirits might delude people: "by exhibiting as present what is not really there, by exhibiting what is there as other than it really is, and by concealing what is really there so that it appears as if it were not."

The finer points continue to be argued among occultists and others even to this day. Rose Gladden, a British exorcist and clairvoyant, thinks astral projection may be behind the activities of werewolves. "Suppose I was a cruel person," she says, "who enjoyed the horrible things in life. Well, as I projected my astral body out of my physical body, all the surrounding evil could grasp me. And it would be the evil

Jean-Loup Charmet, Paris

grasping my astral projection, or grasping my 'double,' which would transform me into an animal or wolf. Evil forces find it much easier to exist within mankind—within an evil man, say—than in a nebulous vacuum. People addicted to were-wolfery were—indeed, still are—the most evil manifestations of humanity."

THERE ARE still individuals today who believe they are werewolves, and some of these lycanthropes have been studied and treated by psychologists and psychiatrists. The November 1975 issue of the *Canadian Psychiatric Association Journal,* noting that this "allegedly extinct condition" had been omitted from most contemporary medical textbooks, reported in detail on several recent cases of lycanthropy.

In the first case, the twenty-year-old patient, referred to as Mr. H, was convinced that he was a werewolf. A drug user, he told his doctor that while serving in the United States Army in Europe, he had hiked into a forest near his post and had ingested LSD and strychnine, the latter a deadly poison that acts as a stimulant when taken in tiny quantities. Both substances are pharmacologically similar to some of the ingredients used by shapeshifters in the past. They had an instant and potent effect on the young man, who claimed to have seen fur growing on his hands and felt it sprouting on his face. Soon he was overcome by a compulsion to chase after, catch, and devour live rabbits. He wandered in this delusional state for several days before returning to the post.

Placed on the tranquilizer chlorpromazine, Mr. H was weaned away from drugs and received adjunct therapy for some nine months, during which time he

Movie Star News

The dreadful grimace of actor Lon Chaney, Jr., in the 1940 film The Wolf Man

continued to hear disembodied voices and to experience satanic visions. Claiming to be possessed by the devil, he insisted he had unusual powers. Tests indicated his delusions were "compatible with acute schizophrenic or toxic psychosis." He was treated with an antipsychotic drug, and when he improved sufficiently, he was referred to an outpatient clinic. After only two visits, however, he had stopped taking the medication and left treatment. Subsequent efforts to contact him failed.

Another werewolf patient, thirty-seven-year-old Mr. W was admitted to the hospital after repeated public displays of bizarre activity, including howling at the moon, sleeping in cemeteries, allowing his hair and beard to grow out, and lying in the center of busy highways. Unlike Mr. H, Mr. W had no history of drug or alcohol abuse. He had once been a farmer and was of average intelligence, as an IQ test indicated. Now, he was seen not only as psychotic but also as intellectually deficient, with a mental age of an eight- to ten-year-old child.

Because of the patient's increasing dementia, the doctors performed a brain biopsy. Their findings revealed an abnormal physiological deterioration of cerebral tissue, known as walnut brain. Mr. W was diagnosed as having a chronic brain syndrome of unknown origin. When placed on antipsychotic drugs, he showed no further symptoms of lycanthropy. Seen later on an outpatient basis, he exhibited quiet, childlike behavior.

The October 1977 issue of the *American Journal of Psychiatry* details the particularly bizarre story of a forty-nine-year-old woman who believed herself a wolf and, with increasing frequency, had begun acting like one. She revealed that just below the surface of a seemingly normal twenty-year marriage she had harbored a consuming desire to indulge in secret, bestial appetites. Her erotic daydreams often involved other women in polymorphous perverse orgies. The wolf was a constant and central figure in her fantasies; she felt its mesmerizing stare fastened onto her by day, its hot breath on her bare neck at night. Soon she began "feeling like an animal with claws."

After a time, she began to act out her compulsions. At a family gathering, for instance, she was suddenly overwhelmed by the wolf passion. Stripping naked and dropping to all fours, she excitedly approached her own mother, and assuming the sexual posture of a female wolf, she offered herself. The woman's state continued to deteriorate; the next evening, after making love to her husband she lapsed into a frenetic two-hour episode of grunting and of clawing and gnawing at the bed. She explained afterward that the devil "came into her body and she became an animal."

Enrolled in an inpatient program, she received daily psychotherapy and was placed on medication. In the first three weeks she suffered relapses, during which she would rave: "I am a wolf of the night, I am wolf woman of the day. . . . I have claws, teeth, fangs, hair . . . and anguish is my prey at night . . . powerless is my cause. I am what I am and will always roam the earth after death . . . I will continue to search for perfection and salvation." Concurrently she experienced the urge to kill accompanied by a consuming sexual excitement.

She now saw the head of a wolf, rather than her own face, when she gazed in the mirror. The medical staff commented on "the unintelligible, animal-like noises she made." There was some improvement, but the patient then relapsed during the full moon. Writing about her experience, she stated: "I don't intend to give up the search for [what] I lack . . . in my present marriage . . . my search for such a hairy creature. I will haunt the graveyards for a tall, dark man that I intend to find." After nine weeks of treatment, she was released from the hospital on a regimen of drugs designed to free her of her delusion.

On the basis of the woman's symptoms, her doctors were able to formulate a psychological profile of the lycanthrope, which, in spite of its modern medical language, is not so different from the conclusions of some of the more enlightened physicians and thinkers of earlier times. The doctors saw the lycanthrope as suffering from "(1) schizophrenia, (2) organic brain syndrome with psychosis, (3) psychotic depressive reaction, (4) hysterical neurosis of the dissociative type, (5) manic-depressive psychosis, and (6) psychomotor epilepsy."

Still, the haunting image of the werewolf—with his red eyes, red nails, hairy body, and scabrous skin—is yet to be explained. And something else must be considered as well: the distinct possibility that some so-called werewolves were in fact the tragic victims of rabies. A strain of virus carried by dogs, wolves, and other mammals, including vampire bats in the New World, the disease strikes the central nervous system. In humans it elicits uncontrollable excitement and produces painful contractions of the throat muscles, which prevent the victim from drinking. Without medical intervention, death usually occurs within three to five days of the first symptoms.

Records from the past suggest the occasional presence of rabies in medieval Europe.

An edict of the archbishop of York, dating from 766, states: "If a wolf shall attack cattle of any kind, and the animal so attacked shall thereof die, no Christian may eat of it." Whether this measure was designed to guard against lycanthropy or rabies is not exactly clear, but it seems a wise admonishment in light of an occurrence four hundred years later in which a presumably rabid wolf bit "two and twenty persons, all of whom in a short space died."

Another physical condition that may have been mistaken for lycanthropy is porphyria, a rare genetic disorder that results in a deficiency of heme, one of the pigments in the oxygen-carrying red blood cells. At the 1985 conference of the American Association for the Advancement of Science, biochemist David Dolphin suggested that the untreated symptoms of porphyria match many of the traits associated with the classic lycanthrope. One of these is severe photosensitivity, which makes venturing out into daylight extremely painful and thus relegates the sufferer to a life of shadows and darkness. Moreover, as the condition advances, the victim's appearance grows increasingly morbid. Discoloration of the skin and hypertrichosis, an unusual and thick growth of facial or body hair, can develop. There is a tendency for skin lesions to form and ulcerate, eventually attacking cartilage and bone and causing a progressive deterioration of the nose, ears, eyelids, and fingers. And the teeth, as well as the fingernails and the flesh beneath them, might turn red or reddish brown because of deposition of porphyrin, a component of hemoglobin in the blood. The disease is often accompanied by mental disturbances, running the gamut from mild hysteria to delirium and manic-depressive psychoses.

Porphyria may have cropped up in certain areas where the gene pool was restricted, and because the disease is an inherited condition, the cases of lycanthropy would therefore be more numerous in some regions than in others. During a period when the general understanding of medical conditions was at best imperfect, the pathetically transformed sufferer could easily become an outcast as well as a scapegoat, with his or her condition ascribed to demonic influences.

Although rabies, porphyria, drug use, and psychosis may largely explain the werewolf phenomenon, the willingness of so many people over the centuries to believe in a creature so far outside the bounds of reality suggests that lycanthropy struck chords deep within the human psyche. Today, now that the wolves have long ceased to be a threat, it may be hard for us to understand our ancestors' fears and secret wishes that bound them to the beast. Indeed now that we have the power to devastate the earth many times over, the ferocious strength of the wolf seems puny by comparison. Yet perhaps the essence of the myths and seeds of demonic delusion have nothing to do with real wolves. Perhaps they have something to say about the shadow wolf that may be lurking in us all.

Vampires

John George Haigh, the "Acid Bath" Vampire

URING THE seventeenth and eighteenth centuries, it was widely believed in Eastern Europe that the dead could be transformed into undead souls who preyed upon the living and could be warded off and killed only by certain methods. Such fears still survive, lurking in some dark corner of the modern psyche, as witness their recurrent appearances in literature and films. The strong erotic element inherent in stories of vampires—who arrive under cover of night to suck the exposed necks of victims prostate with fear and desire—may help to explain the popular fascination with such tales, particularly when they have been romanticized for the screen.

But despite the classic image of Count Dracula, the character created by novelist Bram Stoker that has become the model for most of the movie representations of the undead, not all vampires arise from coffins to feed upon the living nor transform themselves into bats to get from place to place. (The bat form, in fact, seems to have been Stoker's invention.) There are also real, living people who are considered or who consider themselves to be vampires, and who torture or kill unwary victims in a quest for blood.

From earliest times, people have believed that the soul lives on long after a person dies and in some cases retains enough power to reactivate the body. To placate the dead, survivors buried food, drink, and concubines beside them. But the living feared that the most urgent need likely to drive corpses from their coffins was a thirst for fresh, revitalizing blood. Such tales permeated the folklore of many early cultures around the world. But reports of vampires similar to the ones we think of today first appeared in the sixteenth century in the Slavic regions of eastern Europe, in lands now situated in Hungary and Rumania. In 1526, Turkey's Süleyman the Magnificent defeated the Hungarian king in battle. Hungary was then divided into three parts, one ruled by the Turks, one by the Austrian Hapsburgs, and the other, an independent state called Transylvania, ruled by various local lords. In these remote, strife-torn regions the vampire superstition took firm root and flourished.

Transylvania, a remote land where armies fought mightily and nobles built gloomy castles on the craggy slopes of the Carpathian Mountain foothills, has always seemed a mysterious place. Life was often a very real nightmare for Transylvanian peasants who eked out a living from the soil. Anywhere in southeastern Europe sudden plagues could depopulate whole towns. Such events enforced the belief in vampires, which were often blamed for the deaths. The tales that circulated stressed the predators' abominable stench, and the smell of vampires was thought to herald the coming of a plague.

Helpless in the face of an epidemic, terrified people buried the stricken immediately after they died—sometimes, accidentally, even before they had died, perhaps while the supposed corpses were in a comalike state called catalepsy, during which breathing may stop. Occasionally such unfortunate victims would awaken in their graves and attempt to claw their way out. Later, grave robbers or fellow peasants alarmed by some clue that the deceased were vampires would dig them up and discover their bodies twisted and tortured from efforts to escape suffocation.

It was easy for those who opened a grave and found blood beneath the fingernails of a corpse or a mouth agape in an eternal scream to conclude that yet another vampire had been discovered. If a mistakenly buried person was disinterred before dying and actually sat up or otherwise displayed signs of life when the coffin was opened, the indications of vampirism were even more dramatically evident, and a stake driven through the chest would put the body permanently to rest.

European folklore held that certain types of people were more likely to be transformed into vampires than others. Society's outcasts, always viewed with suspicion, were considered likely to return from the grave. So were redheads, people born with cauls, breech babies, children born on Christmas Day—just about anyone born under unusual circumstances or whose behavior was different from the norm. Those with cleft palates were particularly suspect, since the deformity caused a drawing up of the lip. In Greece, where most people had dark eyes, those with blue eyes were considered likely vampires. Suicides were prime candidates to rise again as vampires, as were those who had died after being excommunicated from the Church. The Greek Orthodox church held that the body of someone who had been excommunicated did not decay after death unless the corpse had been granted absolution (in contrast to the Roman church, whose doctrines held that God preserved only saintly corpses from decay).

So strong was the Greek belief in vampires, called *vrykolkas,* that in the nineteenth century, bodies were dug up after three years to make sure they had turned to bones and dust. Greeks believed *vrykolkas* were not really the souls of the deceased but evil spirits that entered the body after the soul had withdrawn. The *vrykolkas* tradition was so strong on the island of Santorini, where the volcanic soil tended to preserve buried bodies, that the Greeks used the expression "send a vampire to Santorini" as a metaphor for redundant action, just as the English speak of "carrying coals to Newcastle." Ancient Greeks had buried their dead with an obol in the mouth, a small coin to bar the way to malicious spirits that might try to enter the body. In the nineteenth century, Greeks similarly thwarted *vrykolkas* by placing a cross of wax or cotton on the lips of the corpse.

Hungarians and Rumanians buried bodies with sickles around their necks, so that if a corpse tired to rise from the grave it would cut off its own head. Rumanians sometimes added the precaution of a sickle through the heart, particularly for the corpses of persons who had never been married and therefore were considered at high risk of becoming *strigoi,* or vampires. Some peoples, including the Finns, restrained corpses by tying their feet or knees together or driving stakes into the grave to pin the body down.

Despite compulsive thirsts, vampires were sometimes thought to be deterred by stratagems that seem almost childlike. Eastern European peasants hung buckthorn and whitethorn—the latter believed to be the shrub from which Jesus' crown was fashioned—on the windows and doors of their houses so that the vampires would become entangled in the thorns and confused. Tradition also had it that millet seeds sprinkled around a grave would force the resident vampire to pick up the seeds rather than search for human victims. Although their breath was said to reek from their foul meals, vampires were thought to dislike strong odors such as that of garlic, so people sometimes put garlic in graves and often wore it about their necks in order to fend off the undead. And like other evil spirits through the ages, vampires were believed to be afraid of silver and representations of the cross, which frequently were hung over doorways or on gates to keep the undead away. People also slept with sharp objects under their pillows to discourage nocturnal visits from vampires or spread human feces on a cloth and laid it across their chests.

If for some reason corpses were incorrectly buried or the charms failed to ward off vampires, the living were compelled to find the revenants—those who returned from the dead—and destroy them. In some cultures, it was believed that a horse would not step over the grave of a vampire. For this test, the horse had to be all of one color, either black or white, and usually had to be ridden by a virginal youth. In Serbia, the graves of vampires were identified as those falling in upon themselves because they were vacant or those with holes in them from which the vampires escaped. Sometimes vampire hunters had to exhume several bodies and determine which was the vampire by the extent of decay.

Whatever the method of discovery, the means of killing vampires were many and varied. Some eastern Europeans opened the grave of a suspected vampire, filled it with straw, impaled the body with a stake, then lit the straw and burned the body until it was reduced to a pile of ashes. Often they cut off the corpse's head, usually using a sexton's spade. They then placed the head at the feet of the corpse or behind the buttocks and, for good measure, separated it from the rest of the body by a layer of dirt. Bulgarians and Serbs frequently placed whitethorn in the navel of the corpse and shaved all of the body, with the exception of the head. Then they slit the soles of the feet and drove a nail into the back of the head.

When a stake was driven through a suspected vampire's heart, witnesses frequently averred that the corpse groaned and gushed dark blood. The escape of air remaining in the lungs when a stake was driven into the chest would explain the noise, of course, but it was misinterpreted as a sign that the corpse was still breathing and therefore was a vampire. The bloated appearance of the alleged vampires and the signs of blood at the nose and mouth or in the coffin are all considered today to be normal signs of decomposition present about a month after death, the time when most of the bodies were exhumed.

Vlad Țepes, also known as Vlad the Impaler or Dracula, dines innocently in this sixteenth-century woodcut from Germany while a massacre is carried out under his orders

Courtesy Time-Life Picture Collection

In this nineteenth-century painting by Csók István, Elizabeth Báthory looks on impassively as her victims are tortured. According to testimony, they literally froze to death.

ONE OF THE most notorious vampires of all time was a sixteenth-century Hungarian noblewoman, the countess Elizabeth Báthory, who became widely known as the Blood Countess. Báthory was born in 1560 in a great castle in north-western Hungary, in the shadows of the Carpathian Mountain foothills near Transylvania. Her family was one of the country's most prominent and powerful, but through the generations ran a wide streak of madness and a taste for decadence; the family tree was festooned with well-known sexual deviates, sadists and masochists, Satanists, poisoners, heretics, and intellectuals.

At age eleven, Elizabeth was betrothed to Ferencz Nádasdy, the scion of an-other prominent Protestant family. Her father had recently died, and her mother sent her to live with the Nádasdy family, where she would be trained for her future role as a countess. By all accounts a precocious child, Elizabeth soon became bored with the domestic routine and found secret thrills in playing with the peasant boys on the estate; by age thirteen she was pregnant by one of them. Her mother retrieved her under the guise of an illness, and she went into seclusion at one of the more remote Báthory castles. The newborn child was spirited out of the country, and shortly after

Elizabeth's fifteenth birthday, she married Ferencz Nádasdy.

Although the newlyweds had the choice of several more salubrious houses in which to make their new home, the countess chose the dank and gloomy Csejthe Castle, in a setting bordered by thick forests where wolves howled at night. Her new husband was soon off campaigning in lengthy wars, and she was left to her own devices at the castle. She whiled away her time engaging in affairs with various men and soon discovered that she found pleasure in inflicting pain on servant girls, especially if they were bosomy and younger than eighteen. Her husband, himself known for his delight in torturing Turkish captives, expressed no objection to his wife's cruelties to the lowly peasant girls, and the couple lived happily enough, producing four children between 1585 and 1595.

When Ferencz died during the winter of 1604, his widow was freed of marital concerns and could concentrate on new and inventive ways to pleasure herself through others' pain. She elaborated on the frequent beatings that she and some trusted members of the household staff administered to her victims, adding various kinds of humiliations and tortures, including pressing red-hot coins and keys into the hands of the hapless girls. The countess, a vain and beautiful woman always searching for new potions that would preserve her youth, engaged a magician named Anna Darvulia to concoct magic elixirs for her. Reportedly, one day a servant girl bled profusely when struck by Báthory, and the blood splashed onto the countess. Báthory noticed to her immense delight that when she wiped off the blood, her skin seemed softer and whiter. She believed she had discovered the secret to remaining young: She must bathe frequently in human blood.

Before long the countess and her helpers—a nanny, a wet nurse, and a valet—began carrying their torture sessions to fatal extremes in the dungeons of her several homes. Their activities were so vilely obscene as to beggar description. A single example will suffice. The countess installed in the cellar of her Vienna mansion a cylindrical iron cage with metal spikes pointing inward, a kind of loose-fitting iron maiden. After a girl or young woman was locked into it, the cage was hoisted to the ceiling. One of the torturers then prodded the victim with a red-hot poker, causing her to flail about against the spikes, while the countess sat below showering in—and, it was said, drinking—the blood. After a time, when the countess's blood baths failed to stem the onslaught of middle age, she turned to blue-blooded victims, young ladies of noble birth, a supply much more difficult to maintain.

Disposing of bodies without attracting anyone's attention always presented a problem, but it grew to be virtually impossible during the height of the countess's madness with the spiked cage in Vienna, when her helpers were forced to simply dump the drained victims in a field. Terrified villagers in the vicinity believed that a plague of vampirism was responsible for the bloodless corpses that kept turning up—and in the broad sense of the word they were, of course, correct.

Eventually, rumors of the horrifying rituals became persistent and widespread. After the bodies of four victims were dumped below the Csejthe Castle ramparts, frightened villagers who had long suspected Báthory were emboldened to complain to authorities. Around Christmas of 1610, Báthory was formally questioned by her cousin, the lord palatine of Hungary, Count György Thurzo, who was anxious to preserve the family from disgrace. The Blood Countess's accomplices were arrested and confessed to the murders. A witness for the prosecution testified that he had seen a list written by the countess of the girls and young women who had been killed, putting their number at no fewer than 650.

After a five-day trial, in which Báthory's name was mentioned only once, her helpers were sentenced to be publicly tortured and put to death. The countess herself was never tried, but was quietly locked away in her own bedroom in Csejthe Castle. Workmen walled up the room's windows and doors, and there the prisoner was confined, with only a food hatch connecting her to the outside world. She died there on August 21, 1614. The only words about Báthory that had slipped into the trial proceedings called her "a blood-thirsty, and blood-sucking Godless woman caught in the act at Csejthe Castle."

AS AWFUL as were the deeds of the Blood Countess, in the centuries since then other "living vampires" have committed acts that seemed no less sensational and frightening, even if in retrospect they pale beside Báthory's excesses. One case that terrified France in the middle of the nineteenth century involved a mysterious night creature who ripped corpses from their graves. The elusiveness of this nocturnal prowler, who seemed not to be deterred by high walls or guards, caused the public to believe a supernatural being was responsible—"the vampire of Paris," as the malefactor was dubbed by the newspapers of the day.

The "vampire" first surfaced in 1849, when guards at Paris's Père Lachaise Cemetery, the final resting place of many famous painters, musicians, and writers, began to catch glimpses of a shadowy figure flitting among the tombstones at night. On a number of mornings they discovered graves and tombs desecrated, the bodies dumped from their coffins and savagely attacked. The authorities, who themselves apparently fueled the newspaper headlines by applying the term vampirism to the case, were unable to catch the culprit. After more graves were disturbed at Montparnasse Cemetery in Paris and at a suburban burial ground, people began to speculate that a phantom vampire was responsible. After all, the high walls of the cemeteries had heavy gates that were kept locked after nightfall.

Faced with increasing public fear, authorities called in the military, and one night not much later, soldiers lying in ambush at Montparnasse Cemetery thought that they spied something in the distance, moving among the graves. Soon they heard the sound of wood being ripped apart. At that, the commander of the group barked an order that sent the men running through the tombstones toward the source of the noise. In the darkness, a figure broke cover and darted for the perimeter of the cemetery. Gunshots rang out, but the fleeing figure managed to scramble over the high wall and disappear. When the soldiers inspected the fugitive's trail by lantern light, however, they discovered traces of blood and a scrap of military uniform.

Knowing now that they were seeking a soldier with an unexplained fresh wound, authorities easily tracked down Sergeant Victor Bertrand. Bertrand, a handsome, well-groomed, blond young man, confessed to an "irresistible impulse" to prowl the cemeteries. But he said he was hardly conscious of what acts he was committing once he got there. The trial of Victor Bertrand on July 10, 1849, drew a glittering audience of Parisian high society. He was judged to be sane but, because he had not physically harmed any living person, was sentenced to only a year's imprisonment. During his term in prison, Bertrand wrote a full account of what he had done. After his release, the public never heard from him again.

If the term vampire seems loosely applied in Bertrand's case, it appears somewhat more appropriate to describe a German named Fritz Haarmann, who in the 1920s became notorious as the Hannover Vampire. Haarmann was the youngest child of a rough, foul-tempered locomotive fireman and, according to "vampirologist" Montague Summers, grew up in the industrial city of Hannover hating and fearing his father. As a youth he was accused of molesting children, but because he was "dull and stupid," the court decided he was not responsible for his deeds and sent him to an insane asylum.

Haarmann escaped and eventually returned home, where he remained until frequent violent quarrels with his father drove him to enlist in the army. Discharged from the service on account of illness, he returned again to Hannover and was arrested there several times—for fraud and burglary, as well as for indecent exposure. After a spell in prison, he was released in 1918 and seemed to start a new, respectable life for himself. He opened a small shop that sold sausages and cooked meats, enjoying excellent business in the time of scarcity that followed Germany's defeat in World War I. And he became a police buff and informant, helping Hannover detectives with tips about the city's petty criminals. He apparently took pleasure in hearing the hausfraus lined up at his shop refer to him in whispers as Detective Haarmann.

He also used his entrée with the police to facilitate the monstrous acts he was later found to have committed. Hannover's main railway station was continually crowded with homeless boys and young men moving from city to city in a largely futile search for work. Because the policemen on duty there knew Haarmann as an ally, he was free to prowl the third-class waiting room in the middle of the night. He would awaken some youth among the scores that were sleeping on the floor, demand in an official manner to see a ticket, ask sharp questions about the boy's place of origin and his destination, then in a sudden turn of sympathetic generosity, dangle promise of a bed and a hot meal that often convinced the weary lad to leave the station and go home with him.

Even those sufficiently experienced and cynical to believe they knew what price Haarmann would extract from them in exchange for his hospitality had no idea, or they would never have accompanied him. For in the privacy of his rooms behind the shop, Haarmann—a heavy man and apparently a strong one—would contrive to pin down his victim and then suddenly sink his teeth into the youth's exposed throat in a fatal bite. Few nightmares could produce a vampire more vicious than this living one.

In what must have been an intensely suspenseful encounter for the murderer, Haarmann's career as a vampire came within a hair's breadth—or more exactly, the thickness of a newspaper—of being stopped by police almost as soon as it began. As far as could be determined later, his first victim was a seventeen-year-old runaway named Friedel Rothe. Friedel had mailed a postcard to his mother, who received it at about the time her beloved son was falling prey to Haarmann. Knowing from the postmark that Friedel was in Hannover, the Rothes tracked down his acquaintances there, who told them their son had accepted an offer of a place to stay from a "detective."

Under pressure from the Rothes, Hannover police deduced that the so-called detective might have been Haarmann and went to his residence. When they burst in unannounced, they surprised Haarmann in an act of "gross indecency" with another boy and had no choice but to arrest him. They did not thoroughly search the premises, however, so they did not find the severed head of Friedel Rothe, which—as Haarmann revealed years later—"was hidden under a newspaper behind the oven. Later on, I threw it into the canal." Instead of being revealed as a killer, Haarmann served nine months for gross indecency and resumed his horrifying practices.

By official count, his deadly teeth claimed at least twenty-four victims before he was caught, although some people who studied the case thought the number might be nearer to fifty. The oldest killed was eighteen years of age, the youngest just twelve. Haarmann collaborated with an accomplice named Hans Grans during much of his seven-year murder spree. Grans, a handsome young man who seemed totally devoid of conscience, frequently brought in the candidates for Haarmann's fatal attentions. He induced Haarmann to commit one murder because he, Grans, wanted the youth's new trousers, another because he coveted the victim's fancy shirt.

Haarmann's practice of disposing of body parts in the waterway behind his home ultimately helped lead to his undoing; a number of skulls and bones found there in the spring of 1924 turned the spotlight of suspicion toward him. Shortly thereafter, it focused sharply on him when he tried to pick up a young man by the name of Fromm at the railway station. Fromm objected noisily and shouted accusations of indecency. Police, who arrested both men, searched Haarmann's place and discovered several bodies in varied states of dismemberment. Haarmann admitted to twenty-seven murders; however, the police apparently could not assemble corroborating evidence for some of them. Yet the actual number of homicides probably did not stun and sicken the citizens of Hannover as much as did one detail of his confession: Fritz Haarmann had ground parts of some of the victims into sausages, which he not only ate himself but also sold to his customers.

At his trial in 1924 on twenty-four counts of murder, Haarmann insisted he was sane but claimed he was always in a trance when he committed the killings. The judge rejected this argument out of hand, citing the concentrated effort needed to hold the victims down while biting their throats. He sentenced Haarmann to death,

Culver Pictures Inc., New York

and the accomplice Grans to life imprisonment. Although the court took no official cognizance of the talk of vampirism that had swept Hannover following the revelations, the death sentence ordered was decapitation.

On April 15, 1925, the neck of the Vampire of Hannover was sundered by the razor-sharp blade of a heavy sword, a most unusual means of execution for twentieth-century Europe, but one that Montague Summers, at least, found not too surprising. "It was perhaps something more than mere coincidence that the mode of execution should be the severing of the head from the body," he pointed out, "since this was one of the efficacious methods of destroying a vampire."

As the twentieth century has lurched along its tumultuous course, cases of mass murders on a scale similar to that of Fritz Haarmann's crimes have become, if not commonplace, at least distressingly familiar in the Western world. In the 1940s, an Englishman named John George Haigh was put to death for murder after confessing to killing nine people, drinking their blood, then dissolving their bodies in acid; inevitably, Fleet Street dubbed him the Acid Bath Vampire. In the late 1950s, a quiet bachelor recluse, Eddie Gein, was found to have skins, heads, and other parts of at least ten corpses in his tumble-down Wisconsin farmhouse. He admitted to murdering two people, claiming he acquired the other grisly mementoes by graverobbing. Throughout the 1960s, 1970s, and 1980s, serial killers and mass murderers have crowded the news—the Charles Manson Family, the Yorkshire Ripper, the Boston Strangler and Los Angeles's Hillside Strangler, the Green River Killer, John Gacy, Charles Starkweather, Ted Bundy, and Jeffrey Dahmer, other names that come to the attention of a shocked public, then fade before an onrush of new candidates for grim notoriety.

Of course, none of these murderers are nowadays spoken of as vampires—not in any serious sense, anyway; headline writers may reach for the term for its sensational value, as they did in the case of the Acid Bath Vampire, but they do not expect it to be taken literally. Now such killers are described instead as disturbed, mentally ill, sociopathic, or just downright evil. People tend to regard them as a strictly modern phenomenon, by-products of our unnatural, stress-skewed society.

And yet their behavior is not really new. It is similar to that which we used to ascribe—mistakenly—to wild animals: killing viciously and wantonly, not for survival but for thrills, or to satisfy some dark and unexplained inner need. In many respects, this seems to be the very behavior that in centuries past characterized people who consequently were believed to be real vampires or werewolves. Is it possible that perhaps the world has not changed so much as we think? That the killer who stalks helpless children with a semiautomatic assault rifle today is basically the same breed as the person whose slaughter of innocents in seventeenth-century Europe would cause neighbors to believe he had been supernaturally transformed into a werewolf or a vampire?

8
AMAZING CREATURES

Sea Oddities

S EA SERPENTS have long inspired fascination and terror. Probably the first of the modern eyewitnesses was the Scandinavian missionary Hans Egede, known as the Apostle of Greenland. Egede reported that he sighted a sea monster on a 1734 voyage to Greenland, and his subsequent description of the creature was remarkable for its sober, matter-of-fact tone. The sea serpent was certainly very large and unusual, but it was no archetypal, fire-breathing, mariner-eating monster. The animal's head reached the top of the mast, but did not tower above or devour it. The body was as broad as the ship and three or four times as long. The minister described the creature as having paddlelike paws and a long, pointed snout and wrote that it spouted "like a whale-fish." The body was said to be covered with a carapace of shellwork, not scales; the lower portion was serpentine in shape, with the tail a "ship's length distant from the bulkiest part of the body."

The next reported sighting occurs in the early nineteenth century, when a sea

Smithsonian Institution, Courtesy Clyde Roper

Amateur naturalist DeWitt Webb poses in 1896 with the remains of a mysterious creature.
Scientists recently determined the carcass was actually that of a whale.

serpent had a brief moment of respectability. Between August 6 and 23 of 1817, as many as a hundred reputable witnesses sighted an enormous marine monster frolicking in or near the harbor in Gloucester, Massachusetts. For a time skepticism all but disappeared; scientists throughout the world followed the story with avid interest.

On August 14 alone, the monster appeared to a group of twenty to thirty people, among them the Gloucester justice of the peace, Lonson Nash. That same day several boats went out in active pursuit, and late in the afternoon, a ship's carpenter, Matthew Gaffney, spotted "the strange marine animal, resembling a serpent." He got to within thirty feet of it, took careful aim with a rifle, and fired directly at the head. An experienced marksman, Gaffney thought he must have hit it, but the serpent appeared to be unharmed. It veered sharply toward the boat, and for a minute the men feared that the creature would attack. Instead, it simply sank like a stone, passed under the craft, and surfaced on the other side, almost a hundred yards away. There it continued to play, apparently heedless of the hunters.

Gaffney later described the monster as probably smooth skinned and certainly dark in color, with a white throat and belly. It was huge—at least forty feet long— and its head was the size of "a four-gallon keg." Moving vertically, "like a caterpillar," it was speeding along at between twenty and thirty miles per hour.

Modern authorities agree that the Gloucester monster could not have been a snake; reptiles cannot undulate vertically or sink straight down. However, the Linnaean Society of New England, which conducted the investigation, was apparently unaware of these facts. Believing that the sea serpent was indeed a snake, the society theorized that it had come to lay eggs on shore. At one point, independent witnesses reported seeing it half on and half off the sandy beach of the harbor, which lent credence to the theory. No eggs ever turned up, but two boys found a three-foot creature that looked like a black snake with humps on its back. The society, sure of its egg-laying theory, was delighted with this apparent proof—the "baby sea serpent." The members examined and dissected it, then christened it *Scoliophis atlanticus,* or Atlantic Humped Snake, publishing a long report on the subject. Unfortunately, in little time a French zoologist, Charles-Alexandre Lesueur, had determined that the *Scoliophis* was just what it appeared to be: a black snake with a spine deformed by disease or injury. The international scientific community had a great laugh at the Linnaean Society's expense, and the whole Gloucester Harbor episode was discredited.

Such incidents soured serious-minded people on the subject of sea serpents. But in 1848, a sighting by several officers in the British navy shook the foundations of British and European skepticism. On August 6, HMS *Daedalus* was cutting through the South Atlantic waters near the Cape of Good Hope, at the southern tip of Africa, when a midshipman spotted something advancing rapidly toward the vessel. He immediately informed the ship's officers, and a total of seven men, including Captain Peter M'Quhae, got a good view of what they all described as a gigantic sea serpent. The visible portion of the creature alone measured more than sixty feet in length, they reported, but it appeared to be only about fifteen inches diameter. Its color was dark brown, with yellowish white at the throat, and it had some sort of mane, like a bunch of seaweed, on its back. Oddly enough, though moving at twelve to fifteen miles per hour, it exhibited neither vertical nor horizontal undulation—nor any other visible means of propulsion. "Apparently on some determined purpose," it held its serpent-like head a constant four feet above the surface and never deviated from its course.

When the *Daedalus* returned home to Plymouth and reports of the sighting appeared in the London *Times,* the lords of the Admiralty demanded a full account. M'Quhae wrote a detailed official report, which also appeared in the newspapers. Uproar ensued. While the sighting had been fairly typical, as sightings go, the credibility of the witnesses was unique: M'Quhae and his fellow officers commanded respect; the British, long used to thinking of the sea serpent as a figment of gullible imaginations, could not so easily dismiss the *Daedalus* monster.

Implicit in every such debate of that era was a basic indictment of the witnesses themselves. Even if their reputations were above reproach, their scientific capabilities were not. Mariners, priests, and ordinary travelers were deemed too unschooled in the principles of scientific observation to be able to judge the validity of what they were seeing. And despite centuries of reported sightings around the world, no trained scientist had ever caught so much as a glimpse of a sea monster. But this line of argument crumbled in 1905, when two respected naturalists, fellows of the London Zoological Society, sighted a huge, unidentified marine creature.

On December 7 of that year, naturalists E. G. B. Meade-Waldo and Michael J. Nicoll were cruising off Parahiba, Brazil, aboard the Earl of Crawford's yacht *Valhalla* when Meade-Waldo noticed a large, six-foot-long "fin or frill" in the water about a hundred yards from the boat. Looking more closely, he could see a large body beneath the surface. Just as he got out his binoculars, the scientist reported, a huge head and neck rose up out of the water. The visible portion of the neck alone was seven to eight feet long and as thick as "a slight man's body"; the head was about the same thickness and resembled a turtle's, as did the eye. Both head and neck were dark brown on top, whitish underneath.

Nicoll's account of the beast was similar to Meade-Waldo's with one important addition: His general impression was of a mammal, not a reptile, although he admitted that he could not be absolutely certain.

Meade-Waldo and Nicoll were rare exceptions. The myth-enshrouded monster has almost always brought ridicule upon its chroniclers and witnesses. It is impossible to estimate how many accounts have been lost when

observers convinced themselves that they had had too much sun or one drink too many—or simply did not want to be ridiculed. The story is told of one sea captain who actually refused even to look at a sea serpent. He was having lunch in his cabin when the officer of the watch summoned him to the bridge to view a strange beast. The captain refused to go, refused even to peek out a porthole. "Had I said that I had seen the sea serpent," he explained, "I would have been considered a warranted liar all my life."

WITH THE ADVENT of powered vessels to take the place of sailing ships, reports of unknown or unidentified animals spotted on the high seas began to taper off. No longer at the mercy of whimsical winds and ocean currents, captains could steer their courses along established shipping lanes—and it is likely, say some cryptozoologists, that the sea serpents could stay away from these heavily traveled areas and thus avoid detection. In the words of the renowned Norwegian explorer Thor Heyerdahl: "We usually plow across [the sea] with roaring engines and piston strokes, with the water foaming round our bow. Then we come back and say that there is nothing to see far out in the ocean." Until the 1960s, the only evidence for sea-monster sightings remained the subjective verbal accounts of those who said they had seen the creatures. Then, in early 1965, proof seemed to be at hand. A French photographer named Robert Le Serrec reported that he had taken the first real photographs of a sea serpent.

According to Le Serrec's story, his encounter occurred just off the coast of Queensland, Australia, on December 12, 1964. He was, he said, crossing the shallow waters of Stonehaven Bay in a small boat with his family and a friend, Henk de Jong, when his wife caught sight of a huge, peculiar object on the sandy bottom, less than six feet from the surface. De Jong at first thought it was a large, twisted tree trunk, but it soon became evident that this was some sort of monstrous creature—a creature shaped like a giant tadpole with an enormous head and tapering serpentine body. Le Serrec took some still photos and then, circling his motorboat closer, began to film it with a movie camera. As the boat drew near, the witnesses could make out a five-foot-long wound gouged open on the motionless animal's back and could

Apparently oblivious to the frigate Daedalus, *a sea serpent passes under the ship's stern on a cloudy South Atlantic afternoon in August 1848. This engraving is based on a drawing commissioned by Captain Peter M'Quhae, one of seven eyewitnesses.*

Culver Pictures

more clearly see the broad head, which greatly resembled a snake's.

At this point the Le Serrec children became extremely frightened. The adults took the youngsters back to shore in the dinghy, then continued their observation of the beast. Since it remained inert, apparently seriously injured or perhaps even dead, they ventured still closer, noting two whitish eyes—located strangely on the top of the head—and regularly spaced bands of brown along the amazing length of the black body. The men decided to dive for a better look, the photographer armed with an underwater camera and his companion with an underwater rifle.

The divers could not get a clear view until they were within twenty feet of the monster. It was truly gigantic—seventy-five to eighty feet long, with four-foot-wide jaws and two-inch eyes that at close range turned out to be pale green. Suddenly, as Le Serrec began filming, the beast began to open and half-close its cavernous jaws "in a menacing manner" and to turn slowly toward the men. Because it was clearly incapacitated, the photographer kept on filming for a short time before he and his

The odd placement of the creature's eyes, along with Robert Le Serrec's shady reputation, led many investigators to brand his photo of an enormous sea serpent an outright hoax

friend made their escape. Back aboard the boat, they discovered that the creature had disappeared. Le Serrec's wife had seen it swim out to sea, undulating horizontally— a motion typical of an eel or a reptile, not a mammal.

On February 4, 1965, Le Serrec released his story, instantly stirring up world-wide interest—and, of course, skepticism. This time, even such an adventurous cryptozoologist as the Scottish-born Ivan T. Sanderson, an author and naturalist with a wide-ranging interest in unusual wildlife, had grave doubts. Although Le Serrec's color photographs seemed genuine enough, his much-touted movies did not turn up for viewing by independent investigators, and rumor had it that they were hopelessly blurred and virtually useless. The sighting could not be explained on the basis of any known phenomenon, and investigators had to consider the definite possibility of an intentional hoax. Especially suspect, in the opinion of French-born cryptozoologist Bernard Heuvelmans, were the unique positioning of the animal's eyes, the handy removal of the children, who might have revealed the ruse, and the contradictory fact that the men were afraid to provoke the creature from the boat but not to approach it underwater.

Further disturbing facts emerged concerning Le Serrec himself. He was wanted by Interpol for leaving France, in 1960, with a lien on his yacht and for absconding with funds put up by would-be sailing companions, whom he left behind. Le Serrec had reportedly told them that he had an idea for bringing in a great deal of money—something "to do with the sea serpent."

When he finally returned to France in 1966, Le Serrec received a six-month jail sentence. Yet several months after his conviction the magazine *Paris Match* printed his color photograph of the supposed sea serpent, attesting to the photographer's reliability and misquoting two experts—Sanderson and a professor named Paul Budker—in support of the Le Serrec claim. Although *Paris Match* did not print a retraction, a rival publication subsequently exposed the sighting as a hoax.

BUT ISOLATED sightings are not the only evidence of mysterious creatures in the deep. Over the centuries, the oceans have deposited many strange and mysterious remains on the earth's shores. Of these, perhaps none was more astonishing or controversial than the enormous carcass discovered on the rocks off the Orkney island of Stronsa (now called Stronsay) by a Scottish farmer named John Peace.

On September 26, 1808, Peace was out fishing in his boat when a large number of birds circling above the rocks caught his eye. Intrigued, he went to investigate. At first he thought that the huge lump attracting the birds was a dead whale. But as he approached, he discovered that it was like no whale he had ever seen. The putrefying monstrosity had several fins, or arms, and when Peace lifted the largest one with his boat hook, he found that it was surrounded by a row of ten-inch bristles.

About ten days later, the carcass washed onto the shore during a storm, and Peace and two other local men began to examine the strange remains in earnest, even measuring various parts of the body. The cartilaginous skeleton was around fifty-five feet long, with a small head, long neck and tail, bristly mane, and six "paws," each with five or six "toes." Another storm subsequently scattered the badly decomposed carcass, but a local artist was able to draw sketches under the direction of the original witnesses.

Eventually, a description of the beast reached Patrick Neill, secretary of the Wernerian Natural History Society in Edinburgh. Neill declared without hesitation that this was the kind of creature described centuries before by the Scandinavian witness Hans Egede—a conclusion no doubt influenced by recently reported sightings of a sea serpent in the nearby Hebrides. Later, before he had even seen the witnesses' depositions or the existing bits of physical evidence, Neill proposed naming the Stronsa beast *Halsydrus* (meaning "sea water-snake") *pontoppidani*. This he did solely on the basis of a paper and some drawings by Dr. John Barclay, a fellow member of the society who had viewed some of the creature's remains in the Orkneys.

Later on, a London surgeon and naturalist named Everard Home obtained all the information, the affidavits, and some pieces of the carcass. Home, despite a reputation marred by charges of plagiarism, was something of an expert on the huge fish known as the basking shark, and he quickly determined that the Stronsa beast was just that. Decomposition, he believed, had created the illusion of the long neck and tail, and also of the bristly mane. The six "paws" were actually four fins and two claspers, the double reproductive organs of the male shark. Home dismissed as error the creature's reported length, too great for any known basking shark, even though the men had taken careful measurements.

However correct they may have been, Home's conclusions angered the Scottish scientists, particularly John Barclay, who had embarrassed himself with his ill-informed paper on the physiology of the "sea serpent." Barclay published a reply and a counterattack—revealing even more ignorance—but Home did not deign to answer. The Scottish public, uncertain who was right, sided with Barclay, who had had the last word—if not the most correct one. Most modern authorities, however, are convinced that Home was essentially correct in his identification. The cartilaginous skeleton was the key clue, since only sharks and their closest relatives have such a skeleton. All the other details fit, as well. Still, according to Bernard Heuvelmans, Home may have oversimplified the issue in dismissing the creature's length; the Stronsa beast indeed may have been an unknown giant shark.

In fact, almost all of the many other unusual strandings examined by scientists over the years have turned out to be decomposed known animals—primarily sharks, whales, or oarfish. A carcass held briefly by a crew of Japanese fishermen in 1977 seemed very promising. On April 10 of that year, the *Zuiyo Maru,* a Japanese ship trawling off the coast of Christchurch, New Zealand, snared a two-ton carcass in its nets. Unfortunately for cryptozoology, a terrible stench and fatty liquid came oozing out onto the deck. The men, who feared that the carcass might spoil their catch of fresh fish, took measurements and photos and then threw the mystery beast back into the sea.

Japanese paleontologists were appalled to hear of this potentially great loss to science. Examining the photographs and the sketches drawn by Michihiko Yano, a fish-

ing company executive who had been on board at the time, the scientists concluded that the animal was possibly a plesiosaur, the supposedly long-extinct marine reptile that some experts believe may have survived to this day. One species is known to have lived off eastern Australia 100 million years ago. The director of animal research at the Japanese National Science Museum, Professor Yoshinori Imaizumi, stated that the remains were "not a fish, whale or any other mammal," and was positive the beast was a reptile, probably a plesiosaur. However, later examination of the data from the Japanese find indicated that the creature was in all likelihood a relatively common basking shark rather than an exotic plesiosaur.

IN TIMES PAST, naturalists tried to fit all sea serpents into a single zoological mold. Today, almost all investigators engaged in the search for sea serpents hold that these creatures are of several different types. Neither do modern researchers believe that all of these animals are actually serpents. Indeed, most are probably not even reptiles; frequent use of the term "sea serpent" persists merely for the sake of tradition and convenience.

Skeptics, on the other hand, of course, lean toward a variety of known phenomena as explanations for sea-serpent reports. The classic porpoises-jumping-in-a-line explanation dates back to at least 1803 and continues to this day, although it would take considerable synchronization for frolicking porpoises to create the illusion of undulating coils. Large land snakes, especially pythons, are supposed to account for some sightings. But even if these snakes were large enough to pass for sea serpents and adaptable enough to survive northern climates, they would still be unable to undulate in a vertical plane, as sea monsters are said to do. Another popular explanation is that the mystery beast is really an oarfish—a monstrous-looking serpentine fish, silver in color, with bright red fins radiating out from the head and oarlike ventral fins. However, although oarfish can grow to lengths of thirty feet, their bright colors and horizontal undulations do not make them likely sea-serpent candidates. The list of known-phenomenon theories goes on and on, including even logs and seaweed.

The debate, too, seems likely to continue—between the multitude of debunkers, demanding solid physical proof, and a small but dedicated band of propo-

This mysterious carcass washed up on the shores of Santa Cruz,
California in 1925. Biologists later concluded that it was the remains
of an extremely rare beaked whale.

nents, clinging to their intriguing fragments of evidence. "Many a man has hanged
on the basis of flimsier circumstantial evidence," wrote two researchers in defending
the sea-serpent issue against the "scoffers who insist that there cannot be any more
large undiscovered animals nowadays and that . . . 'sea-monsters' are the result of hallucination, error or bad faith." But the scientists conceded wryly, "We will admit that
what may pass for sufficient proof in a court of law might not satisfy the criteria of
incontrovertible scientific proof: the body is still missing."

Such proof will never be easy to come by: Suboceanic exploration is fraught
with difficulties and danger—the seas are so vast, and humankind's boats and bathy-
scaphes so small. Indeed, for all our technology, the oceans and many of their inhabitants are still very nearly as enigmatic as they have ever been.

The Quest for the Loch Ness Monster

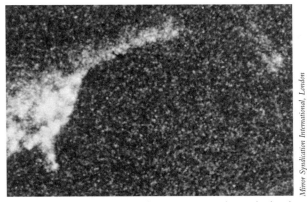

This 1975 photograph by Robert Rines may depict the head and body of a lake monster—or gas bubbles rising from the bottom of Loch Ness

NESTLED DEEP in the Scottish Highlands, Loch Ness is one of Europe's great lakes. Though its length is a modest twenty-four miles and its width rarely exceeds one mile, the fantastic depth—more than 700 feet in places—makes Loch Ness by volume the third-largest body of fresh water in Europe. By all odds, it is the most mysterious. In those frigid waters, rendered dark and virtually opaque by peat, a huge creature is said to reside.

History does not record when the first creature was sighted or who encountered it. Water spirits and other such beings have been a part of Highland legend for many centuries. The early Scots called these creatures water kelpies, water horses, water bulls, or simply spirits, and mothers sternly warned their children not to play too close to the shores of lakes or rivers; the mysterious beast could take the form of a horse, gallop onto the land, entice a child on top of its back, and then plunge with its helpless little rider back into the depths.

One of the first of the modern-day sightings is said to have occurred in 1880, when a seasoned Loch Ness waterman named Duncan McDonald was examining a boat that had sunk in the lake. McDonald was examining the wreck when he signaled frantically to be pulled to the surface. Ashen-faced, trembling uncontrollably, and incoherent with fear, he was finally able to blurt out that he had seen a monster in the murky water. He had gotten a good look at one of the creature's eyes, he reported, and described it as "small, gray, and baleful."

Since then, there have been something like 3,000 reported sightings—from shore and from boats, in every daylight hour—by every imaginable sort of person, singly and in groups of a score or more: farmers and priests, fishermen and lawyers, policemen and

H. L. Cockrell/Camera Press, London

Nessie, or floating log? This 1958 photograph by trout farmer H. L. Cockrell remains in contention

politicians, and even a Nobel prize-winning chemist, the Englishman Richard L. M. Synge, who saw the creature in 1938. Million-dollar expeditions have descended on Loch Ness. Investigators have spent months at a time scanning the lake with binoculars, have launched minisubmarines into its depths, and have probed its gloomy reaches with strobe-light cameras and sonar equipment. One investigator estimated that, for every observation, there have been 350 hours of concerted search, leading to scores of books, some scornfully debunking, others stoutly championing "Nessie," as she—for some reason, the monster has been deemed female—has come to be called.

Nevertheless, the lake has yet to yield an ancient bone, a bit of tissue, or any other definitive testimony to the monster's presence. For all the attention, the puzzles of Loch Ness and its elusive creature are no closer to solution now than they were that day in 1880 when Duncan McDonald was scared half to death by the ominous form he supposedly spotted in the dim, peat-stained waters.

GEOLOGISTS DATE the formation of Loch Ness to the last ice age, between 10,000 and 20,000 years ago, when a great finger of glacier gouged the lake bed out of the earth's crust. How a monster might have reached Loch Ness is almost as great a mystery as what the monster is. The sole waterways connecting the lake with the sea are the Caledonian Canal, first opened to navigation in 1822, and the River Ness. The canal is controlled through numerous locks that are opened only to let vessels through. The river is now too shallow to accommodate a monster-size creature, although it would have been much deeper just after the end of the ice age, before the land rose when relieved of the huge weight of glaciers. A creature would also find a comfortable home in Loch Ness, which is rich in eels, salmon, trout, and other fish.

Nevertheless, it was not until the early 1930s that the monster seemed suddenly to burst forth after centuries of relative quiescence. The first recorded sighting of the beast came on the evening of July 22, 1930, when young Ian Milne and two companions were fishing off Tor Point, near the small village of Dores. The lads were idly casting for salmon when they were startled by a great commotion 600 yards up the loch. "I saw spray being thrown up in the air to a considerable height," reported Milne. The thing bore down on the fishermen until it was 300 yards away, then swiftly turned a half circle and rushed away at a speed of about fifteen knots or more. "The part of it we saw would be about twenty feet long and it was standing three feet or so out of the water. The wash it created caused our boat to rock violently," said Milne. He solemnly concluded, "It was without doubt a living creature, and I can say it was certainly not a basking shark or a seal or a school of otters or anything normal."

Milne's account stirred a mild sensation and prompted a number of letters from correspondents relating previous experiences with a supposedly similar creature. But the excitement quickly faded when no further sights were forthcoming. Then in 1933, the Loch Ness monster made itself known with a vengeance. That year, work crews had repaired and resurfaced the road along the lake's north shore, and some investigators feel that there was a direct relationship between the two events.

On April 14, Mr. and Mrs. John Mackay, innkeepers at Drumnadrochit, were driving along the lake when Mrs. Mackay noticed that the serene surface of the loch had been shattered by a surging, roiling mass of water. As she watched in astonishment, what seemed to be an enormous animal rolled and plunged about for almost a minute before disappearing in a great gout of foam. Soon talk of the monster was rippling through the Highlands. Cynics pointed out that as managers of the Drumnadrochit Hotel, the Mackays stood to gain handsomely from the tourist draw of having a creature in the lake. In truth, the brewery that owned the hotel took advantage of the publicity and sold it, causing the Mackays to lose their positions.

At any rate, the monster kept popping up before the awestruck eyes of local residents and visitors alike—in one case on land. On a beautiful July afternoon, the Spicers, a London couple, were driving near the lake when suddenly a "loathsome" creature with a long neck and measuring about twenty-five feet in length crossed their path. The beast appeared to be carrying a small lamb or similar animal in its mouth, Mr. Spicer said. It was, he added, "the nearest approach to a dragon that I have ever seen." In another instance in September, a party of six people said they watched from a teahouse window while the monster swam about the lake a half mile out. It seemed to have a snakelike head and neck that it pumped up and down and swung from side to side; the people saw two humps and a large tail that lashed the water. They watched in fascination for fully ten minutes before the creature moved slowly off and sank beneath the surface.

The sensation continued throughout the summer, with perhaps a score of sightings involving dozens upon dozens of people. Some eyewitnesses had nightmares for weeks. As Mrs. Spicer described the creature, "It was horrible—an abomination."

The first photograph of Nessie was taken in mid-November by a local, Hugh Gray, who had aimed his camera at a commotion in the lake 100 yards away and had snapped five pictures; four were lightstuck and useless, but the fifth, though damaged, showed a vaguely defined, sinuous form in the water. Gray was hesitant to estimate the thing's size, except to say that it "was very great"; he said that the skin appeared smooth and glistening and of a dark gray color. His negative was analyzed by several photography experts, who declared that it seemed genuine and had not been retouched.

By then the national press had picked up the story, and teams of reporters were racing north to file vivid accounts. Huge prizes were offered for the monster, dead or alive. Such was the crush that on holidays, cars were backed up for miles along the shore road. Prime Minister Sir Ramsay MacDonald planned a special trip north in hopes of catching a glimpse of the monster. In London, a tony seafood restaurant responded to the monster fever by offering "Le filet de sole Loch Ness." And across the Atlantic in America, a woman's clothing manufacturer made quite a hit with an ensemble called "Loch Ness," consisting of a dark green frock and matching jacket with long front tails trimmed in gray fox.

It was an atmosphere ripe for a hoaxer, and inevitably an ingenious prank was

Courtesy Time Inc. Picture Collection

Skeptics claim that the long, dark body shown in this
P. A. MacNab photograph of Urquhart Bay is merely the
wake of a trawler in the loch

perpetrated. In December, a self-styled big-game hunter, accompanied by a personal photographer, arrived in Loch Ness with the declared intention of bagging the monster. No sooner had the two commenced the hunt than they reported finding enormous footprints, only a few hours old, on the shore of the loch. The world waited impatiently for the British Museum's pronouncement. Finally experts rendered their opinion: The footprints, they advised weightily, belonged to a hippopotamus. To be precise, they had been made by a stuffed hippopotamus foot, a Victorian umbrella stand belonging to a local resident with two mischievous young sons. It was never clear whether the explorers were part of the joke or the victims of it.

While the skeptics chortled, more and more people seemed to be seeing the monster. In early 1934, there was a second land sighting. A young veterinary student, Arthur Grant, was motorcycling one moonlit night when he noticed a large dark object on the road ahead. Grant pulled to a stop, dismounted from his machine, and crept cautiously forward. As he approached, he reported, he could see that the object was an animal with a head something like a snake or a huge eel. The creature was watching him, he said, and when he got to within twenty yards, it bounded swiftly away and plunged noisily into the lake. Grant made a sketch of what he had seen; the monster was about twenty feet long, with a heavy body and four limbs, the forequarters small and weak, the hindquarters massive and powerful enough that it had bounded across the road like an immense kangaroo. "It looked like a hybrid," he said.

The reports and the growing consensus about what it might be piqued the interest of a man named Rupert Gould, the first of many who would try to identify the monster once and for all. Gould, who was thirty-seven years old when he retired from the hydrographic department of the British Admiralty in 1927, had published a book about sea serpents in 1930.

Gould was indefatigable, cycling around the lake and conducting interviews with about fifty people who had allegedly seen the monster. In 1934, without ever having sighted the monster himself, he published *The Loch Ness Monster and Others,* the first book on the subject. The Loch Ness monster, Gould said, was a descendant of his old friend, the sea serpent.

Gould's book captured the imagination of Sir Edward Mountain, an insurance company millionaire who had come to the Highlands to fish for salmon. In the summer of 1934, Sir Edward personally financed the first monster expedition at Loch Ness. Its members were twenty local men whom Sir Edward had recruited from the unemployment rolls. Scottish to the core, they solemnly entered their occupations as Watchers for the Monster on the state welfare cards. Sir Edward equipped his team with box cameras and binoculars and posted the men at various points around the lake for five weeks, nine hours a day. The monster watchers reported numerous sightings and took twenty-one photographs. But while King George v expressed interest in the hunt and some members of the royal family visited the lake, nothing conclusive emerged from Mountain's ambitious hunt. Mountain himself, after studying the prints produced by his minions, speculated that the monster might in fact be a gray

Fortean Picture Library, Wales

*R. Kenneth Wilson's 1934 image of the monster's head and neck
may be a photo of an otter or diving bird*

seal that had come up the River Ness in pursuit of salmon, found its way into the lake, and was then unable to get out.

There was one photograph of the monster, however, that could not be dismissed. Earlier, in April, a London surgeon named Robert Kenneth Wilson, on vacation in the Highlands, took four snapshots of something causing what he termed "a considerable commotion" in Loch Ness. When they were developed, two exposures were blank. But the third clearly and dramatically showed what seemed to be an animal's upraised head and neck, and the fourth showed the head disappearing into the water.

Decades later, the third photograph—often called the Surgeon's Photograph—remains the most famous documentation of Nessie. It is also the most controversial. Skeptics sometimes claim that Wilson took the photograph on April Fool's Day; it is also said that Wilson told a close friend he had faked the picture. But years afterward, Wilson's widow staunchly asserted that it was genuine.

As World War II engulfed Europe, the Loch Ness monster was largely forgotten; when sightings were reported occasionally during the late 1940s and 1950s, not many took them seriously. It was as though the furor of the 1930s had exhausted the public's capacity for excitement about such things. It was left to a young Englishman named Tim Dinsdale to rekindle international interest in Loch Ness. One evening in 1959, Dinsdale, then a thirty-four-year-old aeronautical engineer, read an article about the Loch Ness monster. That night Dinsdale dreamed that he walked the lake's steep shores and peered into its inky depths in hopes of finding the monster. When he awoke, he realized that he had found his life's mission.

For the next year, Dinsdale painstakingly analyzed all the available data. Then in April 1960, he set out on what was to be the first of many 600-mile journeys from his home to Loch Ness. This brief visit was to prove his most successful. Dinsdale pursued the monster for six days. Rising near dawn, he watched the lake through binoculars from various points on shore. Each time he drove from one point to the next, he prepared for a sudden sighting by setting up his movie camera, equipped with a telephoto lens, on a tripod next to the driver's seat. When not keeping watch, he interviewed people who claimed to have seen the creature.

On the fifth day, Dinsdale was almost ready to give up. Again rising at dawn, he watched the lake for nearly four hours without success and was hungrily heading back to his hotel for breakfast when he took a few minutes to set up the camera in his car. He was coasting down a hill when something in the lake caught his eye. Stopping abruptly, he snatched up his binoculars and peered intently at a long oval shape, mahogany colored, in the water. Then it began to move. Dinsdale dropped his binoculars and started the camera, filming the monster for four minutes as it swam west on a zigzag course.

(The importance of Dinsdale's film would not be fully appreciated for almost six years. In late 1965, at the request of a member of Parliament, David James, himself a Loch Ness monster hunter, the Joint Air Reconnaissance Intelligence Centre, part of Britain's Royal Air Force, agreed to analyze the film. JARIC estimated that the object was at least six feet wide and five feet high. Most significantly, JARIC concluded that it was neither a surface boat nor a submarine, and therefore "probably an animate object.")

At that time, Dinsdale's film inspired a host of new expeditions, from individual ventures to impressively organized armies of volunteers. The largest and longest-lived was the Loch Ness Investigation (LNI). Its driving force was David James, the M.P. best known for his daredevil escape from a German prison camp during World War II. In 1962, James organized LNI with Constance Whyte, naturalists Sir Peter Scott (son of the famous Antarctic explorer Robert Scott) and Richard Fitter, and Norman Collins, deputy chairman of a British television production company.

Later that year, in what would be the first of many expeditions on the loch, James and two dozen volunteers scanned the lake with binoculars and cameras by day. By night, they beamed army searchlights on the inky waters. As often as not, what they illuminated were other monster hunters, for the lake was becoming positively crowded.

In subsequent years, the LNI, using battalions of volunteers, maintained a round-the-clock camera watch on about seventy percent of the lake from May to October—by James's count, no fewer than 30,000 work-hours. They also pursued the monster with sonar, hovered over the lake in helicopters, and put out pebbles soaked in salmon oil and foul-smelling substances they hoped would act as a sex lure. They piped Beethoven's Sixth Symphony underwater. They recorded noises from the deep and played them back.

For several of the LNI's summers at Loch Ness, the monster hunt was largely directed by Roy Mackal, a forty-year-old biochemist from the University of Chicago

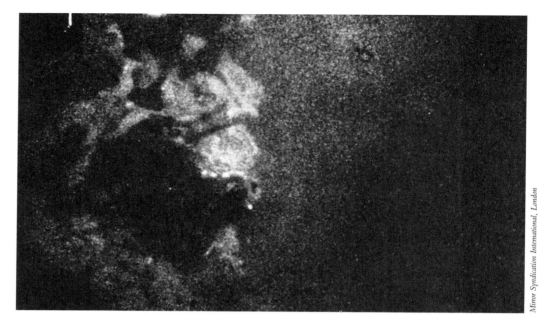

Mirror Syndication International, London

Robert Rines's "Gargoyle Photograph"

who had won renown for his research on DNA. But it wasn't until 1970 that Mackal himself actually saw the monster. He was retrieving hydrophones that had been set out to record underwater sounds when, out of the corner of his eye, he saw the water roil. A rubbery-looking triangular object popped out about a foot from the surface and then disappeared, to be followed by what seemed to be the smooth-skinned back of an animal of some kind. After a minute or so the thing vanished without a trace. Having seen the beast to his own satisfaction, Mackal continued to take an interest in the pursuits of the LNI team, but he also felt free to turn his attention to other elusive beasts.

By the time Mackal began branching out from the search for the Loch Ness monster, another American had become deeply involved. He was Robert Rines, a Boston patent lawyer who was forty-eight years old in 1970 when he heard Mackal speak about monster hunting at a conference Rines attended at the Massachusetts Institute of Technology, his alma mater. Something of a maverick, Rines had originally taken his degree in physics but then had embarked on a successful legal career. In 1963, Rines and a few wealthy friends had founded an organization called the Academy of Applied Science, to support unusual areas of research. The academy had no official university affiliation or established research program, but it did include some individuals with impressive scientific credentials. And many of its interests coincided with those of the Loch Ness monster hunters.

Rines arrived at the lake in 1970. He brought along Martin Klein, a fellow MIT graduate who had invented an extremely sensitive type of side-scan sonar used in searching for sunken ships and in offshore oil drilling. Rines was immediately encouraged; Klein's invention indicated the presence of large moving objects, ten to fifty times larger than the biggest fish known to inhabit Loch Ness. It also suggested the existence of underwater caverns in which the monster might lurk.

The next year, Rines came equipped with an underwater camera synchronized to a powerful strobe light. It had been loaned to him by Harold "Doc" Edgerton, for years the lighting expert for undersea explorer Jacques Cousteau. After two years, in 1972, Rines was rewarded with photographs that were to be among the most important and hotly debated exhibits in the case for the Loch Ness monster.

In the very early hours of an August day, sonar equipment on the LNI boat, *Narwhal,* picked up the presence of a large, submerged object. Minutes later, salmon began frantically leaping about the water's surface, evidently trying to escape some sort of predator. Suspended at a depth of about forty-five feet, the Edgerton camera captured an extraordinary image. The photograph, enhanced by computer at the California Institute of Technology's Jet Propulsion Laboratories, showed what many saw as a large flipperlike limb of an unseen creature. Estimates placed the flipper's length at about eight feet and its width at about four feet.

Three years later, Rines produced more dramatic evidence. On a June day in 1975, his underwater cameras were triggered by two sonar returns about six hours apart. Two months passed before he got around to dropping off the 2,000 picture roll at the laboratory of a friend, Charles Wyckoff, a photographic genius who had developed the high-speed film used to photograph atom-bomb tests. And then Rines and Wyckoff were astounded.

The first of the sonar-activated photographs seemed to show the long, curving neck, bulbous torso, and front flippers of a huge animal. At the end of the long neck, part of which was eclipsed in shadow, was the suggestion of a small head. Wyckoff calculated that the portion of the animal shown must have been about twenty feet long—and the body of the beast extended beyond the frame. More amazing still was the second image; it was a close-up of a grotesquely wrinkled object. Were investigators finally looking at the gnarled face of the Loch Ness monster? The Gargoyle Photograph, as it came to be called, showed what appeared to be two small eyes and two hornlike protuberances, their bilateral symmetry characteristic of a living creature. Wyckoff estimated that the head was two feet long.

The photographs provoked a furor that was unprecedented even by the standards of Loch Ness. But no sooner had the monster hunters won some respect than their credibility collapsed. Word of the photographs was leaked to the press, which promptly ran the news under screaming headlines. Then, scientists at the British Museum, whom David James had asked to examine the photographs, issued their verdict. None of the photographs proved that an animal existed in Loch Ness, scientists said. Instead, they theorized that the image of a body and neck might actually be caused by small gas bubbles in the air sacs of the larvae of phantom midges, tiny, mosquito-like insects often found in Scottish lochs. As for the gargoyle head, they said that it could be a dead horse or even a tree.

Worse, there were suggestions that the photographers were perpetrating a hoax. Sir Peter Scott dubbed the monster *Nessiteras rhombopteryx,* Greek for "the Ness mar-

Lachlan Stuart's 1951 photograph of a three-humped beast was dubbed a hoax by many

vel with the diamond-shaped fin." Wags pointed out that the phrase could be read as an anagram for "Monster hoax by Sir Peter S." Rines countered sharply with an anagram of his own, "Yes, both pix are monsters. R."

All of the important Rines photographs as well as the sonar findings continued to come under heavy criticism. In 1983, two American engineers, Alan Kielar and Rikki Razdan, borrowed the Academy of Applied Science's raft on Loch Ness to set up 144 sonar devices over the surface. Any object more than ten feet long that passed beneath them would set off an alarm, and the sonar would track it automatically.

After several months they returned home empty-handed. When they reviewed the academy's earlier data on Nessie, they concluded that many of the sonar contacts had been caused by boats or stationary objects and that some of the data contained mathematical errors. The engineers also reported with raised eyebrows that a local woman had helped locate the monster for Rines by dowsing. But all of that was trivial compared with their next announcement—concerning the 1972 flipper photograph.

In view of their suspicions, the two engineers had asked the laboratory that carried out the computer enhancement, a process it had performed for closeup photographs of planets taken by space probes, to send them copies of the enhanced flipper photograph. What they received was grainy and indistinct, in marked contrast to the published photograph. News stories about their findings seemed to accuse Rines of retouching. Rines retorted that he had combined various enhancements to come up with the flipper image. That was a standard procedure, he said, and the laboratory backed him up. But the accusation nevertheless tarnished the most convincing piece of evidence that Nessie did in fact exist.

For photographers, the monster is the most frustrating of subjects. The creature surfaces so quickly that even veteran investigators are caught unprepared and stare amazed until it submerges. Sometimes it seems to materialize only in a flicker in the corner of one's eye. Surprisingly often, the apparatus itself malfunctions, or a crucial photographic plate is somehow lost or broken. Because of this apparent misfortune and the creature's elusiveness, some imaginative researchers have suggested that Nessie is not a flesh-and-blood monster at all but some sort of psychic phenomenon.

Another popular theory is that the creature is a plesiosaur, one of a small remnant population that somehow survived the last ice age and adjusted to life in Loch Ness. Proponents of the plesiosaur theory point to the capture in 1938 of a coelacanth, the huge prehistoric fish that was believed to have met the plesiosaur's fate. Nor is the plesiosaur the only ancient creature that has been nominated for Loch Ness. Indeed, it has even been suggested that a species of fish, or perhaps a species of eel, is the most sensible answer to the mystery of Loch Ness. The loch is rich in salmon and eels, both of which can grow to considerable lengths. Furthermore, they can travel swiftly and would rarely surface. But opponents of that theory note that fish could not change depth levels at the rates established by sonar tracking. Eels undulate from side to side, while the Loch Ness monster reportedly undulates from top to bottom. And if the monster were a fish, they say, what would account for the land sightings?

That reduces the field of known creatures to mammals. A likely contender, in the view of some scientists, is one of the orders of mammals, such as seals, whales, or sea cows, that are monster-size and capable of surviving for long periods in fresh water. Mackal, after considering candidates ranging from a large sea slug to a giant, newtlike amphibian, finally seems to have settled on the zeuglodon, a long, serpentine, primitive whale thought to have been extinct for 20 million years.

Solo Syndication, London

This 1934 image by F. C. Adams may reveal a fin emerging from the foam of the loch, but the poor quality of the shot makes analysis difficult

Exceptionally long-necked seals and otters remain the favorite candidates of those bent on explaining the monster in conventional terms. But believers in Nessie as a wholly unconventional creature continue to argue that seals tend to be sociable, frolicking in the water and loping onto land. Otters may indeed be of a more fugitive nature, but they are not so aquatic that they could live and breed in the water as the monster presumably does. Nor can they dive to the 700-foot levels where the sonar has detected moving objects.

If the identity of the monster is a mystery, its numbers are an even greater puzzle. Both monster hunters and skeptics generally speak of a single creature, but two or three of the creatures have sometimes been reported together, and it is widely agreed that a solitary animal could not survive for centuries in the lake. Based on the size of the lake and its food supply, George Zug of the Smithsonian has estimated that the number of Nessie-like creatures in the loch could range from ten to twenty individuals, if they weigh about 3,000 pounds each, to as many as 150 animals weighing 330 pounds each.

While others carry on that debate, the hunters want nothing more than to establish that Nessie exists. And so year after year, Rines and his academy, along with other investigators, have returned to the lake in hopes of putting that single all-important question to rest. But since 1975, nothing has been as impressive as the Rines photographs.

Hunting Bigfoot and the Yeti

PERHAPS THE MOST widely celebrated of the elusive wilderness monsters is the so-called Abominable Snowman—or as Nepal's mountain-dwelling Sherpas say, *yeh-teh,* or Yeti—whose tracks have been often discovered in the frigid lands of perpetual snow in the Himalayan regions of India, Nepal, and Tibet. According to locals, the Yeti is but one of several unidentified creatures that inhabit the highlands of southern Asia.

One of the first recorded westerners to take note of the Yeti was a British army major named L. A. Waddell. In 1889, Waddell found what he took to be large footprints in the snow on a high peak northeast of Sikkim. Ten years later, in a memoir, he wrote: "These were alleged to be the trail of the hairy wild man believed to live amongst the eternal snows. The belief in these creatures is universal among Tibetans." But this account—as well as a smattering of other reports—was ignored in Europe and America for decades, until the creature was popularized by an unwitting error in the translation of its Nepalese name.

In 1921, members of a British expedition climbing the north face of Mount Everest noted, as they reached 17,000 feet, some dark figures moving around on a snowfield above them. When the explorers reached the spot, the creatures were not there but apparently had left behind some huge, humanlike footprints in the snow. The leader of the expedition, Lt. Col. Charles Kenneth Howard-Bury of the British army, later spoke of the incident with journalists in India, noting that his Sherpa guides called the elusive creatures *metoh-kangmi*. In fact, the name was a generic Nepalese term for several mountain creatures said to roam the area, but in the course of transmission to the world the word was mistakenly thought to be Tibetan and was translated as "Abominable Snowman."

Before long the creature became an international sensation. And mountaineers, always interested enough in the conquest of Everest and other great Himalayan peaks,

279

now had another reason to explore the high snowfields—to find the Abominable Snowman. Reported sightings of large tracks, and of the great creatures themselves, began to accumulate. In 1925, an adventuresome Greek photographer named N. A. Tombazi was 15,000 feet up in the mountains of Sikkim when his porters began shouting and pointing. About 200 to 300 yards away, he glimpsed a figure that he later described as "exactly like a human being, walking upright and stopping occasionally to uproot or pull at some dwarf rhododendron bushes."

The unclothed creature quickly disappeared, but Tombazi later found its tracks in the snow. Although shaped like a human footprint, these impressions were both shorter—only about six inches in length—and broader, measuring four inches at the widest part of the foot.

This and other reports that followed in the 1930s gave rise to the thought that there might be more than one kind of creature ranging through the snowy mountains. The tracks reported by Tombazi were smaller than those of a human; others, such as those seen by Howard-Bury, were larger. But all of the tracks resembled human footprints in that they showed five toes and were plantigrade—that is, the entire sole of the foot touched the ground with each step the creature took.

Indeed, the Sherpas had always spoken of at least two different types of creature, and used different names in referring to each. All of them were known as *teh,* the Sherpa word for a flesh-and-blood animal. But one kind, a large beast that travels on all fours and stands up only when it runs, they called *dzu-teh.* Some researchers think this is the relatively common Himalayan black bear that often preys on the yak herds of the region.

For the other, smaller denizen of the high places, the Sherpas have two terms. One, *meh-teh,* means man-beast. The other, more familiar term *yeh-teh* refers to an animal that inhabits rocky places. The Sherpas think of this smaller animal as a nearly human-size, erect creature that lives at the tree line, often venturing upward into the perpetual snow, sometimes moving down the mountainside to pilfer food from a village or prey on the yak herd. Described as having pointed heads, long arms hanging below the knees, and a covering of reddish hair, the Yeti would seem to be a smaller version of North America's Bigfoot, though most investigators insist that the two creatures are entirely different.

To the Sherpas, the Yeti is a familiar figure that they have incorporated into their folklore with more humor than dread. The breasts of the female Yeti, it is said, are so pendulous that in order to run the creature must sling them over her shoulder. Sherpa children are often frightened into obedience by references to these monsters, but they are also advised how to escape their clutches—run downhill, they are told, because in the downhill pursuit a Yeti's hair tends to fall over its face.

In 1951, the Everest Reconnaissance Expedition set out to evaluate routes for an attempt to ascend Everest. At 18,000 feet, two of the climbers encountered fresh tracks, which they followed along the edge of the Menlung Glacier for nearly a mile. According to expedition leader Eric Shipton, writing later in the *Times* of London, "the tracks were mostly distorted by melting into oval impressions, slightly longer and

The Pyramid of Pharaoh Chefren, Fourth Dynasty, in Giza, Egypt

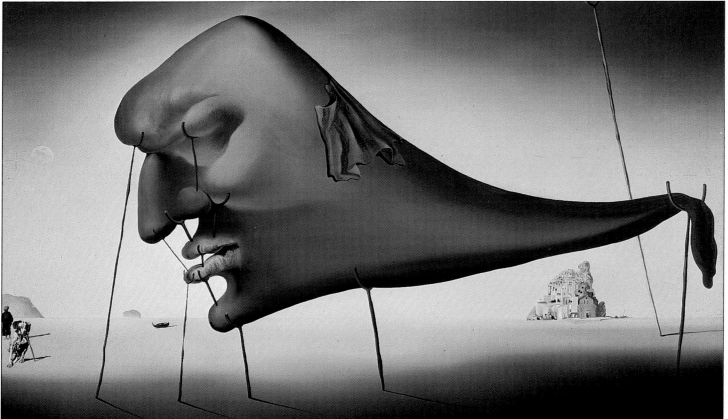

Salvador Dali's Sleep, *1937*

Dotted with volcanic islets, Thera's harbor shows the outlines of an eruption, lending credence to some scientists' theories that the cataclysm that shattered this Aegean island in 1500 B.C. inspired the tale of Atlantis

Photographer Ted Spagna shot time-lapse sequences like Harry & Cat, *pictured above, with a picture every fifteen minutes.*
Neurophysiologists have proven that posture coincides with changes in brain waves during dreaming.

LE·FOU

LE BATELEVR

LAROVEDELAFORTVNE

*The mystical tarot,
clockwise from upper left:
The Fool, seventeenth-century;
The Jester, sixteenth-century;
Death, seventeenth-century;
The Wheel of Fortune,
seventeenth-century.*

XIII

LA MORT

The Gallows tarot card, from a seventeenth-century deck

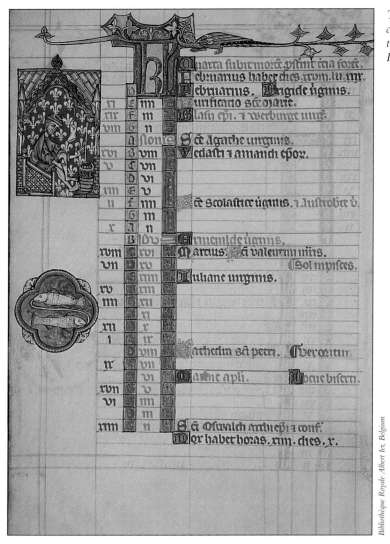

These linked Pisces fish (left center) appear in the calendar of the medieval Peterborough Psalter

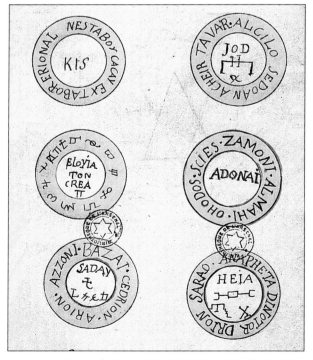

Six magic charms from an eighteenth-century text designed to call forth benevolent spirits

Aries lies at the feet of Spring in a fresco dating from the early 1470s, found in the Palazzo Schifanoia in Ferrara, Italy

The astrological significance of certain planets is often gendered, as shown in this seventeenth-century French print: the female holds aloft the moon while the male proffers the sun

a good deal broader than those made by our large mountain boots. But here and there where the snow covering the ice was thin, we came upon a well-preserved impression of the creature's foot. It showed three broad 'toes' and a broad 'thumb' to the side." The clearest of the impressions measured thirteen by eight inches.

Shipton was a seasoned climber who had scaled mountains throughout the world, and his experiences could not be taken lightly. The publication of his report, accompanied by photographs of the tracks, caused a new explosion of interest in the Yeti. During the following months, several additional sightings of Yeti tracks were reported, all the way from the western Karakoram to the easternmost Himalayas. But skeptics pointed out that melting snow can enlarge small, well-defined tracks, transforming them into bigger, less well defined ones. They also called attention to the fact that bears of the region, when walking, place the hind foot in the spot just relinquished by the forefoot, often leaving an impression that resembles a large human print.

Belief in the Yeti was dealt a considerable blow when Sir Edmund Hillary, knighted for his conquest of Everest in 1953, returned from the Himalayan Scientific and Mountaineering Expedition of 1960–1961. In addition to conducting research on human physiology at high altitudes, Hillary and his team investigated the question of the Yeti. They found a few of the footprints—but the renowned Hillary pronounced them to be ordinary animal tracks enlarged and distorted by melting. The expedition also borrowed a supposed Yeti scalp from a Buddhist monastery, but the scalp turned out to be made of the skin of a serow, an ungainly goatlike animal of the region.

Hillary noted that Sherpas make little distinction between their metaphysical world and objective reality. They firmly believe, for example, that the Yeti can make itself invisible and then reappear at will. In Hillary's view, it all amounted to nothing more than a "fascinating fairy tale, born of the rare and frightening view of strange animals, molded by superstition, and enthusiastically nurtured by Western expeditions."

That same year, a respected British primatologist, William C. Osman Hill, sprang to the Yeti's defense and labeled Hillary's conclusions "rather hasty." Hill found evidence of the Yeti's existence convincing, but he said the animal was clearly a creature of the "rhododendron thickets of the lower parts of the valleys, and it is here that future search should be directed." But perhaps as a consequence of Hillary's well-publicized skepticism, organized searches for the elusive creature became rare. Although occasional reports of tracks found and sightings made continued to trickle in throughout the 1960s and 1970s and into the 1980s, they remain inconclusive.

ACCOUNTS OF another giant have persisted among some American Indians whose tribes took up residence in forested lands, most notably the high forests of the Pacific Northwest. From one of these tribes, the Salish of British Columbia, comes the popular name Sasquatch; the Huppas of northern California call it *oh-mah-ah,* shortened to *omah.* Here there is no linguistic confusion about snowmen; the various names mean, quite simply, "wild men of the woods." And it is in the continent's heavily wooded regions that later white immigrants have also encountered the crea-

tures or observed signs of their passage.

Apparently, reports of such encounters began in the nineteenth century. In 1811, while crossing the northern Rocky Mountains, a Canadian trader named David Thompson saw huge tracks, measuring some fourteen by eight inches, in the snow near what is now Jasper, Alberta. On July 4, 1884, a newspaper in Victoria, British Columbia, reported that a train crew had captured a short, long-armed, manlike creature covered with coarse black hair. They named the immensely powerful creature Jacko. Jacko's fate is not known; he simply disappeared from the record, either a chimpanzee escaped from a circus or, some suggest, a juvenile Sasquatch.

Over the decades, there were sporadic reports of similar encounters, most of them from British Columbia, many of them fantastic. One had to do with several hairy giants who attacked a prospector's shack near Kelso, Washington. But the world paid little heed to such stories; most people who thought about the Sasquatch at all relegated it to the realm of hoax, delusion, or Indian legend.

Then in the 1970s, a new—and, according to most cryptozoologists, utterly preposterous—explanation of the origin of such creatures began to emerge. In 1973, a

The Sasquatch has been a seemingly harmless bystander. In the 75 years the only reports of human encounter has been the kidnapping of an Indian maid and a prospector.

sudden spate of Sasquatch sightings occurred in Westmoreland County, Pennsylvania, among other places in the East and Midwest. On September 27, for example, at about 9:30 P.M., two young girls awaiting a ride spotted a huge, hairy creature standing in the woods. The terrified girls ran home and described a white, eight-foot-tall monster with glowing red eyes that carried a luminous ball or sphere in one hand. Several people later reported that they had seen, that same night, what appeared to be a stationary aircraft hovering over the woods in the area, beaming a light down to the ground. The apparent connection between a rash of Sasquatch encounters and an outbreak of UFO sightings in the area led some to propose that Sasquatch was an extraterrestrial.

The idea seemed to gain support only a month later, near Greensburg, Pennsylvania, when a dozen people reported seeing a large, red UFO descending into a distant pasture. One young man (who used the pseudonym Stephen for his subsequent accounts of the episode) grabbed a rifle and drove off to investigate, along with two ten-year-old twin brothers. As they approached the pasture, the headlights of

Sasquatch footprints have been discovered repeatedly. The tracks have been up to 16 inches long and 8 inches wide, pressed 2 to 3 inches into the ground, with a stride of 5 to 7 feet.

Although the Harrison Lake area is the traditional home of the Sasquatch, reports have come from many parts of British Columbia that the hairy giants have paid them a visit.

Copyright © 1986 René Dahinden

their car dimmed. They stopped and continued on foot until they crested a hill and saw a bright, dome-shaped craft about a hundred feet in diameter hovering just above the ground. They heard a low, humming noise and, from somewhere nearby, the sound of screaming.

At one point, the twins called out in fear, having spotted something in the glow of the huge vehicle's light. Two apelike creatures, standing seven to eight feet tall, were lumbering toward them across the pasture. They had gray fur and glowing green eyes. Twice Stephen fired over their heads, trying to scare them off, but they kept coming. One of the twins ran off in terror, while Stephen fired three rounds into the larger of the two creatures. It whined and raised its hands, and at that moment, the glowing bubblelike vehicle disappeared. The monsters walked away into the dark.

State police and UFO investigators who reached the scene later that night found no sign of monsters or a landing, but did encounter an unpleasant, sulfurous smell permeating the area. A number of investigators had difficulty breathing and became dizzy. Stephen's reaction was even more pronounced; he began to growl and flail his arms, shaking violently, at one point racing off around the field until he collapsed.

Such reported sightings of Sasquatch-like creatures and UFOs at the same time are relatively rare, though persistent, particularly in the Midwest. It is no surprise that they have led to the formulation of some bizarre theories. One of these is that UFOs are the products of electromagnetic energy released by geological stress deep in the earth; this energy, playing on the brain, creates images of UFOs, and by the same process could produce Sasquatch hallucinations.

A less-benign variant of that scenario has been offered by a magician and UFO writer named John Keel. He has suggested that the creatures reported in the vicinity of landed UFOs materialize by drawing energy from the witness, in a kind of bloodless vampirism, emerging into our world fleetingly from some other dimension. According to Keel, this phenomenon could explain the continuing elusiveness of Sasquatch, the chief physical evidence of which consists of some 1,500 tracks leading nowhere.

Such theorizing may be dismissed easily enough, but the existence of so many tracks was evidence enough to lead at least one well-known member of the scientific establishment to proclaim the reality of Sasquatch. John Napier, a British anatomist and anthropologist who had served as the Smithsonian Institution's director of primate biology in the 1960s and was later a professor at the University of London, made a thorough study of the evidence for such creatures. In 1973 he published his findings in *Bigfoot: The Yeti and Sasquatch in Myth and Reality.*

To Napier, the evidence for Sasquatch was all but overwhelming. "No one doubts that some of the footprints are hoaxes and that some eyewitnesses are lying," he conceded, "but if *one* track and *one* report is true-bill, then myth must be chucked out the window and reality admitted through the front doors." The weight of the evidence convinced him, he declared, that "some of the tracks are real," and that "Sasquatch exists."

While Napier was sympathetic to the claims for the Yeti, his scientific caution barred him from taking them at face value. The effects of melting snow on footprints, the relative vagueness of sighting reports, and the Sherpa belief in the dual nature of reality led Napier, like Edmund Hillary, to dismiss the Yeti "as a red herring, or, at least as a red bear." A single piece of evidence—Shipton's clear if enigmatic footprint from the 1950s—continued to bother Napier, but he insisted nevertheless that the Yeti still remained to be shown as real.

Thirteen years after his book appeared, Napier saw what seemed to be convincing proof that the Yeti did indeed exist. The new and tantalizing evidence came from an Englishman named Anthony B. Wooldridge. Early one morning in March 1986, Wooldridge was in the Himalayas of northern India, close to the Nepalese border. At about 11,000 feet, he came across "strange tracks" in the snow, measuring some ten inches long. Wooldridge pressed on until, about 2,000 feet higher, he found that his progress up the incline was blocked by the remains of an avalanche of wet snow. Moving closer to the impassable snow pile, he discovered additional tracks on the other side, leading across a slope to a small bush. Behind the bush, steady and motionless, was what appeared to be an erect creature standing six or more feet tall.

"The head was large and squarish," Wooldridge reported later, "and the whole body seemed to be covered with dark hair." He was able to get within about 500 feet of the presumed creature, which remained unmoving by the bush, and photographed it with his Nikon camera. Then, after observing the startlingly humanlike figure for some forty-five minutes, Wooldridge noted that the weather was closing in and descended from the mountainside.

In England, he showed his photographs to a number of scientists, among them zoologist Desmond Morris, a skeptic when it came to Yetis. Morris found the pictures "puzzling." Napier was less restrained. "In my view," he wrote, "the creature in the photograph is a hominid. . . . The creature cannot be anything but a Yeti."

The Wooldridge photographs are indeed convincing, appearing to show a humanlike figure standing at apparent ease beside a mountainside bush. But such pictures are not always what they seem. In late 1987, not long after John Napier died of a stroke, Wooldridge announced forthrightly that painstaking analysis of his Himalayan photographs, and comparisons with pictures taken later of the same scene, had shown that "the object photographed was almost certainly a rock."

Although Wooldridge's photographs yielded up their mystery relatively quickly, the same cannot be said of Roger Patterson's enigmatic 1967 movie film of the female Sasquatch he supposedly encountered in the Pacific Northwest. The Patterson film has remained a focal point of the Sasquatch debate. If the film was a hoax, as some investigators think, then Sasquatch need not be taken seriously, but if it was legitimate, then Sasquatch exists.

Napier was suspicious of the Patterson footage, finding the alleged Sasquatch's gait and general appearance somewhat unnatural. Another analyst, a British expert in biomechanics named Donald W. Grieve, concluded that if the film had been shot at the standard speed of twenty-four frames per second (fps), the creature it showed might actually have been a human in disguise. However, continued Grieve, the "possibility of fakery is ruled out if the speed of the film was sixteen or eighteen fps. In these conditions a normal human being could not duplicate the observed pattern."

Patterson, as it turned out, was uncertain about the speed setting of his camera. Ordinarily, he kept it at twenty-four fps, since that was more acceptable for use on television. But he remembered after his encounter with Sasquatch that the setting had been at eighteen fps. Perhaps the speed had been accidentally changed when the spooked horse reared back in fright or when the camera was yanked hurriedly from the saddlebag. Patterson, however, could not say for sure.

Later, Russian analysts in Moscow found a novel method of estimating the film speed. As Patterson had dashed toward the creature with his camera whirring, the film recorded how he had bobbed up and down with each step, thus recording the rate of his stride. The Russians calculated that if the film had been shot at twenty-four fps, then Patterson had been taking six steps per second—a faster pace by far than that of a world-class sprinter. According to the Russians, the film had to have been shot at sixteen fps; according to Grieve, that would rule out a hoax.

Patterson died in 1972, but others continued to wrangle over his film. René Dahinden took it to some of the leading practitioners of cinematic deception in the world—the technicians at the Walt Disney studios. If the Sasquatch film was a hoax, said the cinematographers, it was a better hoax than even they could have created. Neither the Disney people nor any other analyst of the film has been able to find conclusive evidence of fraud—what movie people would refer to as "the zipper in the suit."

Further perspective on the famous film footage has come from Grover Krantz, a physical anthropologist at Washington State University. Krantz calculated that a creature of the Sasquatch's size and weight would require a foot quite different from a human's. It would have to be more flexible, he said, and the heel would extend

Patterson/Gilman © René Dahinden, 1968

Taken from a 1967 film made by Roger Patterson and Robert Gilman, this frame shows the mysterious creature in the Bluff Creek area of northern California, where Sasquatch footprints had previously been found. The creature was estimated to be seven feet three inches in height, 600 pounds in weight, and to have left footprints fourteen-and-a-half inches long and six inches wide.

farther back from the ankle. The Patterson film clearly shows the creature's projecting heel—an esoteric biomechanical detail that no former rodeo rider bent on a hoax could have been expected to know.

Krantz, whose pursuit of the elusive Sasquatch began in 1969, has studied many of the more than a thousand reports of sightings and has interviewed dozens of eyewitnesses. About half of them, he thinks, were "lying, were fooled by something else, saw something out of a whiskey bottle or gave me information too poor to evaluate. With the other half, I couldn't find anything wrong." Krantz has also been impressed

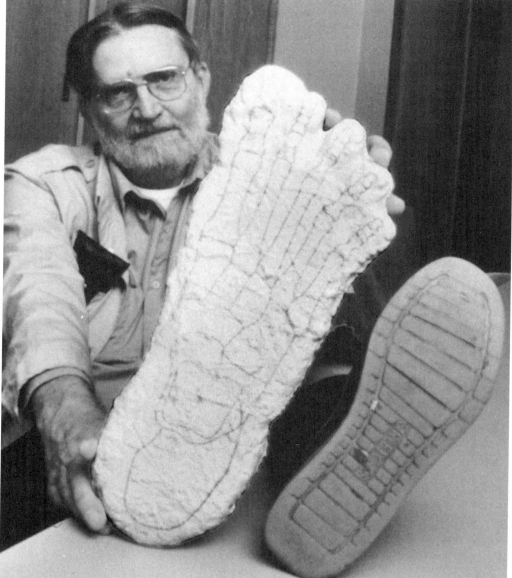

Anthropologist Grover Krantz compares a seventeen-inch plaster cast of an alleged Bigfoot track with his own twelve-inch shoe. From the cast, Krantz was able to posit a bone structure different from that of humans—a structure, he believes, that could accommodate a beast of Bigfoot's size.

by more tangible evidence, such as that turned up in the spring of 1982 by Paul Freeman, a temporary employee of the U.S. National Forest Service.

On the morning of June 10, while tracking a small herd of elk along an old logging road near Walla Walla, Washington, Freeman spotted what he described as a Sasquatch-like figure descending an embankment about sixty yards ahead of him. The creature seemed to notice the human intruder and soon fled, but when Freeman and a party of fellow workers returned to investigate further, they discovered twenty-one well-defined footprints in the hard earth. The men made plaster casts of some of the tracks; six days later, while patrolling in the same general area, they found and made casts of another set of prints.

A number of other supposed Sasquatch tracks have been found in the Walla Walla area since 1982, leading Krantz to maintain that there are as many as six of the creatures ranging through the region. But if Krantz has no doubts about Sasquatch's reality, most scientists remain skeptical. Indeed, eighty-eight percent of the North American university anthropology professors polled in a late-1970s survey would not even concede the possibility that such a creature might exist.

Photography is not conclusive, the scientists insist. There must be physical evidence—a carcass, a skull, or at least a handful of teeth. No one has suggested that Sasquatch is immortal, yet no bodies or even skeletons have ever been found. Hunters, though, respond that one rarely finds the remains of any large animal in the forest, because the bodies are disposed of and scattered very quickly by scavengers. The lack of fossil remains can also be explained; there are few fossils of any kind to be found in the highly acidic soils of the Pacific Northwest.

For all that, there might have been a Sasquatch body to examine by now, were it not for the curious ethical problem the creature poses. Several people who have reported seeing a Sasquatch have said they were tempted to shoot it, but could not, because it seemed so human. In fact, Sasquatch is specifically protected by county ordinances in some jurisdictions.

Krantz, however, maintains that while the creature is surely a hominid, it is clearly not human—it lacks tools, clothes, fire, and language, as far as anyone can tell. For the sake of science, he argues, at least one of the beasts will have to be shot and brought in by the next searcher or hunter who happens to get the opportunity. However, despite the knowledge and understanding that would spring from such a find, the prospect raises daunting questions. Would the elusive Sasquatch be declared an endangered species? Would its forest habitat be protected? Would captured specimens be exhibited in zoos?

So far, such questions remain moot for all but a dedicated minority of travelers, adventurers, and scientists around the world. For them, the stories of what a privileged few have reportedly seen and heard and smelled, as well as the physical evidence recorded on scraps of film and in plaster casts, is enough. In all probability, they insist, those of us who venture into remote regions of the world are carefully observed and for the most part avoided by a large hominoid species—nocturnal, omnivorous, bipedal, and erect—rather like ourselves.

9
MYSTICAL PLACES

The Pyramids

*Seen from the Sphinx at the summer solstice,
the sun forms the hieroglyph for "horizon"—
a sun setting between two mountains—between
the pyramids of Cheops and Chephren*

THE GREAT PYRAMID of Cheops rises in enigmatic majesty from the rocky Giza plateau ten miles west of Cairo. Glimpsed through the branches of the acacia, eucalyptus, and tamarind trees that line the boulevard leading to the plateau, it vaults up from a wind-scraped flat on the edge of the Libyan Desert with dramatic suddenness, a breathtaking mountain of sand-colored stone looming above the lush palm groves of the nearby Nile. Caravan travelers approaching from the desert in ages past saw it for days before they reached it, a tiny triangle on the horizon bulking ever larger in its symmetrical perfection. Close up, its grandeur is overpowering. Numbers can only suggest its immensity—a ground area of 13.1 acres, the edifice itself composed of some 2.3 million limestone blocks averaging two and a half tons each. The structure contains enough stone to build a wall of foot-square cubes two-thirds of the way around the globe at the equator, a distance of 16,600 miles.

The Great Pyramid and the two others that stand near it on the plateau—attributed to Cheops's immediate successors—were erected during the period of Egyptian history known as the Fourth Dynasty, between 2613 and 2492 B.C. Egyptologists believe that Cheops (as the Greeks knew him; his Egyptian name was Khufu) ordered the immense building raised as a tomb and monument to himself. Its outer shell was originally composed of highly polished limestone blocks fitted together with painstaking precision, but these casing stones were stripped off in the fourteenth century and used in the construction of Cairo. At some point in history, the original capstone, forming the top thirty-one feet of the pyramid, was also removed.

Egyptologists have drawn on their knowledge of Egyptian religion to explain the significance of the pyramid shape, contending that it could have been connected with sun worship. The angled walls, they say, resemble the outspread rays of the sun descending earthward from a cloud, and the pyramid thus represents a stairway to the heavens. Some students of the ancient Egyptian Book of the Dead maintain that the pyramid was a secret temple where the elect underwent a mystic ritual transforming them into gods. The initiates would lie for three days and nights within the pyramid while their *ka*—the soul or essence—left their bodies and entered "the spiritual spheres of space." In the process, the candidates "achieved actual immortality" and became godlike.

Questions still surround the issue of how, in an age without pulleys or the wheel, the massive pyramid was built. Archaeologists have guessed that the builders somehow leveled the site and aligned the sides of the building by making repeated observations

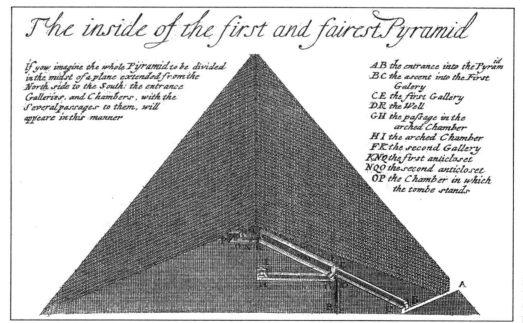

The inside of the first and fairest Pyramid

If you imagine the whole Pyramid to be divided in the midst of a plane extended from the North side to the South: the entrance Galleries, and Chambers, with the several passages to them, will appeare in this manner

AB the entrance into the Pyramid
BC the ascent into the First Galery
CE the first Gallery
DR the Well
GH the passage in the arched Chamber
HI the arched Chamber
FK the second Gallery
KNO the first anticloset
NQO the second anticloset
OP the Chamber in which the tombe stands

*The passages, chambers, and galleries of the Great Pyramid, as shown in
John Greaves'* Pyramidographia, *in 1638*

of circumpolar stars to determine true directions. At quarries a few miles away, masons cut the limestone with stone hammers and copper chisels. Crews consisting of hundreds of workers then dragged the blocks to the site; granite used in some parts of the interior was ferried down the Nile from a site about 400 miles distant and hauled up a causeway from the river. To pull the multi-ton blocks up the sides of the rising pyramid, they may have used a spiraling earthen ramp, although some experts believe they levered the stone upward on planks and wooden runners. The blocks were then fitted together with hairline precision, displaying a remarkable accuracy of engineering.

Speculation on the use of pyramids has persisted since before Christ. The Roman historian Julius Honorius declared that the pyramids were storehouses for grain. Another early writer opined that the structures were extinct volcanoes. The Arabs, who ruled Egypt for centuries, thought they were repositories of ancient knowledge, built by early rulers who feared a catastrophe. Local folktales claimed that the Great Pyramid incorporated both a guide to the stars and a prophecy of the future. Superstition trailed legend: Ghosts patrolled the corridors, the Arabs said, as did a naked woman with unsightly teeth who seduced trespassers and drove them mad.

The Greek historian Herodotus was the first visitor to gather and record information about the Great Pyramid in a systematic way. Herodotus visited Giza in the fifth century B.C., when the structure was already 2,000 years old, and wrote a description of its construction based on his conversations with local Egyptians. Unable to go inside the edifice (its entrance was hidden), he accepted his informants' claim that the pyramid was a tomb built to the tyrannical Khufu. The king's burial vault, they said, lay underground.

One hundred thousand men labored on the pyramid, according to Herodotus, with fresh crews thrown onto the project every three months. They built the causeway from the river to the plateau in ten years; the pyramid itself took another twenty years to complete. Engineers lifted the gigantic stones up the sides of the structure step by step using "machines formed of short wooden planks" on each step. Herodotus did not elaborate on how these machines worked. He was also told that outer casing stones were installed from the top down, after the interior core was in place. These glistening, highly polished stones were covered with inscriptions—later lost when the blocks were carted off to Cairo.

Herodotus was interested in the Great Pyramid primarily as an engineering project. But the ninth-century Arab caliph Abdullah Al Mamun was a young ruler with a scientific turn of mind and a special interest in astronomy. He dreamed of mapping the world and charting the heavens, and he turned his attention to the pyramid when he learned that its secret chambers reportedly contained highly accurate maps and tables executed by the pyramid builders. Perhaps of more interest to the caliph's fellow explorers was the great treasure said to be hidden within.

Arab historians later told the dramatic tale of how the caliph and his team of architects, builders, and stonemasons set to work in A.D. 820. Unable to find an entrance to the inscrutable structure, they launched a frontal attack, heating the lime-

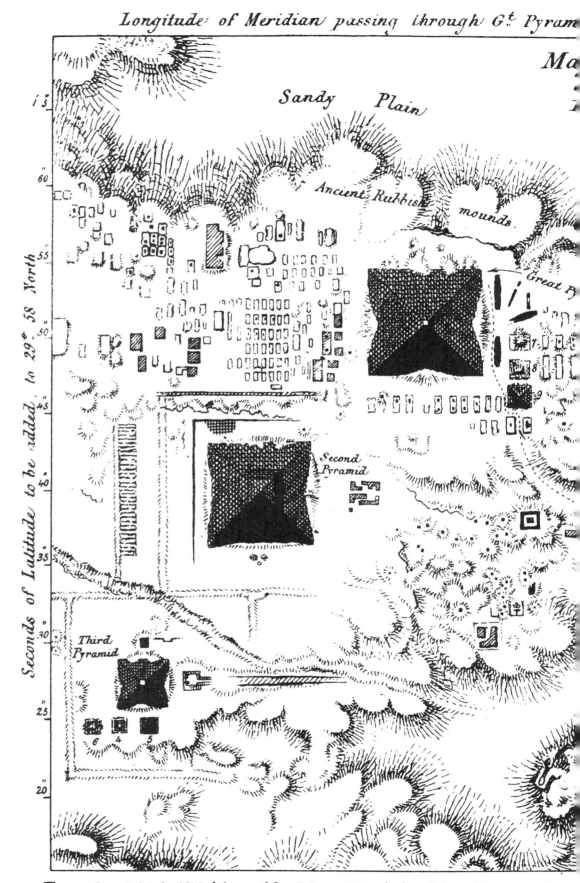

Sandy Plain

Ancient Rubbish mounds.

Second Pyramid

Third Pyramid

6 4 5

Seconds of Latitude to be added, to 29.º 58 North

The numbers 4, 5 & 6, & 7, 8 & 9 are Colonel Howard Vyse's for distinguishing the three

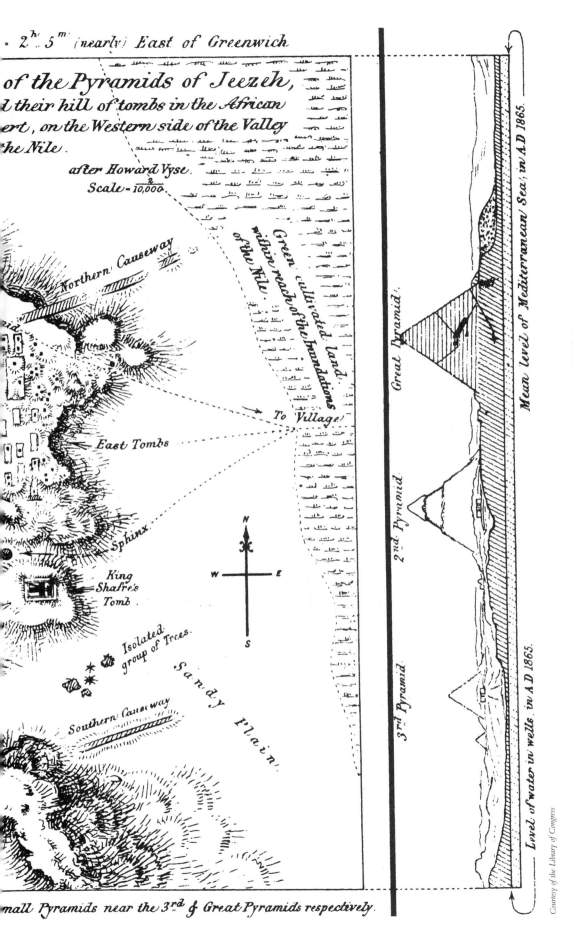

of the Pyramids of Jeezeh,
l their hill of tombs in the African
ert, on the Western side of the Valley
he Nile.

after Howard Vyse.

Scale = $\frac{2}{10,000}$.

Northern Causeway

Green cultivated land
within reach of the Inundations
of the Nile.

To Village

East Tombs

N

W   E

S

Sphinx

King
Shafre's
Tomb.

Isolated
group of Trees.

Southern Causeway.

Sandy Plain.

Great Pyramid.

2nd Pyramid.

3rd Pyramid.

Mean level of Mediterranean Sea; in A.D 1865.

Level of water in wells; in A.D 1865.

mall Pyramids near the 3rd & Great Pyramids respectively.

This early map of the Giza plateau shows the exact north-south alignment of the pyramids stone blocks with fire and then dousing them with cold vinegar until they cracked. After burrowing through 100 feet of rock this way, the explorers finally reached a narrow, four-foot-high passageway that climbed steeply upward. At its upper end they found the pyramid's original entrance, forty-nine feet above the ground, blocked and hidden by a pivoting stone door. Turning around, the explorers followed the passageway downward. After crawling on their hands and knees through the inky darkness, they were chagrined to find only an unfinished, empty chamber.

Excitement was rekindled when Al Mamun's men returned to the passageway and discovered what looked like another corridor slopping upward. Unfortunately, its entrance was completely filled with a large granite plug. The determined Arabs found that they could chip through the softer limestone block around it. As soon as they did, though, they found another granite obstacle and then several more. Someone had been determined to bar intruders from the pyramid's inner sanctum.

After laboriously hacking their way around the series of plugs, the explorers emerged into a low-ceilinged corridor that slanted upward until it intersected a level passageway. This led them to an eighteen-foot-square, twenty-foot-high gabled room that would later become known as the Queen's Chamber (because of the Arab custom of burying women in tombs with gabled roofs). This chamber, too, was empty.

The weary Arabs returned to the ascending passageway and found that it expanded abruptly into a splendid corridor, whose walls of polished limestone, twenty-eight feet high, later earned it the name of Grand Gallery. Still sloping upward, the gallery climbed 156 feet more before it gave onto an antechamber; beyond that was the largest room in the interior, an imposing sanctum thirty-four feet long, seventeen feet wide, and nineteen feet high, later called the King's Chamber.

Al Mamun and his men stepped gingerly across the threshold, doubtless convinced that this was the fabulous prize for which they had all worked so hard. And there, against a red granite wall, they saw it—a large, chocolate-colored stone sarcophagus, so big that the chamber must have been built around it. Thrusting their torches ahead of them, the explorers rushed to look inside. They found nothing. The granite sarcophagus was empty.

THE NEXT assault on the pyramids was a literal one. In July of 1798, disciplined French troops commanded by General Napoleon Bonaparte routed scimitar-wielding Egyptians at the bloody Battle of the Pyramids. Not very long afterward, the young Bonaparte began to attack the secrets of the Great Pyramid on the Giza plateau with a corps of French scientists. Principal among the pyramid students was a young scientist named Edmé-François Jomard.

First Jomard measured one side of the base: 230.9 meters, or 757.5 feet. Then he struggled along to the thirty-three-square-foot platform at the summit of the truncated edifice, tried unsuccessfully to slingshot a stone beyond the base, and patiently measured the height of each stone step on his descent: total elevation, 146.6 meters, or 481 feet. With these figures Jomard calculated the angle of the slope of the pyramid as 51 degrees 19 minutes, and its apothem—the line from the apex to the midpoint of each of its four sides at the bottom—was measured as 184.7 meters, or 606 feet.

The young scientist knew that early writers had described the pyramid's apothem as one stadium long. He also remembered that the length of a stadium, a basic unit of measurement in the ancient world, was believed to be related to the circumference of the earth. His figure for the apothem was thus a number to conjure with. Jomard turned his attention next to the cubit, another ancient measure of length. Herodotus

had written that a stadium contained 400 cubits, so the Frenchman divided his figure for the apothem by 400, which gave him a cubit measure of .4618 meters. Other Greek authorities on the subject had declared the base of the Great Pyramid to be 500 cubits long. When Jomard multiplied his .4618 by 500, the result was 230.9 meters, exactly what he had totaled up for the base length.

Mary Evans Picture Library

To Jomard the message was clear: The Egyptians had an advanced knowledge of geometry. They knew the size of the earth, they derived their units of measure from the earth's circumference, and they built this knowledge into the Great Pyramid.

However, Jomard's colleagues, upon remeasuring the base and height, came up with slightly different results. Further-

The 1877 abandonment of Cleopatra's Needle, the stone obelisk brought to England by Sir James Alexander in the midst of a harrowing storm. Although the obelisk was feared lost, the ship's captain sailed it into the Thames River on January 21, 1878, and it stands on the river's banks to this day. Its twin is found in New York's Central Park.

more, they pointed out, no evidence of Jomard's cubit could be found in other ancient Egyptian structures. In the end, the French refused to abandon their belief that it was the Greeks, not the Egyptians, who founded the science of geometry.

The subsequent accounts of the French scientific safari inspired an explosion of interest in things Egyptian. Nineteenth-century Europeans fell in love with Egypt: Museums vied for mummies, statues, and obelisks; artists grafted pyramids into sylvan landscapes; Empire and Regency fashion designers borrowed Egyptian motifs, and aristocrats had sphinxes and crocodiles carved onto their furniture. The Scottish peer

Alexander, tenth duke of Hamilton, had himself mummified. Americans succumbed to the craze as well: The city of Memphis, Tennessee, took its name from an older river city in Egypt. In 1880, New Yorkers imported an obelisk called Cleopatra's Needle and installed it in Central Park.

Pyramid themes became fashionable just as society, particularly the society of Victorian England, was entering a troubling time, in which modern science seemed to threaten traditional religious beliefs. In response, some religiously oriented scholars seized upon the mysterious structures as proof of the divine hand's presence in the world.

The first major proponent of this theory was a London editor and critic named John Taylor, a former editor of *London Magazine,* whose distinguished circle of acquaintances included poets John Clare and John Keats. Nevertheless, he "frightened away half his friends," according to one, with what was to become a thirty-year-long obsession with the mystery of the Great Pyramid.

Taylor never visited Egypt; instead, he built a scale model of the pyramid to aid his studies. Dismissing the tomb hypothesis, Taylor pored over the figures gathered by Jomard and others in search of unifying principles. He found to his surprise that when he divided the perimeter of the pyramid by twice its height, the result was a number nearly identical to the value of pi (3.14159+), the constant that is multiplied by the diameter of a circle to give its circumference. If the pyramid builders were aware of pi, which was not known to have been correctly calculated to the fourth decimal point until the sixth century, what else did they know? He concluded that they knew the circumference of the earth and the distance from the center of the earth to the poles.

With pi as the connecting link, Taylor determined that the ratio of the pyramid's altitude to its perimeter was the same as that of the polar radius of the earth to its circumference: 2π. The pyramid was a structural expression "to make a record of the measure of the earth that it was built," he declared.

Captivated by Taylor's work, an Astronomer-Royal of Scotland, Charles Piazzi Smyth, warmed to the now elderly Taylor's cause with an ardor equal parts scientific and religious. In late 1864, the forty-five-year-old astronomer left for Egypt to make his own survey and measurements. Smyth spent several nights on the pyramid's summit, making astronomic observations showing that the pyramid was sited within minutes of latitude thirty degrees north. Smyth also observed that the pyramid's shadow disappeared completely at the spring equinox and concluded that this indicated advanced knowledge of astronomy. His measurements of the external dimensions yielded figures that matched pi even more closely than Taylor's had, to the fifth digit beyond the decimal point.

Smyth was in agreement with Taylor's opinion that the Great Pyramid enshrined the ancients' scientific knowledge. Its built-in measures were "more admirably and learnedly earth-commensurable," he wrote, "than anything which has ever entered into the mind of man to conceive." Smyth even went beyond Taylor to claim that measures of time as well as of distance were incorporated into the building of the pyramid. According to the astronomer, the structure's perimeter, in pyramid inches, a distance he identified as ¹⁄₂₅th of a cubit and within a thousandth part of a British inch, equaled precisely 1,000 times 365.2, the number of days in the solar year. The builders had worked all of this out with their breathtaking gift for physics, Smyth wrote, 1,500 years before "the infantine beginning of such things among the ancient Greeks."

In later years, Smyth argued that the pyramid also revealed the distance from the earth to the sun when its height in inches was multiplied by ten to the ninth power, ten to nine being the proportion of height to width of the pyramid. Unfortunately, Egyptologists denounced Smyth; a fellow member of the Royal Society of Edinburgh called his ideas "strange hallucinations which only a few weak women believe." A critic from the United States drolly expressed the skeptics' view that numbers could be marshaled to prove almost anything: "If a suitable unit of measurement is found," he said, "an exact equivalent to the distance to Timbuktu is certain to be found . . . in the number of street lamps in Bond Street, or the specific gravity of mud, or the mean weight of adult goldfish."

Smyth and Taylor's work bred many disciples despite skeptics' jeers. In 1877, an American churchman, Joseph Seiss, wrote that the Great Pyramid's stones harbored "one great system of interrelated numbers, measures, weights, angles, temperatures, degrees, geometric problems and cosmic references." Seiss was particularly struck by the pyramid's unrelenting fiveness: It had five corners and five sides (including the base), and a pyramid inch was ⅕ of ⅕ of a cubit. Was it coincidence, he posited, since we have five senses, five fingers or toes per limb, and that there are five books of Moses?

In 1880, a twenty-six-year-old Englishman named William Matthew Flinders Petrie set out for Egypt with an array of sophisticated instruments, hoping to resolve all speculation about the structure's dimensions and alignment. Flinders Petrie, as he was called, was well qualified by pedigree and training for such a task. His maternal grandfather and namesake, Captain Matthew Flinders, was known for his explorations of Australia. His father, William Petrie, was an engineer who had been so struck by the writings of Taylor and Smyth that he became a dedicated pyramidologist himself, spending twenty years in the design and fabrication of special surveying equipment that would measure the Great Pyramid with unprecedented precision. When he was thirteen, the young Flinders Petrie read Smyth's book, *Our Inheritance in the Great Pyramid*. Enchanted by the notion of varying standards of measure such as the pyramid inch, he took up the surveyor's trade and devoted himself to touring through England and painstakingly recording the dimensions of various buildings and ancient megalithic sites such as the great stone circles of Stonehenge.

In Egypt, Petrie did as so many other pyramid explorers had done before him and took up temporary residence in an empty cliffside tomb. Then he went to work, meticulously measuring and remeasuring every conceivable dimension of the Great Pyramid and its two smaller neighbors. To keep curious—and bothersome—British

BBC Hulton Picture Library

Egyptologist and archaeologist Howard Carter opens a set of doors leading to the sarcophagus of Tutankhamen, also known as King Tut, in 1922

sightseers at bay, he sometimes went about his outdoor tasks clad only in vest and pants, both a shocking pink. In the hot, dusty interior of the pyramid, he often worked nude and late at night, after the irksome tourists had departed. The work was not without its hazards, as a friend, a certain Dr. Grant, found when he joined the surveyor one night. "I had a terrifying time when he fainted in the well," wrote Petrie. "To raise a very heavy man, barely conscious, up a shaft of seventy feet with scanty foothold, when at any moment he might sweep me away down to the bottom was a risk not to be forgotten."

Petrie was astounded by the precision of the pyramid's stonework. Using instruments that were accurate to a tenth of an inch, he reported that the errors in the edifice both in length and in angles were so slight that a thumb would cover them. The walls of the descending passageway were within a quarter inch of being perfectly straight for their 350-foot length. He compared the joining of the casing stones to "the finest opticians' work on a scale of acres." Only in the anteroom of the King's Chamber did the quality begin to deteriorate, leading the youthful surveyor to speculate that the original architect had not finished the job.

The results of Petrie's labors, published in an 1883 book entitled *The Pyramids and Temples of Gizeh,* confirmed the pi relationship between the pyramid's height and perimeter. He found that the King's Chamber also incorporated pi in the ratio of its length to its periphery. But his figure for the pyramid's base was shorter than Smyth's, thus refuting the Scot's theory that the base length reflected the number of days in a year. Petrie also arrived at a different cubit measure, and he found no evidence to support Smyth's cherished pyramid inch.

Having located what he called "the ugly little fact which killed the beautiful theory," Petrie went on to an illustrious career in Egyptology, which eventually earned him a knighthood. His data on the pyramid's dimensions remained the best available until a definitive 1925 survey by the Egyptian government ended the numerical arguments for good. It turned out that the four sides varied in length by no more than eight inches: The south side was 756.1 feet long, the east 755.9, the west 755.8, and the north 755.4. Even more impressive, the sides were almost perfectly aligned to the cardinal points of the compass. The French savant Jomard had estimated the height correctly at 481 feet, but he had miscalculated the angle of the sides, which is fifty-one degrees fifty-two minutes.

But even after Petrie effectively dismantled it, the pyramidologists' theory refused to die; new discoveries continued to surface throughout the twentieth century. British engineer David Davidson managed to reconcile Petrie's findings with Smyth's through a complex set of calculations that factored in the virtually invisible hollowing of the pyramid's walls—which are in fact not completely flat but very slightly concave. Petrie had taken this into account, Davidson said, but had not extended his computations to the original outer casing. When this was done, according to Davidson, Smyth turned out to be right about the perimeter representing the solar year.

The measurement school would continue to arouse accusations of number juggling; Martin Gardner, for example, poked sly fun at the fiveness obsession of Joseph Seiss by applying the same criteria to America's Washington Monument. Not only, says Gardner, is its height 555 feet 5 inches, but its base is 55 feet square and its windows are 500 feet from the base. Gardner's so-called monument foot yields a base of 56.5 feet, which when multiplied by the capstone width gives a number very close to the speed of light. Could this be coincidence? asked Gardner.

T HE QUEST to decode the pyramid continued into the late twentieth century. The most intriguing notion focused not on the Great Pyramid itself but on the pyramid shape. According to some theorists, a factor inherent in that shape, something not clearly understood, seems to exert a force that has peculiar effects on objects, plants, and even people. This idea, which came to be known as pyramid power, derives primarily from a series of observations and experiments reported since the 1920s. Its first manifestation occurred in 1859, however, at the seat of mystery itself, the great mountain of stone at Giza.

Werner von Siemens, founder of the giant German electrical company that bears his name, had stopped at Giza in that year while shepherding a crew of engineers to the Red Sea, where they were to lay a telegraph cable. Ever curious and venturesome, Siemens set out to scramble to the summit of the pyramid; as he labored up the sides, the desert wind raised a pale mist of sand around him. Reaching the top, Siemens struck a victorious pose and jabbed a finger into the air. At that, a prickling sensation ran through his finger and a sharp noise rang out. The effect was similar to a mild electric shock.

Siemens, who knew a thing or two about the infant science of electricity, decided to conduct a test. Wrapping wet paper around a metal-necked wine bottle, he improvised a Leyden jar, a simple device for storing static electricity. When he held this contrivance above his head, Siemens was gratified to discover that the bottle became electrically charged, generating sparks when touched.

In itself, Siemens's electrical experience may not be particularly noteworthy. Under certain atmospheric conditions, others have noticed similar effects atop tall, pointed buildings. But it is more difficult to match the even stranger phenomenon reported in the early 1930s by a French ironmonger named Antoine Bovis. According to Bovis, he had been touring the King's Chamber in about 1920 when he came across the remains of several cats and other small animals that apparently had died in the pyramid. Curiously, the bodies had no odor. When he examined them, Bovis found that the animals had dehydrated and mummified despite the chamber's humidity.

Back home in Nice, the Frenchman determined to learn about this oddity. After building a wooden model of the pyramid, he oriented it due north and placed a recently deceased cat inside. The body mummified in a few days. Bovis repeated the experiment with other dead animals as well as with meat and eggs; in every case, he claimed, the organic matter dried out and mummified instead of decaying.

Even more mystifying was the next revelation. Czech radio engineer Karl Drbal, having heard of Bovis's experiments, repeated them, using a cardboard pyramid to mummify beef and flowers. He then placed a razor blade inside his six-inch model, at a point a third of the way from the bottom (corresponding to the location of the King's Chamber). Drbal expected the blade to lose its edge. To his amazement, he said, it emerged sharper than before. He claimed that in subsequent tests the pyramid shape regenerated blades so that they could be used as many as 200 times.

Drbal speculated that this was produced by an unknown energy that affected the crystals in the blades. Others might have observed that such single-blade marathons have been achieved without mystic sharpening. In May 1926, for example, a Viennese named Oskar Jahnisch informed the Gillette Safety Razor Company that he had completed five years of daily shaving with a single Gillette blade. But after a ten-year delay, an initially skeptical Czech patent office issued a patent to Drbal in 1959 for the cardboard (later plastic) pyramids he called Cheops Pyramid Razor Blade Sharpeners.

The pyramid power idea did not fare well among most scientists. Stanford Research Institute experiments at the Great Pyramid showed that food stored inside deteriorated normally. Geologist Charles Cazeau and anthropologist Stuart Scott conducted research of their own, reporting with amusement that "eggs . . . came out of our pyramid after forty-three days a smelly, runny yellow, and full of sediment. . . . Tomatoes in pyramids fared no better than those in brown paper bags. We were unable to sharpen razor blades."

Still, the pyramid's secrets are elusive despite the best efforts of traditional scientists and far-from-traditional pyramidologists. Whatever we try to make of it, we cannot ignore the Great Pyramid's presence; it haunts and mocks us. William Fix, author of *Pyramid Odyssey,* thinks he knows why: "It is enormous; it is ancient; it is legendary; it is sophisticated; it is the result of great enterprise; it is here for all to see at the crossroads of the earth—and it does not seem to belong to our world."

Stonehenge

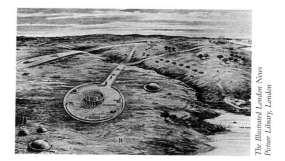

One theory of Stonehenge, illustrated above,
proposed it had served as a trading mart and racetrack

POISED IN isolated splendor on the flat, chalky grassland of England's windswept Salisbury Plain some eighty miles west of London, Stonehenge has intrigued investigators for many centuries. Even the builders of the monument remain unknown: Efforts to prove that they were Egyptians, Phoenicians, Greeks, Romans, Druids, Danes, Buddhists, Hindus, Mayans, survivors of the lost island continent of Atlantis, or even visitors from another planet have all failed.

It is estimated that as many as half of the site's original stones have vanished, with nothing but indentations in the ground to show where they once stood. Many others lie toppled and broken. But as one writer observed 200 years ago, "There is as much of it undemolished as enables us sufficiently to recover its form when it was in its most perfect state. There is enough of every part to preserve the idea of the whole."

The whole is a monument consisting of two concentric rings of upright stones enclosing a pair of nested horseshoe-shaped stone forms. Completing the complex are several solitary stones, including the fancifully named Altar Stone, Slaughter Stone, and Hele Stone; numerous pits; a shallow circular boundary ditch; and a broad roadway that breaches the ditch at its northeastern rim and connects Stonehenge with the Avon River, about a mile and a half distant.

The feature that gives Stonehenge its distinctive silhouette is a group of tall stone so-called doorways, which describe the outer circle and the outer horseshoe. The circle, about one hundred feet in diameter and sixteen feet tall, once consisted of thirty uprights capped by thirty lintels forming an unbroken ring of stone overhead. Even taller than the doorways of the outer circle are the five doorways that once made up the outer horseshoe. Called trilithons—Greek for "three stones"—they range up to nearly thirty feet in height. To erect these massive doorways, the builders somehow had to hoist the huge slabs, weighing perhaps as much as twelve tons each, above the pairs of uprights and then lower them into place with enough precision for the mortised notches on the undersides of the capstones to lock over the stone tenons atop the uprights. Stonehenge gets its name, variously rendered Stanhengues, Stanenges, Stanheng, Stanhenge, and Stanhenges, from the Old English words for "hanging stone."

Just as the builders of the hanging stones have not been identified, so the exact purposes of the place have never been firmly established—although it is believed that the complex almost certainly once served as a temple, one of many such ancient monuments of great stones, or megaliths. By far the greatest concentration of megaliths—some 50,000 in all—is found in western Europe and North Africa, primarily in Britain, Ireland, Spain, Portugal, France, Scandinavia, and Algeria.

These monuments display a wide variety of forms. The simplest are made of single, solitary upright stones known as menhirs, Celtic for "long stones." More complicated are groups of menhirs, sometimes arranged in circles or semicircles, and sometimes in vast enfilades stretching for miles. A third type of megalithic monument is the dolmen, a roofed, chamberlike structure that may be freestanding and above ground or enclosed within a massive mound of earth.

Stonehenge finds its place in the second category of megalithic monuments. But it is by no means the largest or the most ambitiously engineered of Britain's stoneworks and earthworks. Prehistoric Silbury Hill in nearby Avebury, to mention just one imposing example, is an artificial mound 130 feet high that is spread out over five and a half acres. Yet among them, none is better known, more extensively studied, or more subjected to flights of imagination and scientific speculation than Stonehenge. It stands, as novelist Henry James wrote, "as lonely in history as it does on the great plain."

Stonehenge is built primarily of bluestone, a type of blue-tinted dolerite, and sarsen, a variety of sandstone harder than granite. The bluestones, of which there were eight or more slabs originally, have been traced to a Welsh quarry about 130 miles northwest of Salisbury Plain; the sarsen slabs were brought from the Marlborough Downs, about twenty miles north of the site. Since wheeled vehicles were unknown in Britain during the time of Stonehenge's construction, the long-distance transportation involved in moving these massive rocks—some of them weighing as much as fifty tons—is among the more astonishing feats accomplished by Stonehenge's builders and one that has given rise to many conjectures.

An exact chronology of the construction is unknown, owing to the scarcity of data from the site and the margin of error inherent in archeological dating techniques. The best scientific guess is that Stonehenge was built in at least four stages, stretching across the centuries between 3100 and 1100 B.C. Not one but a series of ancient peoples contributed to the monument's construction, as evidenced in the varying choices of building materials and methods and also in the differing ultimate visions of Stone-

Elliot Rockman

Stonehenge, c. 1996

henge. Archeologists believe that in the first phase of construction the monument consisted of a simple circular embankment enclosing a few wooden poles and upright slabs, including the Hele Stone. The second phase was marked by the erection of two rows of bluestones forming a crescent at the center of the site. The doorways and trilithons were created in phase three, and in phase four, about 1100 B.C., the bluestones were reset and the roadway was extended.

Sometime thereafter, Stonehenge seems to have gone into decline, its sacred ground untended and largely unnoticed. Then about A.D. 1130, it was rescued from oblivion by the English clergyman Henry of Huntingdon, who set about to tell his countrymen just what an enigmatic place it was. In his *History of the English,* Henry wrote of "Stanenges, where stones of wonderful size have been erected after the manner of doorways . . . and no one can conceive how such great stones have been so raised aloft, or why they were built there."

Not until the reign of King James I in the early seventeenth century did medieval legend give way to serious investigation of Stonehenge. James paid a visit to the great stones in the summer of 1620 and was so intrigued that he ordered a formal architectural study to satisfy his royal curiosity about the origin and purpose of the mysterious structure. To undertake this Stonehenge study, the monarch chose Inigo Jones, the foremost architect of his day.

Jones had studied painting and architecture in Italy and was well versed in classical principles of design. Obedient to the royal commission, he visited the ancient monument, surveyed the site, and measured the individual stones. Returning to London, he searched his library of architectural writings to identify Stonehenge's builders.

He reviewed and rejected several ideas about the origin of Stonehenge, including the possibility that ancient Britons may have had a hand in it.

Britain before the Roman invasion, Jones averred, was populated by "savage and barbarous people, knowing no use at all of garments . . . destitute of the knowledge . . . to erect stately structures." Like philosopher Thomas Hobbes, he presumed that life for prehistoric humans in the Isles had been "solitary, poor, nasty, brutish and short"—or, in the words of another seventeenth-century writer, "almost as salvage [savage] as the beasts whose skins were their only rayment . . . 2 or 3 degrees I suppose lesse salvage than the Americans."

Such barbarians, Jones was sure, could not have possessed the aesthetic and mathematical sophistication to build anything with as "much Art, order, and proportion" as existed in Stonehenge. His own conclusion: The rocks on Salisbury Plain were the ruins of a temple to the Roman sky-god Coelus, built sometime during the periodic Roman invasion of Britain that began about the start of the Christian era and ended in A.D. 410. Amongst all the nations of the universe, he declared, only the Romans could have created such a marvel.

After Jones's death in 1652, his disciple and son-in-law John Webb edited the architect's notes on his Roman-origin theory into a volume entitled *The Most Notable Antiquity of Great Britain, Vulgarly Called Stone-Heng, on Salisbury Plain. Restored.* This book, the first devoted exclusively to Stonehenge, was a critical and popular failure.

One avid reader of Jones's book was Walter Charleton, a learned scholar-physician in the court of King Charles II. In the course of extended correspondence with a Danish antiquarian, Charleton was convinced that Stonehenge replicated the design of megalithic burial chambers found in Denmark. In a 1663 treatise entitled *Chorea Gigantum, or the Most Famous Antiquity of Great Britain, Vulgarly Called* STONE-HENG, *Standing on Salisbury Plain, Restored to the* DANES, Charleton sought to wrest credit for the stone monument from the Romans and deliver it to the Danish conquerors who

Elliot Rockman

had invaded England in Viking times.

Stonehenge, the doctor wrote, had been "erected by the Danes, when they had this Nation in subjection; and principally, if not wholly Design'd to be a Court Royal, or place for the Election and Inauguration of their Kings." Charleton pointed to the crownlike circular layout of Stonehenge as evidence that it had been connected with coronation rituals and suggested that the high stone lintels had provided lofty gathering places for Danish electors. He even ventured the idea that Alfred the Great had been able to defeat the Danes in A.D. 878 because the invaders had come to the battle weakened by overindulgence at celebrations that were held to mark the completion of Stonehenge.

However, another more controversial—and ultimately more durable—view was soon to emerge, shouldering aside all previous contenders. Stonehenge, so the new theorists proposed, was a temple built by the Druids.

DRUIDS WERE native Englishmen, or nearly so. They made up the priestly class of Celts that had swept westward from the continent to populate Britain as long ago as 2000 B.C. The little that is known about them comes chiefly from the writings of their Greek and Roman contemporaries; the priests themselves seem to have had little use for written language, perhaps fearing it might allow their special learning to fall into the wrong hands.

What made the Druid connection to Stonehenge so controversial was the reputed bloodiness of their religious ceremonies. How could men with such repugnant practices have produced such a sublime work? Many of the classical chroniclers present the Druids as a sinister fraternity, dedicated—as the Roman historian Publius Cornelius Tacitus wrote—to "inhuman superstitions and barbarous rites." Julius Caesar, who wrote extensively on the Druids in his *Gallic Wars,* claimed that they made human sacrifices to their gods by constructing immense wicker cages in human form, "whose limbs, woven out of twigs, they fill with living men and set on fire, and the men perish in a sheet of flame."

Diodorus Siculus, Caesar's contemporary, reflected a similar view. He wrote of Druid rituals in which the priests "kill a man by a knife-stab in the region above his midriff, and after his fall they foretell the future by the convulsions of his limbs and the pouring of his blood." And Tacitus reported further that when Britons were victorious in battle, "This inhuman people were accustomed to shed the Blood of their Prisoners on their Altars, and consult the Gods over the reeking Bowels of Men."

Inigo Jones, in his cataloguing of peoples who could not have built Stonehenge, also took a swipe at the Celtic priests: "Concerning the Druids," he wrote, "certainly Stoneheng could not be builded by them, in regard, I find no mention, they were at any time either studious in architecture . . . or skilful in anything else conducing thereunto." Jones allowed that the Druids may have been philosophers and astronomers, as Julius Caesar had mentioned, but those were branches of learning "consisting more in contemplation than practice," not the sort of studies he considered "proper to inform the judgement of an Architect. . . . In a word, therefore let it suffice, Stoneheng was no work of the Druids."

Forceful as they were, such arguments did not dissuade John Aubrey, an author whose writings ranged across such diverse fields as biography, folklore, and antiquarian studies. His studies of Stonehenge identified an outer ring just inside the earthen trench; the ring consisted of small, barely visible, man-made cavities that had previously gone unnoticed. Known ever since as the Aubrey Holes, these diggings measure up to six feet in diameter and two to four feet in depth, with flat bottoms. They were filled in with rubble, including charred bones that Aubrey took to be human. Admitting that he was "gropeing into the dark" to reach his conclusion, Aubrey said of Stonehenge and other megalithic structures that there was "clear evidence these monuments were Pagan Temples" and a "probability that these were temples of the Druids."

Aubrey's cautious thesis remained unpublished at his death in 1697. But twenty years later, the manuscript of *Monumenta Britannica* came to the attention of William Stukeley, a physician, an antiquarian, and an orthodox Christian.

Stukeley had first become excited about megaliths when he toured several stone antiquities (but not Stonehenge) in 1710. One site, he remarked cautiously, might have been "an heathen temple of our Ancestors, perhaps in the Druids' time." By the time he got to see Britain's most famous megalith, nine years later, he had become thoroughly enchanted with Druidism and with the lore of Stonehenge. He had even undertaken to build a pair of precise replicas, showing the structure in both "its present ruins" and its "pristine state." Once he laid eyes on Stonehenge, Stukeley could not stay away. "It pleases like a magical spell," he wrote. He took exact measurements of the stones and their ground plan, explored earthworks in the vicinity, and did some excavating.

One of Stukeley's most enduring contributions to the study of Stonehenge was his observation that the axis of the complex structure, as defined by the physical orientation of several key features, pointed directly "northeast, where abouts the sun rises, when the days are longest." Subsequent observers have noted that the megalith called the Hele Stone, which stands just outside the circles' entrance, aligns with the center of Stonehenge to mark almost the exact spot on the horizon where the sun rises on the day of the summer solstice. But Stukeley was the first to suggest that prehistoric Britons built their megaliths with precise astronomical alignments in mind.

Along this vein went astronomer Gerald S. Hawkins, a British-born professor at Boston University. Using a computer to check the movements of heavenly bodies against the positions of stones, Aubrey Holes, and other Stonehenge features, Hawkins discovered what he believed to be a total correlation with the extreme seasonal positions of the rising and setting of the sun and the moon. His computer analysis convinced him that the odds against so many astronomically significant placements occurring purely by chance were greater than a million to one.

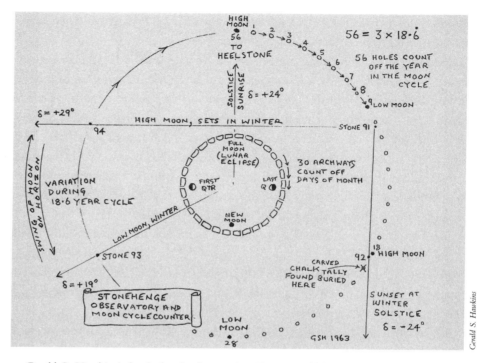

Gerald S. Hawkins' sketch showing how ancient Britons could have predicted lunar eclipses using Stonehenge was a controversial addition to the centuries-old debate

Hawkins published his findings about Stonehenge in 1963. Eight months later, he took his argument even further and suggested that Stonehenge was a kind of Stone Age computer, designed to predict lunar eclipses. The timing of eclipses, Hawkins said, is related to an 18.6-year cycle of lunar movements across the night sky, and he maintained that Stonehenge's ancient astronomers would have been able to track this pattern for three cycles by moving stone markers around the circle of fifty-six Aubrey Holes. In 1965, Hawkins published an expanded version of his theory of Stonehenge in a book boldly entitled *Stonehenge Decoded*.

Debate raged over the findings in *Stonehenge Decoded*. However, another investigator continued to gather data that would eventually win over some of archeo-astronomy's most stubborn foes.

SCOTTISH ENGINEER Alexander Thom, a professor at Oxford University until his retirement in 1961, had been surveying ancient stone structures since before World War II. Not until 1973, however, did he make his first visit to Stonehenge. In previous research, he had discovered that many pairs of structures, sometimes miles apart, could line up like the front and rear sights of a rifle to make important astronomical observations.

When he finally brought his surveying equipment to Stonehenge, Thom concluded that this most famous of all megaliths had been erected as a central rear sight from which prehistoric astronomers could take bearings on six different front sights.

The nearest of these Thom identified as a burial mound just a mile southeast of Stonehenge; the farthest was an earthwork on a knoll nine miles to the northwest.

Thom's theory held that megalith builders throughout western Europe constructed their separate monuments according to certain common standards. Chief among these standards was a unit of measurement Thom called the "megalithic yard," a 2.72-foot length he calculated by measuring and comparing the diameters of numerous stone circles. He also found these early builders to be knowledgeable about geometry as well as astronomy: They had laid out their structures in six regularly proportioned shapes, displaying an understanding of Pythagorean geometric principles centuries before the birth of the great Greek mathematician Pythagoras.

Scholars might have been expected to savage Thom, but when the *Journal for the History of Astronomy* published Thom's Stonehenge findings in 1975, one studied the engineer's carefully compiled data and confessed that he had to recant his previous statements. "It is important that nonarchaeologists should understand how disturbing to archaeologists are the implications of Thom's work," he wrote, "because [his opinions] do not fit the conceptual model of the prehistory of Europe which has been current during the whole of the present century."

It is possible that Stonehenge's mysteries will never entirely yield to human inquiry, that some questions about the monument's origin and purposes are destined to remain unanswered. Perhaps, after all, the definitive word on Stonehenge was given by the seventeenth-century naval official and diarist Samuel Pepys. In 1668, Pepys visited the stones and noted in his diary: "God knows what their use was!"

The Underwater City:
Seeking Atlantis

EVER SINCE the Greek philosopher Plato described it in his writings 355 years before the birth of Christ, the lost continent has been tightly woven into the fabric of the human heritage, a land that has tantalized philosophers and poets, historians and schemers, scientists and explorers for more than two millennia. The story of Atlantis has spoken to generation after generation about the power and wisdom of the ancients. It is a recollection of Eden, of a paradise below the sea.

The subject of more than 2,000 books and countless articles and poems, Atlantis has been traced to a long list of sites and regions in the world: most of the oceans and continents, the Atlas Mountains of North Africa, the Sahara, Malta, Bimini island, Carthage, and Cádiz. Atlantis has also been hailed for spawning a number of civilizations, including Hellenic Greece, those of the Mayas and Incas, and ancient Egypt.

The first known account of Atlantis was supplied by the Greek thinker Plato, who lived from about 428 to 348 B.C. A student of the philosopher Socrates, Plato wrote out his philosophy in the form of dialogues—playlets featuring Socrates as the main character. It is in two of these, *Timaeus* and *Critias,* written around 355 B.C., that the earliest surviving description of the lost continent appears. Briefly mentioned in *Timaeus,* Atlantis became a tantalizing part of the historical record. But *Critias* described Atlantis in detail, the quantity of which gave Plato's account much of its plausibility. *Critias*'s report is filled with precise architectural, engineering, and ceremonial detail. Moreover, Plato laced the dialogue of *Critias* with uncharacteristic references to the tale as "the realm of fact" and "genuine history," taking great pains to make his record of Atlantis seem credible to the readers of his time.

In the earliest times, *Critias* explained, when the gods were dividing the earth among themselves, Poseidon chose the fair and bounteous continent and subsidiary islands that would come to be know as Atlantis. There, with a woman named Cleito, he sired five sets of twin sons; the firstborn child was Atlas, for whom the continent and the surrounding ocean were named.

Poseidon divided Atlantis into ten parts, granting Atlas the biggest and best portion and making him sovereign over his brothers, who were made rulers over the remaining provinces. Atlantis was a land of bountiful plains, extensive stands of timber, and a rich flora and fauna, including great herds of elephants. The ground was seamed with the ore of gold and silver. At the southern end of the continent, the kings built a magnificent city, also called Atlantis, consisting of concentric rings of land and waterways.

In the center, on a high hill where

Colonel James Churchward's pencil drawing of Mu, the legendary sunken Pacific continent Churchward linked to the Garden of Eden and claimed had spawned Atlantis

Mary Evans Picture Library, London

Poseidon and Cleito had conceived Atlas and his twin brother, the Atlanteans raised a great temple to Poseidon, with a statue of the god riding a golden chariot through the sea in the company of dolphins. In the city, there were springs, both hot and cold, some for the use of the kings, others for the citizens, still others for the beasts of burden. The outer rings held a racecourse and houses for the citizens. The inner harbors were filled with the vessels of war.

For generations, the ten kings ruled their respective domains, abiding always by the firm laws set down long before by Poseidon. At alternate intervals of five and six years, the monarchs would meet together and perform a long and complex ceremony in which a wild bull, captured with a noose, was sacrificed and its blood allowed to course down over sacred bronze columns in the temple. Afterward, the kings donned sacred dark robes and discussed among themselves any transgressions between kingdoms that might have occurred in the interval since the last assembly. They inscribed the results of these deliberations on tablets of gold.

It was not long before Atlantis—gifted with wealth, strength, and internal harmony—began to extend its power outward. But at the same time, the divine and virtuous character of its populace had begun to weaken with the passage of years. "Human nature," Critias reported, "got the upper hand." The Atlanteans began to exhibit less seemly qualities: Uncurbed ambition, greed and ugliness grew among the citizens and their rulers as well. Perceiving that an "honorable race was in a woeful plight," Critias said, Zeus summoned the gods to determine what punishment to inflict on Atlantis. "And when he had called them together he spoke as follows:"

Here Critias breaks off. Despite Plato's best efforts to make Atlantis seem real, his descriptive account was soon the subject of controversy. Platonists claimed that Plato's account of Atlantis was straight history; Aristotelians that the lost continent was myth.

During the Dark Ages, European scholars turned their attention almost exclusively to matters of theology. Until the Renaissance, Atlantis was forgotten. Once again intellectuals returned to classical texts and found Atlantis. Meanwhile, seafarers probed the Atlantic. By the time Columbus set sail, mapmakers had endowed the Atlantic Ocean with numerous other islands both real and imagined. When the New World burst upon the European consciousness, some suggested the Americas were the original location of Atlantis. Alternatively, in 1675, Olof Rudbeck, a Swedish scholar, used Homeric sailing directions to Ogygia and located Atlantis in Sweden. The English poet William Blake believed that the Atlantean King Albion led the last of his subjects to Britain, where they became Druids. Ancient Egyptians, Goths, and Scyths were all thought to be escapees from Atlantis; the discovery of blue eyes and blond hair among Africa's Berbers led some to place Atlantis in the Atlas Mountains of modern Morocco and Tunisia. The continent was also identified as part of an ancient series of land bridges that stretched across the Atlantic and even out into the Pacific as far as New Zealand.

As geological knowledge grew, these notions began to look increasingly farfetched. Even students of Plato had their doubts: In 1841, the French scholar T. Henri Martin wrote a commentary on *Timaeus,* calling Atlantis pure fiction. The geography of Europe, Asia, and Africa, he pointed out, showed none of the profound effects that would have followed the cataclysmic disappearance of a sizable landmass; neither were there any shallows where the continent was supposed to have been. Martin concluded that the search for Atlantis was futile. With Martin's authoritative broadside, Atlantis might well have been banished to the realm of myth. But within a few decades, the lost continent found a new, eloquent, and highly unlikely champion.

Born in Philadelphia in 1831, Ignatius Loyola Donnelly was the son of impoverished Irish immigrants. Despite a budding career as a Philadelphia politician, in 1856, after checking out the prospects in several western states and territories, Donnelly left the city of his birth and moved with his wife to Minnesota. Here, Donnelly's political career blossomed. Elected lieutenant governor in 1859, three years later he won a seat in the United States Congress. However, after his political career foundered, Donnelly developed an abiding fascination for the lost continent, turning for solace to his dreams of Atlantis. By 1881, he was beavering away on a book of his own, a book that he called simply *Atlantis.* Laboring long into the night, Donnelly became convinced that Atlantis had existed where Plato had said it was.

Minnesota Historical Society

Ignatius Loyola Donnelly's portrait presides over the Minnesota study where he wrote
Atlantis: The Antedeluvian World

He further concluded that Atlanteans were the first to achieve civilization and that the deities of various ancient mythologies were in fact the actual royalty of Atlantis. As Donnelly saw it, refugees from Atlantis had created the civilizations of Egypt, India, and Central America. Donnelly attributed more to Atlantis than had Plato or any other commentator.

Atlantis was soon available in translation throughout Europe, and many people on both sides of the Atlantic were thoroughly convinced by Donnelly's marshaling of evidence from science, literature, religion, folklore, and mythology. Scientists, however, accustomed to more rigorous research and presentation, were not especially taken with his conclusions. Charles Darwin read *Atlantis* in what he reported to be a "very skeptical spirit."

Donnelly himself knew that his argument was incomplete. Tangible evidence was needed to clinch the case for Atlantis. As Donnelly said at the end of his book: "A single engraved tablet dredged up from Plato's island would be worth more to science, would more strike the imagination of mankind, than all the gold of Peru, all the monuments of Egypt, and all the terra-cotta fragments gathered from the great libraries of Chaldea."

The mysteries of Atlantis have never been plumbed so thoroughly as they were in the first half of the twentieth century by Edgar Cayce. Until his death in 1945, Cayce spent a great deal of his time submerged in deep trances, seeking the causes of people's physical ailments and disabilities and prescribing cures. In the 1920s, Cayce began to stress the existence of reincarnation. Often, when tracking a patient's previous lives, Cayce would allude cryptically to a previous life in Atlantis. In 650 different readings that Cayce gave for different people over a period of twenty-one years, a vivid, consistent picture of the ancient world of Atlantis emerged.

Cayce's Atlantis was exactly where Plato had said it was: "between the Gulf of Mexico in the one hand and the Mediterranean upon the other." It was of continental size, and people lived on it for thousands of years, during which it went through three great catastrophic periods of breakup, the last being about 10,000 years ago, when it disappeared.

These Atlanteans appeared to have developed a highly advanced civilization that was technologically on a par with the industrialized world of the twentieth century. As Cayce intoned during a reading given on April 19, 1938: "Entity was what would be in the present the electrical engineer—applied those forces or influences for airplanes, ships, and what you would today call radio for constructive or destructive purposes."

Cayce also spoke cryptically of an Atlantean substance called firestone, likened by some to materials employed to produce nuclear power. As Cayce explained in a reading given in 1933—more than a decade before the first public demonstration of atomic energy: "The preparation of this stone was solely in the hands of the initiates at the time; and the entity was among those who directed the influences of the radiation which arose, in the form of rays that were invisible to the eye but acted upon the stones themselves as set in the motivating forces—whether the aircraft were lifted by the gases of the period; or whether for guiding the more-of-pleasure vehicles that might pass along close to the earth, or crafts on the water or under the water." These vehicles, Cayce went on, "were impelled by the concentration of rays from the stone which was centered in the middle of the power station."

According to Edgar Cayce's account, the Atlanteans had originally appeared on earth in spirit form and had only gradually evolved into material beings. This was, it seems, the beginning of the end for Atlantis; the more fleshly its inhabitants became over the generations, the more troubled their civilization. Said the sleeping Cayce in 1937: "In Atlantean land when there were those disturbing forces—or just previous to the first disturbing forces that brought the first destruction of the continent, through the application of spiritual things for self-indulgence of material peoples." A faction called the Sons of Belial finally gained control of Atlantis, mistreating the land's producers and casting them into a kind of slave status. Society—like the land itself—began to fall apart. And Cayce suggested that the cataclysmic end was caused not only by geological upheavals but also by misuse of technology. He said in 1936: "In Atlantean land just after second breaking up of the land owing to misapplication of divine laws upon those things of nature or of the earth; when there were the eruptions from the second using of those influences that were for man's own development, yet becoming destructive forces to flesh when misapplied."

Cayce also made a tantalizing prediction. In the late 1960s, he said, the western region of the long-submerged continent would begin to reappear near the Caribbean island of Bimini. In 1968, divers found in the waters just off Bimini what seemed to be a long roadway paved with rectangular blocks of stone. Many believed that the sleeping Cayce's prophecy had come to pass and that this was an actual remnant of the vanished Atlantean civilization. Radiocarbon dating of the monumental blocks indicated an age of some 12,000 years.

Geologists, however, were quick to point out similar rock formations in Australia and even along the very shore of Bimini itself. Like the 2,000-foot Bimini road, said the scientists, these are not man-made structures; rather, they are the result of the formation of beach rock. In this natural process, the calcium carbonate grains left from the decay of sea creatures wash or blow over sand and become embedded there, forming hard rock. Exposure to the sun and slippage of loose sand from underneath cause the rock to fracture in relatively straight lines along the shore and then at right angles, creating the effect of a road made with craftsmanly precision. As shorelines change, such formations become submerged and can appear to be ancient thoroughfares.

Undersea roadways are not the only remnants undermined by modern science. The ability to measure the speed of earthquake vibrations as they reverberate around the earth has led geologists to conclude that the material that composes the earth's crust under continents is vastly different from that of any ocean basin. In tracking such vibrations through the ocean floors, geologists have turned up no sign of a large mass of continent-type material.

DURING THE rule of the Fourth Dynasty in Egypt, about 2500 B.C., a commercial empire dominated trade throughout the Mediterranean basin. On Crete and on other islands in the nearby Aegean Sea, the people of this empire used their amassed wealth to build huge multi-storied temples, to create large cities, to lay out complex waterworks. Their art, on frescoes and pottery, was highly sophisticated—graceful, swirling, bright with gold. By Plato's time, this civilization had disappeared, leaving behind only fragments of myths, until 1900, when Sir Arthur Evans began excavations at the site of Cnossus on Crete. There he unearthed the stunning remains of what may have been Europe's first civilization, called Minoan, after King Minos.

In 1909, a letter appeared in the London *Times* suggesting that the Minoan civili-

Mary Evans Picture Library

Irish psychic Geraldine Cummins, who in 1936 claimed she was receiving mental messages from Colonel Percy Harrison Fawcett. In 1925, Fawcett had disappeared into the Brazilian jungle in search of the remains of the lost Atlantean colony, never to return. In 1948, having found relics of Atlantis in the jungle, the explorer, according to Cummins, reported his own death.

zation had been the basis of Plato's Atlantis, written by K. T. Frost, a professor of classical history at Queen's University in Belfast. The point, Frost emphasized, was to look at Minoan Crete from the perspective of the Egyptians of the time—the source of Plato's information. It would have seemed different from anything the Egyptians were familiar with in Africa or the Near East, a great seafaring empire "united by the same sea which divided it from other nations . . . a separate continent with a genius of its own." Further, to the Egyptians, the center of Minoan civilization would appear to be far to the west, even beyond the four pillars that in the Egyptian world view held up the earth. Frost went on to observe that the great harbor, lavish bathrooms, stadium, and sacrifice of the bulls mentioned by Plato were actual features of Minoan Crete, as was the capture of the ceremonial bull, which can be seen on pottery from Crete.

But suddenly the Minoans vanished. (Frost thought, as a result of a Greek raid on Crete). To the Egyptians, the disappearance of these exotic merchants at the evident height of their grandeur would have been a great mystery, as if "the whole kingdom had sunk into the sea." This picture of a civilization risen to glory and abruptly gone would have been in the written records of the Egyptian historians. This version would have reached Plato.

In 1932, another archaeologist, Spyridon Marinatos, also puzzled over the sudden and unexplained demise of the Minoan culture. Marinatos looked northward some seventy miles to Thera and two other Aegean islands that were known to be the remnants of a volcano that had been active around 1500 B.C., just when Minoan civilization blinked out forever. The three islands are all that is left of a large, round island—a caldera, a volcanic maw, that had exploded so violently that the water depth in the crater is more than 1,000 feet.

Wondering if the event could have been violent enough to eliminate Crete, Marinatos studied records of the volcanic eruption in 1883 of Krakatoa, in the Sunda Strait between Java and Sumatra. This titanic upheaval was heard 2,000 miles away, and it sent walls of water 100 feet high crashing at fifty miles an hour into Java and Sumatra; the rampaging waters charged 1,000 yards inland, sweeping away 300 villages and killing 36,000 people. Marinatos concluded that the eruption of Thera, if it had been as violent as that of Krakatoa, could surely have wiped out the Minoans.

He also reasoned that these kinds of catastrophes had given rise to Plato's story of Atlantis. After World War II, a Greek seismologist named A. G. Galanopoulos picked up the thread that led to Thera. On that crescent-shaped island, Galanopoulos found the ruins of unmistakably Minoan buildings that had been devastated by a volcano. A Hungarian colleague, Peter Hédervári, determined on the basis of collapsed land volume at the sites that the eruption at Thera had in fact been about four times more violent than at Krakatoa. The pumice and ash from such a cataclysm would not only have inundated Crete but would have reached as far as Egypt, about 250 miles distant. It would also have caused torrential rains over a wide area, and locally there would have been so much pumice floating on the sea that the water would have appeared to be filled with muddy reefs for some time. The tsunami, or tremendous sea wave, resulting from the explosion would have seemed for all the world like a flood when it crashed ashore. This catastrophic series of events would surely have been recorded by the Egyptians and associated with the sudden disappearance of the Minoans.

However, Plato was specific about when the catastrophe had occurred, placing it 9,000 years before his own time. He was also precise in detailing the size of Atlantis and its features; the capital city was some 300 miles across, far larger than any metropolis of even modern times. Furthermore, Plato had explicitly located Atlantis in the Atlantic Ocean.

Galanopoulos's reconciliation of these disparities was ingenious. Both the Egyptians and the Greeks used ten-based number schemes, precursors of the modern decimal system. Galanopoulos reasoned that in translation from Egyptian to Greek, the symbol for every number greater than 100 mistakenly had the equivalent of one zero added. Were this the case, the numbers in Plato's account would fit. For example, if 9,000 years really means 900 years, then the date of the catastrophe accords almost perfectly with the eruption of Thera in 1500 B.C. Similarly, a city 300 miles across becomes thirty miles across, a reasonable figure. And a series of large and small islands ten times the size of Crete would not have fit in the Mediterranean as Plato knew it: In his chronicle of Atlantis, the lost continent would exist in the larger ocean that lay beyond the Pillars of Hercules.

And perhaps there does indeed lie in some Egyptian pyramid an undiscovered sanctum containing papyrus with ancient symbols pointing beyond the confines of the Mediterranean, beyond what science knows of the human psyche, to the place where a mystic Atlantis still rests, in the deep.

10
THE DREAMING
WORLD

Windows to the Unconscious

VIRTUALLY EVERY student of the human psyche since Freud and Jung's era has acknowledged the importance of dreams. But the way in which dreams operate—their causes, their function in a dreamer's mental landscape, and their ultimate significance—remains a matter of much dispute. Some, like Freud, believe dreams are manifestations of repressed desires, usually sexual in nature. To Jung and others, dreams are glimpses into a commonly shared unconsciousness and thus hold potential clues to personal self-realization. Still others see them as a psychic device for absorbing new experiences or casting off the frustrations of daily life. A few neuroscientists depart from such psychological interpretations altogether. According to this physiologically oriented school of thought, dreams are simply a mechanical reflex by which the central nervous system clears its circuits. As yet, however, no single theory entirely explains the rich variety of sensations and images that come to us in our sleep.

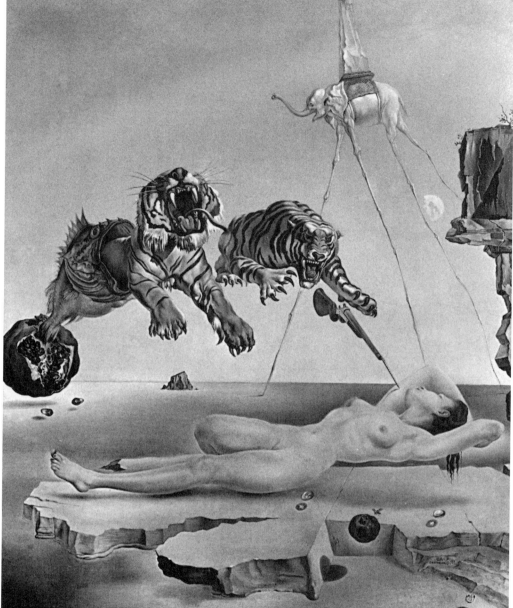

Salvador Dali's Dream caused by the flight of a bumblebee around
a pomegranate a second before awakening

The first attempts to examine dreams in a scientific manner began in the middle of the nineteenth century. One of the very earliest theorists was Jan Evangelista Purkinje, a pioneering Czech physiologist who saw dreams as a natural restorative, releasing the psyche from its mundane workaday cares. "The soul does not want to continue the tensions of waking life," he observed in 1846, "but rather to resolve them." Many disagreed, however. Among the most influential was French psychologist Alfred Maury, one of the first observers to study his own dreams in a systematic fashion. Maury set out to prove by rigorous self-analysis that dreams arise because of external sensations experienced by the sleeper. His approach to this study was to have a colleague sit at his bedside and—once Maury had nodded off—shine a light in his eyes, splash water on his face, or ring a bell in his ear. Maury found the results encouraging. When a lighted match was held under his nose, he dreamed about sailing on a ship whose powder magazine blew up. A drop of water on his forehead led him to a cafe in Italy, in midsummer, where he sat drenched in sweat and drank the wine of Orvieto. A whiff of eau de cologne transported him to the Cairo bazaar. In one famous dream, Maury saw himself caught up in the French Revolution. He was condemned by a people's tribunal and carted off to the guillotine. At the dream's culmination, he felt the knife fall—then awoke to discover that a bedrail had collapsed on his neck.

Maury published his findings in 1861, offering some intriguing opinions on the significance of dreams in relation to human psychology. As sleep begins to take hold, Maury suggested, the sleeper enters a state that is comparable to senility or some forms of mental derangement. Like some very old men and women in their dotage, the dreamer regresses toward childhood. Memories bubble to the surface, and images of long-forgotten people and places crowd the mind's eye. "In dreaming," Maury declared, "man reveals himself to himself in all his nakedness and native misery." But what of the specific images found in dreams and the self-revelations that some believe they convey? Alfred Maury dismissed such considerations as empty and meaningless. Dreams hold no more interest, he wrote, than the noise made by "the ten fingers of a man who knows nothing of music wandering over the keys of a piano."

Several other theorists of this era maintained that dreaming allows sleepers to enjoy pleasures generally denied them during the day. Karl Albert Scherner proposed that dreams occur when a sleeper's sense of fantasy is allowed to run wild, released from the prim control of the waking mind. Why then do nocturnal fantasies sometimes assume such a grotesque and phantasmagoric character? Scherner's explanation was that dreams speak not in words but in symbols. If a woman goes to bed with a headache, she may dream that the ceiling is crawling with loathsome spiders. Scherner contended that dreams often contain recognizable symbols for the parts of the human physiology. A dreamer's lungs might take the form of a roaring furnace, a clarinet or tobacco pipe might represent the male sex organ, and a narrow courtyard could symbolize a woman's genitalia.

By the time Sigmund Freud, in the closing decade of the nineteenth century, began his own exploration into the phenomenon of dreams, there had been nearly fifty years of active inquiry and theorizing on the matter. Among Freud's patients were a number of young women who suffered from hysteria, a puzzling complex of symptoms that ranged from odd aches and twitches to debilitating partial paralyses. Unable to find organic reasons for these complaints, Freud decided that the causes had to be psychological. His patients' tics and phobias, he concluded, were elaborate defenses against the pain of long-forgotten psychic shocks, which they had experienced in childhood and which now festered in the unconscious. The cure, he

*Sigmund Freud (upper right), with family in a photograph taken at his home in Vienna in 1898.
His sister-in-law Minna Bernays, the woman shown here in a lighter blouse, displayed an understanding
of Freud's work that would later be echoed in his daughter, Anna Freud (front, center).*

believed, was to peel back the gauze of memory until the original trauma lay revealed.

At first, Freud would lead his patients back through their recollections simply by allowing them to talk, urging them to ramble from topic to topic by a process he called free association. But before long he discovered that a quicker port of entry was through discussions of his patients' dreams. Each dream provided images that, upon analysis, would release a flood of buried memories, fears, and impulses. These, in turn, would lead back to the roots of the patient's difficulties.

However, some of the methods Freud was developing were propelling him in highly unorthodox directions. Freud's approach to therapy, in having clients rummage through their innermost thoughts and recount their most intimate memories, was highly provocative for that time. Recurring bouts of anxiety plagued Freud's waking hours. "Inside me there is a seething ferment," he confided to a friend, "and I am only waiting for the next surge forward."

Searching for relief, Freud undertook a rigorous study of his own dream life. He found himself recapturing lost childhood memories, and the experience was not entirely pleasurable. He detected some of the same neurotic turns of emotion that troubled many of his patients, and he suffered through periods of depression in which he "understood nothing of the day's dreams, fantasies, or moods." By nature an assiduous scholar, he combed through the body of contemporary literature on the subject of

*Amalie Freud, née Nathanson, was devoted to her
eldest child, whom she called her "golden Sigi"*

dreams. Yet with all his study and analysis, Freud struggled with the task of weaving a cohesive theory on dreams—until July 24, 1895, when he was sitting on the terrace of the hotel Schloss Belle Vue near Vienna, the solution to his problem became clear.

Freud was mulling over a dream of the night before in which he had encountered one of his patients, a young widow named Irma, at a family party. Irma had been much on Freud's mind in his waking hours. Her therapy had run into a snag, and she had gone off to her country estate suffering from spasmodic vomiting and other physical symptoms of her hysteria. Among Irma's guests in the country was a colleague of Freud's, a doctor named Otto. The very day before Freud's dream, Otto had returned to town and confided that Irma was "better, but not quite well." Ever sensitive to criticism, Freud took this remark as a slap at his professional competence. He was filled with anxiety over the matter.

Freud's sleeping mind took flight from there. In his dream, Irma approached and complained of terrible pains in her throat and abdomen. After scolding her for quitting therapy, Freud proceeded to examine her throat. He discovered a very peculiar growth on the walls of her mouth and throat and called upon a highly respected colleague to repeat the examination. The man, referred to as "Dr. M," was joined by Otto, and all the physicians remarked on Irma's affliction. Clearly, she was suffering from a very unusual infection. The dream resolved itself when it became evident that

Jacob Freud poses with young son Sigmund sometime during the 1860s

the cause of Irma's suffering was a careless injection administered by Otto for some earlier illness. Apparently, Otto had neglected to use a clean needle.

While Freud sat at the Schloss Belle Vue and pondered this nocturnal narrative, it suddenly struck him as terribly revealing. The dream was an act of revenge—against Otto for maligning Freud's ability, against Irma for resisting his clinical analysis. It was they, not he, the dream declared, who should be blamed for Irma's alarming condition. Even Dr. M came in for a rebuff, for the dream had pictured him as pale and lame, his usual authority diminished. In a moment of sleep, Freud had outfoxed his competitors and restored his professional pride. "The dream represented a particular state of affairs as I should have wished it to be," he later wrote. "Thus its content was the fulfillment of a wish."

There was still more gold to be mined in Freud's dream of Irma and her ill-fated injection. Minutely examining each image in turn, Freud focused on the chemical compounds contained in the syringe, the names of which had been revealed to him in the dream. One of them was something called propyl, and Freud deduced that his mind had free-associated this name with that of another chemical called amyl, an impurity in some cheap brandies. As it happened, Otto had offered Freud some very modest brandy only the night before. The second compound was trimethylamine, which had been described to Freud as a by-product of sexual metabolism. The analyst detected numerous sexual references in his dream. The syringe, for example, was an obvious phallic symbol.

Freud primly avoided pursuing the sexual clues that he believed to be contained in the dream. "I have not reported everything that occurred to me," he admitted in a single coy footnote. However, sex was a crucial element, a cornerstone of Freudian theory. The hidden childhood traumas of his hysteria patients often turned out to be sexual in nature—possibly because his clientele consisted mostly of wealthy women in a sexually repressed Victorian society.

If so, the deeper implications of Freud's dream are not hard to find. As a number of present-day dream analysts have pointed out, Irma was young, vivacious, attractive, and unattached. Spurning Freud's advice, she had gone off to the country with another man. By the logic of dreams, both parties deserved vengeance.

Freud worked out an elaborate theory of dreams that also focused on the nature of unconscious desires. With children, he explained, desires may be entirely innocent—a special treat denied during the day, perhaps. Freud cited the example of his two-year-old nephew, Hermann. When the boy gave his uncle a basket of ripe cherries that he clearly wanted for himself, he told Freud he dreamed of a cherry feast all his own. The dream wishes of grown-ups, on the other hand, Freud saw as fraught with disturbing sexual undertones and thus likely to take a more devious path.

Sexual urges are so repugnant to the psyche, Freud believed, that a mental censor, which he called the superego, was on the alert to squelch them. The sexual urges are not easily suppressed, however. They change their form, disguising themselves in metaphor and symbolism in order to elude the censor. Freud called this process dreamwork. A young man, for example, might dream of a knight in armor slaying a wicked king. By Freud's interpretation, the king is the young man's father, and the dream expresses both his urge to rebel and a guilty desire to murder his father so that he can sleep with his mother. But the dreamer's mental censor has cloaked this Oedipal scenario in the trappings of heroic saga.

Freud could find a sexual reading for almost any image that occurs in dreams. When an adolescent girl dreamed of a dagger or a snake or a stick or a church steeple—any long or pointed object, for that matter—she revealed her fear of and fascination with the male sex organ. Even the most innocent circumstances might be a

Carl Jung at the age of six, in 1881

© 1979 Princeton University Press, reprinted with permission of Princeton University Press

disguise for forbidden impulses. A cozy house set between two stately mansions suggested to Freud a wish to engage in intercourse. Climbing a ladder referred to a state of mounting sexual excitement. Dreams of flying or of playing the piano both alluded to the rhythms of the sexual act.

Despite his sensitivity to the erotic undertones in dreaming, Freud was not of the opinion that all dreams have sex as their central topic. Missing a train he took as an optimistic sign, for the train stands for death and the dreamer could be thankful when it chugs off on its way. Other dreams speak of birth. On one occasion, Freud was treating a woman who had dreamed about driving into a lake "just where the pale moon is mirrored." In a highly imaginative interpretation, Freud decided that the dream was based on an elaborate pun on the word *lune*—which in French means "moon" and is also a French slang expression for the buttocks. He pointed out that many children share the misconception that babies emerge from their mothers' bottoms. He thus felt that the image of diving into the moon could be read as a symbol of emerging into life, because the symbolic actions in dreams often move in reverse. The dream thus showed that Freud's patient felt reborn—presumably as a result of his therapeutic skill.

The sleeping mind often delivered its message by means of such feats of wordplay, Freud believed, and this talent, together with a tendency to make heavy use of symbolic imagery, was part and parcel of a process that he called displacement. Everything in a dream—people, settings, events—means something other than the obvious. If a young woman dreams of violets, as did one of Freud's patients, it may mean she is frightened of being "violated." Fears and desires that the dreamer refuses to acknowledge may be projected onto other people in a dream. Thus Otto, not Freud, became the villain of the Irma dream. Often, the most minor details will provide the most significant clues to the meaning of a dream. The analyst must therefore trace every image back to its origins, taking the part of a psychiatric Sherlock Holmes. Only then can the dream's facade be penetrated and the analyst move past what Freud termed the "manifest" content to discover the "latent" content concealed inside.

In 1899, Freud published his masterpiece, *The Interpretation of Dreams*. A coterie of pioneering young analysts fell under Freud's sway. Among this group, ardent and articulate, was the twenty-eight-year-old Carl Jung.

JUNG SEEMED handpicked by destiny to be Freud's disciple. All his life he had been subject to the most vivid provocative dreams. As a child in a small Swiss vil-

Carl Jung with family in 1917 at Chateau-d'Oex, Switzerland,
where he was stationed during World War I

lage, the son of a parson, he had nightmares in which balls of light floated toward him like malevolent moons, threatening to engulf him. In later years, his dreams took on a visionary, almost prophetic aspect. When he came of age to choose a profession, he dreamed of an encounter with a magnificent sea creature, like a giant, tentacled shellfish, in a woodland pond. The round, luminous body of this apparition seemed to represent all the wonderment and poetry of the natural world. Jung decided then and there to concentrate in the natural sciences—a determination that soon led him to the study of medicine.

As a scholarship student at Basel University, Jung was beset by doubts and troubled by what he felt were conflicting aspects within his own personality. Once again, in 1895, a dream arrived to smooth the way for Jung. He saw himself struggling forward through a howling storm, in darkest night, with only a small candle to light his way. Gusts of wind kept threatening to extinguish the candle, although he carefully cupped his hand around the flame. Suddenly he felt an ominous presence behind his back. He spun around to face it and saw a gigantic black figure trailing him. Terrified, he awoke.

Immediately, Jung comprehended the message of his dream. The looming black figure was his own shadow, cast by the candle against the storm's swirling darkness. It portrayed the mystical, subjective side of his divided nature. And it seemed to be

Mary Evans Picture Library, London/Sigmund Freud Copyrights

Sigmund Freud (front, left) and Carl Jung (front, right) at a 1909 seminar at Clark University in Worcester, Massachusetts

telling him something. Use the light of your conscious intellect, it seemed to say, to pursue your studies and move ahead in the world. But do not deny your shadow self. Even though it now frightens you, it possesses a deep ancient wisdom. Jung understood that in time his shadow self would come to serve him, as he learned to integrate the two sides of his personality. A few years later, just such a process was begun—when Jung chose psychiatry as his medical specialty.

The young medical student accepted a post in a Zurich hospital in 1900, where his work with patients began leading him in the same direction pioneered by the master psychoanalyst in Vienna some ten years earlier. When Jung studied Freud's book, in 1903, he was struck by how closely it reflected his own ideas. "The interpretation of dreams," Freud had written, "is the Royal Road to the knowledge of the unconscious in mental life," and Jung wholeheartedly concurred. Over a period of years, he became a leading spokesman for the Freudian approach.

As time passed, however, Jung had opportunities to work closely with Freud and gained a deeper understanding of his theories. He began to question some of the older man's most important conclusions. Dreams were an early point of contention. One key Freudian precept was that the majority of dreams are symptoms of psychic illness, the neurotic outpourings of a troubled mind. To Jung this could not be further from the truth. He considered dreams to be as valuable and healthful as fresh air. Indeed, his

Carl Jung's parents, Emilie and Paul

own night fantasies had often proved to be a source of guidance and comfort. Jung found even more troubling Freud's emphasis on sex as the force underlying all dreams. And as for the Viennese master's definition of dreams as a form of wish fulfillment—well, that seemed at best to be no more than a partial explanation. "It is true that there are dreams which embody suppressed wishes and fears," Jung wrote, "but what is there which the dream cannot on occasion embody? Dreams may give expression to ineluctable truths, to philosophical pronouncements, illusions, wild fantasies, . . . anticipations, irrational experiences, even telepathic visions, and heaven knows what besides."

Perhaps inevitably, Jung chose to part company with Freud. Between 1910 and 1913, he gradually made more and more overt his misgivings about portions of the Freudian canon. In stark contrast to Freud, Jung believed that dreams communicate in a comparatively direct, straightforward manner. The nocturnal mind has no need to bury its insights under symbolic camouflage in order to slip them past the watchful eye of the superego. The censoring device described by Freud, Jung contended, simply does not exist. "There is no reason under the sun why we should assume that the dream is a crafty device to lead us astray," he declared. Dreams deal in strange images, to be sure, but only because the unconscious mind naturally thinks in terms that are archaic and visual. Jung argued that we are free to take these images at face value, without engaging in the narrow detective work of Freudian analysis.

A disciple of Freud might, for example, use the technique of free association to follow the clues in a dream about apples in a manner something like this: apples, pears, stairs, bedroom, bed, sex. But a practitioner of Jung's approach would find linkages that were even more flexible. The apple might call to mind a home-baked pie or a gift to one's teacher or food for thought or perhaps the tree of knowledge in the Garden of Eden. Any one of these associations might have a sexual content. Then again, it might not. Jung also defended the possibility that the apple might simply be an apple. More important than any single image, he maintained, was the dream as a whole and its initial impact on the dreamer. To illustrate this point he liked to quote a proverb from the Jewish Talmud: "The dream is its own interpretation."

According to Jung, the unconscious is a multilayered structure that serves as a storehouse for all kinds of instinctive, unarticulated wisdom. Near the surface lies a personal unconscious, which collects individual memories and repressions, much as in Freud's scheme. Then, at deeper levels, the unconscious embraces a more generalized type of psychic information. At bottom lies the collective unconscious, aswarm with images and impulses that are shared by all humankind. In much the same way that genes carry traces of the physical makeup of the earliest human generations, the collective unconscious contains memories and desires that may have had their origin in humankind's earliest experiences.

These primal memories, Jung suggested, repeat themselves the world over—in the myths and folklore of primitive cultures, in children's fairy tales, in the tragic dramas of Greek playwrights, in the symbols of witchcraft, in the rituals of church and state. They deal with the common denominators of human existence, such as birth, death, family, and the rites of passage from youth to maturity. The same motifs occur again and again, across cultures and throughout the centuries. A circle, for example, has always held special meaning—in general, it has represented unity. Jung called such a motif an archetype, and he believed that each of us could gain strength by recognizing the archetypes that appear in our dreams and pondering their significance in relation to our waking lives. "All consciousness separates," he declared, "but in dreams we put on the likeness of that more universal, truer, more eternal man dwelling in the darkness of primordial night."

A Need to Dream

AP/Wide World Photos

Nathaniel Kleitman (left) emerges from a cave after a 1938 experiment with sleep cycles

A KEEN-EYED GRADUATE student at the University of Chicago observed something in 1951 that would dramatically change our understanding of sleeping and dreaming. Physiology major Eugene Aserinsky was studying the sleep cycles of infants when he noticed that during sleep the babies' eyes often continued to move under closed lids long after their bodies had become still. The eye movements would stop for a while, then begin again. Aserinsky thought that these movements might be a more reliable indicator of light and deep stages of sleep than the gross body movements researchers had previously relied upon.

Excited that he might be on to something important, Aserinsky took his data to his physiology professor, Nathaniel Kleitman. Kleitman speculated that the eye movements might also be useful in charting the sleep patterns of adults, whose brain activity could be electronically monitored at the same time. The two researchers quickly set up a sleep laboratory—a simple facility that consisted essentially of a bed, electrical recording equipment, and a technician to keep an eye on the sleeper and the hardware.

Two years of observation, first of Aserinsky's ten-year-old son and then of sleeping adult volunteers, revealed that sleepers had periods of rapid eye movement alternating throughout the night with periods when the eyes moved slowly or not at all. The investigators found that when their subjects were awakened from what was dubbed REM sleep, for the characteristic rapid eye movements, they were usually able to recall dreams in elaborate detail. Subjects roused from non-REM sleep, on the other hand, frequently could not remember even a fragment of a dream. Aserinsky and Kleitman discovered other differences as well. During REM sleep, the respiratory rate and heartbeat sped up and were somewhat irregular. With the onset of non-REM sleep, both functions slowed and became rhythmical.

Aserinsky and Kleitman's 1953 report of their findings in the journal *Science* stirred widespread interest. Previously, sleep had been viewed as part of a simple continuum of consciousness, with very deep sleep at one extreme and highly alert states such as mania at the other. Many scientists had believed—but without benefit of experimental evidence—that a person typically fell into deep sleep a short time after dropping off at night; then, as morning approached, sleep would gradually lighten. Dreams were considered to be occasional, random events that tended to occur shortly before the sleeper awoke.

Now, however, it was clear that sleep was a far more complex phenomenon. From a rather simple observation, Kleitman and Aserinsky had made a radical departure in research, using physiological tools and methodology to study a subject that had for centuries been primarily the domain of philosophers and psychologists. Henceforth, scientists would be able to examine, from an empirical perspective, the ancient questions of when and why people dream.

Based on observations recorded in laboratories across the United States and abroad, researchers can now divide the nightly sleep cycle into several distinct stages revealed by eye movements and changes in brain-wave patterns as detected by an electroencephalograph. On the threshold of sleep's first stage, a transitional period between waking and sleeping known as hypnagogic state, the muscles relax and a person often experiences a sensation of floating or drifting. The eyes roll slowly and vivid images may flash through the mind—perhaps an eerie, unfamiliar landscape, a beautiful abstract pattern, or a succession of faces. As these sensations and visions come and go, a sudden spasm of the body called a hypnagogic startle may momentarily waken the sleeper. Then, as the subject slips into the first stage of sleep, the EEG shows the spiky, rapid alpha waves of a relaxed but wakeful brain giving way to the slower, more regular theta waves of light slumber.

Sleep's first stage is short, lasting anywhere from a few seconds to ten minutes. The theta waves soon decrease and are mixed on the EEG tracing with a combination of two different brain-wave patterns—groups of sharp jumps called spindles, which reflect rapid bursts of brain activity, and waves known as K-complexes, characterized by steep peaks and valleys. Although this stage is considered to be a true sleep phase, a person awakened from it may report having had brief bits of realistic thought or may even deny having been asleep at all.

Between fifteen and thirty minutes after the onset of sleep, large, slow delta waves begin supplanting the spindles and K-complexes of stage two. The change marks the deepest sleeps, called stage three-four. Waking from stage three-four is difficult. An individual typically feels quite groggy and disoriented and, even if an emergency demands alertness, must fight to overcome the compelling desire to fall asleep again. Talking in one's sleep, sleepwalking, and bedwetting tend to happen

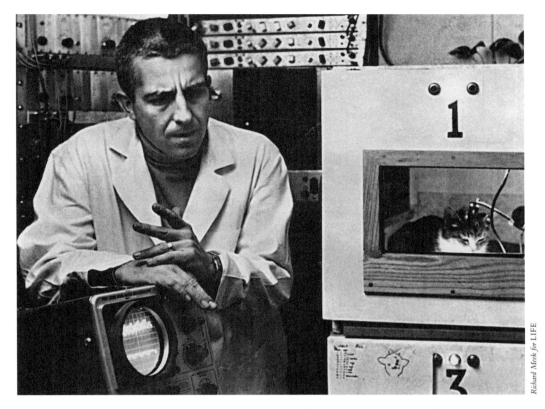

Richard Meek for LIFE

William C. Dement, who pioneered REM research, pictured here with one of the cats he used in a sleep-deprivation study

during this stage because of the brain's partial arousal from deep sleep.

After ninety minutes or so of sleep, most of it spent in stage three-four, the spindles and K-complexes of stage two briefly reassert themselves. The brain then shakes off the rhythms of non-REM sleep and passes into REM sleep—a condition so distinct physiologically from both wakefulness and the non-REM stages that some experts call it a third state of existence. Blood pressure and pulse rate rise, and brain waves quicken to frequencies comparable to those of an awake, alert brain. Yet, despite this activity, the body becomes remarkably still. The eyes begin their rapid movements, but otherwise, except for grimaces and small twitches of the toes and fingers, the muscles are temporarily paralyzed. In fact, a person awakened from REM sleep may even be unable to move for a few seconds. Scientists believe that nature has evolved this paralytic interlude, which seems to be controlled by nerve centers in the primitive brainstem, to protect the sleeper from the harm that might result if dreams were physically acted out.

Most people roused from REM sleep will report that they were dreaming. While it is possible to wake from non-REM sleep and recall images or thoughts that just passed through one's mind, these usually are akin to relatively mundane, everyday thinking and are quite unlike the vivid, dramatic, frequently fantastic images of REM sleep.

The first REM period of the night usually lasts anywhere from ten to fifteen minutes. Afterward, the sleeper drifts close to wakefulness before returning to stage two and beginning the sleep cycle again. Since each non-REM–REM cycle takes about ninety minutes to run its course, the average sleeper experiences four to five cycles per night. As the night passes, the REM periods become progressively longer— some lasting up to sixty minutes—while the time spent in the non-REM stages of sleep decreases. Consequently, almost half of a person's nightly dreaming often takes place during the last two hours of sleep.

All told, periods of REM sleep can account for about twenty percent of an adult's normal slumber. The average individual spends approximately four years of his or her life dreaming and can experience an estimated total of about 150,000 dreams.

HUMANS, AND other mammals as well, appear to have a biological need to dream. This was first detected in 1959, through experiments conducted at New York City's Mount Sinai Hospital by William C. Dement, a psychiatrist and former student of Nathaniel Kleitman. For five nights in a row, Dement awakened volunteer subjects each time they entered REM sleep. He found that, with each succeeding night, the subjects entered REM periods more and more often until, by the last night, Dement had to awaken the subjects at least twenty times. Dement then allowed them a night of undisturbed sleep. As if hungry for dreams, the volunteers spent more of the recovery night than normal in the REM stage. By contrast, a control group of volunteers who had been wakened just as frequently but only during non-REM sleep did not increase their dream time during the recovery night.

Dement's experiments also revealed some fascinating characteristics of REM sleep. He discovered a direct correlation between dream time and real time, laying to rest the common belief that dreams last only a few seconds. Volunteers' dreams usually took about as long to be played out as would comparable episodes in the waking world, as much as twenty minutes in some cases. A related revelation was that a particular sequence of rapid eye movements sometimes corresponds to the way dream images move. The eyes may actually track the dream's action, gazing about within the dream just as they would when watching an event in real life. In one remarkable instance, a subject was observed making about two dozen horizontal eye movements during REM sleep. He later reported that he had been watching a ping-pong game in his dream, and just before he had been awakened, the players had engaged in a particularly long volley.

Exactly what causes dreams to occur is still open to debate. One researcher, Dr. Ian Oswald of the University of Edinburgh, suggests that dreams are the way the nervous system goes about repairing worn-out brain tissue. During non-REM sleep, Oswald found, various growth hormones pour into the bloodstream and course through the body, restoring bone and muscle cells after the day's wear and tear. But when the sleeper starts dreaming, the flow of hormones dwindles to a stop. Presumably restoration work then shifts to the brain, where raveled neurons and synapses are knitted up by means not yet understood. Dreams are the by-product of this activity, Oswald submits.

Other researchers speculate that dreams are the brain's way of keeping house. They suggest that the waking mind is bombarded with so much information that its circuits are in danger of becoming overloaded. The particulars of life crowd in and register themselves in the neocortex. But the neocortex, despite its millions of interlocking nerve cells, has a limited capacity, and the overload causes confusion. Furthermore, most of the data it takes in is quite useless. Who needs to know the color of a matchbook cover, or the contents of the day's junk mail? So during dreams the brain sorts and organizes similar items. Not only individual bits of information but entire patterns of thought get swept into oblivion in a flurry of activity that the sleeper perceives as a dream. Memories that the neocortex judges significant it retains, storing them in its network of brain cells for future reference.

The fashionable analogy for the brain's way of functioning likens it to a computer—the connections among brain cells are equated with the circuitry of microchips in a desktop or mainframe. British psychologist Christopher Evans—who was also a computer scientist—explained how in his 1983 book, *Landscapes of the Night*. While still a student, Evans had his watch stolen and went to the police station to make a report. What make of watch was it, the desk sergeant wanted to know. Although Evans

William Blake's Job's Evil Dreams

had consulted his watch thousands of times, he could not remember.

That night Evans dreamed he was gazing intently at his watch dial. Its every detail appeared in vivid closeup: hands, numbers—and the name of its manufacturer. Evans decided that the needed information had been locked somewhere in his unconscious mind. Perhaps while we sleep, he reasoned, our brains sift through their cerebral data banks, and our dreams are reflections of this nightly browsing.

A similar function takes place in computers, Evans pointed out. Like the brain, a computer processes, stores, and retrieves information. But for maximum speed and efficiency, its operators periodically take the computer off line, shutting down its normal activities in order to scan through its programs, revising and updating them, and cleaning off extraneous data. Sleep is the brain's off-line period, Evans suggested, and the dream a kind of "memory filter," which sorts out the mind's accumulation of impressions and experiences. Some it retains in the brain's active file; others are consigned to a backroom storage area.

The updating process may occur during a single night or, for certain deeply entrenched patterns of thought, it may extend over many months. When Evans gave up smoking, for example, he began having nightmares in which he would find himself at a party with a lighted cigarette in his hand. Gradually, as his nicotine craving subsided, the dreams became less insistent and fraught with anxiety.

Other scientists have proposed that dreams serve as "sentinels of the night," periodically bringing the sleeper out of deep sleep so he or she can awaken quickly and respond to any danger that might have arisen. Another theory suggests that dreams are intimately connected to learning and memory. Studies have shown, for example, that after developing new skills in the day, people experience more REM sleep and slightly increased REM density—that is, their eyes move more rapidly— when they go to sleep. Conversely, the severely retarded have fewer dreams than those who are not mentally handicapped; their reduced ability to handle information, it appears, reduces their need to dream.

Dreaming may also serve as a mood regulator. After repeatedly being deprived of REM sleep, volunteers in laboratory studies are more prone to anxiety and irritability and have a hard time concentrating. Ernest Hartmann, professor of psychiatry at Tufts University School of Medicine and director of two Boston sleep laboratories, has proposed that the mental activity of waking life depletes the brain's supply of critical chemicals. A fresh supply produced during REM sleep, he speculates, helps maintain emotional stability and aids thought processes such as learning and memory.

But REM sleep is not always a restorative, and apparently there can be too much of a good thing. It has been found that some people who suffer from severe clinical depression pass through the initial stages of sleep to the REM phase more quickly, and stay there longer, than do healthy people. And unlike healthy sleepers, who dream most frequently during the last third of the night, depressed people may dream more during the first third, another indication of a malfunction in the body's natural sleeping rhythms.

Scientists cannot explain why such disturbances occur, but they have learned that a depressed person deprived of REM sleep for two or three weeks may find the feelings of despair and apathy lessening. In some cases, this simple therapy can be as effective as an antidepressant medication. A study conducted at the Georgia Mental Health Institute in Atlanta found that fifty percent of the subjects suffering from depression showed marked improvement after REM deprivation. (Those who did not improve also did not respond to medication.)

Researchers have also categorized two distinct but equally frightening disturbances: the nightmare and the much less common night terror. Everyone occasionally has a nightmare—a dream so frightening that he or she wakes up sweaty, short of breath, and with a pounding heart. Such dreams usually occur during the second half of the night, when REM periods are longer and dreams are more intense. Some psychiatrists believe that a nightmare dramatizes problems or anxieties one has recently encountered in waking life; in addition, it evokes related unconscious memories and images, creating an emotionally powerful mix. The common feeling of helplessness probably harks back to infancy, some experts say, when a child is powerless and at the mercy of a world he or she cannot understand or control.

According to Professor Hartmann, "the common thread among those who have nightmares frequently is sensitivity." For a Boston study, he solicited volunteers who experienced nightmares at least once a week. A large number of the subjects were involved in creative work, such as art, music, and theater; others were graduate students, teachers, and therapists. Many saw themselves as rebels or as "different from other people," and some overtly rejected society's norms. "They were all very open and vulnerable," he said, traits beneficial to their careers. But "most had had stormy adolescences, sometimes followed by bouts with depression, alcohol and suicide attempts." Hartmann concluded that people who have frequent nightmares possess a poor sense of their own identities and find it hard to separate fantasy from reality. Some have borderline or potentially psychotic tendencies, he believes.

Night terrors differ from nightmares in both content and timing, and often occur in the deep slumber of stage three-four. Sleepers may rouse with a bloodcurdling scream and sit up in bed, terrified and confused, heart racing. People may also walk or talk in their sleep. While people usually remember specific and sequential details of their nightmares, the victim of a night terror recalls little or nothing of what triggered such extreme horror. Despite the severe panic it engenders, a night terror is short, lasting only a minute or two. (A nightmare can go on several minutes, but probably not longer, since the intense emotional state that results will often awaken the dreamer.) Night terrors seem to run in families; researchers suspect they are triggered by a faulty arousal mechanism: Instead of following the normal shift early in the night from stage three-four sleep to a REM period, the sleeper partially rouses. Children are more susceptible than adults to night terrors, perhaps simply because they spend more time in stage three-four.

Dreams reflect an altered state of consciousness that contrasts dramatically with the rational processes of the normal waking brain. In that respect, the dream state is like other altered states, such as those manifested during deep hypnosis, trances, and meditation, or through the use of mind-altering drugs. But dreaming is the most readily accessible of all altered states, the one that almost everyone enters naturally on a nightly basis.

THE NEW dream frontier is a fascinating, relatively rare state of consciousness called lucid dreaming. Ordinarily, a person knows that he or she has dreamed only after waking. But in the case of lucid dreaming, the sleeper is aware of dreaming as the scenes unroll before the mind's eye, and can also affect the dream's events, characters, and emotional tone.

The earliest known reference to this phenomenon appears in Aristotle's treatise *On Dreams,* in which the philosopher states that "often when one is asleep, there is something in consciousness which declares that what then presents itself is but a dream." In A.D. 415, Saint Augustine recorded the lucid dream of his friend Gennadius. In the dream a young man discussed life after death at length and then told Gennadius, "I would have you know that even now you are seeing in sleep." Some eight centuries later, Saint Thomas Aquinas mentioned lucid dreaming. "Sometimes while asleep," he wrote, "a man may judge that what he sees is a dream, discerning as it were, between things and their images."

The first to methodically examine this aberrant type of dream was Marquis Hervey de Saint-Denis, a professor of Chinese at the Collège de France in Paris. His twenty years of dream research and analysis were summed up in the 1867 work *Dreams and How to Guide Them.* He said that good dream recall, the ability to will himself awake, and an awareness of the dream state had given him a measure of dream control, as his book's title suggested. Sigmund Freud himself praised the professor's research and in the second edition of *The Interpretation of Dreams* wrote "there are some people who are quite clearly aware during the night that they are asleep and dreaming and who thus seem to possess the faculty of consciously directing their dreams. If, for instance, a dreamer of this kind is dissatisfied with the turn taken by a dream, he can break it off without waking up and start it again in another direction— just as a popular dramatist may under pressure give his play a happier ending."

Despite the endorsement of Freud and other respectable scientists, many researchers in the late nineteenth and early twentieth centuries joined the eminent English psychologist Havelock Ellis in discounting the idea of the lucid dream. Dutch psychiatrist and sleep researcher Frederik Willem van Eeden made public some of his findings on lucid dreams in fictional form in his novel, *The Bride of Dreams.* Van Eeden was thoroughly familiar with the lucid dream. In lucid dreams, he said, "the re-integration of the psychic functions is so complete that the sleeper . . . reaches a state of perfect awareness, and is able to direct his attention, and to attempt different acts of free volition. Yet the sleep, as I am able confidently to state, is undisturbed, deep and refreshing."

Van Eeden purposely added an experimental element to his lucid dreams. In a September 9, 1904, entry in his dream diary, he notes, "I dreamt that I stood at a table before a window. On the table were different objects. I was perfectly well aware that I was dreaming and I considered what sorts of experiments I could make. I began by trying to break glass, by beating it with a stone. I put a small tablet of glass on two stones and struck it with another stone. Yet it would not break. Then I took a fine claret-glass from the table and struck it with my fist, with all my might, at the same time reflecting how dangerous it would be to do this in waking life; yet the glass remained whole. But lo! when I looked at it again after some time, it was broken."

The delayed shattering of the glass gave van Eeden "a very curious impression of being in a *fake-world,* cleverly imitated, but with small failures. I took the broken glass and threw it out of the window, in order to observe whether I could hear the *tinkling*. I heard the noise all right and I even saw two dogs run away from it quite naturally. I thought what a good imitation this comedy-world was. Then I saw a decanter with claret and tasted it, and noted with perfect clearness of mind: 'Well, we can also have voluntary impressions of taste in this dream-world; this has quite the taste of wine.'"

Van Eeden often had such lifelike sensations in his dreams. He remarked that "the sensation of having a body—having eyes, hands, a mouth that speaks, and so on—is perfectly distinct; yet I know at the same time that the physical body is sleeping and has quite a different position." He described the experience as "the feeling of slipping from one body into another, and there is distinctly a *double* recollection of the two bodies." He admitted that Havelock Ellis would sneer at the idea, but these sensations suggested that he had what he called a dream body.

However, most researchers thought lucid dreaming an oddity at best. They believed that such an experience was not a dream at all but rather a "microawakening," or a partial arousal during dream sleep. Not until the 1980s, after Stephen LaBerge, a young researcher at Stanford University, established experimentally that a sleeper could alert observers to a lucid dream in progress, did the subject win a measure of respectability and serious attention.

LaBerge claims to have had lucid dreams since childhood. During slumber, he would instruct pirates to return to his dreams night after night to continue their joint nocturnal adventures, and once, when he became frightened of drowning in a dream, LaBerge reminded himself that in earlier dreams he had been able to breathe underwater. Over the years LaBerge continued to have occasional lucid dreams, and in 1977, when he began work on his doctoral thesis in psychophysiology at Stanford, he decided to devise a way to study them scientifically.

An immediate problem was how to gather sufficient data—LaBerge experienced lucid dreams less than once a month. He first tried to increase the frequency of the dreams by using a technique of autosuggestion developed by psychologist Patricia Garfield—he would tell himself before retiring, "Tonight I *will* have a lucid dream." Using this method, LaBerge discovered that he was able to induce about five

Bridgeman/Art Resource, New York

Evelyn de Morgan's Night and Sleep

lucid dreams per month. By routinely reminding himself of his intention to be lucid during his dreams and by evolving his own technique, called Mnemonic Induction of Lucid Dreams, or MILD, LaBerge boosted his rate to more than twenty lucid dreams per month. On especially productive nights, he could induce four lucid dreams. LaBerge's procedure is fairly simple. After awakening from a dream, he memorizes its content, a practice intended to hone the ability to recall dreams. Then, for ten to fifteen minutes, he reads or performs some other activity that demands wakefulness. As he is about to fall asleep once more, he tells himself, "Next time I'm dreaming, I want to remember I'm dreaming," and imagines himself taking part in the dream he has just had, with the awareness that he is dreaming.

Intentionally inducing lucid dreams was LaBerge's first major research achievement. His second was to herald the arrival of a lucid dream by sending a clear signal during sleep, cleverly calling on the few muscles that are not immobilized during the REM stage. Initially using himself as his principal subject at the Stanford Sleep Laboratory, LaBerge selected as his signal two vertical sweeps of the eyes. Each night he recorded his brain waves, eye movements, and the slight muscle activity of his chin and wrists on a polysomnograph (a type of lie-detector device). One night after a series of tries, LaBerge examined the record of the previous night's session and found a telltale group of zigzags tracing the eye signal he had wanted to send. To prove that the eye movements were not REM related, LaBerge devised a second, more elaborate, signal to be sent by his clenched fists. In LaBerge's version of the Morse code, tightening his left hand equaled a dot and tightening his right equaled a dash. An electromyograph (an instrument measuring muscular activity) recorded LaBerge's predetermined message—his initials delivered in Morse code.

Color and light, according to van Eeden's report, are more intense and sensations in general are sometimes heightened in lucid dreams, compared with ordinary dreams. LaBerge and other contemporary investigators also agree that the lucid dream contains a powerful, mainly positive emotional content. Van Eeden's recollections are filled with words such as bliss, gratitude, piety, thankfulness, serenity, and calm. A contemporary of van Eeden, an Englishman named Hugh Calloway, reported that during his first lucid dream, "the vividness of life increased a hundredfold. . . . Never had I felt so absolutely well, so clear-brained, so divinely powerful, so inexpressibly *free!*" When a lucid dream does occasionally inspire negative emotions, they, like the more common positive feelings, are also unusually strong.

As a lucid dream draws to a close or lucidity fades, the dreamer frequently dreams of waking up. Such a false awakening can occur dozens of times within a single dream, and the lucid dreamer may go to great lengths within the dream to test whether he or she is still asleep. One subject reported, "I dreamed my wife and I awoke, got up, and dressed. On pulling up the blind, we made the amazing discovery that the row of houses opposite had vanished and in their place were bare fields. I said to my wife, 'This means I am dreaming, though everything seems so real and I feel perfectly awake.'" But the dreamer could not convince his wife that it was a dream, so he decided to prove it to her by safely jumping out of their bedroom window. "Ruthlessly ignoring her pleading and objecting, I opened the window and climbed out on to the sill. I then jumped, and floated gently down into the street. When my feet touched the pavement I awoke. . . . As a matter of fact, I was very nervous about jumping; for the atmosphere inside our bedroom seemed so absolutely real that it nearly made me accept the manifest absurdity of things outside."

Lucid dreaming comes naturally to about five to ten percent of the population. What traits these dreamers share is not yet clear, but researchers believe they may have identified a few. Jayne Gackenbach, an experimental psychologist at the University of Northern Iowa, found evidence that female lucid dreamers tend to be creative and adventurous during their waking lives—many of them relish such risky activities as scuba diving, rock climbing, and parachute jumping. And she suggests that both female and male lucid dreamers are less likely to be depressed or neurotic than the general population, although male lucid dreamers seem to be more prone to anxiety than their female counterparts.

Gackenbach and other psychologists report that people who do not spontaneously have lucid dreams can develop the ability if they are motivated and have good dream recall. Techniques such as MILD and presleep hypnotic suggestion and the use of special devices may aid the novice. LaBerge has designed plastic goggles with sensors that set off a pulsing colored light when the wearer enters REM sleep. The light arouses the dreamer just enough to make him aware he is dreaming. British psychol-

Jean Auguste Dominique Ingres's The Dream of Ossian

ogist Keith Hearne's compact device, which he calls his dream machine, uses a wire sensor clipped to the sleeper's nostril to detect the rapid, irregular breathing of REM sleep. The machine then sends four mild electric shocks to an electrode on the dreamer's wrist. The sleeper has been told in advance that the four shocks stand for a four-word sentence—"This is a dream."

Having the kind of pleasant, vivid experiences that lucid dreamers report seems reason enough to learn how to induce this type of dream, but there appear to be other reasons for bringing the notoriously unruly dream process under some degree of control. Dream researchers see a variety of therapeutic possibilities. In fact, lucid dreaming is already being put to use to combat recurring nightmares. This technique, strictly speaking, is not an invention of sleep laboratories. More than two hundred years ago, Scottish philosopher Thomas Reid was plagued night after night by frightening dreams. Wanting to be rid of them, he decided that he would try "to recollect that it was all a dream, and that I was in no real danger." Reid began to remind himself before he fell asleep that whatever he experienced during the night would be only a dream. "After many fruitless endeavors to recollect this when the danger appeared," he recalled, "I effected it at last, and have often, when I was sliding over a precipice into the abyss, recollected that it was all a dream, and boldly jumped down. The effect of this commonly was that I immediately awoke. But I awoke calm and intrepid, which I thought a greater acquisition."

People with a natural bent toward lucid dreams are also apt to experience vivid, kaleidoscopic images during the hypnagogic state, the drowsy interface of waking and sleeping. The body relaxes, blood pressure drops, and the heart rate and breathing slow. The individual may hear a cacophony of sounds—crashes, explosions, indecipherable voices, or the repetitious calling of his or her own name—and experience a sensation of falling, accompanied by a hypnagogic startle; fragmented, nonsensical phrases may escape the lips. A hypnagogic episode may be accompanied by a frightening paralysis, and perhaps by a sensation of pressure on the chest, which can immobilize the sleeper long after the hallucinatory sensations have dissipated.

The history of Western art is rich in anecdotes implying a link between hypnagogic imagery and creativity. Composers Johannes Brahms, Giacomo Puccini, and Richard Wagner, for instance, all said their musical ideas sometimes took shape during states of consciousness that a number of psychologists believe were hypnagogic. Nineteenth-century novelist Mary Shelley is said to have based her best-known work, *Frankenstein,* on horrifying hypnagogic imagery. And scientific and technological insights as well seem to have surfaced during such episodes. Thomas Edison was famous for taking a catnap whenever he became stuck on a particular problem. Holding little steel balls in both hands, he would drift off in his favorite chair. As his mind relinquished consciousness his hands would relax, droop, and finally drop the balls into pans strategically placed on the floor. At the noise Edison would jerk awake, often with an idea for solving the problem that had perplexed him minutes earlier.

Sleep appears both to enhance learning and to aid retention of the information. Studies have shown that when subjects sleep immediately after memorizing facts, they retain more material—and can relearn it more easily after a twenty-four-hour lapse— than if they stay awake for a few hours after the learning period. Sleep, it seems, helps match fresh experience to related material the mind has already mastered and forges a link between the old and the new.

The Dream Gallery

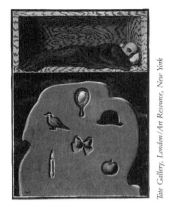

René Magritte's The Reckless Sleeper

Jungian Archetypes

I N ADDITION to our immediate consciousness," wrote Carl Jung, "there exists a second psychic system of a collective, universal, and impersonal nature which is identical in all individuals." Inhabiting this collective unconscious, he posited, are what he called archetypes, the primordial images, or symbols, imprinted on the psyche at the beginning of time and since passed on to all humankind. The mother, father, child, and hero, with their associated motifs, are all examples of such archetypes, expressed the world over in myths, fairy tales, and dreams.

Dreams that present true archetypal images are rare, according to Jung. He found that they are likely to appear at pivotal points in a person's life, such as early childhood, puberty, early adulthood, midlife, before death, and at other times of crisis. Archetypal images in dreams, Jung held, give definite form to a particular psychic content of the unconscious, thus enabling it to enter the conscious mind. Professional analysis is usually required to interpret the full implications of archetypes. They often appear as symbolic images; the mother, for instance, might take the form of an inanimate object. But even if archetypal dreams are not understood, Jung believed, they would nonetheless "stand out for years like spiritual landmarks."

The Mother

Like all archetypes, the mother has both positive and negative connotations. In the following dream of a thirty-seven-year-old woman, the protective, nurturing aspects of the mother prevail:

"I was wandering through the woods, lost. I felt like Gretel in 'Hansel and

Gretel,' but Hansel wasn't there to protect me. Suddenly I heard a rustling behind me. I was terrified and didn't dare move. Out of the woods came a beautiful woman. She seemed ageless. She smiled and gently pulled me into her lap. I knew that she was connected to nature and had magical powers. I knew that I would be safe. I had a strong urge to suck her breast. I was ten years old in the dream."

A dream of being lost in the woods frequently symbolizes the beginning of a new phase of life and expresses the anxiety of leaving behind the familiar. In the case of this dreamer, she had just left a much-trusted female analyst. Her dread of working with a male analyst apparently stemmed from the fear and mistrust she felt toward all men. Her father had left home for good when she was ten—her age in the dream. And the cruelty she had felt from her mother during her childhood made her feel abandoned by both parents, much like fairy-tale Gretel in her dream.

The comforting mother figure in this dream—whom the dreamer associated with her female analyst—indicates that the patient had healed the psychic wounds related to her mother. The appearance of this positive archetype signals that the patient is now ready to move on to the healing of the wounds that were caused by her father's desertion.

While the imagery in this dream is straightforward, the mother archetype can take several forms—both human and nonhuman. In its positive form, it may appear as a kindly mother, grandmother, or aunt, or as a church, a cave, or a garden. Associated with these images are maternal solicitude and sympathy, growth, nourishment, and fertility. Negatively, the mother may take shape as a witch, a dragon, or a shark and connote anything destructive and hateful, secret, dark, or hidden, as well as anything that devours, seduces, or poisons.

The Father

The father archetype commands center stage in the following dream of a fifty-three-year-old man:

"I was with another man, a shadowy figure. We went into a house. We saw an old man there. He was a former Mafia don. At one time he had headed the Mafia families. Now he was old, tired, and sickly. I realized that some time ago I too had been connected with the Mafia. Later, we realized that a contract had been put on the old man. We took pity on him and offered to help him, to help him hide out, to stave off his inevitable end. He insisted that we not do that. What would be, would be, he said. Finally the hit man entered the room. I pleaded with him for just a bit more time. The old man was ready, but I was not."

The significance of this dream reaches back into the dreamer's childhood, where he grew up in a sternly patriarchal household. As a boy and then as a man, the dreamer believed he had to deny his own burgeoning sense of masculine authority in order not to lose his domineering father's love and approval. As a result, he felt weak and ineffectual well into middle age. The emotions and memories unleashed

by this dream served as a turning point in the dreamer's life. He realized that the old man in the dream symbolized his father, who was willingly relinquishing his power so that his son might lay claim to his own. The dreamer interpreted the old man's insistence on not being saved as a sign he need not feel he was sacrificing his father's love by asserting his own masculinity.

This dream reflects Jung's view that the father as much as the mother plays a crucial psychological role in "the destiny of the individual." The power of one's father, according to Jung, derives from his embodiment of the father archetype. As an archetype, the father represents the ruler, lawgiver, or protector. It often appears in dreams as a king, an elder, or a heavenly father, or as heaven, the sun, a weapon, or a phallus. On the negative side, the father archetype may assume overbearing, devouring, or destructive qualities.

The Child

A depressed and angry forty-year-old woman had the following dream, in which the child archetype figures prominently:

"I was sitting on a bench in a park. It was a beautiful day. I was thinking about how I was going to accomplish all the things I had to do that day. Suddenly there was a little girl in front of me. She was about six years old. She radiated joy and happi-

A depiction of a mother archetype, from Gustav Klimt's Beethoven Frieze

ness. She was dressed all in yellow. She said to me in a tone I absolutely could not resist, 'Will you play with me?' I smiled. She took my hand."

The radiant little girl in this dream represents the arrested child within the adult woman. Her parents had divorced when she was six—the age of the little girl in the dream. From that point on, her mother treated her as if she were a burden, and little joy remained in the child's life. She grew into a somber and morose woman who had trouble with both her professional and private lives. The dream symbolizes her inner child breaking through from the realm of her subconscious to intrude upon her conscious frame of mind. By asking her to play, the child reveals the dreamer's desperate need to learn how to play again and enjoy life.

The dream above illustrates Jung's view that "the child motif is a picture of certain forgotten things in our childhood." Here, the dreamer had literally forgotten how to play. But, Jung continued, the archetype represents not only what has been but what can be. The occurrence of the child motif in a person's psychology, he wrote, "paves the way for a future change of personality." In the case above, as the dreamer set about learning to play, some of her unhappiness began to fall away.

In religion and mythology, the child–hero and child–savior—such as Hercules, who strangled two threatening snakes when he was a babe, or Jesus, who saved humankind from eternal damnation—are common themes. The child archetype may take the hero or savior form in dreams, or it may manifest itself as the dreamer's own son or daughter or as any other youngster. It may appear to be of exotic origin or may even appear surrounded by stars or with a starry crown. In its negative manifestation, it may present itself as the child of a witch, with demonic attributes.

The Anima

Just as both men and women's bodies inherit a mix of paternal and maternal chromosomes, so their unconscious minds, Jung believed, comprise both male and female elements. In dreams, this hidden, contrasexual aspect materializes as an archetypal figure of the opposite gender of the dreamer. The feminine character in men Jung termed the anima, and the masculine nature in women, the animus—both Latin terms that mean soul. The following dream, from a middle-aged man, revolves around the anima:

"I was walking down the street and saw an old house with a strange door. I felt compelled to open it. Inside, there was an empty room, with the opening to another room at the end of it. As I entered the second room, I saw something lying on a cot. It seemed lifeless. I went over and looked more closely. It was a beautiful woman in a long white gown. She opened her eyes and smiled and said, 'I've been waiting for you for a long time.' A golden glow seemed to surround her."

The woman in the dream symbolized his inner anima and the positive feminine characteristics—openness, spirituality, earthiness, creativity—he had been repressing. Her apparent lifelessness and then her words indicate that she had long existed as a dormant psychic potential deep within the dreamer's unconscious.

Jung assigned the anima archetype an extremely important role, that of guiding a man to the depths of his soul. Coming to terms with the anima—which may appear in dreams as a goddess, an elf, a mermaid, or any female persona—supposedly provides spiritual inspiration and a more balanced view of life. In the above dream, the anima seems to be offering the dreamer this opportunity. But, like all archetypes, the anima may take negative form as well, appearing in dreams as moody, irritable, and oversensitive—the stereotypical "inferior" woman, in Jung's terms. Its appearance may signal that those destructive characteristics are dominating the dreamer's personality and that he might need professional help in overcoming them.

The Animus

The animus—the archetypal male figure that reflects the masculine principle in women—dominates this dream of a woman in her mid-thirties:

"I was sitting in my living room watching television. There was a fascinating man who was the husband of a woman in the drama. I thought to myself, 'I wish I knew someone like that. He seems to have such spiritual depth.' Just at that moment, he came right out of the TV set and walked right up to me. He didn't say a word but just smiled and handed me a golden key. He then turned around and walked back into the TV. I was astounded."

The attractive man emerging from the television in her dream represents her positive animus, of which she was previously unaware. And the golden key symbolizes her potential to unlock her inner mystery and find within herself qualities of great value. As the dreamer later explored her fantasies about the nature of the man in her dreams, she began to work at integrating into her personality the positive characteristics she felt he had projected, such as compassion and empathy.

A positive animus, then, serves much the same purpose for women as the positive anima does for men: Properly cultivated, it can open doors to inner wisdom and emotional and

Girandon/Art Resource, NY

Ferdinand Hodler's The Dream

spiritual depth. Like the anima, however, the animus may also appear as an unfavorable force, the characteristics of which are also defined by cultural stereotypes of gender-appropriate behavior. A negative animus, in Jung's traditional view, causes a woman to be opinionated, argumentative, rigid, controlling, and excessively critical of herself or others. Its archetypal materialization in a dream might be taken as a warning that this negative masculine side threatens to rule one's nature.

Jung believed that there was a proper balance to strive for as regards the anima and animus. In general, the goal was to work toward integrating the positive qualities associated with them into one's consciousness and to guard against letting their negative aspects dominate.

The Hero

The hero archetype makes an abstract appearance in this dream of a timid, self-doubting male lawyer:

"I was on vacation, walking along a beach. I saw something sticking out of the sand. I looked closer. It was a torn and crumpled piece of paper. I picked it up. It read, 'Go to the land of your fathers. There you will find words.' It was an odd message. It made no sense. As I looked at it, I realized that if I took the *s* off the end of words and put it onto the front, it would read sword. At least the sentence made sense now, even if it didn't apply to me."

This dream shows the subtlety of dream symbols: The prescription for the

Erich Lessing/Art Resource, New York

A hero archetype, from Gustav Klimt's Beethoven Frieze

dreamer's psychological ills was revealed through a seemingly trivial symbol—a discarded piece of paper. But what that scrap communicated was that it was time for the dreamer to stop relying mainly on the intellect—words—and to claim the authority of the hero, as symbolized by the word *sword*.

Hero myths, common to all cultures, tend to follow the same formula: Born into humble circumstances, the hero soon exhibits superhuman strength, goes on to struggle triumphantly against the forces of evil, then often meets his death. The hero archetype reflects the sort of maturation process suggested by the myths. Its appearance reportedly signals the dreamer's awareness of his inner strengths and weaknesses, knowledge essential for the development of a healthy personality.

Although the hero archetype generally appears in dreams during adolescence and young adulthood, it may stay hidden for a while in the subconscious. The dreamer above, for instance, was thirty-seven. Over time he realized the heroic implications of his nocturnal vision—through his analytical work—and began to take charge of his life.

The hero motif may appear in dreams as a standard mythological character or as a modern-day hero, perhaps an athlete. Or it may take the role of an ordinary person acting bravely within the dream's context. When the hero continues to occur in an older person's dreams—a fifty-year-old man, say, seeing himself as a young athletic champion—it may signal that the dreamer is clinging to the illusion of youth rather than integrating a mature balance of power and wisdom. Women also have hero dreams, which are becoming more prevalent as women take on more assertive roles.

The Shadow

A thirty-three-year-old man who had been fired from his job for his role in a political scandal and saw himself as a victim related the following dream, in which the shadow archetype prevails:

"I was in a room, having a conversation with someone—I'm not sure who, it could have been me, too. I left the room, then for some reason turned back to reenter it. I opened the door and saw myself standing on the far side of the room. Looking to the left, I saw the back of another person. He turned around, and I saw he was also me. He seemed very startled to see me. As I looked at him, his face began to change into something quite grotesque—a monster-animal. I was horrified at the face of the monster and horrified to realize that all these people I saw were different sides of myself. The person on the far side of the room saw my horror and said: 'I told you not to come back; you should have knocked before you came in. Now you know.'"

The shadow archetype, which is symbolized as the same sex as the dreamer, generally represents the darker, repressed side of one's character—the part most people choose not to face in waking life because it is inconsistent with their self-image. The dreamer above, for instance, saw himself as a doer of good deeds and blamed his troubles on others' persecuting him. This explicit dream revealed that unbeknown to him, there were unconscious sides of himself that were nothing less that monstrous. Up until then, the man had successfully hidden, or repressed, those destructive facets from himself. By exposing his shadow in all its awful truth, this dream forced the man to accept responsibility for his actions.

Although shadow archetypes often appear in dreams as frightening or unsavory characters to be avoided, they can offer a dreamer useful revelations about his inner self, which he can then integrate into his waking life. Knowing that his shadow appears cold and forbidding, for instance, may encourage a person to be warmer and more compassionate in relations with others. True to archetypal form, a shadow may have positive as well as negative aspects. A meek person's shadow, for instance, may come across in a dream as a strong and assertive character who possesses qualities the dreamer might do well to assimilate.

Common Dreams

AMID THE kaleidoscopic swirl of unique dreams that emerge from each human mind are a handful that occur to almost all dreamers. Dreams of falling, being chased, soaring through the air, and losing teeth seem to be common manifestations of shared human experience. "Our dreaming self has apparently never lost sight of a basic truth," writes one dream researcher. "Namely that, despite the manifold ways in which the human race has fragmented itself in the course of history, we are, nevertheless, all members of a single species."

Some dreams are typical of a particular culture. The examination dream, in which the dreamer stares uncomprehendingly at a test paper, is a familiar expression of anxiety in industrialized societies. But the dream of being pursued spans cultural borders. The Masai may dream of being chased by an animal and the New Yorker of being stalked by a man with a knife, but the fear of being attacked is so basic that such dreams occur in almost all societies.

Yet even common dreams, each dramatically colored by individual circumstances, mean something slightly different to different dreamers. And as demonstrated by these typical dreams, each can be interpreted in a multitude of ways, according to various schools of psychological thought and dream theory.

The Fear of Falling

Almost everyone has at some time been jolted awake by the alarming sensation of falling from a great height. This unsettling phenomenon may be triggered by a dip in blood pressure, movement of fluid in the middle ear, or a limb dangling off the bed. But dreams involving a fall as part of a scene, such as tumbling off a cliff or out of a window, are nearly as common and seem to have deeper roots. Some psychologists speculate that they go back to when a toddler takes his first shaky steps, and the precarious sensation imprints the brain with an indelible metaphor for insecurity. Sociobiologists look back even further—to a primordial vigilance against tumbling from the tree while sleeping.

Whatever their cause, dreams of falling are powerful images that lend themselves to many interpretations. Sigmund Freud offered two. In women, he theorized, falling symbolized surrender to erotic temptation—the dreamer viewed herself as a "fallen woman." Otherwise, falling was an example of wish fulfillment, reflecting a desire to return to infancy when a child who fell was picked up and held in reassuring arms.

Psychiatrist Emil Gutheil suggested that falling could be a metaphor for the loss of equilibrium in many forms: loss of temper, loss of self-control, a falling away from

Pieter Breughel's (the Elder) sixteenth-century La Tentation de Saint Antoine

accepted moral standards. Noting that such dreams are almost invariably accompanied by anxiety, Gutheil added that a pleasurable falling dream—one in which the dreamer drifts safely to the ground—should be classified instead among flying dreams.

Contemporary theory holds that falling usually reflects insecurity—a sense that there is nothing to hold on to. People in the throes of a divorce or whose jobs are in jeopardy may dream of falling from a precipice. A child who overhears a quarreling parent threaten to leave home might have nightmares of tumbling into a deep hole. To men who fear impotence, falling can represent the failure to achieve an erection.

Finding Yourself Naked in Public

The traditional Freudian view of nudity dreams held they were inspired by an unconscious, infantile longing for the free, unclothed moments of early life. But today, dreams of public nakedness are considered more likely to indicate that the dreamers are metaphorically exposing what they believe to be their faults or that they feel vulnerable to some situation in their lives. Such dreams may also connote honesty, expressing a desire to strip away one's facade and be seen for what one really is.

The tone and content of nudity dreams offer important clues to their meaning. For example, a dream of showing up naked at the airport the night before a journey might be no more than a reminder to pack underwear. If you are naked at a party or in the office, it can mean that you feel exposed to friends or coworkers. Clues may be found in the attitude of the other people in the dream. Disapproving onlookers signal guilt; indifferent ones may indicate that something you are concerned about revealing is not very important. In some cases, onlookers clearly approve of the dreamer, as they did in the case of one college student who dreamed he disrobed to the cheers of friends. The triumphant dream—which occurred soon after the young man had his first experience of sexual intercourse—was evidently a message that he was delighted with himself for shedding inhibitions.

Running for Your Life

The dream of being pursued or attacked—often accompanied by the feeling of being helplessly rooted to the spot—is common to all societies. In the United States, surveys indicate that attack/pursuit is one of the two most common anxiety dream themes among such diverse groups as college students, prisoners, and military inductees (falling is the other one).

Like falling, pursuit is a dream metaphor for insecurity. Yet people who dream frequently of being chased or attacked seem seldom to dream of falling, and vice versa, leading some investigators to speculate that the two dreams are flip sides of the same psychological coin.

The psychoanalytic tradition suggests that they represent two fundamentally different subconscious anxieties: fear of the loss of love in the case of falling dreams and fear of castration or, for female dreamers, sexual attack in the case of attack dreams. Another interpretation holds that a woman who dreams of being pursued is expressing a longing to be wooed. The fact that she is being "chased" is viewed as a punning reference to the word *chaste* and reflects contradictory desires to be courted and at the same time to maintain her virginity.

Questions that dreamers can ask themselves in order to explore possible interpretations of the pursuit dream include: Are circumstances closing in on you? Are you at the mercy of feelings that threaten to get out of control? Are you being victimized by someone else's aggression? Do you have feelings of guilt and a fear of being caught? Are you attempting to get away with something? Are you in the same position you were in as a child when you felt endangered by forces that were more powerful than you?

Taking Flight

Soaring through the air like a bird has been an intriguing feature of human dreams since ancient times. To the Babylonians, a man who took flight in his dreams would find riches if he were poor, freedom if he were a prisoner, and health if he were ill. Lydian soothsayer Artemidorus Daldianus said dreams of flying gave the dreamer a sense of elevation above others—as well as a promise of happiness and riches.

Characteristically, Freud saw sex in flying dreams—connecting the sensation of flight with orgasm and with sexual prowess. Because suspension in the air suggests ghosts and angels, Wilhelm Steckel, an early student of Freud's, linked dreams of flying with thoughts of death. Alfred Adler interpreted the dreams as revealing a will to dominate others, and Carl Jung believed they symbolized the desire to overcome a problem or break free of restrictions.

Contemporary dream research tends to ally itself with Jung's thinking. "People under a compulsion, people who are forced to endure unhappy circumstances (unhappy marriage, unhappy job or the like) experience their desire for freedom in their flying dreams," writes Emil Gutheil. "To fly then, means to be free." Bolstering such thinking is the fact that elderly people seem to dream of flight more frequently than do younger ones—apparently reflecting their desire to slip the bonds of increasing physical infirmity.

On Stage and Unprepared

In a recurrent dream that understandably unsettled him, playwright George Bernard Shaw found himself standing on a stage as the lead actor in a play that was about to begin. As the curtain rose, the master of repartee and biting dialogue realized to his horror that he had nothing to say. He did not know his lines.

To Emil Gutheil, who related it in his book *The Language of the Dream,* the nightmare revealed that the playwright—who in his waking hours was a man of fabled self-confidence—harbored a deep-seated anxiety about his ability to rise to the occasion when confronted with tasks to which he did not feel equal. To other dream researchers the dream might also have suggested that the great playwright subconsciously feared losing his prodigious verbal skills.

Whatever the interpretation, Shaw's dream, in which an inner drama of anxiety and inferiority is played out in a theatrical setting, is a typical variation of the even more common dream in which the dreamer sits down to take an examination, looks at the test paper, and realizes, to his horror, that he cannot answer a single one of the questions. Salespeople may dream of being examined or having stage fright the night before a sales presentation; athletes often have such dreams before competing in a sporting event.

In other cases, a dreamed exam or unprepared stage appearance is a metaphor for being put to the test on some personal issue. Noting that such dreams often occur at the "threshold of important decisions," Gutheil writes that they are frequent among those individuals whose self-confidence is at stake—a young man about to marry who doubts his sexual adequacy or his ability as a provider; someone entering a new job who is unsure of being able to handle new responsibilities. He notes that an examination dream may also signify a sense of being tested morally—"the 'final' examination as to one's 'good' and 'bad' deeds before the Highest Examiner."

Do-it-Yourself Dreams

Remembering and examining dreams can be of great benefit. Yet most people do not routinely remember their dreams when they wake up in the morning. Indeed, some people insist they never dream at all or do so only on rare occasions. Science has proved them wrong, however, with studies showing that everyone dreams and that we may have as many as four or five dreams per night.

The problem for dreamer and "nondreamer" alike is that our memory of dreams tends to evaporate quickly as time passes, beginning with the moment we awake. No one knows for sure why this happens; scientists speculate the process of forgetting begins even while the dream is in progress, so that any dream memory is only of the most recent dream action.

One antidote to this ongoing loss of dream memory is to keep a dream journal. The journal can be a notebook or a tape recorder placed on a table next to the bed. Upon awaking, you can write down or dictate as much of your dreams as you remember, adding to the entry later in the day if more night images resurface in your mind.

RECALLING YOUR DREAMS. Before you can keep a successful dream journal, however, you may need help in jogging your memory. It helps to be patient when learning to recall dreams—you may have spent a lifetime ignoring dreams, and it could take days and even weeks to begin remembering them. One tip for sharper dream recall involves going to bed with a clear head; being too tired can cloud memory in the morning, and studies have shown that alcohol and drugs, including sleeping pills, taken before bedtime alter the time spent dreaming.

Experts also suggest allowing yourself some quiet, reflective moments upon awaking. Lie still, keep your eyes closed, and relax. Then ask yourself, "What was I just dreaming?" You may remember only a fragment of an image, but further memory sleuthing might lead back to a complete picture. With those images fresh in your mind, reach for the dream journal.

RECORDING YOUR DREAMS. Sometimes the simple process of writing or speaking of your dreams triggers other images and details, so it's best to record dreams soon after waking. In fact, the process of recording your dreams can begin *before* you

A dreamlike landscape in Pieter Breughel's (the Elder) sixteenth-century
Les Justes Libérés de Limbes

go to sleep. Some dream therapists suggest jotting down your thoughts and feelings about the day just prior to bedtime. This not only helps you become more comfortable with the journal-writing process; these notes may also help you see how your dreams correspond to what you experienced during the day.

When recording an actual dream, do not stop to think of what it might mean; just concentrate on getting down the dream's plot. Try to recall details of places or characters, but do not struggle for precise descriptions—you can go back afterward and fill in particulars or nuances, impressions or emotions. Also record any fantasies, quotes, songs, and poems that appeared; you might want to sketch or paint your dream images so that you can study them from time to time.

In reconstructing your dreams, do not try to shoehorn them into the mold of reality. Logical sequences and cause and effect often do not apply. Accept the order of images and events as they seem to have occurred, and enter them that way in the journal.

Once you have finished, be sure to write down the date of the dream and, if you can, the approximate time it took place. Dream fragments may come back to you later in the day or even a few days later; record them in the margin beside the original entry. Sometimes images appear over and over in dreams—a house or a clock, for example. Many experts suggest assembling a glossary of such images, listing each symbol and any associations that come to mind, and how it appeared in each dream. These images may have some personal significance that will be revealed as you study them and their places in your dreams.

MEDITATING ON YOUR DREAMS. Carl Jung believed a message could be found in almost every dream if one took the time to examine it carefully. Current dream analysts are in agreement that focusing attention on a dream—even just taking the time to recall it and write it down—can often lead to a greater understanding of its meaning.

Practitioners also suggest you examine entries in your dream journal for recurring symbols, characters, or themes. Many believe each image in a dream represents an aspect of the dreamer's personality and suggest role-playing each image. Free-associating about a puzzling dream element—allowing any other words, images, or ideas it evokes to float to the surface of your mind—sometimes produces a nugget of self-revelation as well. So may extending an unresolved dream—replaying the dream in your imagination and giving it a conclusion.

Dreams are a symbolic language emanating from the depths of the inner self; taking the time to think about them and their possible messages may provide valuable insight. But some authorities believe true dream interpretation should be pursued only with the help of a trained professional. The messages of the unconscious can be upsetting or frightening, they believe, if revealed too rapidly or without proper guidance.

11
A MANUAL FOR THE
MAGICAL ARTS

Portents in the Palm

FOR THOUSANDS of years, in diverse cultures, people have believed that an individual's destiny is previewed in the hands, that every palm, from the time of birth, holds in its own unique network of mounts and valleys, lines and markings, the key to life's potential. It is also said that as the person matures, significant events in his or her life will be reflected in the palm. But these marks of the past and guideposts to the future are usually indecipherable to all but a few—those who can supposedly divine the course of someone's life through palm reading.

Palmistry has changed little over time. Its proponents claim that it enables people to understand themselves better. It may also reveal inherent strengths and weaknesses in character—useful knowledge when facing life's challenges—and provide clues as to how one's nature can affect health, career, and relationships. But most of all, many palmists contend, hand analysis enables people to make choices that will bring them pleasure and self-fulfillment.

In a reading, palmists usually compare the subject's right and left hands. The lines and overall form of the so-called passive hand are thought to reflect one's innate potential, while those of the dominant hand—typically the one used for writing—are said to reveal choices the individual has made and what may lie ahead. A thorough palmist generally discerns from the hand's shape and markings a likely life pattern, a set of tendencies, or particular events that may occur.

Hands are often classified as one of four types, named by some practitioners of the art to correspond to the traditional four elements of nature—air, earth, water, and fire. The classifications are based on the shape of the palm and the length of the fingers in relation to it. Palms are typically rectangular or square, with either long or short fingers. Fingers are considered long if the middle finger (called the Saturn finger in palmistry) is at least as long as the palm itself, and short if that finger falls short of the palm's length.

The **Air Hand** is characterized by long fingers and a square palm etched with many fine lines. People with air hands tend to be expressive, emotionally stable, and intellectually curious. They may gravitate toward professions involving communication, such as writing, education, or public relations.

The **Earth Hand**, signified by a deeply lined square palm and short fingers, may reflect a serious, practical person who delights in physical activity. These individuals tend to enjoy manual occupations, such as carpentry, farming, and working with machinery.

The **Water Hand**, with its long fingers extending from a finely lined rectangular palm, often reveals a sensitive, creative, quiet personality. Studious or relatively low-pressure occupations—such as research, office work, or retail sales—may appeal to these individuals.

The **Fire Hand**, recognized by its short fingers and rectangular palm filled with clear lines, denotes an energetic, impetuous person. People who have fire hands seem drawn to professions that involve challenge, risk, and creativity, such as medicine, law enforcement, or the arts.

The shape of an individual's fingertips, palmists maintain, provides further insight into his or her character. There are four distinct fingertip shapes—conic, round, square, and spatulate. Conic fingertips, which taper off almost to a point, imply a sensitive and impulsive nature, as well as a lover of art and beauty. The individual may also be highly intuitive, relying more on that gift than on powers of reason. A well-balanced disposition is usually denoted by round fingertips. This individual adapts easily to change, is receptive to new ideas, and reacts to situations with equal measures of mental and emotional reasoning. People with square fingertips tend to thrive on order and regularity and to express themselves clearly and with confidence. They desire security and stability for themselves as well as for their loved ones. Fingertips that are narrow at the first joint and then flare to a wide tip are known as spatulate. Individuals with spatulate fingertips are usually considered to be

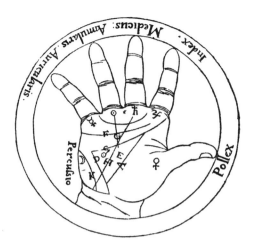

A flexible, independent thumb

independent, energetic, and enthusiastic; they love action everywhere in their lives, even seeking it in the books and other materials they read. These generally down-to-earth personalities often make true and loyal friends.

Palmists observe that some fingertip shapes are typically associated with certain hand types. Individuals with water hands, for example, frequently possess conic fingertips, while square fingertips are commonly found on individuals with air hands.

A mixture of two or more fingertip shapes on an individual's hand is also common. These so-called mixed hands suggest a person who is versatile, adapts quite easily to new situations, and may excel in a variety of occupations.

The thumb is regarded by some palmists as the key to personality. It is thought to reveal so much, in fact, that some Hindu palmists study only the thumb when analyzing an individual's character. Most practitioners of palmistry, however, insist on weighing the thumb's length, placement, and flexibility in relation to the entire hand.

In general, the thumb reveals an individual's energy level and strength of will. A long thumb, reaching past the knuckle of the index, or Jupiter, finger, may indicate a forceful personality and an abundance of energy. Someone with a short thumb may lack self-confidence and have little ability to complete projects.

A tense thumb

The thumb's significance is also affected by its placement on the hand. A low-set thumb, one that creates an angle of sixty to ninety degrees between the thumb and index finger, reveals a personality that is flexible, independent, logical, and well-directed. Someone with a high-set thumb, creating an angle of thirty degrees or less with the index finger, may be tense and self-contained.

Another indication of ego strength is in the thumb's tip. If the tip is flexible, bending back easily from the first joint, the person probably adapts easily and is

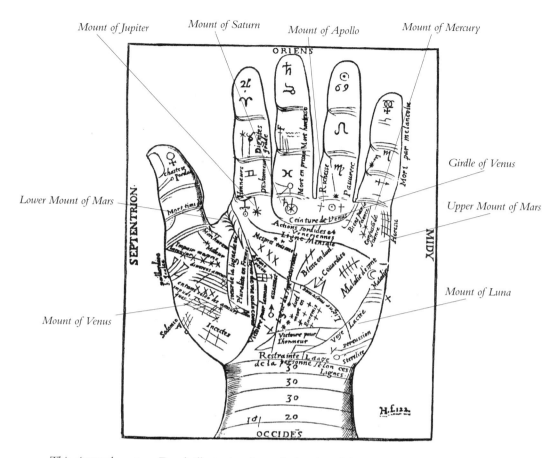

This sixteenth-century French illustration shows the location of the mounts and lines in palmistry

generous, although not indiscriminately so. If the thumb is extremely flexible, the individual might be extravagant or show a lack of restraint.

A thumb that bends only slightly under pressure may indicate a practical personality and a strong will modified by open-mindedness. The owner of a rigid thumb may be stubborn and resistant to new ideas and experiences. However, this person is usually very reliable, stable, and responsible.

A THOROUGH READING by a professional palmist should include an analysis of the palm's mounts, the fleshy pads found at the base of the thumb and each finger and on the outer edges of the palm. The larger the mount and the more directly it is centered under the corresponding finger, the greater its supposed influence on the personality. Prominent bulges are considered strong or highly developed mounts, while those that are flat or only slightly raised are judged normal or well developed. A depression in the palm instead of a fleshy pad constitutes a weak mount.

• **Mount of Jupiter**   At the base of the index finger, the mount of Jupiter reveals an individual's degree of self-confidence, social sense, and leadership ability. If the mount is well developed, healthy measures of assertiveness and ambition are indicated, as well as an even temper, generosity, and self-assurance.

An unusually strong mount may tip the scales toward vanity, narcissism, and an overbearing attitude. However, if the prominent mount is modified by factors in the lines and fingers, the individual may simply exhibit strong leadership skills. An under-developed mount may suggest a poor self-image, lack of respect for authority, and a tendency toward idleness.

• **Mount of Saturn** Found at the base of the middle, or Saturn, finger, this mount governs the introspective aspect of the personality. A well-developed Saturn mount reveals an independent nature, that of a person who enjoys solitude as well as the company of others. Self-awareness and emotional balance are indicated, as are fidelity and prudence.

A highly developed mount may indicate an unhealthy tendency toward self-absorption. And lack of a Saturn mount may denote indecisiveness, a pessimistic tendency, and a poor sense of humor.

• **Mount of Apollo** This mount, located at the base of the Apollo, or ring, finger, is said to govern all forms of creativity. A well-developed mount implies strong artistic abilities and a love of beauty. These talents may not apply solely to the fine arts but may also include culinary expertise or other forms of expression. A prominent Apollo mount may signify a tendency toward extravagance and materialism as well as vanity and self-indulgence. Low physical energy, a lack of aesthetic values, and a disregard for creative pursuits may stem from a weak Apollo mount.

• **Mount of Mercury** Communication is ruled by the mount of Mercury, at the base of the pinkie. A well-developed mount implies a talent for self-expression and a lively disposition. A large mount has no negative connotations, but an underdeveloped one may mean a lack of business acumen and difficulty communicating. A mount with short, straight lines may denote a caring, compassionate nature.

• **Lower Mount of Mars** This fleshy area located just inside the thumb joint is considered a barometer of the individual's assertive nature and ability to overcome obstacles. A normal mount indicates courage and aggressiveness; an overdeveloped mount may indicate a hot temper as well as an abundance of sexual passion. A weak lower mount of Mars suggests a quiet, passive nature and timidity in the face of challenge.

• **Mount of Venus** A fleshy ball at the base of the thumb, the mount of Venus is considered by some to be the seat of basic emotions. This mount is said to indicate physical and sexual energy, an appreciation of beauty and the arts, and the ability to love and be loved.

A firm and rounded mount of Venus suggests compassion, sincerity, warmth, and vitality, as well as a love of the outdoors. An overdeveloped mount, especially

Fate line   *Relationship lines*   *Mount of Apollo*

one with reddish skin color, reveals physical energy and sexual passion, and a healthy appetite for food and drink. An individual with a small or weak Venus mount may suffer delicate health, a lack of exuberance and intensity, and perhaps a lack of sensitivity. Frequently, palmists say, a strong love relationship can cause this mount to increase in size.

• **Upper Mount of Mars** Located just beneath the Mercury mount, the upper mount of Mars reportedly measures an individual's determination and resistance. A firm, well-formed mount reveals courage, self-reliance, and a somewhat stubborn nature. An extremely large mount might indicate inflexibility and, perhaps, a tendency toward violence or cruelty. A weak mount may reflect a lack of assertiveness, the sign of an individual who is easily manipulated by others.

• **Mount of Luna** A well-developed mount of Luna, located opposite the Venus mount and just above the wrist, suggests a balance between imagination and realism and a love of peace and harmony. The more fully developed the mount, the greater the individual's gift of intuition and imagination and the stronger the nurturing instincts; for some, restlessness is also implied. A weak Luna mount may suggest a steadfastly realistic personality who seldom indulges in fantasy.

• **Girdle of Venus** This line, located beneath the Apollo and Saturn fingers, denotes an amorous sensibility.

THE COMPLEX network of lines discernible in every palm is allegedly capable of steering each of us along life's course. Palmists analyze these lines not only to reflect the development of an individual's character traits as he or she matures but also to reveal insights into the future. And armed with this knowledge, the believers say, a person can actually affect future events. The lines of the palm are constantly changing: Old lines may fade or grow clearer and new ones may appear, sometimes in a matter of weeks. By modifying behavior and changing attitudes, palmists maintain, we can change our lines—and thus our lives—to achieve our predestined potential.

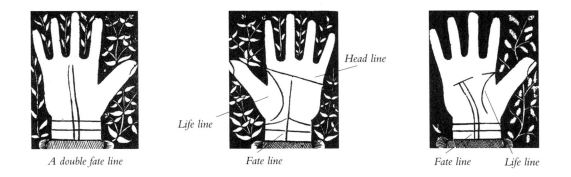

A double fate line   *Fate line*   *Fate line*   *Life line*

Life line   *Head line*

• **Head Line**   The head line, reflecting intellectual capacity and potential, usually begins below the Jupiter mount and traverses the palm. An analytical nature is typified by a straight head line, while a downward-sloping line suggests creativity. A forked end indicates a balance between imagination and realism.

Average intelligence and good reasoning powers are symbolized by a head line stretching at least two-thirds of the way across the palm. A longer line is said to reveal keen insight and a range of intellectual interests. A wide gap between the head and life lines at their origin may reflect impulsivity and impatience; the closer the lines, the more tentative the person.

• **Heart Line**   An ideal heart line, indicating a warm and demonstrative nature, begins at the hand's outer edge, beneath the Mercury finger. It traverses the palm near the base of the finger mounts, curving upward slightly before ending between the Jupiter and Saturn mounts.

A upward curve implies a physical or instinctual sexuality, while a straight heart line suggests that romantic imagery is important in love. Two or three branches at the line's end are thought to indicate a balance between emotions, realism, and physical passion.

A wide space between the heart and head lines reflects extroversion and an unconventional outlook on life; a narrow space might imply some lack of self-confidence, difficulty expressing feelings, and a secretive nature. If the heart line is longer than the head line, the person could be ruled more by emotions than reason.

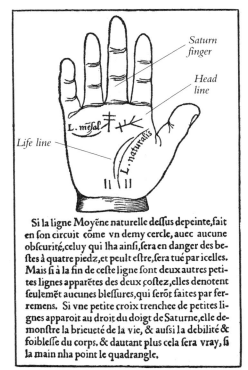

Saturn finger

Head line

Life line

L. méſal

L. naturalis

Si la ligne Moyēne naturelle deſſus depeinte, ſait en ſon circuit cōme vn demy cercle, auec aucune obſcurité, celuy qui lha ainſi, ſera en danger des beſtes à quatre piedz, et peult eſtre, ſera tué par icelles. Mais ſi à la fin de ceſte ligne ſont deux autres petites lignes apparētes des deux coſtez, elles denotent ſeulemēt aucunes bleſſures, qui ſerōt faites par ferremens. Si vne petite croix trenchee de petites lignes apparoit au droit du doigt de Saturne, elle demonſtre la brieueté de la vie, & auſsi la debilité & foibleſſe du corps, & dautant plus cela ſera vray, ſi la main nha point le quadrangle.

A sixteenth-century palmist's reading

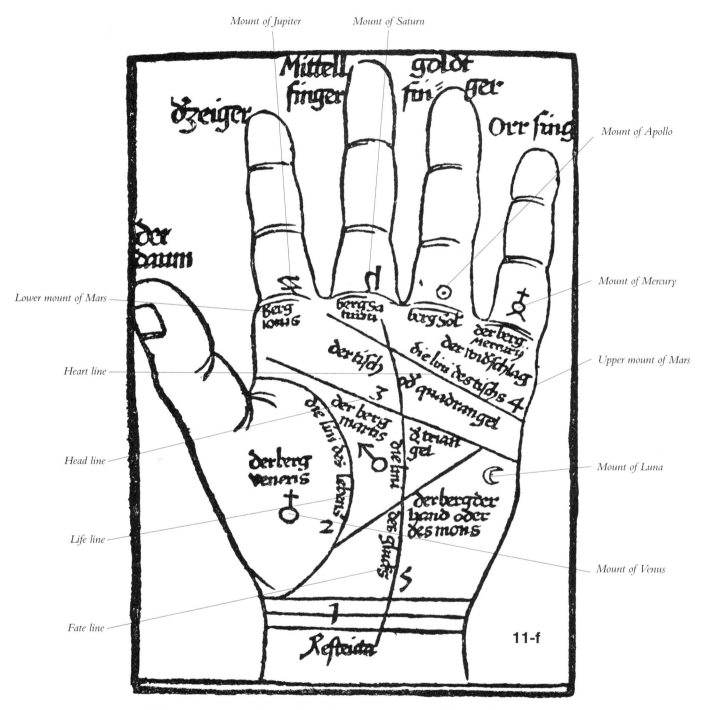

This sixteenth-century German illustration shows the location of lines and mounts on the palm, with corresponding glyphs from the zodiac

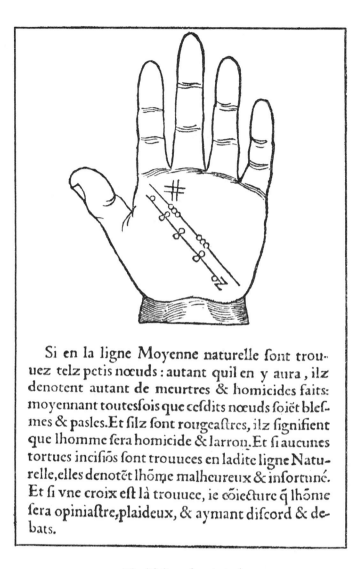

Si en la ligne Moyenne naturelle font trou-
uez telz petis nœuds : autant quil en y aura, ilz
denotent autant de meurtres & homicides faits:
moyennant toutesfois que cefdits nœuds foiët blef-
mes & pasles.Et filz font rougeaftres, ilz fignifient
que lhomme fera homicide & larron.Et fi aucunes
tortues incifiõs font trouuees en ladite ligne Naturelle,elles denotët lhõme malheureux & infortuné.
Et fi vne croix eft là trouuee, ie cõiecture q̃ lhõme
fera opiniaftre,plaideux, & aymant difcord & de-
bats.

The life line of a criminal

A chainlike heart line may signal a person who falls in love easily but fears commitment. Romantic upsets are suggested by short diagonal lines crossing the heart line; small
islands—points where the line splits in two, then merges once more—especially near the
Jupiter mount, could imply significant romantic disappointments, such as divorce.

• **Relationship Lines**   On the outer edge of the hand, between the heart line and the
base of the Mercury finger, one or more short, horizontal lines may be found. Called
relationship lines, they supposedly indicate important commitments. The lines can
signify deep friendships as well as intimate relationships. The stronger the line, it is said,
the more potential for the union.

Lines denoting current or past relationships are usually indelibly etched in the

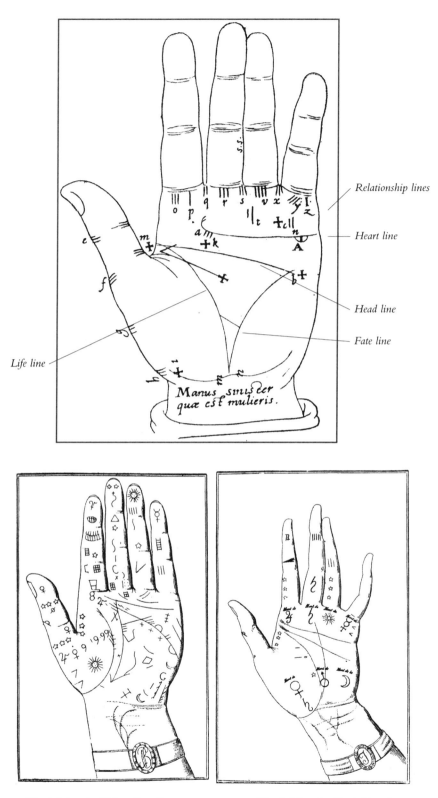

Relationship lines

Heart line

Head line

Fate line

Life line

Manus sinister quæ est mulieris.

LEFT: *The left hand of Napoléon Bonaparte*   RIGHT: *The left hand of Joséphine Bonaparte*

A Bohemian predicts good fortune in this seventeenth-century French engraving

palm, but those signaling future ones may change periodically. A line may become clearer to show deeper feelings, or new lines may appear. To estimate the age at which a relationship may occur, note the line's position between the heart line and the base of the Mercury finger; a point about midway may mean age thirty-five.

• **Life Line** An indicator of disposition, physical energy, and well-being, the life line usually originates between the mounts of Jupiter and lower Mars and follows the curve of the mount of Venus. A broad arc around the Venus mount is thought to indicate a warm and emotionally responsive nature; a shallow arc, cutting into the mount, suggests an aloof, inhibited, or unresponsive individual. If the life line ends curving toward the Venus mount, the individual is said to be domestic, drawn to the comforts of home. A line curving toward the mount of Luna suggests a restless personality, one who loves adventure and travel.

The life line itself, if deep and clear, denotes a strong physical constitution, good health, and vitality. Any islands may signal periods of ill health or indecision. Breaks in the line are sometimes interpreted as an illness or accident or as a change in the individual's life-style.

While the length of the life line has often been used to predict a time of death, reputable palmists believe such predictions are virtually impossible—and irresponsible—to make. The line shows tendencies, they say, not facts, and the length of the life line is no guarantee against life's uncertainties.

- **Fate Line**   Also known as the career or destiny line, this line reveals an individual's level of satisfaction with a profession or other chosen task. Ideally, the fate line begins just above the wrist and moves upward toward the mount of Saturn. Generally, the higher in the palm the fate line begins, the later in life the person will find his or her true vocation.

If the fate line originates in the mount of Luna, it portends a career that depends on the decisions of other people—as in politics, for example—or the potential may exist for a number of careers and possible relocation. If the line arises from the mount of Venus, the family may play a part in the individual's profession.

The more content an individual is with his or her chosen path, the clearer the fate line may be: a weak, fragmented line may reveal a person who feels restless or unfulfilled. Breaks in the fate line are interpreted as a hiatus in one's career or a change of direction, and islands may reveal a temporary obstacle in the path. An additional vertical line running close to the fate line may suggest a second career or strong avocational interest.

A person will remain active throughout life, it is thought, if he or she possesses a long fate line. If the line comes to a stop at the heart line, however, the individual's ambition could be thwarted by emotions; if the line ends at the top of the head line, his or her success may be stymied by some sort of intellectual blunder.

Tarot, Talismans, and Runes

The Tarot

WITH THE complex, controversial, and abstruse Tarot, certainties are elusive. Nevertheless, it is generally agreed among believers that the cards have a dual significance: They are at once mystical and divinatory.

Their supposed occult nature rests primarily with the twenty-two cards of the Major Arcana, or Trumps Major. These are regarded widely as allegories for the soul's journey from ignorance to enlightenment, or the human sojourn through life, or as mystical keys to the secrets of the universe and the place of humans therein. For thousands who believe in its power, the Tarot also evaluates the past, elucidates the

present, and predicts the future. Both the Major Arcana and the fifty-six-card Minor Arcana—which is divided into suits of Wands, Cups, Swords, and Pentacles—are used in divinatory readings. Some say the cards tap the psychic awareness of the reader, the inquirer, or both. Others contend the cards carry their own meanings, intrinsic and absolute.

But what meanings? Hundreds of different Tarots are used today, and interpretations of cards may vary from deck to deck and from reader to reader. Each reader—and each inquirer—brings his or her own imprint to the cards. Moreover,

The Pope	*The Lovers*	*The Chariot*	*The Scales of Justice*

perceived meanings can be altered by the cards' positions relative to each other and by whether a card falls upright or inverted. With the Tarot, nothing is simple. Mastering all possible meanings of all cards as they appear in various decks is an arduous job, but it falls short of preparing a would-be Tarot reader to practice cartomancy. The next step is deciding which cards in the deck should be used and how they should be laid out. Some employ all seventy-eight cards, others only the Major Arcana. In either case, the cards may be arranged in any number of configurations—most commonly, the three-card spread, the seven-card spread, and the ten-card spread.

In general, divination with the Major Arcana is said to reveal one's spiritual condition and potential, while the Minor Arcana cards deal with more mundane realities: occupation, social position, domestic situation. Many see the Major Arcana as the soul's map in its quest for self-awareness and integration into the cosmic whole. The cards are tools, and diligent meditation on them can unlock mystic truths.

Hermit or Wise One	*Strength*	*Temperance*	*The Devil*	*The House of God*

The Stars	*The Sun*	*Judgment*	*The World*	*The High Priest*

King of Wands

Queen of Swords

Knight of Cups

Ten of Wealth

Jack of Wealth

Ten of Wands

Pope Joan

The Empress

The Emperor

The Power of Talismans

IN HOPES of swaying Fortune, medieval Europeans commissioned engraved, coin-shaped objects called talismans. Such charms, carried in a pouch, were thought

Star of David talismans

to attract favorable influences. Most Western talismans reflect the tradition of the Cabala, the mystical body of ancient Hebrew wisdom that holds that all things in creation are related to one another through a network of correspondences. By incorporating special symbols, inscriptions, or materials associated with a planetary or spiritual power, a talisman is supposedly imbued with like power, which can then be wielded by the charm's owner.

The seven heavenly bodies regarded by the ancients as planets are thought to influence a particular area of human life. Thus each talisman is designed to express the power of Saturn, Jupiter, Mars, Venus, Mercury, the Sun, or the Moon. To strengthen the bond between talisman and planetary force, charm makers use mystical symbols and pay heed to such traditional beliefs as the metal, color, and day of the week said to correspond to the planet.

Each planet is also associated with one of seven archangels and with a benevo-

Sigil charm to protect wearer from danger

lent spirit, called the Intelligence. On a talisman, these names supposedly invoke divine assistance. Every planet has a so-called magic square, or *kamea,* made up of rows of numbers. The sum of any row—vertical, horizontal, or diagonal—equals the same number, one sacred to that planet. Charm makers assign numerical values to letters, usually the Hebrew alphabet, to plot out names on the kameas with connecting lines whose diagrammatic forms are called *sigils.*

Some talismans feature other nonplanetary symbols and magical elements said to harness unearthly energies.

• **Saturn** Saturn is said to influence business and politics, property deals, agriculture, mining, archaeology, and the building trades. It also corresponds to morality and the shouldering of responsibilities. Some say that Saturn talismans protect women in childbirth and prevent death by poison or conspiracy.

Metal: Lead
Color: Black
Day of the Week: Saturday

Archangel: Zaphiel
Intelligence: Agiel

*For getting out
of prison*

*For resisting
evildoers*

*To counter sudden
death*

*To regain youth
and money*

*To discover
hidden treasures*

To regain memory

 • **Jupiter** Power, legal and commercial transactions, financial speculation and the acquisition of wealth, marriage and remarriage, education, religion, and philosophy are all associated with Jupiter. Additionally, Jupiter talismans may be used to protect travelers, foster friendships, preserve health, banish anxiety, and establish sympathy in others.

Metal: Tin
Color: Blue
Day of the Week: Thursday

Archangel: Zadkiel
Intelligence: Yophiel

 • **Mars** The planet Mars is thought to influence police matters, war, sports, engineering, machinery, and male sexuality. It is also said to favor surgical undertakings as well as development of physical strength and courage. A Mars talisman is believed not only to protect its owner from enemies but even to help overthrow them.

Metal: Iron
Color: Red
Day of the Week: Tuesday

Archangel: Camael
Intelligence: Graphiel

• **The Sun** The Sun is associated with nobility, leadership, career advancement, large commercial ventures or business undertakings, the judiciary, banking, fatherhood, and the performing arts. It is thought to promote self-confidence, health, virility, friendship, and powers of divination and to help dissolve hostile feelings.

Metal: Gold
Color: Gold
Day of the Week: Sunday

Archangel: Raphael
Intelligence: Nakhiel

• **Venus** Under the dominion of Venus fall matters of love, courtship, and marriage. This planet is also said to influence personal and business partnerships, the negotiation of contracts or settlements, the visual arts, leisure pursuits, female sexuality, and an individual's income. Its powers allegedly protect women from cancer and all from poison.

Metal: Copper   *Archangel:* Aniel

Color: Green   *Intelligence:* Hagiel

Day of the Week: Friday

• **Mercury** Talismanic magic says Mercury governs road, rail, and air travel, commerce, healing, the media, mathematics, science, and industry. Intelligence and eloquence are also attributed to the planet, as is the power of prophecy. Some claim that a Mercury talisman will aid deceitful undertakings, such as theft.

Metal: Mercury or zinc   *Archangel:* Michael

Color: Purple   *Intelligence:* Tiriel

Day of the Week: Wednesday

• **The Moon** The Moon is said to correspond to all matters pertaining to water, including navigation, voyages, and maritime trade. This heavenly body is also thought to influence motherhood, fertility, children, the home, and other domestic issues. Those wishing to start new ventures or enhance their psychic powers may benefit from a lunar charm.

Metal: Silver   *Archangel:* Gabriel

Color: Silver   *Intelligence:* Malka Betharshesim

Day of the Week: Monday

Formed by two interlocking triangles, the hexagram is associated with divine order and destiny. The symbol is believed to protect against fire, deadly weapons, and the perils of travel. The hexagram is best known for its use as the Jewish Star of David—in Hebrew, Magen David, or David's Shield.

The circle, one of the most powerful of all occult symbols, represents infinity, eternity, unity, the universe, the Sun, heaven, and perfection. Inscribed on most talismans, the circle serves to contain and concentrate the magical energy necessary to summon the appropriate powers or spirits.

An embodiment of the number three, the triangle relates to body, soul, and spirit; father, mother, and child; past, present, and future; wisdom, love, and truth. In Christian doctrine, the triangle represents the Holy Trinity of the Father, Son, and Holy Ghost.

```
ABRACADABRA              ABRACADABRA
ABRACADABR               ABRACADABR
ABRACADAB                ABRACADAB
ABRACADA                 ABRACADA
ABRACAD                  ABRACAD
ABRACA    ABRACADABRA    ABRACA
ABRAC     BRACADABR      ABRAC
ABRA      RACADAB        ABRA
ABR       ACADA          ABR
AB        CAD            AB
A         A              A
```

• The magic word abracadabra, whose meaning remains mysterious, is sometimes the sole element of a talisman. It is thought to bring good luck as well as to effect healing. As part of what is called a diminishing spell, the word is written repeatedly, with each successive line dropping a letter to form an inverted triangle. The charm will supposedly diminish the wearer's illness at the same rate the word abracadabra dwindles.

• Magic squares in which letters spell out the same words vertically and horizontally are often found on talismans. Best known is the enigmatic SATOR square, which dates to Roman times and is still used for protective magic. The ROLOR talisman created by a fifteenth-century magician purportedly enables the wearer to fly like a crow.

```
S A T O R          R O L O R
A R E P O          O B U F O
T E N E T          L U A U L
O P E R A          O F U B O
R O T A S          R O L O R
```

• AGLA   These letters are an acronym for **Ate Gebir Lellam Adonai**, Hebrew for "Thou art mighty forever, O Lord." They invoke God's name and allegedly infuse a charm with divine power. In the Middle Ages, AGLA was used to ward off fever.

The pentagram symbolizes the human body, with its five points corresponding to the head, arms, and legs. With one point upward, the shape is also associated with God and is used to invoke the powers of goodness. When inverted, with its single point downward, it represents the forces of evil.

Perhaps the oldest talismanic symbol in the world, the cross is an emblem of prosperity, life, and divine protection from evil. Some believe it represents the four quarters of heaven and can thus invoke heavenly powers. Christians associate it with eternal life and resurrection.

*A Druid
wheel cross*

Since long before its association with Nazi Germany, the swastika has been a worldwide symbol of longevity, good luck, and happiness, and followers of magic use it to attract those qualities. The ancient symbol also represents the four winds, the four seasons, and the four directions of the compass.

Anyone creating a personal talisman must first decide what purpose the charm is to serve—to help further one's career, for instance, or enhance athletic abilities. Once the goal is fixed, the planet thought to influence that sphere of life can be determined and the undertaking can begin.

A beetle scarab

The charm maker starts by engraving a circle on a section of metal corresponding to the planet—or simply by drawing a circle on a piece or appropriately colored paper or parchment. The next step is to inscribe—on either side or both—any of the symbols associated with the targeted planet. The talisman creator can then add any shapes, words, names, or verses that exemplify the forces the charm is intended to invoke. Although Hebrew is the traditional talismanic script, any language may be used.

Once the talisman is complete, adepts say, it must be purified to remove any unwanted energies. Metal talismans may be passed through fire, although bathing them in clear water is said to be just as effective. Paper talismans may be held up to the wind or passed over smoking incense. Next, according to tradition, the talisman must be consecrated to charge it with magical powers. This ceremony should take place on the day of the week related to the planet, believers say, but otherwise may be tailored to personal taste. It can be performed nude or clothed, indoors or outdoors, by candlelight or moonlight, say adepts—as long as the consecrators do something out of the ordinary and speak their intent aloud.

After consecration, the charm is supposedly ready to work its magic. Talismans are usually stored or worn about the neck in a silk pouch, the color of which should relate to the planet invoked.

Runes

MORE THAN 2,000 years ago in the cold, rugged lands of Scandinavia, shamans seized evanescent, magical ideas and gave them form in symbols they called runes. These sticklike characters, scratched onto pebbles and bits of wood, functioned as talismans and implements for divination, protecting and guiding those who sought their wisdom.

Legend holds that the runic mysteries were first revealed to Odin, the supreme deity of the Norse pantheon. God of magic and learning, he quested eternally for greater knowledge, even giving up one of his eyes to drink from a spring of wisdom. To acquire the secrets of the runes, he made the greatest sacrifice of all: Mortally wounding himself with a spear, he hung by his feet from a windblown tree for nine days and nights. As the moment of death approached, eighteen runes appeared to him. Giving a shout, he seized them, only to then expire. But Odin was resurrected, it is said, to share the secrets of the runes.

The original runic symbols developed into the letters of the earliest Germanic alphabet, known as the Elder Futhark. Even when put to this practical use, the markings retained their old occult meanings. The word "rune" derives from the Old Norse term for secret, and runes were ubiquitous during the Viking era as tokens of magical power. People covered their homes with the symbols to ward off evil; warriors engraved them on the hilts of their swords, hoping for strength in battle; midwives scratched them on the palms of women in childbirth to ensure safe delivery; and shamans used them to commune with the dead, to cast spells, and even, reportedly, to fly. Itinerant priests and priestesses wandered from town to town reading the future in the symbols etched in wood. At villagers' requests, the seers would cast their pieces onto white cloths, then interpret them according to well-established rules.

Use of the runes waned as Christianity spread through northern Europe. Only in the early twentieth century did German mystics and magicians revive the custom. Today, rune priests believe that the symbols function as an oracle, interacting with those who seek their counsel on an unconscious level to clarify situations and divulge options. Many people give runes a place alongside such favored divination systems as the I Ching and the Tarot. In fact, some students of magic posit that the Major Arcana of the Tarot had it origins in runic magic.

Runes can be purchased in specialty shops that carry the paraphernalia of magic. But modern rune priests tend to recommend that you make your own; they believe that the process bonds you to the runes and thus leads to more meaningful readings. A variety of materials can be used in creating runes. The symbols can be carved into chips of wood (yew, ash, and oak were sacred to the Nordic priests) or etched onto pebbles, chips of quartz crystal, bones, seashells, or ceramic tiles. Runes can also be painted on paper or cardboard. Ancient rune priests used blood in applying the markings, but any natural pigment will suffice.

Once you have a set of runes, there are various ways to consult them. Usually, the pieces are kept in a suede or leather pouch, from which some or all of the runes may be drawn for interpretation.

The manner in which runes are cast depends in part on the needs of the inquirer. For example, someone seeking quick insights into his or her current situation might choose to interpret a single rune selected from the set at random. On the other hand, someone who needs a more detailed assessment might toss the entire set and interpret all the runes that land face up.

Fehu   Fehu, the first rune, is a powerful symbol of bounty. Depicting the horns of cattle or oxen, the rune originally represented material wealth in the form of livestock. It may also have signified the plow and fertility of the fields. Today, Fehu indicates prosperity of any kind, material or spiritual. As a rune of fertility, it may also suggest an actual or symbolic birth.

Uruz   An ideogram for the aurochs—a large, long-horned wild ox that is now extinct—Uruz represents the strength and freedom of that animal and symbolizes creative power, sexual energy, and physical health. When Uruz appears in a reading, it counsels the inquirer to think about harnessing his or her energies in the interest of per-sonal growth.

Thurisaz   Thurisaz represents a thorn and bears painful messages, warning of cruelty, deceit, or a rude awakening to a previously hidden truth. Associated with Thor, god of thunder and lightning, this rune symbolizes cathartic destruction. But while it predicts unhappiness to come, Thurisaz also indicates that the way is clear for new beginnings.

 Ansuz   Most mystical of all the symbols in the Elder Futhark, Ansuz represents the mouth of the wise god Odin, discoverer of the runes. It marks the link between Odin and modern rune magicians, signifying truth, verbal expression, and clarification. Inquirers who draw Ansuz should take heed: An important message may be forthcoming.

Raidho   Raidho is the rune of travel. It originally represented a chariot, signifying the path of the initiate as he or she climbed to higher levels of magical knowledge and experience. Today, Raidho indicates a physical or spiritual journey or quest. Drawing this rune suggests that the inquirer is moving toward the realization of a goal.

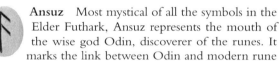 **Kenaz**   Fiery passions may be in store when the inquirer selects Kenaz, the flame of a torch. Associated with Freya, the Norse goddess of love, this rune represents the positive aspects of human passion and sexual love. It also indicates creativity and generation on a physical level. As the torch, Kenaz offers illumination, lighting the way through darkness.

 Gebo   Gebo, meaning gift, traditionally pertained to the gifts of the gods, one of which was rune magic. Modern interpretations of this rune include gifts of any sort, even selfless actions. Gebo's intersecting lines also indicate union or partnership, possibly of a sexual or magical nature.

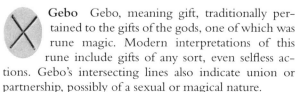

 Wunjo   Joy is predicted when the rune Wunjo is drawn. It suggests happiness and harmony among people and delight in one's accomplishments. A symbol of restoration, Wunjo also promises clarification of things previously unclear and the opening of areas formerly blocked. The inquirer who draws Wunjo may expect changes for the better.

Hagalaz   In opposition to Wunjo is Hagalaz, or hail. In its icy storm, the inquirer may suffer setbacks and hardship. However, change and liberation are part of its message: If current upheavals are handled wisely, they will lead to a brighter future. Symbolizing the Nordic concept of a cosmic ice egg filled with magical power, Hagalaz promises joy and warmth, but only after a thaw.

Naudhiz   This symbol represent human struggle in the face of adversity. Naudhiz, meaning need, indicates an overwhelming compulsion to achieve something. The inquirer who draws the rune is invited to examine his or her motivations and to separate true needs from desires. Trust fate, Naudhiz counsels, for it will ultimately guide you to what you need.

 Isa   Isa, or ice, represents life in stasis, where change and growth are absent. The symbol, a single line, suggests the individual ego, coldly separate from others; it also denotes the sustaining force during times of stress. Thus the ice rune urges the inquirer to consider areas of his or her life that may be frozen and suggests reliance on inner strength in struggling free.

 Jera   Jera means "the year" and its symmetrical symbol suggests the seasons' cycle. This rune offers the inquirer a waiting period, allowing time in which growth may occur naturally. Cyclic development, natural fruition, and the passage of time are watchwords for Jera.

 Iwaz   Sacred because it symbolizes the yew tree from which Odin hung to capture the runes, Iwaz signals the traits inherent in that evergreen. A hardy, long-lived conifer, the yew protects against evil, according to Scandinavian legend. Drawing Iwaz assures the inquirer continued growth even in the face of adversity.

 Perthro   Perthro depicts a dice cup, contributing an element of chance to the runes. It relates to the Old Norse concept of ørlög, the layers of past action—either individual or cosmic—that shape the present. The inquirer is challenged to accept the fact that in certain areas fate controls all.

Elhaz The symbol for Elhaz is a stylized hand with the fingers splayed, a universal symbol of protection. The inquirer who draws Elhaz will be blessed during tribulation and will face temptation without succumbing. This rune also forms a bridge between human consciousness and the divine, alerting the inquirer to prepare for enlightenment.

Sowilo Sowilo, the sun, counters the freeze of the ice rune Isa. It predicts challenging periods of growth, embodying the inquirer's most difficult goal but also promising a path leading toward that objective. Sowilo foretells transformations that, like the sun's heat, can be extremely intense.

Tiwaz Rune of the Norse god Tyr, Tiwaz stands for his qualities of bravery, truth, and justice. According to myth, Tyr once sacrificed his own hand to the jaws of a wolf in order to save another god from destruction. Drawing this rune signifies that sacrifice and courage may now be required in the name of justice.

Berkano A stylized depiction of a woman's breasts, Berkano, or the birch goddess, is the runic symbol for the concept of mother earth. It relates to the cycles of life—birth, coming of age, marriage, and death—and promises the blessings of peace and fertility. Its association with the birch tree pertains to the inquirer's physical and spiritual environment.

Ehwo Ehwo, the two horses, symbolizes the means of reaching a physical or spiritual destination. Composed of two elements, the symbol speaks of the trust and loyalty shared by horse and rider and predicts the harmonious cooperation of two forces pursuing a single goal. The peaceful union of two people in an emotional relationship may also be foretold by Ehwo.

Mannaz Mannaz is the runic symbol for the self. One expert describes it as the mystery of the divine embodied in the individual. The power of human intelligence, rationality, and memory are highlighted here. Although it generally relates to a single person, Mannaz may also address a couple that functions as a single unit.

Laguz A rune of initiation, Laguz, the lake, signifies water. It was originally associated with the pagan baptism of newborns. The rune also suggests emotion, intuition, and dreams, and the inquirer who draws it should pay special attention to the messages of the unconscious mind.

Ingwaz Representing an old Germanic god who consorted with the earth mother, Ingwaz signifies fertility and gestation. It warns that adequate time—a gestation period—must be allowed in order for difficult tasks to be completed. At the end of such a period, however, the inquirer will emerge from this chrysalis of toil to experience deliverance.

Dagaz Dagaz is the day: a message of awakening, clarity, and transformation. It promises a short waiting period for the completion of a process. Dagaz has been described as the break of dawn, a mystical moment in which all opposites—darkness and light, pleasure and pain, life and death—can be expected to meld. The inquirer may await a revelation when it is drawn.

Othalo Othalo means ancestral property or homeland and relates alternatively to the inquirer's family or to his or her spiritual or professional heritage. Othalo encourages the inquirer to examine the ways in which his or her roots inform the present; the rune also recommends evaluation of the beliefs and habits learned from one's elders.

Wyrd Wyrd, the blank rune, is not part of the Elder Futhark, but it is often included in purchased rune sets. Similar in meaning to Perthro, Wyrd stands for fate and mystery. When drawn in a reading, it represents an unattainable quantity, reminding the inquirer that some knowledge is beyond reach and must remain forever a mystery.

Numerology

IN THE ancient practice of numerology, a person's birth chart consists of four basic numbers—three drawn from the name given at birth and one from the birth date. Numerologists analyze these numbers to discover clues about the individual's character, destiny, and life cycles. A personal chart reading, similar to those performed by professionals, can be done by simply calculating these four numbers and checking the following capsule descriptions. Although people are the usual subjects, the process can be applied to anything that has a name and date of birth or origin—a cat, a business, a nation, or even an idea.

The first step in this intriguing exercise is to translate the name into its numerical equivalent, using the number-letter conversion table shown below. Each letter is assigned a single-digit number based on its sequential place in the alphabet: The letters A through I are numbered one through nine, and the remaining letters are reduced to one of those digits through simple addition. For example, J as the tenth letter reduces to a one (10=1+0=1), and U as the twenty-first letter reduces to a three (21=2+1=3).

The three birth-name numbers are determined by adding the numerical values of three different sets of letters in the name: first, all the vowels that occur; then, all the consonants; and finally, the total of all the letters. The numerical total of the vowels—*a, e, i, o,* and *u*—in the name is called the Soul Number. This is thought to

1	2	3	4	5	6	7	8	9
A	B	C	D	E	F	G	H	I
J	K	L	M	N	O	P	Q	R
S	T	U	V	W	X	Y	Z	

reflect the person's true inner self, encompassing ambitions and motivations, judgment and attitudes, and feelings. The total of the consonants, on the other hand, produces the Outer Personality Number, which relates to physical appearance, health, and the impression the person makes on others through dress and behavior.

The total of the entire birth name is known as the Path of Destiny Number. It indicates the sum of the individual's capabilities and achievements and how he or she will affect others. The Path of Destiny Number also influences the course a person will take to attain career goals—whether the career involves raising a family or running a corporation—and describes the types of people who will be encountered along the way.

Numerologists believe that although the birth name remains the foundation of nature and destiny throughout life, a name change can dramatically alter the mix of letters and numbers and thus expand the person's experiences, attitudes, and role in society. A woman who changes her last name at marriage, for example, may become more adaptable and flexible in her new circumstances because she is taking on a new set of numbers that will be used along with her birth name. Numerology points to a shift in personal numbers as a factor in such transformations. Similarly, movie stars and writers may take on new public identities—and private personalities—through name changes they hope will provide a certain image. Archibald Leach and Joyce Frankenburg certainly have a different ring from Cary Grant and Jane Seymour, the stage names these two performers chose.

Although a person's name may change over the course of a lifetime, the birth date is constant. And it is the sum of numbers in this date that produces the fourth and most important number in a numerology chart—the Life Lesson Number. This number reveals the lessons and truths a person is meant to learn during his lifetime; it signals the essential purpose of his existence.

The Life Lesson Number is obtained by writing the birth date in numbers and totaling them until they reduce to a single digit. If your birth date is November 4, 1947, for example, you would figure your Life Lesson Number by writing the date as 11-4-1947—making sure to use the full year, not the abbreviation '47—and then adding the digits until they reduce to a nine ($1+1+4+1+9+4+7=27=2+7=9$).

The birth-date number is also the key to interpreting what numerologists call "personal-year cycles"—a set of reigning patterns and influences such as assertiveness, harmony, security, resignation, and the like. These patterns are said to be set in motion on the day a person is born and continue in nine-year cycles for as long as he or she lives. The personal-year cycle explains where energy should be focused during any given twelve-month period—a kind of psychic homework assignment for the year.

A simple method of determining the current personal-year cycle is to go back to the person's last birthday and add the numbers in that date, as demonstrated above. The patterns associated with this number will prevail from the birthday up to the next birthday, and then the cycle will move forward one number; at the end of year nine in the cycle, the person begins again with year one.

Whatever Life Lesson Number is determined on the day of birth, that number is repeated in the person's ninth year—and every nine years thereafter. For this reason, the birth year and the ages of 9, 18, 27, 36, 45, 54, and so on are important years—periods when events occur that underscore the major theme of a person's life and remind him again of the lessons he is here to learn.

Once the four numbers in a personal birth chart are determined, the final step is to look up their interpretations. Each of the numerical descriptions that follow begins with the number's supposed essence, followed by its influence as a personal number in one of the four categories. If you are examining your Soul Number, for example, the definition describes your inner nature. If it is your Outer Personality Number, the description represents how others see you. If you are looking up your Path of Destiny Number, the influence applies to your career course. And if it is your Life Lesson Number, the definition suggests the lessons you need to learn. And finally, the personal-year cycle describes the prevailing pattern of events and attitudes for any year—past, present, or future.

• **Essence of One:** *Activation.* One is the seed, the beginning, when the life force is self-compelled to move out to explore and confront newness. It is original and individualistic because it is uninfluenced by previous experience. Because it does not know that things cannot be done, it proceeds with complete faith to do them. One is the pioneer, facing the unknown with an innocent courage. It draws upon its own creative well to solve any problems that arise.

Personal Number One: You are an extreme individualist and a self-motivator, and therefore feel comfortable following your own ideas and instincts. Your individuality is the drive behind your need for freedom and independence. You express leadership creatively and with originality. Not wanting to take a secondary position, you handle the entire operation and leave the details to others. You learn more from experience than from instruction and advice, which you dislike. Your ardent nature can cause swings in your emotional behavior. Yet the intensity of your focus, together with your courage and intelligence, make you a tower of inspiration in difficult times. You should avoid becoming arrogant, selfish, and stubborn.

Personal-Year-Cycle One: This is the beginning of a new nine-year cycle in your life. Major changes have occurred and you are still in the process of sorting them out physically and emotionally. You feel compelled to center on yourself, which may be a difficult mental transition if you have been trained to think of others first. However, your needs should come first now—the decisions you make during this cycle will influence your life for the next four to nine years. Even if there are people around you, you may feel isolated and alone. Do not let this be a concern, because your sense of separation allows you to make important decisions uninfluenced by others. People may offer advice, but you will not take it. You feel more independent, assertive, and willing to take chances. This is the year to express your individuality, to attempt those things you have only dreamed of to this point. One important person, attracted by your new attitude, may come into your life.

• **Essence of Two:** *Attraction.* In its dynamic advancement, One is attracted to another One, and they become Two. Two is the gestation period where the seed from One is collected and assimilated, and things begin to form. It is the mirror of illumination where knowledge comes from opposites: night and day, female and male. Two is the principle of marriage between two distinct entities.

Personal Number Two: You are a diplomat with a strong desire for peace and harmony. Since you are so strongly tuned in to the moods and feelings of others, you collect and assimilate their ideas, which can make it difficult for you to make decisions. You are so sensitive that you naturally interact with others gently while staying in the background and remaining unobtrusive. The subtle forces of nature stir you deeply; music and other soothing art forms fulfill your deep sense of rhythm and harmony. You have an expansive imagination that creates a magic mirror in which you can see every detail. Your cooperative and patient nature, along with your sincerity and your ability to see both sides of things, makes you the perfect partner. Avoid oversensitivity, indecision, and feelings of inferiority.

Personal-Year-Cycle Two: This year requires a calm, receptive attitude on your part. Because you have the ability to see opposing points of view now, you become the peacemaker or mediator. You become aware of the needs of others and are willing to settle any differences that may have arisen as a result of last year's assertiveness. You may find it hard to make decisions now, preferring to remain more in the background. This is a good period for partnerships because of your sensitivity. Marriage may occur during this cycle. Your subconscious is very active, so you should explore and develop your intuitive abilities. Flashes of insight and understanding will aid you in solving difficult situations. Sudden recognition is possible for some act or work you are presently doing or perhaps have long forgotten. Legal dealings, sales agreements, legacies, and claims may occur now. It is a curious year, when life flows along quietly—until sudden, exciting events occur that can require overnight decisions. Your motto this year should be: Expect the unexpected. And listen to your inner self. Creative magic lies waiting to be explored.

• **Essence of Three:** *Expansion.* The marriage of Two results in growth and unfoldment in Three. The most imaginative and creative of the numbers, Three is the mother-father-child. This family unit is symbolized by the triangle, known as the first perfect shape in mathematics—that is, the first closed plane that can be constructed with straight lines. The triangle represents the three-fold nature of divinity in most cultures.

Personal Number Three: You are an extremely expressive individual who can influence others with your ability to communicate in a flamboyant style. Somewhere there is a stage waiting for you. Whether you are speaking, writing, or acting, your bright, warm nature draws others who bask in your enthusiasm and energy. You are aware of appearance because performing depends upon the impression you make on others. You dream big, and your faith is often rewarded because positive thinking produces positive results. Because of your expansive nature, you meet people from different cultures and social strata, increasing your already broad and all-encompassing thinking. Do not scatter your energies, and avoid exaggeration, self-indulgence, and foolish optimism.

Personal-Year-Cycle Three: This is your year of activity, expansion, travel, and luck, You need room to move and express yourself, to experience life, freedom, and the joy of living. You may travel to another part of this land or to another country and meet people who enlarge your idea of the world. Some of the individuals you meet now can be important business contacts in the future. You are aware of your appearance and may indulge in a new wardrobe, hairstyle, or other beauty improvements. Since this is often called a lucky cycle, your one ticket may win the prize. But do not overindulge. Overexpansion leads to bankruptcy. If you use good judgment, however, this is a fertile cycle that could include the birth of a child, a creation of the mind, or an expansion of your bank account. In the midst of this social cycle, you will be invited to parties and functions where you suddenly become the center of attention. People respond to you positively, which feeds a growing feeling of well-being within you. You have more faith in yourself and your abilities.

• **Essence of Four:** *Security.* Four symbolizes the boundaries that provide security for the Three. As the square, the second perfect shape in mathematics, it suggests solid foundations and perimeters that contain and protect. The determined and conservative Four works hard to provide strong fences and square meals for the nourishment of the Three family.

Personal Number Four: You are practical, cautious, and reliable, the salt of the earth. You feel responsible for building solid foundations upon which the future depends. That is why you respect law and order. It also explains why your cupboard is never bare and you have something saved for that rainy day. You can be depended upon to be at the job every day and to finish any task assigned to you; you exemplify Khalil Gibran's line from *The Prophet,* "Work is love made visible." You take pride in your work because it is an expression of yourself. You are concerned with the land and need to be connected in some manner, through a garden, nature trips, or environmental issues. Financial matters are of concern to you as well; they are another expression of the worth of your talents. You should avoid stubbornness, overwork, and hoarding.

Personal-Year-Cycle Four: The emphasis this year is on work, order, budgeting, foundations, close physical relationships, the body. You have an urge to organize all areas of you life, so you begin cleaning the attic, cellar, closets, the garage, the office. This action is a symbolic gesture indicative of your subconscious need to build an orderly and strong foundation in your life. Material things become important now because they add to your sense of security and satisfy your heightened physical needs. You may purchase goods or property, or decide to build or remodel. Exercise good judgment and organize your funds carefully. Your body is a physical possession, and since you may have put on a few pounds last year, now is the time to bring out the sweat suits, the diet book, and the bathroom scales. Health can be a concern, so rest, eat well, exercise properly, and have a physical examination. This can be a money cycle, but funds that come in are in direct proportion to the amount of work you do. Work well and you will be rewarded.

- **Essence of Five:** *Experience.* Four, firmly entrenched in its home, now begins to explore the environment. The Five needs freedom and independence so that it can indulge its senses in the experiences of life. It has an insatiable curiosity through which it filters its encounters and ultimately makes choices that will influence its future.

Personal Number Five: You are a communicator. Impulsive and restless, you need the freedom to move freely through your life so that you can gather experience and information to feed your curiosity. You promote ideas and like change for the learning opportunity it provides. Mental stimulation is essential for your well-being. Your mind moves quickly, imitating and adapting to immediate influences so that you are able to blend in with any group. You can talk on most subjects with ease because of your vast experience, and you are a natural mimic, delighting others with your impish actions. Versatile and adaptable, you are the super salesperson and life of the party. You are efficient but dislike monotony and routine jobs. Because you have the power to communicate effectively, you should remain sincere and truthful.

Personal-Year-Cycle Five: You are restless and ready for change. Life suddenly becomes so busy that you feel as if you are on a merry-go-round, attending meetings and parties, running errands, answering mail and the telephone, and generally being available for others who suddenly need you. Communication is a key word this year. Get involved and meet people, because from these experiences you will gather the information you need to make important decisions that can affect your life for the next four years. If you are dissatisfied with your life, you can make changes more easily now. This is a turning point. Opportunities will arise in which you can find solutions to any current impasses. Because your mind is so active, this is a good time to take courses to satisfy your need for more experience. Your romantic desires increase, sending out magnetic waves that attract the opposite sex. Various love interests become possible. Your nervous system is in high gear, so avoid alcohol and drugs, and be careful of accidents. This is your year for fun and excitement, romantic encounters, decisions, and change.

- **Essence of Six:** *Harmony.* After tasting experience through its five senses, Six realizes the importance of love, compassion, and social responsibility. The home, built in the Four, must now be filled with love and meaningful relationships. Home also

5

6

becomes part of the community in which law and order are established to ensure social harmony.

Personal Number Six: You are an artistic individual whose sense of harmony may express itself in the home, the arts, or community service. You need and show love in your home, where family is all-important. Your sense of beauty may be evident in the way you decorate your home, or in crafts and cooking. Your innate ability to go right at the crux of the matter makes you the counselor to whom others go for answers to their problems as well as for the nurturing compassion you provide. If your profession is outside the home, you seek to bring harmonious order to the world through beautifying the environment, counseling, the arts, or through the legal system, which seeks balance in justice. You love people and are concerned, generous, and tolerant. Be careful to avoid becoming a recluse or a doormat for others, playing the martyr.

Personal-Year-Cycle Six: This is the nesting phase where the emphasis is on home and family. In the natural order of things, after last year's possible romantic encounters, marriage and the birth of children are possible. Even if this does not apply to you, your attention shifts to the domestic front, and changes occur, such as family members moving in or out, children going to school or marrying, relatives wanting financial or emotional support. Responsibility for the family increases. Because your sense of justice is heightened, people may tell you their problems and ask your advice. Court decisions that restore balance are possible. Beauty and harmony become important in your life, so you may redecorate your home, surround yourself with works of art, and enjoy attending museums or the ballet. Community projects can satisfy your social sensibilities now. And close relationships with your partner, family, and friends are possible if you extend love and compassion.

• **Essence of Seven:** *Analysis.* Now that the physical is taken care of, Seven goes within itself to contemplate its place in the universe. It begins to think and to analyze past experiences and present situations, and it wonders what lies ahead. Seven realizes that the skills it has developed must be perfected in preparation for the future. Seven is physical rest and mental work.

Personal Number Seven: You are a thinker and an idealist who thoroughly analyzes knowledge from many sources before accepting any premises. Noises and crowds disrupt your meditative nature; therefore, you spend time by yourself so your creative imagination can roam freely seeking perfection. Your intuitive abilities combined with your naturally analytic nature make you a prophet, able to anticipate future needs and events. You understand human nature and are not easily fooled by external appearances, and thus can make others uneasy. Because of your introspective demeanor, you are a puzzle to many. As a rule, you will not accept orthodox beliefs but will search for your own—although you may find these within the walls of conventional educational or spiritual institutions. Try to listen to other ideas and do not allow your naturally aloof manner to alienate you from those you love.

Personal-Year-Cycle Seven: It is time to rest. You feel more tired and less social than usual and want to be alone to think about where you have been, where you are now, where you are headed. You may spend time with one or two friends who complement your contemplative mood. This cycle says it is time to go within and think. You have to maintain your everyday routine to some extent, but do not push your affairs aggressively—if you persist in scurrying about in the outside world, you may become ill. You can set your material worries aside; the things you have been worrying about for the past six years will take care of themselves. Your mind is keenly alert, and you should perfect any skills that you have; they will be useful next year. But for now, study, read, and take courses in philosophy, religion, numerology, astrology, or other metaphysical subjects to help you understand your place in life. Your intuitions are keen, and dreams, visions, and telepathic experiences are all possible.

- **Essence of Eight:** Reward. The strength and skills gathered in the past seven numbers are now put to the test. Well grounded physically, emotionally, and mentally, the Eight reaches out into the world to establish its authority in positions of material power. The rewards for its past efforts come in equal proportion to the wisdom of past choices. This is the karmic period where Eight reaps what it has sown.

Personal Number Eight: You are the executive type in whichever sphere you move. Sensing your organizational and managerial abilities, people automatically look to you for leadership. You know the value of a dollar, so your sound fiscal judgment can place you in positions of financial management. By working hard and exercising discipline and caution, you can achieve positions of great power. You do not rely on luck; you depend upon your own resourcefulness and perseverance. You know no halfway measures; your ambition drives you to achieve success. You must accept responsibility and handle it fairly because your actions have obvious repercussions in the world around you. As a steward of material resources, you must handle them wisely and with respect. Scheming and ruthless actions and personal advancement without regard for others lead to defeat.

Personal-Year-Cycle Eight: This year you will get what you have earned. Pursue your career goals with confidence and determination, because now you will be noticed. If you have planned well, you will get that promotion, raise, or recognition. Honors, awards, and legacies are also possible. You are finding out how effective you are in the material world. It is a year of pressure and responsibility in career and in finances. Depending upon your past actions, the reins of power can be placed in your hands—and possibly large sums of money. Personal relationships are also intense. To fulfill the needs of this cycle—as opposed to your Five Cycle, where romantic activities were for the purpose of experience—your relationships now must embody respect and equality, the physical and the spiritual, body and mind. You can find wholeness here, but whatever this cycle presents to you, an examination of your behavior during the past seven cycles will reveal how you arrived at this point.

9

- **Essence of Nine:** *Release.* After experiencing the world of material power in the Eight, Nine now knows that physical things are transitory and must be returned to the giver. Having learned that life is cyclical, Nine gives back freely and without fear those things it has gained so that the universe will be richer. Nine is the humanitarian carrying the light of wisdom.

Personal Number Nine: You are the humanitarian who feels compassion and love for others regardless of social, economic, or racial barriers. Because you understand that you are part of a greater whole, you give generously of your time and resources. You seek wisdom rather than mere knowledge, desiring to make the world a more loving place in which to live. Because you belong to the universal family, you know that you have to live impersonally and let go of things when it is time. People are drawn to you because of your tolerance, inner wisdom, and breadth of vision, which is often prophetic. You must live your own philosophy because you are an example for others. The necessities of life may come easily so that you are free to follow your humanitarian impulses. Avoid self-serving interests, which can only lead to a lack of faith in life's bounty.

Personal-Year-Cycle Nine: This is the final year in your nine-year cycle, a cleansing period in which those things no longer necessary in your life must be discarded to make room for a new round of experience in next year's Personal-Year-Cycle One. Major changes occur now. People may leave your life, you may change jobs or have to relocate, and things you have grown used to may have to be given up. Your attitude changes dramatically. Use some of your energy in charitable deeds. Give back to life some of what you have been given so that you can experience firsthand the joy of giving. These acts are integral to the transition process. Old friendships become especially meaningful now; new ones can develop. You may receive gifts for your past efforts. Many goals have been accomplished, and you should tie up loose ends. The past eight years have added to your pool of wisdom. Sprinkle others with your sympathy, compassion, and understanding, and be open to the cleansing wash of change. An exciting new year lies ahead, beginning with your next birthday.

12
ASTROLOGY

Sun Signs

BECAUSE OF its life-giving quality, the sun is believed by astrologers to be the heavens' most powerful predictor of character. Thus the sun sign—determined by the sun's place in the zodiac at the time of one's birth—is the astrological designation almost everyone knows. Many people see their characters perfectly delineated in traits ascribed to their sun signs. Perhaps this is so because astrology expresses some mythic truth. Or it could result from the ease of fitting one's personality into the vague, elastic terms of most astrological language.

Aries ♈

MARCH 21—APRIL 20

ASTROLOGERS LIKEN those born under Aries to the season of spring itself, a time of awakening, emergence, shedding of restraints, impulses toward life. Arians are vital, instinctual, and young—the zodiac's perpetual children, youths in search of identity. As such, Rams are likely to be joyful, dynamic, assertive, outspoken, and brave. They celebrate life. On the other hand, they may also be intolerant, impatient, impulsive, and overemotional, deficient in the capacity for self-reflection and concentration, and inclined toward taking impulsive and ill-considered risks. Enormous energy is Arians' great gift. Channeling it outward, past self-absorption and toward enlivening the world around them, is the great challenge confronting Rams.

Arians hate constraint, boredom, apathy, and ambiguity. Nuance escapes them; shades of gray confound them. They are most comfortable with emphatic contrasts—black and white, yes and no, good and bad. Subtlety is foreign to their natures. Confrontational, provocative, and at times even outrageous, they delight in testing limits and breaking rules. They despise pretense in others; if it exists in themselves, they simply fail to recognize it. They tend to prompt conflict and to revel in it, but their fights are usually over principle and their roles are heroic. Arians are the zodiac's warriors. Wary of joining groups and following leaders, they are also quintessential individualists, and they care deeply for individual rights. Astrologers deem it no accident that the Declaration of Independence was written by an Arian, Thomas Jefferson.

The symbol of the Ram is as metaphorically significant as its season, spring. It is the way of Aries to butt its way forward, scornful of obstacles, careless of consequences. The raw, erratic force of Arians can be destructive, and it is the task of those born under the sign of the Ram to direct their power toward mature and constructive ends.

Taurus ♉

APRIL 21—MAY 20

IN THE fullness of spring, the inchoate energy of Aries resolves into the orderly pursuits of Taurus, the Bull. Taureans are as prudent and tenacious as Arians are careless and flighty. Methodical and faithful, even ponderous, Taureans peacefully tend and nurture spring's garden, bringing forth harmony from chaos. The glyph, or picture-word, symbolizing Taurus represents not only the Bull's head, but the womb—Mother Earth, spring's fecundity, sexuality in the service of procreation.

Taureans are the zodiac's sensualists. They revel in tastes, textures, colors, aromas, sounds. They love good food, comfortable living, aesthetic pleasures. All beauty delights them. But in a deeper sense, their sensuality brings them into close attunement with nature itself. They appreciate its loveliness; they are the wise stewards of

Astrologers draw a birth chart in this sixteenth-century illustration from Utriusque Cosmi Historia

its maternal beneficence. Astrologers believe Taureans were born to value, learn from, and care for the physical world—that they are materialists in the very best sense of the word.

But there is a negative side to Taureans' materialism. They may be possessive, controlling, and overconcerned with money, security, creature comforts, and convenience; they may even be prone to ostentation and avarice. In matters of the heart, they sometimes treat their partners as personal property, and they are capable of fierce jealousy and even violent anger. Depending on certain aspects of Taureans' astrological charts, they may be melancholy by nature, world-weary, brooding, and pessimistic, or they may be hedonistic and inclined to exaggerated extroversion and a lack of self-control. These unattractive traits are apt to come to the fore, however, only when Taureans confuse stewardship with ownership.

Astrology holds that plodding Taureans lack agility and liveliness of mind. They are said to be bullheaded and fixed in their ways. But their slow and burdened mental gait should never be mistaken for stupidity. Unlike Arians, Taureans think things through. The sign of the Bull has produced some of the world's most profound thinkers, among them Karl Marx and Vladimir Ilyich Lenin, Immanuel Kant, Søren Kierkegaard, and Sigmund Freud.

Gemini ♊
MAY 21–JUNE 21

AFTER THE heaviness of Taurus comes the airy agility of Gemini, the Twins. Taureans are bound to the earth, but Geminis soar in the ether of abstractions, ideas, and—most of all—words. The Twins are the zodiac's wordsmiths, the lovers of language, the poets and bards, the verbal magicians. In the zodiacal quadrant where

Astronomer Tycho Brahé in his observatory, in 1587

Gemini falls, Aries initiates life's energy, and Taurus gives it solidity and form. The Twins expand it, extend it, and turn it toward interconnection and communication.

Gemini, ruled by the planet Mercury, weds a silver tongue to a quicksilver temperament. Twins crave experience, variety, mobility, change, company, banter, and intellectual play. They are endlessly curious and experimental. They loathe routine and fear stagnation. They can, and usually do, express cogent opinions on almost any subject, although their knowledge is apt to be superficial. Mentally quick, they nonetheless often lack the Taureans' capacity for deep, productive, singly focused thought. Befitting their sign, the Twins are skilled at seeing two sides, or all of the possible sides, of any question.

In love they are dubious partners, characteristically flighty and inclined to be overly intellectual, clinical, and cold. It is the Twins' bane that once they find their wider world they may feel achingly alone in it, despite their apparent extroversion. Given their charm, ready wit, and facility with words, they can easily present themselves as capable and confident. Only those closest to them are likely to see the insecurity that their confidence masks.

They are often actors, in life as well as by profession. They like to experiment with roles, discarding them as the glamour wears thin or new possibilities beckon. The advantage of this characteristic is that Geminis usually stay young in spirit throughout their lives. Ironically, they often come into their own in their middle years, when they have learned to distill what is important from what is merely idly charming. Until they reach this point, they must struggle with the sign's particular demon: all talk, no action. Thus the chore of Geminis is to learn perseverance and cultivate depth. They must aspire to substance as well as style. They must take themselves, and their words, seriously.

Cancer ♋

JUNE 22–JULY 22

WITH THE coming of the summer solstice, unfettered Gemini is drawn downward by the tidal pull of Cancer, the Crab. Cancer's ruling planet is the moon, linked in astrology to nature, gestation, motherhood, and the creation and preservation of life. Cancer represents the passive but profoundly powerful female force in nature—the all-nourishing, or all-devouring, mother. The Crab symbolizes the sea, cradle of all life.

Where Geminis are expansive, Cancerians are family centered, tradition bound, tied to the past, fearful of the future and the unknown. Security is one of their major goals. While Geminis laugh at life, Cancerians tend toward melancholy and introversion; they find the real world threatening and like to retreat into dreams and fantasies and to shelter themselves in the relative safety of the past.

Memory is one of Cancerians' special gifts. The taste and smell of certain biscuits were enough to call up the whole fictional world that Cancerian Marcel Proust created in *Remembrance of Things Past*. Cancerians love all things old and are wonderfully retentive; thus they make fine historians.

The symbol of the Crab is highly emblematic of Cancerian nature. Metaphorically, Cancerians have a hard outer shell and a soft interior. They need to feel safe if they are to put aside their brittle exteriors and expose their considerable vulnerabilities. They risk little and flinch easily. They are wary, defensive, and quick to withdraw into their shells. Like the crab, they approach the world obliquely, sideways. They tend to be exclusive in their social contacts; at the same time, they are particularly touchy about being excluded by others. And they never forget a slight: Cancerians keep score. They expect their kindnesses to be returned. If they are disappointed, they become withdrawn and hostile. It is then that the Crabs' pincers come into play, nipping at the vulnerabilities they sense in others.

At their best, Cancerians of both sexes are among the most loving of people, profoundly intuitive, and quick to grasp and respond to the emotional needs of others. They inspire and nurture growth—of children, animals, plants, projects, homes, ideas, cultures.It is Cancerians' task to find the safe haven in which their sign's exquisite sensitivity can bloom and flourish.

Leo ♌
JULY 23–AUGUST 22

AT THE height of summer's fullness, there springs from the nurturing cradle of Cancer majestic and fiery Leo, the Lion—producer, director, and star of life's drama. In Leo's passionate theater, pageantry, ceremony, and celebration are the order of the day. The spotlight is the Lions' birthright and applause their due. They live to perform and to create on the grand scale. But they have a dilemma: How do they differentiate between creating high art and merely living high melodrama?

For young Leos, the play's the thing. They want to experience everything—or at least to imply that they have. They need a watchful audience to feed their craving for constant attention and admiration. More mature Leos come to value their creativity enough not to squander it in vain displays or emotionally exhausting scenes. They learn that they are not only the actors, but the playwrights as well, with a responsibility to direct their theatrics into productive roles.

Leos are both impulsive and emphatic. They are at home with absolutes, edicts, and flamboyant proclamations. They tend to construct rather overdrawn personal dramas around the issue of authority. They are quick to confront and challenge a power figure, yet they are wholly amazed if they suffer wounds in the ensuing fray. Metaphorically, Leos struggle to emerge from the mothering domination of Cancer; at the same time, they are apt to retreat to the authority figure for reassurance when the world proves too harsh. However cocky in their headlong assaults on life, Leos

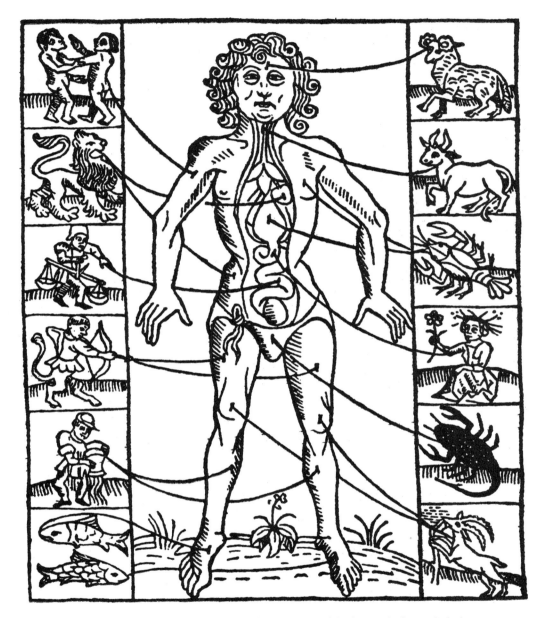

Many Renaissance physicians believed that each part of the human body was linked to the zodiac. This fifteenth-century French illustration shows the correlation of each astrological sign to a part of the human body.

sometimes feel that only a parent can fully appreciate their brilliance or soothe their injured pride. As assertive as Arians and as clever as Geminis, Leos, like Cancerians, enjoy building. But where Crabs seek an edifice for security, Lions want a monument, a material testament to their greatness, their uniqueness, and their majesty. Larger-than-life historical figures abound under the sign: Napoléon Bonaparte, T. E. Lawrence ("of Arabia"), Fidel Castro, Benito Mussolini, Mata Hari. Lions are also industrial leaders, literary masters, and pacesetters of style: Henry Ford, George Bernard Shaw, Carl Jung, Aldous Huxley, Robert Graves, Herman Melville, Percy Bysshe Shelley, Dorothy Parker, and Jacqueline Kennedy Onassis.

Virgo ♍

AUGUST 23–SEPTEMBER 22

VIRGO IS sometimes associated with Demeter, the Greek goddess of the harvest, who made the earth lie fallow for half of every year. However, astrologers say Virgo's original symbol was the Sphinx, the mythological poser of riddles. So too do Virgoans question, turning inward to seek larger meanings about causes and purposes in life and looking for worthy goals to pursue. Whereas Leos aim for the full

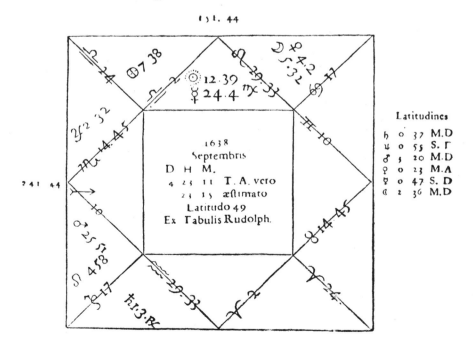

The nativity chart of Louis XIV, born in September of 1638

development of the ego, Virgoans seek complete realization of the mind. They are logical, practical, and methodical. Their intellect subjugates their instincts. They have strong senses of order and organization and a love of the technological and the minute. Virgoan Samuel Johnson clearly exhibited the sign's passion for detail in compiling his famous dictionary.

Virgoans are theorists, masters of extrapolation and deduction. They are also perfectionists. They want their environments, as well as their lives, to be tidy.

If Leos are profligate with their love, Virgoans are extremely thrifty. They are rather aloof and repressed, even puritanical, viewing passion with a highly suspicious eye. They are demanding in their choice of partners. If Virgoans do not find precisely the right person, they will probably prefer to stay unattached. Another pitfall for all Virgoans is their tendency to rehearse for life rather than live it. As they see it, they are never prepared enough to take full advantage when an opportunity presents itself.

Virgoans' real challenge is to expand their perspective beyond details, to see the larger order and underlying pattern of creation and to marvel at its abundance and diversity. Virgoans who accomplish this will know the goals worthy of service.

Libra ♎

SEPTEMBER 23—OCTOBER 22

IF THE first half of the zodiac was concerned with the development of the self, the second half deals with the relation of self to others. This is especially true for Libra, in which relationships are all. Librans are emotionally rich, gifted with tact and delicacy, and skilled at making and keeping friends. Because they are wonderfully careful not to harm or give offense, they invite confidence and trust. But for all their loving natures, Librans have a talent for emotional distance—Librans are at once involved and objective. They can look coolly on matters of the heart.

Still, Librans' whole beings are centered on connections—not only between people, but between humans and the things around them. Like Taureans, Librans love beauty, but more as a backdrop than as an end in itself. Librans want a lovely setting where graceful events can unfold. To the extent that they are artists, their palettes are social settings and people their media. Charming themselves, Librans value charm in others. They love gossip and parties and make wonderful hosts. The Scales' influence is particularly strong in women who preside over salons where people of note connect with one another. Moreover, guests at such salons are likely to include a number of Libran wits. Examples past and present include writers Oscar Wilde, Truman Capote, and Gore Vidal.

But people born under this sign are also social in a more profound sense. When scales are out of balance, Librans feel compelled to right them. They prize social justice, though their tactics will more likely involve compromise than confrontation. Mahatma Gandhi and former First Lady Eleanor Roosevelt epitomized the Libran love for both social justice and peace.

Like all the signs, however, Libra has a less attractive side. Fully evolved Librans are judicious, but immature ones are judgmental; a fondness for meddling can make Librans a source of irritation to their friends. Librans display great certitude when it comes to telling other people how to behave. Unfortunately, they are not as certain of their own paths. Vacillation is probably Librans' greatest fault. The Scales, after all, have two sides, and Librans seem always beset by the tug of opposites. Librans need to fight the indecisiveness that threatens to sap their strength and dim their charm. They must care less indiscriminately for approval, and they must pay as much attention to their own development as they do to that of others.

Scorpio ♏

OCTOBER 23–NOVEMBER 21

AUTUMN IS the season of Scorpio, one of the most complex of all the zodiacal signs. Life, death, and resurrection are inextricably linked in Scorpio. Powerful, instinctual Scorpios sting and destroy, but as their natures evolve, they also rebuild and create. It is significant that this sign has not one symbol, but three—the Scorpion, the Eagle, and the Phoenix.

Profound perceptions and violent urges characterize Scorpios. They are often impelled by overwhelming unconscious forces that can find no coherent outlet. When this happens, they may become bitter and depressed. In complicated, multi-faceted Scorpio, sexuality is expressed as eroticism, even aggression. This formidable and sometimes perverse sexuality is a potential pitfall for Scorpios. Giving it free reign, they risk wreaking havoc with themselves and others. On the other hand, repressing it can engender terrible anxiety and feelings of guilt. Scorpios both male and female are deeply seductive individuals, driven by their erotic needs. They tend toward fiery, ephemeral passions and are prone to fierce jealousy and possessiveness. They are not well suited to marriage, which, over time, they find tiresome. In friendship, as in romance, Scorpios sometimes do not know their own power. They may sting others without meaning to, then turn their venom on themselves in remorse. They may incite more fear than affection, and they tend to have a few intense relationships rather than a large circle of casual friends.

Each of Scorpio's three different emblems contributes distinctive qualities to the sign's nature. Aggression and instinct dominate the Scorpion guises: The deadly arachnid is destructive, viciously competitive, violent, and cruel. The essence of the Eagle, on the other hand, is the shrewd insight most Scorpios possess. With their Eagle's eyes, Scorpios see what others miss. Scorpios' perceptiveness finds sublime expression in many fine writers and thinkers. These include Fyodor Dostoyevsky, Albert Camus, Dylan Thomas, Evelyn Waugh, and Kurt Vonnegut. They discern hidden motives; they ferret out secret flaws and vulnerabilities. And they are not above exploiting others' weaknesses to their own advantage. Among Scorpios' most important tasks, astrologers say, are ridding themselves of the tendency to be judgmental and tempering their insight with compassion. Those who manage this difficult assignment manifest the virtues of the Phoenix, the redemptive third aspect of the sign.

Scorpios have the capacity for high spiritual development, but, astrologers believe, their path toward it is the most difficult in all the zodiac. They must be alchemists, transmuting dark instinct and selfish impulse into purified desire, striving to discipline and channel their great power toward constructive ends.

Sagittarius ⟫→
NOVEMBER 22—DECEMBER 20

SAGITTARIANS ARE the zodiac's explorers, teachers, and zealous advocates. Half-man, half-horse, the Sagittarian Centaur symbolizes the potential for unifying the animal and the spiritual components of humanity, bringing them into harmonious balance to create the complete individual. Sagittarians try to create unity from duality.

In 1572, Catherine de Médicis, an avid follower of the occult, had an astrological tower built on her property to her exact specifications. It is the only structure of its kind devoted solely to astrology.

On the wheel of the zodiac, Sagittarius is situated directly opposite Gemini, and the restless Archer shares certain characteristics with the restless Twins. Both are curious, fascinated by ideas, and enchanted by information. Both are adventurers, hating all things routine or methodical. Both want to break parochial confines and be citizens of the world. But as the astrologer Dane Rudhyar once observed, "Gemini has tolerance but no real understanding; whereas Sagittarius can have understanding even when he is most intolerant." Archers crave variety, whether in people, countries, or cultures. But even as they quest for experience, they are seldom satisfied with what they find. For Sagittarians, the point in life is the voyage: the outcome never seems to match the richness of the process.

The traveler emerges as storyteller in the work of such nineteenth-century writers as Emily Dickinson, Jane Austen, and Louisa May Alcott. Sagittarian men of the same and earlier eras turned their actual journeys into great literature. Mark Twain, Joseph Conrad, Jonathan Swift, and Gustave Flaubert were all born under the Archer's aegis. Perhaps the ultimate avatar of Sagittarius was poet-artist William Blake. Indulg-

Astrologers watch the heavens in this
eighteenth-century illustration from Amsterdam

ing the Sagittarian love for working in more than one medium, Blake used words and paint in his fiery assault against all that would confine or limit the human mind.

Sagittarians are also fascinated by systems of thought and ways of organizing information. They delight in the diversity of different cultures and disciplines—even when they view them, as they usually do, with a skeptical eye. Learning is Sagittarians' passion; teaching is their gift. The curious Archers are researchers and investigators—amassing all sorts of information, sorting it, and reprocessing it to make it accessible to others. Best of all, they are able to pass along not only their knowledge, but their love of learning.

Capricorn ♑
DECEMBER 21—JANUARY 19

CAPRICORN BEGINS on the winter solstice—a time of brooding, dark, introspective power. Capricorn is ruled by Saturn, the planet of cold rationality, and Uranus, the planet of strong will. Thus natives of the sign are apt to be defensive loners, spurred by a single-minded ambition that can carry them to great heights. Their progress may be slow, but it is virtually certain.

Capricorn's totem is the goat. When astrological symbolism arose, it took into account the two kinds of goats—the domestic one and the free-roaming wild goat. The two are emblematic of Capricorns' dual natures. If they feel chained and duty-bound, they are dour and taciturn. But if Capricorns discover their own paths, they have a feisty strength and harsh humor that will help them climb any mountain.

Capricorns are seldom impelled by a desire for money or possessions, nor do they take much pleasure in fleeting success or fame, however brilliant. They want durable power and lasting monuments. Their chilly rationality helps them keep control of their own emotions and of all situations that might distract them. They have a fierce work ethic and great managerial ability. They are capable of intense concentration and matchless determination. On the way to their goals, they are indifferent to obstacles or privations and are seldom swayed by the feelings of others. They press ahead at any cost.

Capricorns have no use for the past. They move inexorably on, permitting themselves neither regrets nor nostalgia. As lovers or spouses, Capricorns will provide material security only at the cost of emotional drought. They are often too cool, solitary, and self-sufficient to make loving partners.

There is a grim and gothic side to the sign of the Goat. Capricorn Matthew Arnold, for example, wrote that there is "neither joy, nor love, nor light, nor certitude, nor peace, nor help for pain." The writings of Capricorn Edgar Allan Poe also express this dark aspect. Even the Goats' humor is usually of the black variety, typified in the cartoons of Capricorn Charles Addams.

Capricorns are so insular by nature that they can get perilously out of touch with other humans, and if this happens, their fate may be to seclude themselves atop their cold mountains like hermits. But the season of the Goat, the dead of winter, also contains the promise of spring. Capricorn Martin Luther King, Jr., left behind the enduring monument of his dream of social justice. "He's allowed me to go up to the mountain," Dr. King proclaimed shortly before his death, "and I've looked over, and I've seen the promised land."

Celebrated astrologer and prophet Nostradamus at the age of fifty-nine, shortly before his death in 1566. As the astrologer of Queen Catherine de Médicis of France, Nostradamus was the rage of high French society in the sixteenth century. Recent interpreters claim he successfully predicted the political impact of leaders such as Stalin, Hitler, and the Kennedy brothers.

Aquarius ♒

JANUARY 20—FEBRUARY 18

AFTER SOLITARY Capricorn comes Aquarius, the most outgoing and receptive of all the zodiac signs. Aquarius lies opposite Leo, the sign that seeks full realization of the ego. The Aquarian dream is to merge that ego with the very cosmos. Aquarians are the mystics, the idealists, the reformers, the humanitarians, the innovators, the inventors—and most of all, the communicators of their groups.

Aquarians are generous, flexible, freethinking, and curious about ideas that run counter to tradition. Given their humanitarian impulses, they are often strongly dedicated to the cause of human fellowship and are capable of total self-abnegation in the service of the common good. Many Aquarians strive to live more on the spiritual plane than on the material one. Nonetheless, their spirituality and profound insight are usually tempered by rationality. This fortuitous coupling produces great creativity, which may find an outlet in the service of an ideology, or lend itself to other interests, including science and technology.

Aquarians are concerned with information and communication of all sorts, and love pictures—art, television, film. In their need to connect with the group, Aquarians always strive for speed and immediacy. The two wavy lines of their glyph symbolize not only water, but fast-flowing currents of energy—or perhaps, in the case of Aquarian inventor Thomas Edison, electricity. It was Edison who also invented motion pictures, the medium in which Aquarian directors D. W. Griffith and Sergei Eisenstein did their trailblazing work.

Aquarians push back boundaries and introduce new ideas. Aquarian Wolfgang Amadeus Mozart brought music to perfection previously unknown. Charles Darwin revolutionized thought about humanity's place in creation. Charles Lindbergh flew alone across the Atlantic when common wisdom held that such a feat was all but impossible. Aquarian writers Charles Dickens, Jules Verne, James Joyce, Gertrude Stein, and Virginia Woolf were all innovators in literature.

A major Aquarian demon is oversensitivity to the group. This weakness can cause Water Bearers deep doubts about what their true feelings are. Another Aquarian risk is that of overindulging their nonconformist impulses. If they lack rationality, they are capable of foolish, destructive attacks on tradition. At their best, however, Water Bearers, beginning with imagination, shape reality. And they work toward their most prized image, an all-inclusive society in which each individual is a happy, productive contributor to the group.

Pisces ♓
FEBRUARY 19–MARCH 20

NEARING FULL circle, the zodiac's wheel arrives at Pisces, the Fish. Those born under this sign inhabit the zodiac's twelfth house—the house of the ego's union with the eternal.

Pisces' glyph—two fish, hooked together but swimming in opposite directions—is a metaphor for the Piscean character. One part of it swims wide, toward the edge of the universe, while the other dives deep, seeking some mystical substratum to reality. Ideally, there is a rhythm to the journeys: The Fish reunite and share their discoveries before setting out again on their separate missions. Lacking the rhythm, however, the metaphor signifies unbalanced extremes: the voyager wandering aimlessly and the unhappy introvert deep in the abyss.

The Fish as cosmological voyagers are exemplified by some of history's great students of the universe—Copernicus, Galileo, Albert Einstein. Einstein was Pisces at its most evolved—a complete human being, scientist and mystic, who joined intuition to rationality.

But not all Pisceans are so comfortable in the cosmos. Some are sensitive to the point of hypersensitivity—even, astrologers say, to the point of being psychic. (Edgar Cayce, the most famous psychic of the twentieth century, was a Piscean.) Piscean minds are so receptive that as children Pisceans may have trouble distinguishing their own thoughts from those of others. This confusion can spur a headlong retreat from reality: Pisceans may become withdrawn, submissive, anxious, and disorganized.

When it does not run to extremes, however, Piscean intuition is strong and redemptive, endowing the individual with intellectual and artistic gifts. On a larger scale, it instills profound understanding and compassion. Pisceans are in touch with what the culture has forgotten or repressed—the magical, irrational world of unconscious longing and subterranean dreams. Pisceans have the ability to retrieve the dreams from the depths and return them to consciousness, revealing a cosmic unity that alleviates human alienation. Composer Maurice Ravel was a Piscean, as was master balladeer Nat King Cole.

The Fish mark the end of the progression of the zodiac from birth (Aries) to reunification with God or the cosmos, which astrologers liken to the sea.

Unraveling the Planets

O BSERVING THAT THEY seemed to steer independent courses across the firmament of fixed stars, ancient peoples believed the planets to be gods. Their appearance and behavior were reflected in the divine roles ascribed to them. The one tinged blood-red, Mars, was the god of war. The small planet that darted to and fro but never strayed far from the imperious Sun was the gods' messenger, Mercury.

The planetary gods lived out great mythical dramas that were reflections of human emotions and experiences. They loved and fought, betrayed and were betrayed, died and were reborn. Astrologers have believed for thousands of years that the planets' movements not only describe the gods' behavior and the events related in these myths, but also coincide with manifestations of the same archetypal elements in the lives of human beings. The positions of key heavenly bodies at the time of an individual's birth and at later crucial stages are thought to be more than symbolic; they occur in synchrony with forces that shape life in ways that can be advantageous if understood and painful if not properly anticipated.

The famed psychologist Carl Jung held that the mythical archetypes are ingrained into the collective unconcious of the human species. Only people who understand themselves and the archetypes, he declared, can avoid the pain of blindly reliving the myths. Astrologers believe the planets offer a route to that understanding.

In astrology the term "planet" applies to the ten bodies in our Solar System that appear to circle the Earth, eight actual planets plus the Sun and Moon.

The Sun

MYTHOLOGICALLY, the Sun in ancient times was every-where seen as a powerful, life-giving god, represented in many cultures with arms or rays reaching down to convey vitality to mortals. Perhaps the sun god with the most enduring influence was the Greeks' Apollo, who traversed the heavens in a fiery chariot and later was adopted by the Romans for their own pantheon.

Apollo grew to manhood quickly, slaying a dragon while only days old. He became the ideal of virile, youthful beauty, fathering a number of children by both women and nymphs. He could also be a dangerous suitor to those who rejected him, however. Apollo turned the nymph Daphne into a tree after she spurned him, and he bestowed centuries of longevity—but not youth—on a woman named Sibyl; she finally shriveled until only a disembodied voice was left. The Greeks recognized the god's duality: He was at once Phoebus Apollo—Bright Apollo—and Loxian, meaning "the ambiguous one."

Like Apollo and the physical star itself, the Sun in astrology has a dual nature. Highly visible, it is nonetheless contradictory, a benevolent source of life and beauty that is at the same time capable of great destruction.

Astrologically, the Sun governs the essential self, ambition, spirit, will, energy, power, and organization. Among the traits it is said to confer are creativity, pride, generosity, and dignity. But it is also linked with egotism, pomposity, arrogance, and overbearing condescension. It represents dry, hot masculinity in a partnership of opposites with the Moon, which is cool, moist, and feminine (a traditional view some modern astrologers reject as sexist). The Sun is consciousness, the "lighted" part of the mind, to the moon's unconsciousness, or intuitive knowledge. In the human body the Sun has special influence on the heart, circulatory system, and spine, and on health and vitality in general. The Sun, along with the Moon, Mercury, Venus, and Mars, is one of the inner, or personal, planets, which are thought to have the most direct influence on the lives of individuals. Its position in the zodiac at the time of birth, of course, determines a person's natal sign—the sun sign, an important element in the total astrological view of one's personality. The Sun rules the sign

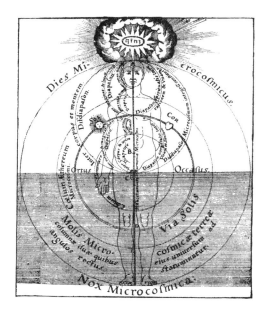

The Sun corresponds to the heart in this seventeenth-century rendering of night and day on the human body

Leo, which is its specific dominion, and is personified in kings, other rulers, and heads of state, as well as fathers, teachers, male partners, and older friends.

Each of the astrological planets has its own ancient symbol, or glyph. The Sun's glyph, is a circle—an image of wholeness—and a point, for the center or focus of life.

The Moon

THE HEAVENLY body closest to us has always been at once familiar and mysterious. The most universally notable characteristic of the Moon is its regularity; it changes from a new moon to full and back again every twenty-nine-and-a-half days. Ancient peoples used it to keep track of passing time. To the Babylonians the Moon was Sin, god of the calendar and wisdom. The Greeks dreaded the unlit, new-moon period of each lunar cycle when Selene, one of several goddesses identified with the Moon, was taken down into the underworld for three days.

Since remote times people have credited the Moon with power over nature's processes. That the Moon causes tides has long been known, of course, and by extension it was thought to affect body fluids. Its long-supposed links to menstruation—the average length of a menstrual cycle nearly matches the lunar cycle—may be one reason most ancient cultures saw the Moon as female.

The most important moon goddess was Apollo's twin sister, the Greek hunter Artemis, known to the Romans as Diana. When her father Zeus, king of the gods, offered her gifts, she chose eternal virginity, with its unencumbered freedom, and a short skirt that made it easier to chase wild animals. Armed with a silver bow, she roamed the mountains unfettered, the essence of woman as person, not woman as man's mate.

Another Greek goddess, Hecate, was associated with the dark side of the Moon. She was the queen of ghosts and other dark and hidden things, ruler of magic and deep wisdom.

Ancient astrologers had no way of knowing the Moon's minimal importance in the cosmic scheme; they saw only that the orb was one of the two dominant objects in the sky. Thus they paired the Moon with the Sun in a female-male du-

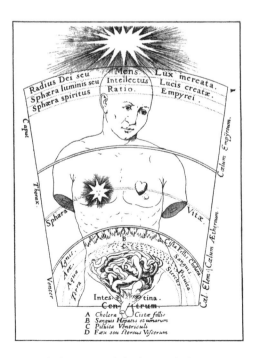

The heavens and the human body, 1619

ality. Astrologically, the Moon represents the soul and the unconscious self. It is seen as feminine, watery, and emotional in opposition to the Sun's dry masculinity. The Moon correlates with fertility, maternity, the family, growth, death, and decay. In horoscopes it is associated with duality, light and dark qualities, rhythms, changeability, sensitivity, and memory.

The Moon rules Cancer, but since it moves so rapidly through the entire zodiac each month, astrologers think it also sets the tone for other signs. Physiologically, it is said to relate to the stomach, breasts, and ovaries, to lymph and other bodily fluids, and to the cerebellum. The moon has several glyphs, among them the crescent of the new moon.

Venus

SINCE IT SOMETIMES appears in the sky in the evening and at other times in the morning, Venus was once thought in some cultures to be two different bodies, the Evening Star and the Morning Star. Perhaps the hours it keeps, which bracket the period humans favor for lovemaking, is why the planet has traditionally been associated with goddesses of love—Ishtar to the Mesopotamians, Aphrodite to the Greeks, Venus to the Romans.

Venus was born from the sea, full-grown and irresistibly beautiful. Wed to the blacksmith god, Vulcan, she presented him with three children actually sired by the vigorous and aggressive god of war, Mars. Hearing that his wife was betraying him, Vulcan forged a net of fine bronze threads and secretly rigged it to his marriage bed. He then announced he was going on an island holiday, but returned a few hours later to catch Venus and Mars snared in the net.

Vulcan unwisely called in the other gods to witness his wife's infidelity. There apparently was some snickering as they gathered around the entangled pair. The sun god Apollo nudged Mercury and said he doubted that Mercury would mind being in Mars's place, net or no net. Observing Venus's glorious nakedness, Mercury replied that he would not mind at all, even if there were three nets. The god of the sea, Neptune, his own heart stirring, undertook to guarantee that Mars would make restitution to Vulcan, paying the cuckolded husband what Vulcan had laid out as a bride price. If Mars defaulted, Neptune said generously, he himself would pay the bride price—and take Venus off Vulcan's hands.

But Vulcan was still smitten by Venus, and he kept her. The episode gained him nothing but some new rivals. Venus later bore children by both Mercury and Neptune and spread her favors to a number of others, gods and mortals. She was the embodiment of unrestrained natural sexuality, and the love and lovemaking that she promoted were sources of joy for humans. She inspired passion as a form of worship. But like other archetypal deities, Venus also had a dangerous side. The urgent yearnings she stirred caused people to sacrifice family and duty. She was called the "dark one" because of tragedies resulting from the passions she inspired.

Still, Venus is chiefly associated astrologically with things admirable and desirable: love, beauty and the love of beauty, appreciation of the arts, the feminine nature in women and men, harmony and unison, peace and reconciliation, and the enjoyment of pleasure. It is thought that when Venus is in the right place in a horoscope at birth, an individual will be gentle, warm, sentimental, graceful, and artistic. Negative Venus influences are said to make a person vulnerable to laziness, indecisiveness, an excessively romantic and impractical attitude, carelessness, envy, and jealousy.

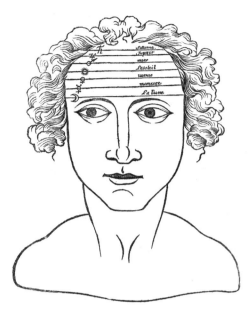

Glyphs of the five original planets, plus the Sun and Moon

Venus rules two signs, Taurus and Libra. Its special correspondences to the human body include the throat and the kidneys, as well as physical beauty. Venus's glyph—a circle above a cross to indicate the ascendance of the spirit over matter—has come to be recognized as a universal symbol for the female.

Mars

MARS'S REDDISH hue results from corrosion: crystalline rocks on the surface that have been broken down and oxidized. It was natural for ancient people to link the shimmering red ball in the night sky to ill-tempered deities whose traits suited that color.

The Babylonians said the planet was Nergal, god of war, with dominion over blood, fire, and heat. To the Greeks, the reddish orb was their war god Ares, a quarrelsome, arrogant deity who was admired for his unquestioned bravery and widely hated for his enjoyment of bloody conflict. Accompanied by two aptly named sons, Phobos and Deimos—Fear and Panic—he plunged wherever carnage was promised. (The planet Mars's two moons are named for that terrible pair of offspring.)

The Roman god Mars assumed many of the characteristics and myths attached to his precursor Ares but enjoyed a more revered status than the Greek deity. He held sway over agriculture as well as war and was the second-highest-ranking god in the Roman pantheon, after Jupiter. March, the first month of the old Roman year, was named after Mars. During that month his priests wended in procession into the countryside, marking not only the spring advent of the agricultural year but also the annual resumption of military campaigning, which was normally suspended during the winter months.

The human impulses represented by the Ares-Mars archetype are evident, of course, every time armies clash in battle. But the archetype is also at work in all accomplishments that require great effort, vigor, and tenacity: the stuff of rugged individualism.

Not surprisingly, the planet Mars in astrology represents, on the one hand, roguery, anger, aggressive self-assertion, personal ambition, and lust for power. On the other hand, it stands for assertive creativity, courage, and the quest for achievement.

Mars rules the signs Aries and Scorpio, and is thought to signify men in general. It is especially relevant to the careers of soldiers, police officers, and athletes, as well as such people as clerics and artists if their work requires, or is marked by, notable courage. An individual under the influence of the planet may lack subtlety and depth and be prone to excitability, impatience, and wrath.

Physically, Mars is associated with red blood corpuscles, the muscular system, the adrenal glands, body heat, and sexual organs. The planet is often considered responsible for an aggressive sex drive.

In the glyph for Mars, the cross of matter is transformed into an arrow and drawn atop a circle to represent the ascendance of the material over the spiritual. It is generally viewed as a universal symbol for the male.

Mercury

PERHAPS BECAUSE Mercury is so tiny and clings so close to the Sun, ancient mythology imbued the god Hermes—as Mercury was called by the Greeks—with some of the attributes of a wayward child. The love child of Zeus and the nymph Maia, a daughter of the Titan Atlas, Hermes grew into a small boy only minutes after his mother laid her newborn down to sleep. As soon as she turned her back, he tiptoed out and promptly rustled a herd of cattle belonging to his half brother, Apollo. The sun god was outraged, but Hermes charmed him and soothed his wrath by playing a tune on the world's first lyre, which he invented on the spot by stringing stolen cow gut across the inside of a tortoise shell.

As he grew, Hermes learned to put his quick wit to good use. He once rescued Zeus's lover, Io, from a hundred-eyed monster named Argus by playing his pipes so tediously that he finally put the beast to sleep. Because he was so resourceful, Hermes became the messenger of the gods, endowed with a winged helmet and winged sandals to speed him on celestial errands.

The Greeks considered Hermes the cleverest of all the gods. He was thought to have invented the alphabet, the musical scale, astronomy, and boxing. In addition, he was called the lord of travel and commerce and the patron of alchemy, the magic art of transforming base metals into gold.

The Romans welcomed Hermes into their pantheon as Mercury, who, along with his other duties, governed trade. The god's skills as an alchemist were extended by the Romans to the mastery of medicine. Thus Mercury carried the caduceus, a wand encircled by two entwined snakes and imbued with the power to heal the sick.

Like the liquid metal bearing its name, Mercury symbolizes fluidity overcoming rigidity. Thus Mercury is the champion of new beginnings, upsetting conventional attitudes, and blazing trails for invention and change. Mercury's message is one of personal transformation, a bridging of the gap between the self and its potentials.

The term "mercurial" refers to people with lively and changeable temperaments. Mercury correlates with a tendency to be critical, argumentative, or sarcastic. The planet also denotes gifts of great perceptivity, intellectual versatility, and skill at communicating knowledge. Mercury is the magician, the alchemist who magically transforms words into substance. The planet is said to figure strongly in our computerized age, with its advances in information and communications. Astrologers maintain that people whose charts feature a strong Mercury presence can be found in journalism, teaching, the travel industry, secretarial work, education, carpentry, engineering, and, of course, medicine.

Mercury rules the signs of Gemini and Virgo. It is also said to relate to the intellect, the nervous system, and the thyroid gland, as well as the senses of hearing, sight, and touch. Mercury's glyph is a cross surmounted by a circle capped by a semicircle, uniting mind, spirit, and matter, but giving primacy to intellect.

Jupiter

LORDLY JUPITER was named after the Roman king of the gods, known as Zeus in the Greek pantheon. Zeus was ruler of Mount Olympus, the home of the gods. Legend has it that he came to power by overthrowing his tyrannical Titan father Cronus, an act sometimes interpreted as the triumph of human reason over animal instinct. Greek images show Zeus as a bearded man in a sky blue cloak, sometimes astride an eagle. The god holds thunderbolts emblematic of his power.

Although he existed on the most lofty spiritual plane, Zeus also had his carnal side. He was married to his sister Hera, the Romans' Juno; but he was a philanderer of Olympian appetite and stamina, cavorting with numerous divinities and mortals of both sexes. Even so, the Greeks regarded him as guardian of the social order, particularly the supremacy of men over women. The Roman Jupiter was the lord of day and—like Zeus—the lord of lightning bolts, which were his direct messages to humanity. And Jupiter smoothly evolved from ancient myth into his astrological role, standing for masculine authority. He is the wise man, brightening the world with meaning.

These sixteenth-century French illustrations show the location of the planets on the human face. Certain marks or traits were thought to govern temperament.

Jupiter is associated with religion and philosophy, benevolence, compassion, justice, law, and honesty, as well as wealth and social status. People whose horoscopes feature Jupiter prominently are established and respectable, but as conscientious individuals will flout conventions in the name of higher principles. They are said to operate on a grand scale, and may run to extravagance if unchecked. Moreover, they have a tendency to throw around broad concepts without examining the fine print, which can make them blindly optimistic.

Pastors, philosophers, scientists, doctors, philanthropists, judges, lawyers, teachers, and chief executives are believed to be influenced by Jupiter. The planet supposedly conveys an aristocratic demeanor and facility with languages, traits appropriate to superb diplomats.

Jupiter rules Sagittarius and Pisces and oversees the circulation of the blood. The glyph that represents him, a half circle rising over a cross, is symbolic of the mind's triumph over matter.

Saturn

OMINOUS SATURN is the most distant planet from Earth still visible to the naked eye. The sixth planet from the Sun, it was a cold, solitary pariah in deep space—alone, but an awesome presence nonetheless. Saturn is the second-largest planet, after Jupiter.

The Greeks identified Saturn with Cronus, chief of the race of giant gods called Titans who ruled before the Olympians. Fearful of a prophecy that one of his children would dethrone him, the grisly Cronus ate each child right after it was born. But his wife Rhea saved the infant Zeus by offering Cronus a stone in the baby's stead, and Zeus grew up to fulfill the augury. Cronus ended up as a bitter outcast, whom the Greeks portrayed as a stooped Father Time.

The Romans grafted Cronus onto an agriculture god they inherited from the Etruscans. The result was Saturn, a god of time and farming. His festival, the Saturnalia, was held every December to celebrate the winter solstice.

But Saturn never entirely shed its ancient negative associations. The word "saturnine" means gloomy and taciturn. Still, astrology finds the planet a complex and vital constricting force that stabilizes Jupiter's expansive optimism. Saturn may indicate adversity, but often it is in the service of a more realistic perspective.

Saturn's influence can inspire or devastate. In positive circumstances, it confers persistence and endurance, prudence, thrift, and managerial skills. Saturn's strong presence in a birth chart may denote a person who is fond of routine and possibly is destined for a career in the military, government, business, or religion. A negative Saturn influence, however, warns of repression, selfishness, cruelty, deviousness, and greed.

Saturn rules Aquarius and Capricorn. It is also said to govern the body's aging process and such predations of time as rheumatism, hardening of the arteries, degeneration of organs, loss of teeth, and ailments of the gall bladder and spleen.

Saturn's glyph, like Jupiter's, incorporates the cross and half circle. But in Saturn's case the cross is paramount, making matter ascendant over mind and bringing intangibles down to earth.

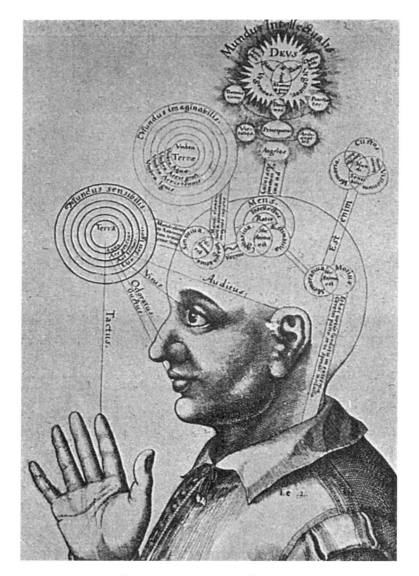

The macrocosm and the intellect, 1619

Uranus

Uranus was the first planet to be added to humanity's concept of the Solar System in recorded history. Named after the Greek god Ouranos, a tyrant whose son Saturn castrated him and then cast him out of the heavens, Uranus seemed to astronomers to act as a disrupter of the old order. Obviously, its very discovery upset the eons-old notion of a seven-planet system. Moreover, the discovery roughly coincided with the French and American revolutions.

As the first of the outer, or transpersonal, planets, Uranus is believed to wield influence beyond the individual, infusing entire cultures and eras with rapid and profound change. Heralding disruptive transformations, the planet is, astrologers say, an icon for the final third of the twentieth century.

A major Uranian presence at birth supposedly denotes an individual determined to change society rather than conform to it. He or she is apt to be inventive, rebellious, unorthodox, freedom-loving, progressive, original, and resourceful. Workaday incarnations of the Uranian spirit include electricians, inventors, and technicians.

But Uranus is not without its negative side. People influenced by the planet may be so bent on disruption and reform that they can be antisocial, even in a good cause. Their need to be different from others sometimes makes them rebels for rebellion's sake, and their restless energy can find outlet as sarcasm, brash impulsiveness, and moodiness.

Uranus rules Aquarius and the brain, especially the pituitary gland. The planet's glyph is a cross atop a circle, flanked on each side by a half circle. The symbol signifies spirit ruled by mind and operating in materiality, synthesizing attributes of all the planets.

Neptune

COLD AND SLUGGISH Neptune takes 162 years to orbit the Sun. It is thought to have a mass more than seventeen times that of Earth and to be made of ammonia and other frozen gases. It has two moons. The larger one, named for Neptune's son Triton, orbits backward.

The prototype of Neptune was worshiped by the Greeks as Poseidon, god of the sea and all waters. Although he lived on the ocean floor in a golden palace, Poseidon was primitive and unruly and would rise up in the form of earthquakes and tidal waves. But the god of the sea could be nurturing as well as destructive. Poseidon was a god of male fertility, his waters the father of crops. The Greeks also venerated him as a tamer of horses. As the Romans' Neptune he was worshiped primarily as the lord of irrigation.

Modern astrology associates Neptune's ocean kingdom with the forces of the unconscious mind and his horses with the power of raw instinct. Astrologers believe Neptune is the bridge leading from the conscious mind to the collective unconscious, that theoretical storehouse of shared memory and understanding common to all humans. Mystics believe the collective unconscious is a source of human creativity and renewal. But storming its bastions can be risky, they say, since unconscious thoughts surfacing abruptly can result in mental disruption, or even insanity.

Still, Neptune's mythical ocean is said to convey enormous empathy and a capacity to understand the depths of human personality. People with strong Neptune influences are thought to be blessed with the potential to rise above their own concerns in order to serve family or society. They are also apt to be dreamers, a trait that adds to their possible success as spiritual and artistic leaders, actors, filmmakers, and poets. And given their mythical connections, they may be seafarers, deep-sea divers, or explorers for offshore oil.

For all its virtues, Neptune has its dark side; its power is believed to exaggerate evil as well as good. Violent as an earthquake, its influence erupts to cause people to do things they are unprepared to control and might later regret.

Neptune rules Pisces and has dominion over the brain's pineal gland, spinal fluid, and amniotic fluid, that inner sea that supports unborn infants. The planet's glyph, a trident composed of an inverted cross and a semicircle, is an astrological warning that only the spiritually adept can safely approach the deeper knowledge represented by distant planets.

Pluto

DISCOVERED IN 1930, Pluto is the smallest planet—smaller than Earth's moon—and it has no known atmosphere. Pluto is the Roman version of the Greek god Hades, whose name means the "unseen one." Hades' underground kingdom, which bore his name, was the realm of the dead. Its gates were guarded by the three-headed dog Cerberus, who both mortals and ghosts tried to escape. On a foray outside his dark realm, Hades fell in love with the daughter of the earth goddess Demeter, Persephone, and carried her off to be his wife. In her grief Demeter let the Earth lie fallow, thus creating the seasons of late fall and winter.

Pluto is considered to be a source of revelation about higher realities. It is similar to Jupiter in its call to action in the name of principle. Those born under Pluto's influence may feel impelled to root out injustice. Pluto corresponds to useful dissatisfaction, the sort that spurs one toward self-improvement. Those who heed its message, say astrologers, may benefit by learning from tragedies and pitfalls and by seeking new beginnings.

But the planet's explosive power can be subverted. Those who fail to recognize and accept the negative aspects of their own personalities, for example, tend to crusade against what they perceive as evil in others while ignoring their own faults. In such cases, the crusades can have violent and disastrous results. At their very worst, people with heavy Plutonian aspects in their horoscopes can be criminal or sadistic, wholly without morals or scruples. The planet figured prominently in the horoscopes of the depraved Roman emperor Caligula, Adolf Hitler, and Joseph Stalin.

Pluto is co-ruler with Mars of Scorpio and Aries. It influences the male and female generative organs, the immune system, and genetically related diseases. Several glyphs have been proposed for the new planet. The most commonly accepted one is a cross surmounted by a half circle cupping a full circle, to depict spirit being forged in the crucible of matter.

Wartime Mysticism:
Hitler's Third Reich
and the Occult

Adolf Hitler with troops

FROM THE END of the First World War through World War II, many people in Europe—particularly those in Germany—showed a new interest in psychic powers, astrology, and spiritualism. Some Germans turned to seers and the seance table for the same reason they embraced the tyrant Adolf Hitler: for hope. The pain of their defeat in World War I, exacerbated by stringent peace terms and a hugely inflated economy, had left them with an oppressive sense of despair. They flocked to anyone who painted a bright picture of the future. The Nazis themselves, although they publicly scorned paranormal endeavors and eventually persecuted fortunetellers, nonetheless privately tolerated occult activity in their own ranks. They even ordered research in 1939 into psi phenomena and dowsing.

In the rest of Europe, psychics and astrologers found themselves deluged with clients, especially after World War II began. And British intelligence forces, sensing Nazi ambivalence toward the paranormal, launched an occult propaganda attack intended to misdirect Nazi officials and undermine German morale. Opportunists in Germany were quick to capitalize on popular interest in the paranormal—and to attach themselves to the increasingly powerful Nazis. Erik Jan Hanussen did both.

Born Hermann Steinschneider, son of a Jewish itinerant performer, Hanussen learned at an early age to please a crowd. He claimed to possess psychic powers and soon styled himself as a clairvoyant. Changing his name to Erik Jan Hanussen—and boasting descent from Danish nobles—he joined the Nazi party in Berlin in 1931 and stared a propagandist newspaper. He also set up what he called his Palace of the

Occult—a flamboyant hall of magic where he staged dramatic seances sometimes attended by Nazi officials.

On one such occasion, Hanussen fell into a trance, then described a great hall that his audience recognized as the Reichstag, the lower house of the German parliament. According to the seer, flames were leaping from the building—flames set, he averred, by those jealous of Hitler's power.

The very next night, February 27, 1933, the Reichstag was torched. Hitler's Communist opponents took the blame, although history has shown that a Dutch communist working alone was responsible. Hanussen's startlingly accurate prophecy was chalked up to his psychic prowess rather than to complicity, but less than a month later, Nazi storm troopers shot him dead: He had offended a Nazi leader by asking him to repay a debt.

In 1939, Nazi propaganda minister Joseph Goebbels hit on a clever tactic for psychological warfare: propaganda based on prophecies of the sixteenth-century French astrologer Nostradamus. Swiss prognosticator Karl Ernst Krafft was to carry out the plan.

Krafft had already proved himself a talented seer. On November 2, 1939, he had predicted mortal danger for Hitler between the seventh and tenth of the month. On November 8, Hitler spoke at a rally commemorating the anniversary of the Munich Beer Hall Putsch. Minutes after he had left the gathering, a bomb exploded behind the podium from which he had spoken.

Krafft was detained by Nazi police, but he convinced them he was a seer, not a murderer, and was soon assigned to the Nostradamus project. He put a dubious pro-

Elsbeth Ebertin, a popular German astrologer, with her book A Look into the Future, *which in 1923 asserted that Adolf Hitler would rise to still greater power*

*Hanussen (center) holds his clients in thrall at his Palace of the Occult,
where he supposedly predicted the Reichstag fire*

Mario Fenyo

Adolf Hitler melts lead over a candle in a traditional German ritual on New Year's Eve in 1939 in order to "read" the shape formed when the lead dropped into the water

Nazi slant on many of the astrologer's vague predictions, in one case even construing a mention of the grand duke of Armenia to be a reference to Hitler. Krafft may also have fathered the later notion that Nostradamus had predicted the German blitzkrieg that resulted in the 1940 occupation of Paris.

Rumors of Hitler's reliance upon astrologers circulated for the duration of his rule. Although in hindsight it appears that the Führer did not regularly dabble in the occult, some of his subordinates did, and their interest in the subject subtly affected the history of the Third Reich.

Heinrich Himmler, chief of the Nazi protection squad (SS), is said to have consulted with an astrologer before making important decisions—and to have asked when might be an opportune time to supplant Hitler. But Himmler's grandest display of occult belief was in his police force. The SS was a true secret society, rife with all manner of mystical trappings, from arcane symbols to elaborate rituals.

British propagandists cleverly faked an astrology magazine to resemble a popular German publication

Himmler restored a seventeenth-century fortress, Wewelsburg Castle, to serve as the SS high temple. Smitten with Arthurian lore, he built a round table and a memorial hall for his "twelve knights"—his best men. He also built a sanctuary for the Holy Grail and sent a young scholar on an inconclusive quest for it in 1937.

Another high-ranking Nazi, Hitler's deputy Rudolf Hess, supposedly relied on the counsel of an amateur astrologer. In a desperate attempt to secure Hitler's favor, Hess planned a secret mission and allowed his occult adviser to select a fortuitous day. On May 10, 1941, Hess flew alone to Scotland, hoping to forge an accord between the Germans and their fellow Aryans in Great Britain. The mission failed miserably and cost Hess his career.

During the late 1930s, as Hitler's forces waited hungrily for the opportunity to pounce on neighboring Poland, two psychics in that country were becoming well known among their compatriots. One, Wolf Messing, successfully foretold the failure of the German attack on Russia, and is also thought to have correctly predicted the circumstances of Hitler's death.

These bleak foreshadowings nearly cost Messing his life. After the German occupation of Poland, the Gestapo imprisoned the seer and sentenced him to death. Messing managed to escape, however, and later claimed that he had foiled his captors by exerting psychic control over them, compelling his guards to gather in his cell and stay there while he slipped away.

Another Polish psychic, Stefan Ossowiecki, managed to elude capture even though he lived near a Gestapo office. Ossowiecki claimed to have seen auras in his youth and purportedly possessed gifts of clairvoyance and psychokinesis.

When the Germans bombed Warsaw in 1939, leaving parts of the city a skeletal ruin, Ossowiecki chose to remain in order to help his fellow Poles. People reportedly lined up outside his apartment every day in 1940 and 1941 to inquire about vanished loved ones. In many cases, the psychic was able to mentally locate the missing persons; in some cases he led the inquirers to their loved ones' graves.

As the war raged on in 1941, the British launched a cunning campaign designed to erode enemy confidence. An element of this plan—which consisted largely of bogus German radio broadcasts and publications—was the use of slanted occult propaganda.

One broadcast, "Astrologie und Okkultismus," featured a German-speaking actress who claimed to receive messages from dead German soldiers that she then transmitted over the airwaves. The broadcast soon ceased, apparently because the actress was unable to refrain from chuckling while reading the scripts. With more success, the British Political Warfare Executive Office printed counterfeit German astrology magazines. Subtly written to confuse or dishearten the German public, the prophecies were dated to past months so they would appear to predict current events.

At about the same time, British naval commander Ian Fleming—who later wrote the James Bond stories—purposefully leaked a false rumor to the Germans: The British, he revealed, were using pendulum-wielding psychics to dowse the location of enemy U-boats. This seemed plausible to the Germans because it coincided with an increase in British sinkings of submarines. In truth, the sinkings resulted not from the input of psychics but from new technology and the fortuitous capture of a German decoding device. The unwitting Germans hired a dowser of their own in a vain attempt to answer the British triumphs, but their efforts were, as history has borne out, for naught.

INDEX

Note: Page numbers in *italics* refer to illustrations or their captions.